CRUNCH & DES

CLASSIC STORIES OF SALTWATER FISHING

CRUNCH & DES

CLASSIC STORIES OF SALTWATER FISHING

PHILIP WYLIE

*Edited
and with an Introduction by
Karen Wylie Pryor*

LYONS & BURFORD, Publishers

Printed in the United States of America

10 9 8 7 6 5 4 3 2 1

Library of Congress Cataloging-in-Publication Data

Wylie, Philip, 1902–1971.
    Crunch and Des : classic stories about
saltwater fishing / Philip Wylie : edited and
with an introduction by Karen Wylie Pryor.
        p.   cm.
    ISBN 1-55821-080-6 : $24.95
    1. Saltwater fishing—Fiction. I. Pryor,
Karen, 1932–
II. Title.
PS3545.Y46C78   1990
813'.54—dc20   90-46153
                                                CIP

C O N T E N T S

PREFACE
MY FATHER, PHIL WYLIE

My father, Philip Wylie, was two writers. He was, first, Wylie the ferocious visionary, a preacher of the brimstone sort. This Wylie's vituperative attacks against American shortsightedness—such as "Science has Spoiled my Supper" and "Our Polluted Paradise"—were written a full generation before nutrition or ecology became national concerns. His book *Generation of Vipers*, a sermon on American hypocrisies, was virtually memorized by American servicemen during World War II. Phil's mastery of epithet—"A woman whose urine would etch glass"—inspired a generation of imitators and put at least one new pejorative, "Momism," into the English language.

Yet Phil was also Wylie the gentle storyteller, who could amuse a little daughter at bedtime with ridiculous but moral fairy tales, and whose short stories about two Miami fishermen, Crunch and Des, beguiled *Saturday Evening Post* readers for almost thirty years. More than once I have faced some irate Wylie fan who insists that the two authors could *not* have been the same person. Usually it is a Crunch and Des enthusiast: It is understandably hard for some people to imagine that the author of these merry, almost magical tales could have turned out the polemics "the other Wylie" was famous for. But the stigmata are there: His fabulous lexical gifts, used in these tales for white magic rather than black—"A blond of the maple-fudge variety"; "gin-clear water"; "the cloying crimson of a Florida sunset." And above all, his descriptions of the fish, such as the marlin that "bounded out of the water, immense and shocking. Silver and blue. A fish with a bill like a baseball bat and eyes the size of teacups. Enraged." An archetypal marlin; a Wylie fish.

Phil loved fishing. Any kind of fishing. He was happy to dig worms and catch "punkinseeds" in a farm pond, and often did so with my children in his later years. When he first started doing well as a writer he did not spend his money on fast cars and fancy furniture, but on fishing, hiring charterboats to hunt for marlin and sailfish in the Gulf Stream off the Florida coast. Thus began the fishing stories. Forty-nine, including several three- and six-part serials, appeared in the *Saturday Evening Post*, and twenty more were published elsewhere.

Phil often based a story on a real event. An experience of his favorite charterboat captain, Harold Schmidt, and his mate, provided the basis for the first Crunch and Des story, "Widow Voyage." Sometimes he borrowed real people: The hero of "Once on a Sunday" is a portrait of Phil's father, my Grandpa Wylie, who was just such a craggy-faced, benign Scottish Presbyterian minister. Sometimes life borrowed from Phil: Shortly after Miss Jones caught her tarpon from the drawbridge ("Light Tackle") a real person caught a record fish under similar circumstances, tying up car and vessel traffic in all directions. The traffic cop who showed up ignored the traffic and instead helped the fisherman to the shore and then waded in, uniform and all, and beached the fish—a detail, Phil said, that he would not have dared to invent.

World War II changed Miami. There were indeed enemy ships offshore, and oil, wreckage, and worse on the beaches. Fishing boats like the *Poseidon* were pressed into patrol service and sometimes saw combat. Several stories in this collection reflect those events. In "The Shipwreck of Crunch and Des," the development of fishing gear for life-raft survival did proceed much as described. The elite group of international big-game fishermen who put those kits together included Phil Wylie; Wylie himself had been temporarily lost at sea, while testing life raft fishing gear.

Phil was a careful journalist and a gifted observer; his accounts of fish and fish behavior are textbook-accurate. But the Crunch and Des stories, though accurately set and as vivid as dreams, are not "realism"—they are romantic idylls. Dangers—storms, stingrays, uncooperative bankers—never cause permanent damage. The red-faced selfish tycoon is sent home chastened; the scurrilous boat captain who steals customers, fishes illegally, and doesn't keep his boat clean either mends his ways or is banished from the Gulf Stream Dock, that timeless fishing Eden. Crunch and Des may be wrongheaded, but they are always right in the end. The guy almost always gets the girl. And everyone catches fish who deserves to do so. These stories entertain the mind and satisfy the soul.

Phil's characters, sometimes appearing over and over again, are not so much stereotypes as archetypes. Crunch is the epitome of honor, Des of strength; wisdom comes from Crunch's wife Sari (an idealization of my beloved and beautiful stepmother, Ricky Wylie). Heroes and heroines are often in disguise; Phil relished the protagonist—metaphorically, himself—whose mild-mannered exterior concealed the man of steel (in fact he tender, affectionate Philip Wylie I knew.

Some of these stories are period pieces; I have let them stay that way. For example, the words we use in speaking of women and of different races have changed. Phil used the verbiage that was considered most polite at the time; I hope the reader will recognize his good will and forgive the anachronisms. Money amounts are anachronistic too, inevitably. In the early stories, Crunch and Des charged customers thirty-five dollars a day to hire the *Poseidon*. By the last story, a day's deep-sea fishing cost one hundred dollars. Today, in 1990, this kind of fishing costs six hundred dollars—or more—a day. At any price level, it has always been out of the reach of all but the well-to-do.

Since this chain of tales began, the price of a meal or a day's work may have changed; the Miami sunsets have not. You can still catch a bonefish in Biscayne Bay, and the marlin still run past Bimini. It's a joy to me to anticipate new readers for these stories, which publisher Nick Lyons and I consider to be the best of Crunch and Des. For the reader about to breathe Wylie's velvet air, hear the chug of charterboat engines, and cross the indigo-blue edge of the Gulf Stream for the first time—I envy you. Good fishing.

KAREN WYLIE PRYOR

originated this "Superman" character in a 1930 novel, *Gladiator*). Ult
mately, many of these stories *are* fairy tales. Miss Jones, the jobless libra
rian who is thrust into the world and goes fishing with her last dollar, ha
a predecessor in Snow White. The disagreeable rich man with the love
daughter, a favorite character ("Danger on Coral Key"), is the tradition
powerful king with a captive princess, to be won through deeds of darir
by a poor but honest peasant lad.

Fishing provides the deeds of daring. In these stories Phil demonstrat
the thrills in every kind of fishing Miami has to offer, from battling gia
tunas off Bimini to casting for bonefish in the Florida Keys. He can mal
bait-fishing for your supper ("Spare the Rod") just as exciting as boating
four-hundred-pound blue marlin, and that's because he felt that way hir
self. I have seen Phil as tense as a big-game hunter, plug-casting f
pan-sized mangrove snappers under the pilings of a dock. I've seen hi
just as thrilled with the resulting catch as with an International Gar
Fish Association record billfish. And he worked at passing that enthusias
on to others, including me.

When I was six, visiting my father and stepmother in Florida, Phil s
a fish trap off the seawall in Biscayne Bay behind his house and caug
for me a small octopus, a creature that transfixed me with its mysteriou
ness as it promptly squeezed itself right through one-inch-mesh chick
wire and returned to Biscayne Bay. When I was eight, Phil bought i
my first aquarium—guppies and mollies, tetras and zebra fish, and a lit
turquoise catfish, all species I still admire. When I was twelve Phil taug
me how to rig lures for trolling in the Gulf Stream (they had to be *p
fect*) and when I was fourteen he taught me to cast accurately—in 1
backyard in South Miami, using a hookless plug, with an old tire fo
target—so I could go bonefishing with him.

Phil thought he would make a fishing enthusiast of me; he made
marine biologist instead. He puzzled over that in the dedication to one
six earlier anthologies of Crunch and Des stories. Phil had been watch
my spouse and me netting one-inch fishes out of tide pools for laborat
study. He finally decided that he could dedicate a book of fishing stor
to us because that *was* fishing—of a sort.

I enjoy Phil's writing (he made me a writer, too, and I'm grateful
that). I even like most of the vitriol; he was being angry, of course,
he was also being funny, an aspect of his work that both his fans and
detractors often fail to appreciate. But I have always loved best th
stories of Crunch and Des. Here is the scientist I try to be, demonst
ing what Phil's friend Konrad Lorenz has called the naturalist's cru
"unreflecting joy" in watching living organisms, be they palm trees, p
cans, or plug-casters. Here, hovering in the background, is the ger

WIDOW VOYAGE

CRUNCH WHISTLED lovingly. "A beauty," he said, balancing himself on the riverbank by grabbing a palm frond. "A sheer, pure beauty!"

"She'll do," his companion answered. He wiped sweat from his forehead with a bandanna and nodded to himself. "Only a real sea boat has lines like that! She's a duzie!"

The object of their affection scarcely merited such praise. Indeed to give it any, required imagination and hardihood. Before them lay the hull of the *Evangeline IV*.

A mere glance would have revealed that it had been under the water for some days, another that it had been partially burned, and a third that it was holed and plugged in the stern. The cabin was a carbonized melee. The engines had been lifted out and sold to some other optimists. So had her twin screws, her steering gear, her compass and her chromed fittings; even her name was partly missing, so that it spread on her forward bulwark in quasi-Esperanto: *Ev ng l ne IV*.

"We'll clear that stuff out this afternoon—"

Crunch nodded. "Then cut the stern out, put in a sliding door to haul the big ones through, build a new cabin—a trunk cabin, by golly!"

"Get an engine!"

The mention of an engine silenced them. A good engine would cost six or seven hundred dollars. They had put their savings—two hundred dollars—in the hull. They had signed a note for two hundred more—a note due in six months. And Crunch's wife was going to have a baby sooner than that. Only, it was she who had taken the money from the bank.

"Buy that bottom," Sari had said. "You may never get another chance. It's worth a thousand, easy." She'd thrust her chin out nearly an inch, and Crunch had argued for three days, but he had known by the chin that all argument was simply vanity.

So now they jumped silently aboard the *Ev ng l ne IV* and through the

1

hot afternoon they wrenched loose and poured upon the oily bosom of the Miami River an aquacade of damaged jetsam—cushions and window frames, linoleum, partitions, shelves, bedsprings, rudder cable, rope, bent brass, planks, canvas, and even broken dishes. But everything that might be usable was carefully transported to the bank.

When the light failed, they straightened up. The demolition had largely cleared the hull, but what remained looked more like the archaeological residue of a Viking longboat than the foundation for a successful business—the business of scouring the open sea, under charter, in quest of sailfish, marlin, broadbill, dolphin, grunts.

Crunch rubbed his arms and, in the omniprevailing screen of twilight, changed his shirt and pants. So did his companion, who would serve as mate aboard the fishing boat they planned to resurrect from the salvaged vessel. Then they walked over to the Gulf Stream Dock.

Miami's Gulf Stream Dock is a gaudy spectacle. Gaudy even against the neon-spangled harbor and the perfervid sky line behind it. It extends three hundred feet into Biscayne Bay and has mooring slips for fifty boats. Behind each cruiser is a placard bearing its name. Lights glitter on wet planks, on the functional bodies of the day's catch, and floodlights beglamour the colored dresses and the pastel beach costumes of the crowds that stroll there. Small lights wink from slowly swinging portholes, and brighter bulbs illuminate cockpits and the fishing tackle—delicate gear affected by masters of the craft, and the appalling equipment with which sea giants are fought; reels as big as ice-cream freezers and rods as thick as baseball bats.

Here the public comes to rent deep-sea fishing boats. Here, every morning, wild-eyed expectation puts out toward the South Atlantic and returns at night as triumph, or alibi. The place reeks of romance and fresh fish.

Voices from the busy brilliance greeted the boat builders—friendly voices and grudging ones: "Hi, Crunch! Hello, Desperate!"

"Hello, fellows!" Crunch's eyes found Mr. Williams. He was standing beside the scales with a group just back from the Stream.

"Thirty-two pounds, Mrs. Merson!" He chuckled. "Nice dolphin!"

The woman's eyes sparkled. "I thought I'd go overboard!"

Mr. Williams nodded as if Mrs. Merson's dolphin were something unprecedented and altogether amazing. He turned. "Hi yuh, boys!"

"Fine."

Crunch gazed thoughtfully at the water, the theatrical clouds, the rigid volplane of a homebound pelican. "Be a light northeaster tomorrow. About like today."

Mr. Williams said, "Yup. Plenty of sailfish off the whistling buoy."

There was a pause. Crunch had spent two years in the prize ring. Light-heavy. He hadn't liked it, but he'd needed money. Rather, his mother had. At the moment, he would have preferred taking a ten-round shellacking.

He said, "We bought that hull."

Mr. Williams' two hundred and thirty-eight pounds seemed to condense. His usually jovial voice was strangled. "I know it! I saw you two fools tow her up to the river this morning!"

"She was a good boat," Desperate said unevenly.

"Sure, she was! So was the *Merrimac* before the *Monitor* went to work on her!"

"We wondered, if maybe, when we got her fixed up—"

Mr. Williams interrupted. In his tone was pain that ached through the soft and fervent evening: "This is like a judgment for trying to help my fellow man! I take you two birds off freighters! I teach you how to fish! How to do everything from cut baits to nurse seasick schoolteachers! I knit your reputations by hand! I offer you my own boat to run—the *Porpoise* herself—which is the *Normandie* of the charter business. But no. Oh, no! You have to prog up a derelict—burned in the bargain!"

"She's only been under a few days," Desperate murmured.

"It's not you I blame!" Mr. Williams compromised even that small solace. "It's Crunch! Thirty years old! A big guy! A tough guy! But no wise guy! What are you going to build her with?"

Crunch blushed and slowly flexed his right arm. The makers of his shirt had designed it amply, but, even so, the material was strained perilously around his biceps.

It did not impress Mr. Williams. "I suppose you've considered that it generally takes about four thousand bucks—in money—to build anything a normal human being would risk his neck in!"

"We got some tackle lined up," Desperate began. "Rudders, a swell mast, outriggers. Sam's letting us use his place when we're ready to haul out."

"You intend to pedal her?" Mr. Williams chuckled.

"I'm—we're—Sari and I are going to have a baby."

"Fine time to start thinking of that!"

Crunch leaned against a piling. It was as bad as he had expected it would be. But he was beginning to feel sore. It wasn't exactly soreness, either, but a deep, burning sensation—the kind that had won him his nickname. Won it in small boxing clubs, where nicknames are more likely to be "Drop" or "Fade-out." Light fell on his eyes; Crunch had eyes like the blue flame of a welder's torch.

"We're building this boat, see?" he said. "I'd have worked for you this season—only I want my own boat more. Especially with a kid coming. I thought when we got her ready—"

"Which'll be about 1960!"

"—if you were going to have a place on the Gulf Stream Dock, you might let Desperate and me—"

"—tie up here? Why, man, they won't know it's a fishin' boat! They'll think it's a case of mossbunkers!"

Crunch shrugged. "O.K. If that's the way you figure." He turned to walk away. He'd set his heart on the Gulf Stream Dock, but there were other anchorages.

Then he felt Mr. Williams' hand on his shoulder. Mr. Williams' other hand was held out straight. "I'll talk to the corporation next week! I hope you build a solid-gold boat and catch every four-eyed fish in the sea! I wish I had some dough—"

"Thanks," Crunch said.

That was all. Mr. Williams tried to decide whether his reticence was normal, or due to the fact that Crunch couldn't say any more; it meant a great deal to be on the Gulf Stream Dock. He wondered, too, how he could persuade the corporation's committee to save room for a nonexistent cruiser to be raised, like the *Phoenix*, from burned boards. And by grit alone.

Crunch and Desperate made a tour of the dock and gleaned from their friends a summary of the status quo in fishing. From those who were not their friends they gathered black looks and a few mediocre wisecracks. That group included several captains and mates; the charter business is competitive, uncertain, and highly individualistic. But all their conversation was stuff to make a fisherman's heart beat harder.

Marcy was hosing down the *Willalou*. He waved and shot water at them before he shut it off. "Nice outside today! The sails are swarming. Mac hit into an Allison's tuna. He was fishing a party from Pahk Avenoo. Some fat dame hung it, and you could hear her squeal clear to Fowey Light. We trolled by, hoping to hook its pal, and she was doing all right. On it for over an hour, screaming and yelling, and then I guess the tuna did the usual."

Crunch and Desperate nodded. The usual. Dove deep, wrapped his tail in the leader wire, kinked it, pulled hard, and went on alone to wherever Allison's tunas go.

Randy said, "Hear you've bid in on a fire sale! I saw the *Evangeline* hit and explode. A big woof—and that rich playboy who owned her was in the water with his friends. Coast Guard picked 'em up. What's left of her?"

"You'll see soon enough," Desperate replied.

Randy sliced the port side fillet from a mackerel. "Yeah? Say, listen, you guys! You fished Mr. Perkins on the *Porpoise*, but I've got him now. If you bring that cremated derelict over here, don't try to take him away from me!"

Neither of them responded.

A cluster of people stood around the stern of the *Valkyrie*. They pushed their way through—poor people from the fringes of Miami, eager to buy fresh fish; rich men and their ladies, come down from the Beach to arrange for a day of trolling in the Stream; tourists, natives, kids; and a man who kept repeating, "A self-respecting trout fisherman wouldn't touch this marine stuff!" There was also a pretty blond girl who didn't say anything, but kept staring incredulously at the sawed-off bill of a sailfish which she held in her hand.

"What's the attraction?" Desperate called.

Squeak Parsons pointed disgustedly with his mop. On the dock behind the *Valkyrie* lay the formidable carcass of a nine-foot shark.

"Caught him on a big rig," Squeak said—and his voice was like his gesture.

Fishing for sharks, excepting one or two breeds, is considered no sport at the Gulf Stream Dock. It's like—they say—hunting cows in a New England pasture. Horrid, sharks may be, but game they certainly are not.

"My party wanted to see what it was like," Squeak explained.

Blubber Ellis was splicing a line. He merely nodded.

Crunch grinned a little. There had been some disaster for the placid Mr. Ellis that day. Usually he was on the dock in the midst of the crowd, dilating the dramas of his past.

"What'd you get?" Crunch asked.

Blubber made a noise—a noise like that of a saw on a knot.

"Skunked?" Desperate sounded sympathetic.

The note appealed to the huge and unhappy captain. "Is it mah fault if these rich damn Yankees ain't got the brains of a crawfisherman? This morning some guy from Boston comes up and charters me foah the day. Said he'd fished in every sea except the Caspian. So Ah don't advise him none. An' what happens? A white marlin comes along an' hits his bait. It'd of been the first caught this year! 'Drop back to him!' Ah yells. Does he drop? No, sir! You can see the marlin turn to gobble that little bittie ballyhoo. Sun's overhead an' the water's clear as gin. But this half-wit yanks the bait right away from him. You'd think that marlin would have gone off scared then. But he comes back. An' the fellow yanks the bait away. The third time the marlin tried to gulp it—Ah can see th' expression in his eye, which is plumb furious—but Mister Yankee feels the spike tap, an' still don't let out line! He strikes so hard instead that the dinged ballyhoo—hook, leader an' all—snaps back an' whips around the out-rigger, clean out of the water!"

"Tough," Desperate said. He sounded like a man who was on the verge of a great emotion.

"Tough!" Blubber gazed ruefully at them. "Tough! Before that marlin leaves, he cuts twice at the ballyhoo swingin' in the air! An' Ah can't get the line free in time to hook him!"

Crunch and Desperate walked away. "It's a lie," the latter said, after a while.

"Maybe," Crunch answered. "And maybe not. I saw a white marlin take a swipe at a flying gull, once."

They caught a trolley car out to the Northwest section, where faded apartment houses and small frame cottages vied for unattractive promi-nence with garages and ironwork shops and half-forgotten, vine-choked lime groves. Sari was standing in the door of their small apartment. She'd tied up her hair in a ribbon from an old middy blouse and her dark curls stood like a coronet. She wore a hibiscus at her waist, held by her apron strings.

"Did you get the boat?"

Crunch nodded.

"Swell! How was fishing?"

"How do we know? We won't be doing any for a long time." He hugged her shoulders hard with one arm and said the habitual things. "Imagine a fishin' skipper with a wife named Sari! Or even one that looks like you!" The teasing quality of his voice camouflaged his everlasting awe.

"Did you bring any fish?" Sari asked.

They looked at each other guiltily.

"Well, we've got plenty without it. But the boys'll give you all we can eat, and we're going to be able to eat quite a lot, from now on."

They sat down to dinner at the kitchen table—which was also the living-room table. Crunch refused a second helping of beets. Sari ate them—"just to get rid of 'em." And afterwards he said, "What's at the movies?"

She chuckled. "We could go over and look at the posters. But we can't give the man three quarters and go in."

"That's right. Not till 1960, Mr. Williams says."

Mr. Williams looked down at the *Ev ng l ne IV*. The boys hadn't heard him come along the riverbank through the palms and Australian pines. They were too busy; Crunch assiduously following a pencil line along a piece of mahogany with a keyhole saw, and Desperate tacking canvas around the forward hatch. Already, moss and barnacles and sea mats had attached themselves to the hull. Every sign of its accident was gone, but the once-doughty cruiser was a shambles. Mr. Williams swallowed hard. He didn't like unpleasant things in life. They were pretty nice fellows too. Lunatics, maybe, but the kind you had to admire. Crunch's blond hair flew with his sawing. *Wife cuts it*, Mr. Williams thought. Desperate materialized copper tacks between his teeth with the regularity of a metronome.

"Hi yuh, sailors!"

Saw and hammer stopped. "Come aboard!" Crunch yelled happily.

The older man laughed. There wasn't any deck in the cockpit. Just crossbeams and braces. Doubled, he noticed, for extra strength. But no place for a fat man to stand.

"Look at her!" Crunch said. "A fellow gave us that mast! Aluminum! We're going to get some fancy linoleum for the deck. Lady on a yacht refused it. Wrong shade of gray. Desperate swapped three sweaters for a mess of cleats and brass strips. They're used, but we're having them chromed. I picked up a wheel from a racing car in a junk yard, and enough glass to make side panels. Real plate glass! Last week we took a skiff out where the *Ellen B.* sank, and dove up—" he pointed—"a bell, and a lot of wire, and fifty fathoms of new inch rope, still wrapped."

"Barracudas didn't bother you?"

Crunch snorted. "They don't come near you, if you don't splash too much! I got an octopus on my leg, but he was a little guy. Portuguese man-o'-war's worse!"

"Where'd you get that steering rig? Looks new."

"It is new, though I talked the chandler into a discount. You gotta have A-1 steering equipment."

"He give you credit?"

Crunch shook his head. "If we could get credit at a marine hardware store, we'd be on velvet. We paid hard cash. Didn't you hear? We ran into a fellow needed his house painted. Offered us a hundred bucks. We got a couple of flood lamps on long cords off a photographer I know, and finished the whole shebang in two days and three nights. How do you like the trunk cabin?"

Mr. Williams knew boats. He also had vision. "Going to be all right. In fact—if you don't mind my saying so—I'm surprised. If you can get her finished this way, and find a power plant—" He broke off. "I talked to the corporation."

"Yes?"

"I hate to disappoint you, Crunch. They just don't believe you two birds can build anything that'll be good enough for the Gulf Stream Dock."

"When they see her—"

"That's the trouble. When they see her, I'll be booked solid for another year. Everybody wants to get on that dock! I had to tell 'em you didn't know where your next nail was coming from. They just gave me a ha-ha for suggesting it."

"But, Mr. Williams, I've run your boat at the Gulf Stream Dock for a long time. The only customers I know fish out from there."

"That's another thing. The fellows on the dock—most of 'em—would hate to see you roll up with a boat. They're dividing your business now, and times are none too good. Besides, look at the record you made the last couple of years in the fishing tournament. If you start repeating that—"

"It was just luck."

"Yeah? Then they'll be scared your luck'll hold. Scared you'll take some of their trade. They raised the deuce when I said I was going to hold a place for you."

Crunch shrugged. "Nice guys! Though I can't say I blame 'em. And quite a few have been over here, giving us stuff, lending us tools."

"I'm sorry. Say, how's Sari? Haven't seen her around for quite a while."

"Not coming around, these days." Crunch looked at Desperate, who had been sitting on the cabin during the parley.

"Well, son, that just makes it so much tougher!" Mr. Williams went away, then, precipitately.

"He's a good-hearted guy," Crunch said.

"We won't be on the Gulf Dock," Desperate answered slowly. "How we going to get back our old customers?"

Crunch was a little grim. "Write 'em letters."

"Yeah. We can try." Desperate pounded a tack.

Sam's Boat Yard was some distance upriver from the cove where they berthed the *Ev ng l ne*. That was where Sari phoned, and Sam himself came running through the weeds. It was on one of the black days too. The day when they'd come down by trolley at 5:30 in the morning— tired, as usual; thin, from working too hard and eating too little—and found the boat on the bottom. Holes drilled through the planking in every compartment. Somebody—one of the fearful and jealous captains, doubtless—had spent a couple of hours there at night. They'd been diving down all morning, putting corks in the auger holes, and then pumping. Their backs ached and their hands were not just blistered but bleeding. Desperate had been close to crying, and Crunch had been talking about killing somebody if he ever found somebody.

Sam ran through the weeds. He hadn't bothered to drop his blowtorch. "Hurry!" he yelled. "Oh, Lord, hurry!"

"Sari?" Crunch asked.

Sam gulped and nodded. "Gone to the hospital already!"

Crunch picked up some waste and tried to clean his hands. Desperate blew his nose. It is not funny when a squarehead cries. Crunch put on his jacket and considered changing his pants, but didn't. He went away, and Desperate kept pumping. All afternoon. All night, finally. He forgot he was pumping. He thought he was just waiting for something, and toward dawn he had trouble remembering what it was.

Eventually the pump sucked air. He got a sponge and began sloshing water overboard. The *Ev ng l ne* was floating again. He sat down and smoked a cigarette. Vaguely, he heard the first trolley stop. And Crunch came running through the weeds in the track Sam had made, nodding his head, for some ridiculous reason. His bellow scared up a pair of mockingbirds. "A boy! And Sari's fine! Eleven pounds, even!"

Desperate fumbled in his watch pocket. "Great," he said. "Look, Crunch. I been hoarding a little on the side." The bills were sweat-wadded. "Twenty-two bucks. Not for hospital bills or the doc. We can handle that later. For Sari and the kid. Maybe even some flowers."

Crunch saw, as he took the bills, that the *Ev ng l ne* was dry. A palsy seized him. His teeth chattered. His arm muscles quivered.

"Get some water," he said, "and pour it over me."

Desperate poured.

"Another bucket."

Crunch sat down, dripping. "A big little guy, like his old man. Look, Desperate! Do you mind if we name him—"

"After me?" The squarehead cursed softly. "I do. Though, if you can't think of anything, being in a sort of tizzie, you can use my middle name."

"What's that?"

"William."

"Bill," said Crunch. "That's a good name for a tough guy, isn't it?"

"Oh, probably he ain't so tough."

"No?" The blue eyes blazed with outrage for a moment. Then he laughed. "Bill Adams. It's O.K. I'll tell Sari tonight. Let's work!"

Desperate knew, then, how tired he was. But he whistled while he worked, and stopped only when he heard Crunch chuckle. He couldn't whistle then, because the sound made him grin.

Bill was six weeks old when his father decided to give up his dream. Everything that could be borrowed and begged, everything that could be created by human energy, had been tenderly bestowed upon the derelict. She was a trim cruiser again, forty feet long, not counting the harpoon pulpit, with aluminum-painted outriggers, mahogany cabin walls, a registry number, a sky-blue trunk cabin, cream interior, bunks, galley, stove, two day beds bought on time, top controls, and even a new name, which Sari had remembered from high-school ancient history—*Poseidon*. "He's the Greek god of the sea," she had said. "And that includes fish." Even the most bitter of their rivals had admitted it was a spectacular job. Only, there were no engines in the *Poseidon*.

Sari had named her and, in another sentence, reluctantly relegated her to limbo: "The milkman wouldn't leave anything for Bill this morning."

Desperate had walked out of the house, then, and spent his last quarter at the grocery store.

And Crunch had walked out later too.

When Desperate came back, Sari was playing with Bill, and she kept her head down. "Where do you think he went? Maybe he'll kill the milkman! Maybe he'll get drunk—and I wouldn't blame him! Or you, Desperate! Starving, working like that!"

"A guy," Desperate replied with difficulty, "offered us two thousand for the *Poseidon*, as is."

Sari didn't answer.

Crunch took a trolley downtown. The guy might be at the Gulf Stream Dock. If he weren't, it was only a short walk to his hotel. Crunch dropped slowly from the trolley—one hand on the rail sufficing for the maneuver—and strolled out on the pier. The boats were all in, lights on. The sun had gone, but the sky was still carmine. With two thousand bucks he could pay up everything and start young Bill out decently in life. He and Desperate could get jobs; if not in the fishing fleet, then . . . well—There'd been an advertisement for trolley motormen. He'd run one in Schenectady.

He strolled out, thinking of a bell clanging, streams of automobiles separating, the hiss of air brakes. "Plenty of room in the rear!"

People were crowded around Randy's *Vanity*. Must be something special. Mechanically, he pushed in to observe.

A big man with a café-society accent began yelling at Randy. "In my opinion, you cut off that fish deliberately! Criminal negligence! It was a record fish! A monster!"

Randy blinked and looked palely at the crowd. "I'm sorry, Mr. Closser. I didn't do it intentionally."

"I was Randy's passenger," another man said. "It wasn't his fault. He was getting a hook out of my sleeve, and his mate was helping."

The big man was breathing hard and growing redder. "I don't want to hear this fool's excuse! My fish had taken out a lot of line! He ran his boat over the line and broke it!"

Suddenly he swung and knocked Randy back into the water. There was a silent, suspended instant. Randy came up, swimming in the tide. Someone threw a rope. Closser looked at his fist, smiled, and walked down the dock.

Crunch followed him. So did Randy's passenger, although Crunch did not notice that. He didn't notice anything. He had never liked or trusted Randy. But Randy was a little guy. And it was more than that. For three months Crunch had been fighting against odds that had proved insuperable. The gall of disappointment and frustration seethed inside him. He walked, and kept whispering, "The lug. The mean lug." He followed the lug into the parking yard, watched him unlock a long yellow roadster, walked closer, and spoke. "That's the right color car for you, Mr.—Closser."

The man whirled around. "Look here!"

"Randy's a fisherman, mister. He wouldn't of lied. If he cut off your fish, he's sorrier than you are. His customer said the same thing."

"Do you want what he got?"

Crunch came to his senses a little then. He had been a fighter. Fighters don't fight with the laity.

The big man mistook his silence for circumspection. "I thought not! It isn't healthy! When I was in Harvard I was the intercollegiate loose heavyweight champion."

Then Crunch felt the burn again, deep, terrible and glorious. "A man who had the opportunity to go to Harvard," he replied, "should know better than to be a louse." At least afterward he maintained he had said "louse."

They all came up—captains, mates, customers, rich men, poor women, sportmen, the newspaper boy—everybody. They said it was a better fight than the promoters had ever staged in Miami. They said Crunch hit him so hard the last time he took off the crushed coral in the parking yard like a hooked mako. They said he went so high you could see the sky line under his feet. It wasn't so, but he did fall flat, and got up a while later and drove off without troubling anyone.

Mr. Williams took Crunch into his office and called a doctor. Two bones were sticking through the back of Crunch's right hand.

"You shouldn't have done that," Mr. Williams said. "Captains fighting passengers! Give us a bad name!"

"I'm not a captain any more! I guess I had a bellyful of life! Had to hit somebody!" They poured iodine on his hand, and his eyes turned gray. "Sorry."

Then Randy's passenger came in. He looked at the torn blue shirt, the iodine and the gray eyes—which were coming back again to blue. "You a captain down here?"

"Was," said Mr. Williams fearfully.

"Got a boat?"

"Have one. No engine."

The man nodded. He was a tallish man, thin, no sunburn, and he wore gold-rimmed glasses. He looked like a banker, or, maybe, a broker. One of those New York men, alert, quick; good fishermen, sometimes. This one was about fifty.

"No engine?" he said after a while.

Mr. Williams tried to make an excuse: "He and his mate were tops at the charter business till they got swelled heads and tried to build their own boat. They got licked on dough. He's through! It's too bad, but I guess he couldn't take it. And he just plain had to sock somebody."

"My name," said the man, "is Taylor. This was the first day that I ever tried deep-sea fishing. And I like that right of yours. I like it. I've been run out of my office by my doctor for a couple of months. If I chartered you in advance—say four weeks—would that? . . ."

Crunch looked at his hand. "Yeah," he said, "it would."

"How soon could you be ready?"

"A week?"

"I'd like to get in on the first day of the Miami tournament. Is it possible?"

"We'll try. But with this mitt . . ."

When he returned to his home and opened the door with his left hand, Sari raised her eyes and stared for a minute. Then she whispered to Bill, "There's your father. He's been fighting. And he's drunk. Maybe he isn't quite as good a guy as I've been telling you he was."

So Crunch grinned. "Not drunk. Not a drop. I get this goofy expression from being happy." He took out a ten-dollar bill. "Where's the squarehead?"

They lost track of time. Slip Wilson and Bugs Holover and Cap Johnson came to help them. Slip even gave up a charter on one of the days. Bugs worked all night. The engines were lowered on the blocks. The reduction gears were attached to the shafts. Desperate put in the panels and hooked them up.

Mr. Williams drove over to the river on the eve of opening day. "I have your number in the parade. Think she'll be ready?"

"Try to be," Crunch said.

"Wish I had a berth for you at the dock. Looks like you've had a break. I suppose you know this Taylor owns a newsreel company?"

Crunch shrugged and lent his good hand to holding a storage battery. "I don't care what he owns, so long as it pays dividends and he likes fishin'!"

"Did he tell you he was taking two cameramen out with him to shoot the boat parade and any fish he catches?"

Crunch looked down at Desperate, whose arms knotted as he turned a bolt. "Hear that?" He wasn't pleased. "First trip, and we get a job put up on us! What if we don't have a strike all day? It's happened before! Every sports page will run the news that the *Poseidon* entered the tournament with two cameramen, and came back with all her bait! That's a sweet handicap for her maiden voyage!"

Desperate grunted. "Can't we make the guy wait till after our first trip?"

"It is kind of putting the lug on you boys," Mr. Williams agreed. "I'd hate to drag baits for two cameramen all day. But, then, it's really not the boat's maiden voyage. She was the *Evangeline*, remember! Kind of a 'widow' voyage!" He laughed.

"Maybe we won't have her ready anyhow," Crunch said dispiritedly. And he went back to work.

At 8:30 the next morning, Mr. Taylor was waiting on the sea wall near the Gulf Stream Dock. Waiting anxiously. The fifty fishing cruisers were wound with crepe paper, spangled with gold and silver paper stars, and bristling with fishing tackle. A vast throng on the pier yelled, sang, waved, took pictures, and prepared to embark for the flotilla parade. A band struck up "Dixie" aboard the glass-bottom boat, and the fleet pushed off. Once every year, to open its fishing tournament, Miami decks itself in bunting, and sails out on its indigo ocean in everything floatable, from rowboats with kickers to yachts with crews of fifty.

As the crowd thinned and vanished, Mr. Taylor fidgeted. His cameramen drove up and unloaded their equipment.

"The boys'll be along," he said convincingly. "Soon. Very soon, now."

It was 9:15 when the *Poseidon* appeared, cutting across the bay, both motors roaring, a wave at her bow. Mr. Taylor felt weak with relief.

And Crunch made a bleak apology as he held his boat off the sea wall: "Sand in our gas, friends! We can still make the parade, I hope." They did, by a narrow margin. They were last in line, but, Mr. Taylor thought, far from least.

It was a peaceful day outside, with wheeling gulls and golden sargasso weed floating on the fantastically blue water. Slow fishing—which is not unprecedented in January—and Mr. Taylor relaxed. It was midafternoon before he bothered to think that his two cameramen had photographed no piscatorial drama worthy of national release. Nothing but the boating of a kingfish, and a long shot of a dolphin shaking out the hook.

He understood the effect of such failure only when Crunch traded places with Desperate at the top controls, and said, "Well, at least she behaves all right."

"Sure," Mr. Taylor said. "Best boat in the fleet! You two birds have genius! So why worry about a sailfish? We've got plenty of days to get 'em in."

Crunch gazed into the two blue distances of sea and sky. "Yeah. But it's a pity, since we have these photographers—"

"We can take 'em again." Mr. Taylor tried to smile away Crunch's disappointment.

"I guess so. But it's the first day of the contest. And our first trip. Besides, nobody has a sail yet."

"How can you tell that?"

"When we catch one we run up a flag." He scanned the fleet. "Haven't seen any."

Then Mr. Taylor knew chagrin. He shouldn't have brought the photographers. They interfered with the mysterious thing called "luck." They were an embarrassment to Crunch. He began praying for a sailfish.

And he was deep in some mystic ritual when Desperate's voice rang thrillingly from above: "Watch it!"

"Watch it!" eventually became unforgettable to Mr. Taylor. He looked at his bait, trolling under the clear water, occasionally breaking the surface. He looked, and grew tense from head to foot. There was something behind and underneath it. A mere shadow.

Crunch was whispering, "Get ready to drop back when he taps it."

Then the tap, as the sailfish slapped the bat with his bill. Mr. Taylor tremblingly threw down the lever that let the reel spool turn free, and his bait, as if killed by the sail's slap, drifted astern. There was a silence. The reel unwound. He tried to count to ten. Then suddenly the unwinding reel sped faster. "He's got it," Crunch whispered at his shoulder. "Slam on the drag and sock it to him."

After that, Mr. Taylor became confused. The reel stopped unwinding. The line went taut. He remembered vaguely that he stood up and whipped back the rod, that there came an alarming answering pull, that Crunch half carried him to the big center chair and sat him down. He remembered that the reel was making a sound like a wounded banshee. He remembered how the rod bent and how he struggled to hang on. He remembered being afraid that all the line would be run off the reel, and that presently, with sickening suddenness, the line went slack. He thought it had broken.

But Crunch yelled, "Wind, man! Wind! He's coming up to jump!"

So he wound, and looked out on the water, and saw what some men have spent months to witness—the awesome leap of a sailfish, sword flailing, jaws wide, indigo dorsal spread full, the wide-forked tail churning itself free of the water. The fish hung in the air for a second; huge, scintillant, miraculous. Then it was gone. It came again, walking across the sea on its tail.

He remembered other things. A surging dive that melted line from his spool. Exhausting efforts to regain it inchmeal by heaving back slowly on the rod and lowering it quickly to crank back precious inches of slack thus created. Cramps in his reel hand. Sweat running down his face, and Crunch wiping it away without taking his eyes from the place where the line sizzled through the sea. He remembered the first time he managed to heave the leader wire out of the water and thought he had the fish, only to see it rush away again, a hundred yards in a few seconds.

And at last—it seemed hours later—the intensity of the struggle decreased. The fish was drawn near the boat. Its sail broke water. It lay over on its side. Crunch begged him to "keep it coming," and, paradoxically, to "take it easy." Then Crunch reached, grabbed the wire in a gloved hand, bent low and lifted. The sailfish, beating the bulwarks with its tail, was heaved bodily across the gunwale and dispatched by a single blow, which Crunch administered with a milk bottle.

"Didn't have time to turn up a billy on Sam's lathe," he explained.

It seemed a fantastically trivial statement to Mr. Taylor, until he realized it was Crunch's effort to hide his own excitement. They stretched out the fish, ecstatically praised its colors, and bent it into the seven-foot fish box. Only then did Mr. Taylor realize that his cameras had been grinding all the time. The *Poseidon's* widow voyage would make the newsreels.

Three days later the *Poseidon* was standing on the ways at Sam's Boat Yard. Desperate and Crunch were toiling underneath her stern, putting on bigger rudders and otherwise preparing for a trip with their customer to the Keys. Sari had brought Bill down; he lay on the grass, watching the white clouds navigate the southeast trades. His mother unpacked a far from frugal lunch and listened while her husband filed noisily on a dull piece of bronze, and talked above the sound: "You're going to be a widow, honey, like the boat! This spring. Guy saw us in the newsreels yesterday and wants us for several weeks in Bimini!"

A car stopped. Mr. Williams stepped out. His expression was secretive. "Got a note for you, Crunch." He studied the *Poseidon's* naked planking. "You guys ought to quit fishing and build boats! Nobody ever got rich in the charter business!"

"We like it!" Crunch opened the note, read it and handed it to Desperate. "Dear Adams," it said. "Ever since you cleaned up on that Closser rat, I've felt like a heel. Business has been slow for me. I figured if you got a boat you'd take Perkins back. I bored those holes. Now I got a chance at a good berth in Key West for the spring and I'm pulling out. Maybe Mr. Williams will give you my spot at the Gulf Stream. Randy Forbes. P.S. You can't prove I sunk your boat."

Desperate giggled. "The dumb Benny! Doesn't this note kind of prove it?"

Crunch took the note from his mate. He tore it slowly into many pieces. He tossed them into the air, and the wind carried them out onto the oily river. He looked up, then, at Mr. Williams.

"Randy's left my pier," he said, "for the reason of 'business elsewhere.' And other reasons not known, but suspected, by me. Want the place, Crunch? Thirty bucks a month, including light and water." His eyes were twinkling. "Nice dock; be a credit to the *Poseidon*."

Another car stopped on the road beside the ways. Mr. Taylor walked over. He gazed at Sari, at Bill and at the lunch. Then he called to his chauffeur, "I'm eating here! Come back at six!"

The mate looked surprised. Mr. Taylor untied a bundle. There were work clothes in it. "Thought I'd help you guys do a little painting, Desperate. Nobody in my business knows it, but I painted signs for a living once." He grinned at the squarehead. "Which reminds me of a query that crossed my brain last night. I don't know what your real name is."

"Smith."

"I mean, first name."

Desperate glanced about to be sure Sari and Crunch and Mr. Williams were beyond earshot. He stared doubtfully at Bill for a moment. Then he gathered himself. His eyes met Taylor's. "Nobody in my business knows my name." He paused again. "Desmond," he said truculently.

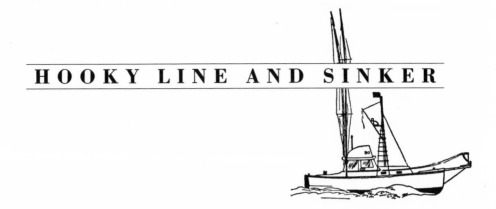

HOOKY LINE AND SINKER

THE *Poseidon* STRAINED against her stern lines as the tide attempted to pull her away from the Gulf Stream Dock; her harpoon pulpit dipped in an expectant salute to the surrounding bright morning and the far-off cobalt horizon; the halyards on her outriggers shivered in the light breeze. Farther down the dock, the *Go West*'s motors coughed, thundered softly and carried her into the Government Channel which led out toward the cobalt streak. In the *Go West*'s stern cockpit two plethoric and somewhat ponderous gentlemen grinned and rubbed anti-sun lotion on their faces; a day's fishing lay ahead, and Miami faded astern.

Crunch looked up from his work. "Wally's got Mr. Wheatley again today."

He picked another balao from the icebox and measured it against a large hook. Then he inserted the hook and wound the bill-like nose of the small fish tight against the shank with copper wire. A chromed leader ten feet long completed the rig—a bait that would swim like a live fish. But woe unto any marine giant who tried to swallow it.

"Here comes those Jameses," Desperate murmured. He was looking down the dock. A young man and a very pretty girl were walking somewhat diffidently in the distance, feasting their eyes on the sights of fishermen, fishing boats and fishing gear.

Crunch nodded. "Someday when we have nothing better to do we'll take those kids outside."

"You will not!"

They turned.

Sari, very lovely in slacks, but with a nonetheless hostile aspect, stood behind young Bill's baby carriage. Crunch winked at his infant son and leered at his wife.

"You should be at home washing dishes and cleaning house," he said; "not down here on the dock taking up the time of busy men."

The hostility increased. "If I didn't keep tabs on you two morons, we'd starve! You still owe for some of the boat, and for our furniture, and you have a wife and child to support! The charter-boat business isn't a gold mine. And you idiotically bought that radio telephone—"

"Are we going to listen?" Crunch asked Desperate solemnly. "Look, Sari. If we get in trouble, you'll be glad we have a ship-to-shore phone. If we get delayed out there with a big one on, we can call, and you won't worry. It brings in business; people like it—" He pronounced each threadbare point with undue emphasis.

In the next slip, Captain Emery interrupted the good-natured family dispute, "Hey, Crunch! Fishing today?"

"Yeah. Customer I don't know, name of Granger."

"Want to lay ten bucks we have a better day on the *Firefly?*"

Sari answered that: "No! Not now! Not ever! Crunch isn't betting. We're trying to make a living, Captain Emery."

The skipper of the *Firefly* pulled his hat down over his ears, grinned and murmured, "Excuse me."

Sari continued her wifely homily. "Those James kids are sweet; I talked to 'em a couple of times. But when we get rich enough to dole out charity, Crunch Adams, I'll let you know. And I'll do the doling!"

Crunch nodded and came up on the dock. He made a pass at Bill with his right—the right that had earned him a living in the prize ring for two unpleasant but necessary years.

"O.K., Sari. I just thought someday when we didn't have a charter we could take them out for a couple of hours. The gal was sick, so that James lad gave up a swell job in the North to bring her here. Now he grubs in a bank, and their only fun is coming down here to watch us go out and see what we bring in. They've read every book in the library on fishing. They even know what people catch in Siam and Japan! I feel so sorry for 'em I almost hate to talk to 'em!"

Sari sighed. "Yeah. I know how you feel—and how they feel too. But we can't do favors, Crunchie, till we get ahead!"

She kissed him and wheeled Bill along the Dock, smiling in answer to numerous cheery greetings. She spoke to the Jameses, too, when she passed, and she left them looking at a cobia caught the day before. They studied it carefully and walked along to the place where the *Poseidon* lay.

"Good morning, Captain," Mrs. James said.

Crunch waved. "How are you, folks?"

"Oh, wonderful, just as usual." She pointed to a roll of heavy white paper under her husband's arm. "Jeff worked out a new theory about where sailfish feed, last night."

Jeff's flush was deep, but not quite so deep as his enthusiasm for his idea. "Of course," he said, "I'll never have a chance to prove it."

"Come on aboard." It was Desperate who gave them the invitation.

"Could we?" The girl looked down the dock worriedly. "Aren't you all set to go out?"

"Sure. But our party hasn't shown up." Crunch held out his hand to Mrs. James, and then to her husband, who scorned it politely and dropped into the cockpit. "What you got there?"

Both the Jameses took a moment for the mere enjoyment of being aboard the boat. They'd been on board others at the Dock, but never before on the *Poseidon*. They exclaimed at the sword of a broadbill mounted over the compass and sniffed the exhilarating blend of paint, salt, rope and varnish. Then Mr. James, still embarrassed, unrolled the paper.

"It's a hydrographic map," he said. "Covers the coast along here."

Crunch spread it out for him on one of the day beds aboard the *Poseidon*. He and Desperate bent forward earnestly, as if nobody in the charter-boat fishing fleet had ever thought of studying the Government soundings and their relation to the habits of fish. But Mr. James surprised him. It wasn't an old theory.

"I've studied a good deal of physics," he said. "You know, I used to be an engineer. And I've worked out a chart to show the effect of varying depths and winds on the submarine drift of the Gulf Stream. It's all theoretical stuff, but I've checked it as much as I could, with catches made for the last few weeks. Where the fish were hung; how the wind was blowing that day—velocity and direction. Take, for instance, last Thursday a week, when the fleet brought in all those white marlin. There was a northeaster. Eight miles, almost steady. Barometer at 30.01. Temperature from 71 to 77. The Stream was in toward shore, running about two miles an hour. Now look at the bottom." He pointed to his map of the ocean floor. "It would be scoured up along these lines. The weeds and small fish would probably congregate here—and here—" he pointed with a pencil—"which is just where they hung seven of the nine whites they caught that day."

"Isn't that amazing?" Mrs. James said proudly.

Crunch nodded in a sage and approving manner. No use to tell a person so rabid about fishing—a person who couldn't afford an hour of fishing—that years of experience had taught him that all such theoretical consideration of winds and tides was futile. The fish simply came and went, struck or failed to strike, according to natural laws that transcended mere physics.

Desperate, equally skeptical, nevertheless feigned approval.

"Mr. James," he said, "someday fellows like you will put fishing on a completely scientific basis! We'll know exactly where to go, when. We'll just sail out and massacre 'em.'"

The young man's pride was adequate reward for that kindness. "It's at least possible—"

"Possible! It's the coming thing!" Crunch was paternal.

Mrs. James laughed. "Jeff's terribly bright . . . Tell 'em what you thought about conditions today!"

Her husband's demur was instant. "They have their own ideas."

But Crunch seemed to want nothing more than the James data. "Go ahead! We might give it a whirl!"

"I'd certainly feel flattered if you did. But—well, where did you plan to go?"

Crunch scratched his head. "Well, with this southeast breeze, I thought we'd spend an hour out at the end of the ship channel, till the tide changed; then head north, maybe as far as Baker's Haul-over; then cut away out in a big circle . . ."

Mr. James was shaking his head. "Nope. Not if I'm right. South is your direction—and in close. Head for Fowey Light. Ought to be a lot of small stuff well in—dolphin, bonito, some kings, scattered white marlin, and whatever sails are around today."

"We'll try it," Crunch replied. "And thanks for the tip."

"Oh, that part was fun. Janet and I are batty about fishing—on paper. I guess we're pretty much of a pest here at the dock." He smiled apologetically. "It's the only amusement we can afford; being sort of 'buffs' for fishing."

"You could try wetting a line from one of the causeways," Crunch suggested. "I'd be glad to lend you a couple of outfits."

Mrs. James shook her head. "We did try, and we did get some snappers. But I guess Jeff would rather dream and plan about going after the big ones than catch all the little ones in the sea . . . Come on, darling! It's 8:30! . . . And thanks!"

Crunch helped them ashore. "That man," he said to his partner, "is crazier about fishing than I am! I call it a rotten shame."

"The girl likes it too."

"Sure."

Fate at that moment entered the proceedings in a small way. A boy in a scarlet uniform with the name of a Miami hotel on his cap hurried down the dock, looking at the boats. When he saw the *Poseidon*, he stopped. "That's it," he said aloud. "*Poseidon.*" He approached. "Message for the captain. You it?"

"Yeah," Crunch said. Internally, he sank. A cancellation. Thirty-five bucks lost, and a day to be spent idle at the pier.

The boy regarded Crunch—open blue shirt, blue trousers, sandals. "Hell of a looking captain!" He held out an envelope.

Desperate swore softly and looked over Crunch's shoulder.

Dear Skipper:

I'm having to take the night plane back to Kansas City. Business. Don't know whether I'll make Miami again this season or not. I hadn't got up my party when the news came, so here's my check for the charter, and I'll look you up next year. Thanks for a swell day I didn't get a chance at.

G. J. GRANGER

Crunch eyed the messenger who was hovering so purposefully, and whose insult had been so direct that Crunch decided to waste no dime.

"Go back to your hotel, son," he said coldly, "before those red pants set fire to the dock."

Then, abruptly and with force, he turned toward Desperate. "Say!"

"Just what I was thinking!" Desperate gazed down the pier, smiled a little at his skipper, and hopped ashore. He caught Mr. and Mrs. James as the theoretical angler was hailing a bus and kissing his wife good-by at the same time. He explained the situation. Under her tan, Mrs. James went pale. She looked imploringly at her husband.

But he was just smiling. "It's mighty nice of you two fellows. Terribly nice. I'll never forget it. But I got to bring home that twenty-eight a week, and the bank is always casting about for excuses to reduce its personnel in the springtime."

Desperate's eyes were guileless. "You could of been fighting an attack of acute indigestion all night."

Janet interrupted passionately: "Of course you could, Jeff! You haven't missed a day since you got here! You could have a tummy-ache, or a migraine, or anything! We'll never have another chance! Oh, Jeff!" She began to shed a few strategic tears.

Jeff took a nickel out of his pocket. He tossed it and caught it. Putting the matter up to destiny, like a man, Des thought. But Mr. James didn't look to see which side of the coin came up. He simply stepped into the dockhouse and dropped the nickel into a telephone slot. They heard his voice above the clangor of passing traffic: ". . . awfully sorry, Mr. Briggs . . . terrible attack . . . fine tomorrow, I think . . . Yes, sir."

Aboard the *Poseidon*, Crunch was being twitted by Captain Emery. "She won't let you bet, eh?"

"My party didn't show up. I'm taking out some kids, I think."

"Wears the pants, does she?"

Crunch shrugged. "Just the same, if I were betting, I'd bet on my two passengers. They've never fished."

"And I'm fishing a couple of the smartest light-tackle men in South Florida, but you'd bet on amateurs!"

"I said I would. Because fishing is one part skill and three parts luck. Those Jameses stand as good a chance as your professional anglers, almost, if they decide to go."

"Maybe your wife would let you bet a nickel, as a sort of token. Then, if your kids go out and beat Weymouth and Grenoble today, you can make my nickel into a locket. Or wouldn't she let you risk a nickel?"

Crunch flushed. "It isn't like that. Nothing like that. We're trying to get ahead!"

Emery chuckled. "It sounded like Mrs. Scrooge herself, to me."

"Look." Crunch got up, still flushing. He spoke quietly and intensely: "Want to bet the whole day's dough—thirty-five bucks—you get a better haul than I do, if I go out?"

That frightened Emery. Finally he said, "All right. I will. Yes."

And the Jameses returned. Desperate strode delightedly in their wake. Crunch didn't mention his bet. Instead, as he held up a hand to help Mrs. James, he said, "They give him a day off?"

And Mr. James lied, without thought, and to his eventual distress: "Sure. Told me to go ahead and take a day. Said I could make it up later! Gee, this is the most exciting thing that ever happened to me in my life!" He glanced at Desperate with a request for backing in his eyes. No need of letting Crunch know he'd told the bank he was sick. Des winked. And Janet smiled.

"They're nice at the Union Dade," she said.

Crunch nodded without giving the matter further consideration, and threw the stern lines ashore. The *Poseidon* headed out in the lead of Emery's *Firefly*, to fish beginners against old-timers for a wager.

He headed the *Poseidon* east until he had left all the channel buoys astern, except the big whistler that marked the turn from the ship lane. The wind was southerly and Crunch pointed into it, after a long look at the rest of the fleet, miles to the north.

He was thinking about his bet and about the fact that the other captains didn't concentrate their boats to north'ard if there was good fishing elsewhere; he kept only a casual eye on Desperate, who lowered the outriggers and attached baits to the lines on two sturdy rods. His face relaxed a little when he saw the enthusiasm with which the Jameses watched each step of the various maneuvers—so familiar to them from their books—but experienced now for the first time. And he even grinned faintly when Des put over the first bait.

Mrs. James shut her eyes and crossed her fingers and murmured, "Pray, Jeff! Start praying for luck right now, and don't quit till we come in! This may be the only chance we'll ever get!"

Tough to be that poor. Tougher still that it cost so much money to troll in the deep sea. And no way to avoid that. Crunch's eye automatically followed Mrs. James' line from the rod tip up to the tip of the outrigger, where a clothespin on a halyard held it in a firm pinch, so that the bait skipped along the surface of the water far abeam of the *Poseidon*'s wake. His eye dilated when it came to the bait. The balao hadn't been dancing for a half minute, but there was a fish coming for it, a big dolphin, leaping clear of the water, green, gold, and fast, on a course at right angles to the *Poseidon*'s. It dawned on Crunch that the Jameses might be lucky.

"Get ready!" he said at the same time.

To a beginner in the art of deep-sea fishing, such a phrase is disconcerting. It lacks cogent direction. It merely alarms. The girl stiffened from head to foot. She grabbed the upper part of her rod with both hands and levered it back in the socket on the seat of her chair, so it stood up straight.

She said, "Oh, my!" Then she saw the dolphin's last leap—a long one, like a greyhound's—and saw it slam at the bait. She said, "E-e-e-e-e!" in a gentle scream.

Mr. James, similarly afflicted with buck fever, offered several conflicting directions. "Hold hard!" he shouted. "Reel like hell!" he added. "Lean forward! Pull back!"

His wife's line snapped free of the clothespin, and a hundred feet of slack floated down on the water. It began to grow taut immediately, as the fish ran off diagonally astern and the *Poseidon*'s inertia carried her ahead, although Desperate, steering from the cabin roof, had thrown her out of gear. Crunch ran to the girl's side. "Reel," he said calmly. "Reel fast and gather up that slack."

Mr. James stood up and stared. "I don't think he took the bait," he said with bitterness.

Crunch glanced at him. "No? Then what's dragging that line under water?"

The girl screamed again. The line had come tight. The reel began to give forth a tormented sound. She cranked with zeal and saw at the same time that the spool of her reel was turning in the opposite direction. Theoretically, she should have understood—the fish was pulling harder than the point at which the drag had been set, but, in the heat of battle, the loss of line against her best effort seemed dangerous.

She pressed her thumb on the spinning reel and yelled again, "Ouch! I'm burned!"

"Idiot! her husband bellowed. "Half-wit! We may not see another fish all day, and you're going to lose it!"

"Take it easy," said Crunch.

Desperate walked forward on the decking over the cabin and peered into the volcanic cockpit. There was amusement in his eye, and when he caught Crunch's, he winked. Then his attention went elsewhere.

Mr. James, with a concentration that would have been admirable in a naval battle, was trying to use spiritual force to make his wife do the right thing in this great crisis. Not that he knew what the right thing was. Indeed, as the dolphin broke far out on the water, and then went into a series of aerial convulsions, he yelled, for a reason he was never later able to explain, "Give him slack! Give him slack!"

However, Mr. James still clung mechanically to his own rod, and it was that which attracted Desperate's gaze. The *Poseidon* had stopped. Mr. James' line had lain limply for a minute or two, dangling in the water from its outrigger, which was itself now like a mighty fish pole. However, Desperate saw that the bait had stopped its normal slow sinking and was being drawn rapidly downward by some force which was not aquatic.

Indeed, as he looked, the loosely hanging line pulled up the clothespin in the outrigger and snapped out. He opened his mouth to mention it, and he hesitated. Mr. James had been pretty imperious about his wife's amateurish and skittery behavior. Let him look to his own laurels.

Ordinarily, the outriggers serve two purposes: they troll the baits in calm water outside the boat's wake, and they permit an automatic "drop-back," so necessary for bill fish, which first merely hit the bait—knocking the line from the clothespin and thereby dropping a hundred or so feet of slack on the water—and then return to swallow it—which they usually will not do if the bait is carried onward by the boat's motion after the first hit. In this case, however, the outrigger served no purpose except to prevent Mr. James from feeling his strike.

Mr. James' recognition of the fact that he, too, had a fish was vocal. A heavy surge bent his rod in a considerable arc. He very nearly lost his hold on it. And his reel started at once to make banshee sounds. So did he. "A-a-a-w-e-e-e-e—wow!" he said.

Desperate spoke quietly but firmly, "Crunch, it's a big one."

Mr. James had been holding his rod nonchalantly across his lap; now he was on his feet, experiencing trouble in keeping it from going overboard. The butt was gouging his vital organs. Both men were needed to get it set in the socket of his chair.

Mr. James thereupon forgot about his wife and her fish. He stared, instead, at his reel spool. It was making unguessable revolutions per second. In fact, it spun so fast, the line strands could not be seen and seemed merely to be melting away, like the snowball in the proverb.

"Turn the boat!" Mr. James yelled. "He's taking everything I've got."

Crunch looked up. "Turn her," he said.

Desperate put the boat in gear, gunned it and shoved the rudders over. The *Poseidon* swung around and began chasing Mr. James' fish.

Word came from Mrs. James almost instanter: "I've lost him!"

"Wind," Crunch said fervently. "We're after the other fish, and that's putting bellies in your lines! Wind, both of you."

"My wrist hurts," said Mrs. James.

"Wind anyway!" her husband yelled.

"You, too," said Crunch.

"He's jumping!" Mrs. James reported.

"Mine's sounding!" Mr. James said. "And there's hardly any line left! Can't we do something?"

Crunch scanned the sea. The *Poseidon* was pouring along in pursuit of Mr. James' fish. But it was a big fish, because even with the throttles open, it was still tearing line from Mr. James' reel.

Then, far ahead and to starboard of the *Poseidon*, Crunch saw a sight common in Bimini waters, but rare off Miami. A heavy "blue"—a marlin—soared into the air, angrily shaking his head, throwing barrels of water with his flukes, walking along the placid blue surface, vanishing and reappearing. On his second leap, he turned a complete somersault. On his third, he rolled twice in mid-air. Crunch glanced anxiously at Desperate. And Des only bit his lip.

This was luck, indeed, but luck not for beginners. It was luck worthy of all the strength and kill of an old hand. The rod was light for the fish, and so was the line. Twenty-four thread. It would break under a strain of seventy-two pounds. And the marlin looked as if he would go three hundred, which meant he was capable of exerting double the strain the line would stand, on a dead pull. Of course, the pull wouldn't be dead; the drag would slip. Still—

Crunch looked at Desperate again. He had stopped biting his lips. That was the apogee of apprehensive facial condition for Des.

"Won't somebody help me?" Mrs. James asked piteously.

Nobody even heard her.

Crunch leaned down to Mr. James and spoke in a fatherly manner—a gentle, tender manner: "He's a pretty big one."

"Did you see him?" Mr. James began to shake.

"I had a glimpse of him," Crunch answered placidly. He sounded so offhand that Mr. James doubted his fish was very big. If he had known

Crunch better, if he had seen the perspiration running down Crunch's forehead, he would have realized that the captain was capable of no more terrible excitement. "Take it easy," Crunch added.

"He's jerking my shoulders loose!"

"Throw her out!" Crunch said to Des. "His first run's ended!"

"Praise God," Mr. James murmured. So did Des, to himself.

Crunch then dived below. He came up with a leather harness which he slipped over Mr. James' head and attached to two eyelets on the reel. The strain of the bowed rod was thereby taken from his arms and transferred to his back. He gasped. He let go of the rod for a minute, holding it entirely on the harness, and rubbed his hands on his trousers.

"Sweaty," he explained. "Slippery."

Crunch brought a cloth. The marlin had swung around in a wide curve and was now astern again. Mr. James began pumping—heaving back slowly against the fish and then dropping his rod tip quickly while he wound in the slack thus gained. That much of his theory was beginning to register.

Mrs. James' voice came rather grimly: "I suppose, Captain, being a man, you only care about men catching fish. I suppose it wouldn't interest you to know that I have a big fish on my line, too, and that my thumb is bleeding where I burned it on the reel. And that my fish keeps jumping madly here and there, and I haven't the slightest idea what to do about it, except to try to keep a tight line."

"That's right," Crunch said quickly. "Keep it tight." And he paid her no more attention. Instead, he tested the drag on Mr. James' reel and watched the water intently at a point some two hundred and fifty yards astern.

"He's taking line again!" Mr. James cried alarmedly.

"Yeah. He's going to jump."

"Jump! What is it? A sailfish?"

"Well—" Crunch didn't want his angler to die of shock— "it's a kind of big sailfish."

The lie was futile. The "sailfish" suddenly decided to exhibit itself— not ahead of the boat, where Mr. James couldn't see it, but astern and in full view. I came out of the water with a surge—bounded out—immense and shocking. Silver and blue. A fish more than ten feet long, with a bill like a baseball bat and rolling eyes the size of teacups. Every time it leaped, Mr. James was racked as if an invisible Joe Louis had walloped him between the shoulder blades; and every time it leaped, Desperate prayed to his strange and personal Scandinavian gods. Crunch only wiped off more sweat.

He tried hard to see how it was hooked, for on that fact depended much of the battle ahead. If it was hooked insecurely, then, in one of its submarine power dives, it would surely pull free, or in one of its sea-splitting leaps it would toss the hook clear. But the marlin twisted so swiftly in the air that Crunch could make no adequate determination. It was still on, and that was something.

It jumped straight up, its bill fifteen feet clear of the sea. It bounded horizontally, twenty feet at a crack. It stood on its tail and shimmied. It shook its head like a colossal bulldog. And Mr. James, involuntarily, shook, bounced and shimmied with it.

This fusilade of jumps had other, wholly unanticipated effects.

In the first place, Mr. James, having witnessed the thing to which he was bodily attached, lost all reason.

"It's a marlin, isn't it?" he said hoarsely.

Crunch merely nodded.

And Mr. James collapsed morally. "You better take it," he said. "The biggest fish I ever caught weighed four pounds."

Crunch shook his head. "It's yours," he answered, "and you're doing fine. But don't waste your strength."

Mr. James sobbed.

His wife had also seen the titanic emergence. It had simply paralyzed her motor functions. "Nobody," she had said insanely, and yet with a certain sort of logic, "has a right to try to catch anything like that on a rod and reel!"

"It's been done," Crunch answered. His back was turned to her as he bent over Mr. James, murmuring encouragement and instruction.

Desperate, however, left the controls long enough to peer into the psychic bedlam. "Have you lost that dolphin?" he asked.

"Dolphin?" said Mrs. James.

"Yes. The one that you were fighting."

She looked dazedly at the rod in her hand. Her line had been slack for some moments. And her reel was jammed; she had wound in all the line in one place; it had piled up and made itself into a brake that acted against the metal rods which held the reel together.

"I'll come down," said Des.

"You stay up there," Crunch said harshly. "We've got a lot of line out!"

"Just pull out the line with your hand," Des said then, to the inert fisherwoman, "until that pile doesn't scrape any more. Then wind in on the side where there's room for it. Maybe he's still on."

Janet did so. She pulled out the piled line and wound it up carefully — not with the idea of encountering her fish again, because she had been told that if you give any fish slack, he'll get free — and she rewound the spool evenly, so that it would not jam again. In that process she was surprised. She did not pull in a bare hook. Instead, she encountered life and fury when her hook was still fifty or sixty yards at sea. The dolphin, having rested, took to the air again.

He leaped and he ran. When he stopped running, he was almost as far away as Jeff's marlin. "Oh, my!" she said. "I'd rather watch Jeff!"

Des grunted. "Be plenty of time for that!"

And Crunch yelled, "Give her the gun! He's coming toward us!"

The marlin did come toward them, at what was literally express-train speed, his high dorsal fin cutting the water like a periscope. Mr. James spun the reel with a frenzy that belied his aching arms and numb fingers. Des gave the *Poseidon* every drop of gas she would take. It wasn't enough. The fish doubled back on the line. Crunch whispered, over and over, commands to the angler to get in line, and his voice was a mixture of supplication and threat.

But a man's best reeling speed added to the *Poseidon*'s sixteen knots is trifling compared to a marlin's top velocity when he is aroused. It has been estimated at sixty or seventy miles an hour — some say a hundred — and the fish swam in until Crunch grew pale. It looked as if he were going to ram the stern. That had happened in Bimini once or twice — a blow that rocked the boat; a bony bill a foot or two long, broken off after being struck cleanly through two inches of mahogany planking and left there as a souvenir. Certainly the marlin had the idea of attack in his enraged mind. But he changed it when he was not more than fifty feet astern. There was a sweep, a geyser of water as he hauled up; and he broke again, jumping high, fast, violent, and so close to them on the last leap, that a bucket of water was flung into the cockpit.

On the last leap, too, Crunch had stood up and grabbed the heavy gaff, holding it like a bat, ready, in case. In case the marlin came aboard. That had never happened, so far as he knew, but it had almost happened several times. And nobody could say just what the result would be if three or four hundred pounds of powerful billfish landed among several people in very close quarters. It wasn't a calming idea.

"He's gone," Mr. James said, after a moment of quiet. Mr. James sounded relieved.

Crunch looked. "Threw the hook, I guess. Are you sure?"

"Positive. Line's slack."

Desperate had cut the motors again.

Mrs. James spoke. It had been quite a while since she'd said anything. "All the time we were trying to keep Jeff's fish from running us down," she murmured in quiet pain, "mine was running away. Now, I'd say there's about ten feet of line left on the reel. I can see the little shiny spindle here and there. I may say, too, I don't care much. My feet hurt from pushing on the stern. My back will never be the same again. One arm is paralyzed. My thumb is a bloody pulp."

Her husband stared at her. "And suppose you'd been hung on a marlin all that time, instead of that — minnow?"

Crunch sagged back against the cabin wall. "Gone, eh? Well, reel in and we'll start over. If you'd got that fish, mister, it would have been the first 'blue' caught in Florida waters this year. You'd have topped the tournament. But you can always say you hung one —"

He never finished. Mr. James had not lost the "blue." It had merely submerged fifty feet or so and rested. Being inexperienced, he had not thought to wind in his line to make certain his quarry was gone. He had accepted the long period of slack as proof positive. Now, however, the rod bent, the reel yowled, and the marlin took off in a vertical power dive until he approached bottom at some sixty fathoms. He then turned and zigzagged among the reefs in a generally northward direction.

Mr. James bent with pain. He clung to his rod, not with stubbornness, but with the grim resignation of a man who has been sent over the top on a glorious but probably fatal mission.

Crunch screamed in a mighty jubilation.

Des lighted a cigar he had been saving for three days. It was in somewhat wispy shape, but it drew. In the ensuing hour and a half, he smoked it down and burned his lips before he tried to throw it away. When he did that, he burned his fingers.

It was a memorable hour and a half. Somewhere during it, Des hopped down and gaffed for Mrs. James a very handsome forty-pound bull dolphin. Even Mrs. James scarcely noticed that episode. The dolphin ran off the marvelous series of color changes, for which the breed is celebrated, without an audience. He lay still and regal at last, alone and without mourners. Mr. James and his fish held the spotlight.

There came a time when even Crunch was worried. After all, Mr. James had been clerking in a bank for months. He was not in perfect physical trim. Men had been known to walk ashore after a tussle with a big one and shake off the mortal envelope. Deep-sea fishing is not recommended for persons with heart disease, for example. Mr. James had suffered, visibly. But, on the other hand, he had seemed singularly tenacious, and in his lithe frame there were muscles. The warm Florida sun bathed him, he perspired, the breeze blew on him, the indigo water splashed alongside, he seemed to be in excellent shape, but Crunch finally lost his argument with himself.

"Look, Mr. James," he said; "if you're taking too much of a beating, I'll sit in on the fish for you."

James turned. Something had happened to him in the latest half hour of the struggle. His face was set, calm, unutterably determined. "If you touched the rod or reel, it wouldn't be my fish, would it?"

"Not according to the rules."

"Touch it, and I'll break your neck!"

Crunch nodded. Then he looked up at Des and winked.

"I was stroke," said Mr. James, "of the hundred-and-fifty-pound crew in my college. This is child's play."

"Oh," Crunch answered. "Fine."

When the marlin spent himself to his last erg, calorie and decibel, Mr. James manfully pumped him alongside. By that time, Crunch and Desmond were half maddened with the expectation of victory. Any fish so well hooked that he could not free himself with long minutes of slack should rightfully be theirs.

"Heave him up a couple more times," Crunch said, "and I'll get the leader. Then it'll be your fish, even if I lose him."

Mr. James heaved, lowered and wound. The marlin lay out on the water, limp, glassy-eyed and unprotesting. Mrs. James stood by the gunwale, yelling at him—though afterward she swore she had not said a word. Crunch pulled out a panel in the *Poseidon*'s stern, which opened a square hold almost to the water line. He put on gloves. He reached out suddenly and grabbed the leader wire just as the swivel came up close to the rod tip.

"Throw off your drag," Crunch muttered, "in case he runs again."

Des, also wearing gloves, hopped down to aid.

"I'll grab his bill," Crunch said, "and haul his head inboard. Des will grab, too, and help . . . Mrs. James, you stand ready with the billy, and we'll put him out with that. Let's go!"

Only it didn't happen that way. Crunch pulled the fish through the water gently with the wire leader. Then, just as he was about to grab the fish's bill, the hook came out.

Accidents like that are frequent. The marlin had been hooked in the bony corner of his jaw. Two hours of battling had eroded a hole there and the hook had dropped free. All four of them saw it. And the marlin began to sink, too tired to swim, a fighter temporarily groggy from effort. He sank a foot, two feet. Crunch dropped the leader and just stared at him. Desperate did not move. Mr. James shivered and tears began to well in his eyes.

Then Crunch made a little history. He was not the first to perform the act, nor will he be the last. Men spend fortunes and chunks of lifetimes to "get a blue." Charter-boat men spend all their lives in hopes of catching a few—a dozen, perhaps. And this one, by all rights, had been caught fair. To lose him after such a struggle was intolerable.

Crunch grabbed the end of a stern line and dived in. He held the line in one hand. With the other he reached down in the blue water and grabbed the rough and heavy bill. The marlin, thus unfamiliarly assaulted, made a last valiant effort. His tail broke water, churning foam. Crunch was visible in the near depths, dancing involuntarily about. But Crunch had been a fighter — a good fighter. If the marlin was strong, so was he. And if the fish was exhausted, Crunch was fresh and full of fury.

Des had already picked up the rope and was pulling. His muscles writhed. Janet grabbed it also. And Jeff tried, but his gear and his debility kept him from rising. In a second or two Des had Crunch's hand. Then Des had the bill of the lashing fish and Crunch was coming aboard. Together they pulled the marlin into the cockpit and dispatched it.

Crunch stood there, panting, soaked, grinning. And he spoke to Mr. James. He spoke with fervor and even a little awe. "Nice work, James! Beautiful! Shake!"

"Me?" said Mr. James vaguely.

"Sure. You caught him. I almost lost him. You ought to kick my pants for letting that hook drop out."

Mr. James stirred weakly. "I'll be . . . " he said softly.

Then Janet realized that it was all over, crossed the cockpit, kissed him, and began to laugh and cry at the same time.

Her husband rested the rod on the gunwale. He unbuckled his harness. Crunch relieved him of it. He stood up uncertainly, stretched, said, "Ouch!" and looked down at the fish. He said, "Hmmmm."

Crunch ducked below and came up with a blue flag, and a bandage for Mrs. James' thumb. The "bloody pulp" turned out to be only skin deep. He attached the blue flag to the halyard on the outrigger and ran it up.

"It's the first marlin ever caught on the *Poseidon*," he said quietly. "You two ready to start fishing again?"

Mr. James gaped. "Do we have to?"

"It's customary. Only noon. I'll rustle some beans though."

"Good idea," said Mr. James. "Janet and I will just go upon the top and

When the Jameses were resting comfortably, albeit excitedly, on the monster which stretched the length of the cockpit, at the mighty bill, the fierce forked tail, the yawning jaws. "I caught it," he said. "I! Imagine!"

When the Jameses were resting comfortably, albeit excitedly, on the cabin top, Crunch went over to the dials of his ship-to-shore telephone. He picked up the receiver-transmitter and listened. He gave his letters. "Gimme," he said, "The Miami *Dispatch*." He waited. "Fishing editor," he murmured presently. He gazed at the Keys, winding greenly southward on the far horizon. He watched a man-o'-war wheel in the sky. He whistled a little. "Hello! This Bob Breastedt? . . . This is Crunch

Adams. . . . Yeah. I'm outside. . . . Sure I got something to report. We just boated a 'blue.' About three hundred . . . and on twenty-four thread. . . . I know it's the first this year. . . . Fellow by the name of Jeffrey James. . . . Works in the Union Dade Bank. . . . Oh, about two hours and fifteen minutes. . . . Jumps? Better say thirty. There were more. . . . Anything special?" Crunch pondered a moment. "Sure. The guy only caught a four-pound fish before in his life. . . . Yep. First trip, first blue marlin. That's the height of something, isn't it?"

He hung up. He went aloft and sat down beside his exuberant guests. "Well," he said genially, "I just reported our catch to the fishing editor of the *Dispatch*."

It had a wrong effect, somehow. He heard the girl's breath catch. He saw Jeff start. "I suppose they'll print it?" Jeff said slowly.

"Print it! Why, it'll be on the front page! There'll be a gang of reporters down at the dock to take your picture when we come in tonight!"

"I see. There isn't any way we could . . . " Mr. James looked at the surprise and discomfort on Crunch's face. "You see, I told my boss I was sick. And if he knows I went fishing . . . "

Crunch's eyes wandered away toward the ocean again. "You mean you told old man Whitbie—" He started to say more, but didn't.

Jeff smiled ruefully. "Not Whitbie! I've never even met the president of the outfit. My boss is a sourpuss named Briggs."

"Oh," said Crunch, "I see. I'm sorry if I kind of spoiled your day."

Janet leaned over and looked down at the fish. "You haven't," she answered. "You couldn't! If he gets fired, there are other jobs! I'm well. Maybe now he will go back North. But he's caught a marlin, and I guess he'd lose twenty jobs for that!"

Crunch didn't answer. He brought up lunch after a while. Then the Jameses resumed fishing.

Their luck for the rest of the day was normal—two bonitos, a kingfish, a mackerel, and another dolphin—the largest under ten pounds. A sailfish showed once behind the baits and went away without striking. Janet said she was glad. It had been her bait. "If I'd caught him," she said, "think of the dreadful anticlimax!" But their spirits were not what they had been at first. And when Crunch started toward the Government Cut at 5:30, their courage ebbed visibly. Crunch overheard them once figuring out whether or not their cash resources would pay the bus fare to Buffalo. He explained the situation to Desperate. And it was a very quiet group that was warped up to the Gulf Stream Dock—for champions.

With the motley and enthusiastic crowd as a background, and the aid of other captains and mates, Crunch and Desperate brought the marlin ashore. They hung it on the high crossbeams and weighed it. Three hundred and thirty-six. Eyes bulged. Questions crackled. Several hundred people pushed, marveled and exclaimed. Jeff and Janet stood in the *Poseidon*'s stern and answered as fact as they could. Then the reporters came, with more questions and with cameras. Jeff was posed holding the rod and standing beside the fish, smiling, looking up, smiling at his wife, frowning sturdily, holding a fin, and smiling at the fish. A man from a radio station told them they would have to make a statement on the air that night. Customary, he said. Bewildered, they agreed. The head of the Tournament filled long blanks and elicited information for press dispatches to the rest of the world.

Jeff took it all stoically. "Might as well be hung for a goat—" he said.

And then Janet nudged him. "Look!"

He looked. It was Mr. Whitbie, the president of Union Dade, elbowing his way toward them, his face firm and implacable.

"He's come down personally," Janet whispered, "to show you up. Probably he thinks a public lecture will be good for morale in his bank. Talk back to him, Jeff! Please do!"

Mr. Whitbie was beside them and the crowd all around. Mr. Whitbie inspected the fish and then Jeff and finally Jeff's wife, with the same cold eye.

"You're an employee of mine," he said finally.

"I was, anyhow," Jeff answered.

"Hmmmm. Looked you up. Heard from Briggs you said you were sick today."

Janet interrupted: "Look here, Mr. Whitbie. Jeff is fishing crazy! He adores it! He—he knows more about it than any man in Florida. He's read everything! And if you don't think he can fish, look at the marlin! You pay us a measly twenty-eight a week. And Jeff's only here because of my health. We got a chance to go out free today, thanks to Captain Adams . . . "

"Hmmmm," Mr. Whitbie repeated. "Nice dolphin. Jeff get that, too?"

"I did," said Janet. "And it's second in the Tournament so far! And if you're going to fire Jeff, do it, because the photographers want some more pictures." She gestured toward a number of men, kneeling with cameras.

"Fire him?" Mr. Whitbie's manner changed perceptibly and suddenly. "My dear young lady! I've been trying to get a 'blue' myself for two weeks every year for five years. Breastedt phoned me when he got the ship-to-shore message from young Adams. Fire your husband! I came down to find out all about how he did it!"

Janet gulped.

Mr. Whitbie turned to examine the marlin's head. "By George! Loosely hooked, eh? Must have kept a perfect taut line, eh? James, any man who is a fisherman is a hell of a lot more! I'd like to have you and Mrs. James for dinner. And—" He raised his voice to address the photographers: "Get a couple of pictures with me in it beside these folks! I'm the president of the bank where this boy works!" There was a ring in his voice which belied his alibi to Janet and Jeff: "Good publicity for the bank, you know!"

Crunch had heard every word. It had been a better denouement than he had dared to suggest. Because all afternoon, knowing that Whitbie was as rabid a fisherman as could be found in Florida, Crunch had combined wishing and logic in a passionate hope that the Jameses had not made a fatal error by playing hooky.

Now Sari nosed the perambulator through the crowd to the box on which Crunch sat. Sari looked angry. Desperate saw her and faded into the thickness of people. "You took these people out—for nothing!" she said.

He sat still. "I did not! Granger paid me, for one thing. And for another, I won thirty-five bucks extra from Emery! He had two sails, but I beat him hollow!"

Sari did not deign to glance at the marlin hanging in the center of vast collective awe. "I heard about that. I made Emery keep his money. I said you weren't allowed to bet—and you aren't! You charter-boat men can't afford luxuries like betting a day's earnings!"

"O.K.," Crunch answered. "O.K. I'm sorry. He got me peeved."

Sari sat on the box. She was suddenly startled. "Why, Crunch! Your clothes! They're salty! Did you fall overboard?"

"I dove. The marlin broke away after I got hold of the leader."

Her eyes widened. "And suppose there'd been a couple of mako sharks chasing after that marlin, like there often is? Then what?"

"Then," Crunch answered, "you could get a second husband with some sense!" His voice was mocking. His eyes were full of laughter. In the baby carriage, young Bill saw him and seemed to smile also. So did Sari. That was the picture the cameraman caught for the *Dispatch*.

THE OLD CRAWDAD

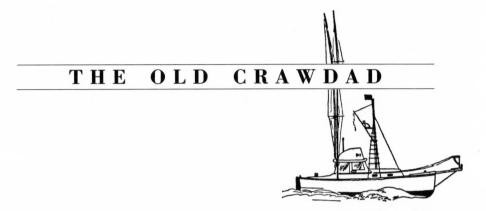

Mr. McLaen hated Miami. It made him unpopular there. "Crawling with insects," he said, when an unusual west wind blew in a few black flies from the Everglades. His married daughter anxiously explained that the trade winds generally kept back the vermin. But Mr. McLaen merely peered down from his daughter's *cabaña* and called the celebrated beach below a "swarming purlieu"—which was going pretty far even for a man whose taste in phrases was on the gaudy side.

His daughter was depressed by that. Her name was Evelyn and she had two charming children as well as a young husband whom she considered more than charming.

"I'd hoped dad would like it here," she said sadly. "Because if he doesn't . . ."

Her husband looked at his father-in-law's haughty back. He spoke without reserve: "Your old man is a human meat grinder. He doesn't like me. He doesn't like Florida. He has the temper of a water buffalo."

"He's a lamb," Evelyn replied. But her gray eyes were rueful. "Up at home—in Michigan—"

"There!" said her husband. "Michigan! He thinks there is only one state—Michigan! Night and day for two weeks!" He made a sound like the collapse of a stovepipe. "If I wanted him to invest in timberland in Michigan he'd go for a county. But since it's sugar cane . . ."

Evelyn tried to soothe him. "Some people don't like the tropics. Dad's one. We'll just have to give up the sugar-cane idea and go back to St. Louis again."

She rose hastily then, because Ellis, who was four, had waded experimentally into the sea where the water was deeper than Ellis.

Mr. McLaen was having trouble with children too. He had walked to the diving board at the end of the pool, a fine figure of a man of fifty-nine, with a deep chest and beetling, red eyebrows, and he had dived as

35

expertly as any youngster. Unfortunately, his plunge was intercepted by a child's balsa-wood surfboard.

He came up treading water and bellowing. "Lifeguard," he roared, taking no heed of the many onlookers, "this thing!" He hurled the board ashore. It hit a cement cornice and cracked. "Have you no rules in this pool?"

A lifeguard hurried forward.

"I'm sorry, Mr. McLaen!"

"You're sorry! In the Great Lakes area, you'd be sacked for such negligence! A noisome pesthole!" By that time, the child had retrieved his split board and was bawling. There was a rush of mothers, waiters, infants and others to the vicinity. Mr. McLaen sputtered to himself, "Miami! A nitwit's Mardi gras!"

All in all, it made a bad day for Evelyn and Ralph and the two little Owenses. The last straw, which was laid on before supper, came in the form of a palm beetle in grandfather's chair. He sat on it. His daughter began to worry about her father's heart, and to regret fiercely the hour in which her now frayed young husband had decided there was a future in Florida sugar cane.

"Dad's not used to being a house guest," she explained in a tone that was placating, but fairly hopeless. "He's accustomed to running things. Up home—"

"I know." Ralph couldn't put heat even in sarcasm. "He's a sort of chronic president. An order giver. A policy shaper. Temperamental, if you consider it temperamental to throw an ash tray because you've sat on a beetle; but a heart of gold. Gold brick!"

Thus the Owenses progressed into domestic squabble.

The subject of their discussion was not present. He was striding through the twilight of Miami, pounding with his cane, looking neither to the right nor to the left, and not giving any heed to the orange clouds or the glimpses of blue water in the bay. Not, that is, until the Gulf Stream Fishing Dock hove in sight dead ahead. Then he gave heed indeed, for he realized that his formidable stroll was less to calm his wrath than to find a fresh object for it. The pier was such an object: Crowded with people, hemmed by the bright cockpits of fishing boats, and heaped with trophies from the day's catch. Mr. McLaen went out on the planking like a tank.

It was natural that he chose Desperate for his victim. Desperate was a quiet-looking young man. He had a vague way of staring at people which was disconcerting to some and vexing to others. He never stood, but leaned or sprawled, letting his support, be it chair or railing, absorb his weight. Sometimes when Desperate was thinking, his mouth opened. Frequently, he chewed gum. All that appealed, negatively, to Mr. Mc-

Laen. He would not have tackled Desperate's partner and skipper—
Crunch Adams. Anybody could see that Crunch, master of the *Poseidon*,
was not a person to trifle with. And the disgruntled magnate from Michigan intended, consciously or not, to trifle a little.

He frowned so that his eye thatch met in the middle and he walked
with a leering simulation of curiosity toward the place where Desperate
leaned. He said, "Good evening, young man."

Desperate, scenting a customer, came to near-attention. He smiled
amiably and said it was a wonderful evening. Like most, he added.

Mr. McLaen cleared his throat.

"Looks as if the fishing had been good today."

"Pretty fair."

It had been excellent. But Desperate was no man to tempt providence
by boasting. Besides, he was modest.

"My name's McLaen," said the other man. He pronounced it to rhyme
with "fine."

Desperate said, "How do you do?" and continued, "Interested in a
trip out?"

Mr. McLaen hesitated. With his cane, he pointed at some fish which
were being dressed by the captain of the adjacent *Firefly*. "What do you
call those?"

"Those are kings. Kingfish. Some people call them king mackerel."

"Hmmm. And those?" The cane swung in a short arc.

"Bonitos. They're members of the mackerel family too."

"Edible?"

"The kings are. The bonitos aren't. We're having a run of kings now.
They're also caught commercially here."

Mr. McLaen winced. Desperate noticed it, and wondered why. He was
beginning to detect a difference in the approach of this gentleman, but
he could not guess its significance.

"I fish a good deal," said the tall man.

Desperate smiled pleasantly. Any man who fished a good deal was
almost certain to be a right guy. He waited. Fishermen are likely to
advance confidences piecemeal. Mr. McLaen had the shoulders for anything. Tuna, if he felt like it. Maybe he was thinking of a Bimini trip.

"But not," said Mr. McLaen in a voice suddenly loud and irate,
"for squid!"

"Squid?" Desperate repeated perplexedly.

"Squid!" the other man thundered. "Squid and cod. Lings, halibut, had-
dock, flounders—whatever you drag out of the ocean on this insane tackle!"

The *Poseidon*'s mate flushed lightly. Mr. McLaen had named no Gulf
Stream gamesters, and Mr. McLaen was pointing to a proud acquisition—

a brand-new heavy rod, reel and line on display in the cruiser's cockpit. "We only use that on big stuff," Desperate said. He felt apologetic, and he didn't like the feeling.

"It would make a fine winch, that reel!" Mr. McLaen's voice had started a drift of people in the direction of the *Poseidon*. He seemed to have a peculiar knack for drawing crowds. "And the line!" he went on. "What do you use that for? Lariats? Be first-rate for calf roping."

"Some of the fish," Des answered moodily, "are bigger than calves."

Mr. McLaen was worked up by that time. Also, he had an audience. "My dear young man," he said scathingly, "it is quite conceivable that a person could catch a whale—if the whale would take a bait—and the line were a hawser—and the angler could run the animal down with one of these motor boats. It is conceivable, but it is not sport. It is not fishing. It is a form of assassination." He raised his cane again and pointed down the pier. "Look. Scores of fish. Salt-water fish. Turgid monsters, ugly and badly made. Hulks. You take people into the sea with this—this—salvage apparatus, and you haul fish out of the water and you say you are fishing! You call yourselves sportsmen! Why, the very temperature of the water hereabouts precludes any gaminess in the fish! It's a kind of wrecking operation that you practice! A rodeo! A roping contest!"

Desperate was blushing deeply by that time and looking down at the planks. To his simple way of thinking, an assault of this sort could be remedied by one method alone: A straight sock on the chin. But Mr. McLaen's age, and Desperate's sense of his dignity as a mate, prevented that. There was nothing to do but stand by and let people laugh.

They did. The ignorant laughed because they thought that the distinguished-looking man was probably right. The sophisticated laughed at the mate's discomfiture. And Mr. McLaen had no way of realizing that the apparently ashamed youth in front of him was on the very equator of homicide. He took a quick bow from his audience and barged recklessly ahead: "You're not anglers, really. You're trawlers! You chaps are a libel on the commercial fishermen who earn a decent living catching these—things."

"I thought," Desperate finally replied in a cool tone, "you said you were a fisherman?"

"I am. Yes, I'm a fisherman. I've won several cups and medals for what little skill I have. At the moment, indeed, I hold a championship or two. Not, however, for hauling these torpid monsters from the sea by main force. I was taught by my father that fishing is a gentleman's sport and that it demands skill. Skill with rod, reel and line. Skill in casting. The stamina to wade cold streams for hours in a northern woods. The ability to select the right lure, to cast it accurately, to strip line, to maintain a difficult stance! A hundred skills! I was given the impression that angling is more than just sunning yourself in a chair while engines fish for you."

"Oh," said Desperate. "Trout."

Mr. McLaen glared. "Trout! A profanation on the lips of a salt-water fisherman! Trout, young man! Rainbows! Browns! Steelheads! And salmon—if I may mention it here!"

"I've heard of them," said Desperate.

"Heard of them!" Mr. McLaen's voice shook. "I daresay! You may even have seen a nine-foot rod—or a fly reel! You may have read of men who could cast so accurately that they could fetch back dollar bills at thirty paces!"

Desperate sighed and nodded. It wasn't a threatening response. But he was on familiar ground. His anger did not abate, although the attack had been wanton and ignorant; however, it congealed with purpose. He met Mr. McLaen eye to eye. His voice was quiet. "I've seen some of you fellows fish. And a few Florida men have taken sailfish on salmon rods from rowboats. But most of you bait fisherman aren't good enough to—"

"Bait fishermen!" Mr. McLaen's voice squeaked.

"M-m. What you hang in your club walls we use for bait down here."

The chuckle in the crowd was for Desperate.

Mr. McLaen bristled. "In Michigan," he said, "we take a trout, young man. We don't lead it out of the water on a leash."

Desperate turned suddenly and jumped down into the cockpit of the *Poseidon*. From there, he hurried to the cabin. He was so perturbed that his hands were shaking. Presently, he came back with what he had sought. It was a rod, shorter than a fly-casting rod, but as light as any. Attached to its butt was a large reel. The reel was loaded with six-thread line—line the thickness of ordinary grocery string. He handed it silently to Mr. McLaen.

The magnate from Michigan swished it in the air. "Miserable balance," he said.

"A fellow," Des replied, "took a sixty-one-pound white marlin with that rig last week."

"Towed it in," the other man retorted. "Or else you ran the boat up to it. And in this warm water they can't fight."

"I doubt," Desperate continued gently, "if you could boat a ten-pound dolphin on it."

Mr. McLaen had been fiddling with the handle of the reel. Its purring sound seemed to fascinate him. But when Des spoke, he snorted. "Why, I wouldn't be seen fishing on the ocean! My salmon club would probably throw me out. Michigan would be convulsed! Dolphin, eh? I'd prefer to play a harnessed house cat with my four-ounce fly rod!"

"Sure. You might catch the cat."

Mr. McLaen's steely eyes brightened to the challenge. "See here. How much do you charge for a fish-towing expedition in one of these power launches?"

"Thirty-five a day." Bitterness welled in Des. Nobody could call the *Poseidon* a power launch. "If you have it," he added. "In your case, though, I'll make it ten if you're not satisfied and pay the difference myself."

Desperate said that and shivered. The difference would be half a month's pay. Crunch would be furious. But the insult was worth the risk.

The old gentleman looked as if he might froth at the mouth in a minute. He was fumbling in his pocket. "Busy tomorrow?"

"No."

He pulled out an amalgamated chunk of money. There were hundred-dollar bills in the lump. He sorted out three tens and a five. He handed them to Desperate. "I'll be here at four," he said. "Four thirty, if you prefer!"

Desperate gulped. "We usually go out around eight or nine."

The older man blew his cheeks. "Eight or nine! There you are! What fish worth taking would rise at noon? That isn't fishing, young man! It's herding sheep! Good evening to you!"

He plowed his way through the crowd. The people dispersed slowly, arguing the pros and cons of Mr. McLaen's subject. Captain Emery, who had finished dressing the kings, winked. "Nice going, Des."

But Desperate was not amused. His mouth was a firm line. His face was spotted with red. He kicked back his yachting cap with the heel of his hand. "If I don't teach that old nail chewer a lesson tomorrow, I'll smother myself in my bunk!"

About an hour later, when Desperate had relaxed somewhat, Crunch and Sari and young Bill appeared on the dock. Crunch hurried up to his mate. "Woman named Mrs. Owens phoned me at the apartment," he said. "What's this about you making her old man so mad he came home and busted open a front screen because it was locked? He's a big shot in Michigan, this Mrs. Owens says, and she says will we please take good care of him and get him some fish tomorrow because he's got to like Miami—"

"That guy," Desperate interrupted with hideous solemnity, "is never going to forget Miami, if I have anything to do with it. He's going to loathe the word Miami. It'll haunt him!"

"But why?"

"He said," Desperate answered, "we weren't sporting. He said we were trawlers. He said we caught practically dead fish. He called the *Poseidon* a launch."

Crunch was startled. "Yeah?"

"He's a trout fisherman." Desperate expectorated the words.

Crunch's wife Sari was worried. "But if he's so important, boys . . ."

It had no weight with her husband. He was smiling at his mate and colleague.

"Is that so?" he said amiably. "A trout fisherman, eh? Well, well, well. Think of that!"

There was justice. Desperate said that, the minute Crunch showed up the next morning. During the night the wind had hauled around from the northwest to the northeast and risen steadily. Not to a gale by any means, but to a fresh, incessant breeze in the teeth of which the Gulf Stream was pouring a river of water. They knew what that meant: big, steep seas, bright blue skies, gulls slanting on the air, white crests, good fishing, but bad sailing for a landlubber.

Cheerily they prepared to go out, purchasing fresh balao for bait and filling the two iceboxes. On the possibility that Mr. McLaen would dislike the Stream that day, Crunch also bought four pounds of shrimp. Then they sat in the two side chairs astern, waiting. Crunch thought of something. "What's this oaf's name?"

"McLaen," Desperate replied. "Rhymes with swine."

"That him?"

Desperate looked. Mr. McLaen was stalking down the pier. He wore a rawhide shirt, breeches, woolen puttees, heavy high brown shoes, a bandanna tied around his neck, and an old, floppy-brimmed slouch hat which would neither shade his eyes from the sun nor stay on his head in the wind.

Crunch covered his grin with his hand. "Think we'll find any rainbow trout out there?" he asked.

"Come on," Des replied. "We'll cut this guy down to our size."

The man from Michigan lowered himself aboard. His shoes, ideal for fording a stony stream, slipped on the linoleum deck. Crunch caught him. "Maybe you'd better take those shoes off," he said. His customer grunted and sat down. "And the shirt too," Crunch continued.

"It's blowing, man! This shirt is a fine windbreaker!"

"Sure. But the cockpit's not very breezy on most tacks, and the sun's going to be hot."

The *Poseidon* headed into the Cut. Mr. McLaen took off his shoes. Then his woolen puttees and socks. His shirt came last. Crunch saw his relatively untanned torso and gave him a shirt of Desperate's. At the mouth of the Cut the water was boiling. Heavy seas roared in against the ebbing tide. The *Poseidon* heeled, rose, banged down, took spray clean over the cabin, shuddered, and came up skidding on the next wave.

Mr. McLaen looked at Desperate with alarm. Desperate wasn't even holding on to anything. He seemed engrossed with the business of trimming a bait.

The man from Michigan decided that the thing to do was to grin. He grinned. Then he thought about fishing—from a chair that was shooting around like a roller-coaster car. "Must be kind of difficult, at that," he said loudly, "to handle a fish in such weather."

Desperate shrugged. "Nothing, when you compare it to slippery rocks. Of course if you weren't set right and you got a big strike you might get pulled overboard." Desperate didn't add that no customer, to his knowledge, had ever fallen overboard. He did not say that both he and Crunch would consider themselves eternally disgraced if Mr. McLaen so much as fell down while he was a paying guest on their boat. He just allowed his passenger to ruminate over the idea.

The *Poseidon* was clear of the boil and tumult between the stone jetties. Clear, and at sea. She rode the combers sturdily. But Mr. McLaen, viewing first irregular walls of blue water and then the sharp profile of the ever-retreating Miami skyline, felt insecure. Not only insecure, but queasy. "I suppose people do occasionally get sick on these craft?" he ventured.

"Oh, a few." Desperate cut bait. Mr. McLaen, for the first time in his life, felt an antagonism to the odor of fish, however fresh.

"What do you do in such an event?"

Desperate looked up. "Depends. If they're game, we keep on for a couple of hours and sometimes they get well. If they fade out completely we take 'em in."

Mr. McLaen gritted his teeth. All he could see was wheeling sky and vast pyramids of water which took form and vanished before he could be certain of what the form had been. The motors were humming headily. A large dark bird with a forked tail floated into his vision and circled sickeningly. He realized that he was lying down, more or less, on one of the day beds. He realized, also, that he was perspiring. Clammily. He did not know that his initiation was too abrupt for a beginner. He did not know that fewer people suffer from *mal de mer* on clean, open small boats than on ocean liners, after the first few trips have relieved them of their initial anxieties. He knew only that his will was at war with his inclinations.

"Comfortable?" Desperate asked presently.

"This is great!" Mr. McLaen replied.

The mate found himself reluctantly admiring his passenger. Obviously, to Desperate's experienced eye, it was anything but great for the trout fisherman. He had turned the unromantic color of bituminous ash. His head was beginning to loll.

"We have a few hazards and troubles in connection with deep-sea fishing," Desperate said conversationally, after another interval. "Adds to the sportsmanship of it, don't you think? For example, if you hang one on light tackle and have to fight him standing up, with the boat slewing around in these seas, it gets tricky. Of course it may not be as hard as trout fishing."

"Sounds exciting," Mr. McLaen said.

But that was about all he said. He had never before been at sea in a small boat. He had scorned small boats on the Great Lakes: No fish worth going after there. Not in his opinion, anyway. He lay quietly. He realized that death was near at hand. It was going to be a slow and ugly death, with a white-and-indigo universe revolving around and over him, surging, eddying, diving, dropping, lifting him up agonizingly against the whole weight of his body and sinking out from under him just as he had begun to hope for stability. Stability, in fact, became an illusion that had belonged to another, better world.

He saw Desperate looking at him. He attempted to smile. A sea frosted with golden weed swelled up and tilted the *Poseidon*. It polished off Mr. McLaen. He hastened to the rail of the boat.

A few minutes later, he lay on the bed again with his eyes closed. Dimly, hopelessly, he toyed with the idea that the mate might soon summon him to fish. That was out of the question. He thought that perhaps he would be unconscious before it came time to admit he couldn't sit there and troll. He hoped so. The *Poseidon* began a new and unfathomable series of slides and convolutions. He groaned a little. And suddenly, all was tranquil. The heaving had stopped. The boat was running smoothly through quiet water. His head began to clear. He drew a breath and the air was fresh and good. He opened his eyes.

Desperate was sitting on the fish box in the stern, his solemn Scandinavian profile expressionless. Beyond Desperate, Mr. McLaen saw a large sign that said, DOG TRACK.

The mate turned. "We ran in," he said. "No sense in staying out if you feel that bad."

A rush of human warmth came over Mr. McLaen. These Florida boatmen were not, after all, the callous and sadistic salts of legend. When a fellow was about to die, they brought him in to water that was calm and turquoise and mighty good to look at. Not like the sailors he had read about in sea books who let you lie unconscious for hours if you happened to get seasick, who laughed at you, kidded you. Mr. McLaen presently tried his feet. They were pretty firm. His stomach had found its accustomed niche in his abdomen. He looked at his watch. Ten. Thirty-five dollars for an hour and a half. A bargain. He would have given a thousand to have been able to get ashore without losing face. And they were making it pretty easy.

"Feel better?" Crunch asked from the deck above.

Mr. McLaen peered. "Have you been standing up there through all that surf?"

Crunch smiled. "That was nothing. I mean for us. Do it often. All day. But when you're not used to it it sometimes gets you."

The man from the inland waters stretched himself. "I feel pretty fine — now. I guess I'm too old for that sort of stuff. And I'm perfectly willing to hand it to anybody who can take it. They're born lucky."

Desperate disliked that. His customer was hedging again. "You probably wouldn't care to do any bay fishing," he said provocatively. "In calm water—in the dinghy?"

"Bay fishing? For what? Catfish?"

"Bonefish."

"Never heard of 'em."

Desperate nodded.

"Most people haven't. You catch 'em on the shoals. They're supposed to be pretty gamy."

"How big?"

"Oh, a big one would run nine or ten pounds. I've even heard people say it reminded them of trout."

Mr. McLaen, who had thought within the past hour that he would never smoke again, found himself biting off the end of a cigar. "Trout?" he said. "Nonsense!"

"People on the dock would think we were pretty smart if we managed to bring in a bonefish or two," Desperate continued. "But I suppose you're all tuckered out."

"Tuckered out?" Mr. McLaen was altogether himself. "See here, young man. I tramp all day with the best of 'em. Up mountains or down ravines. I've crossed glaciers on foot to fish, and packed canoes up the edges of hundreds of miles of white water. Take me to these—these carp."

Desperate looked up at Crunch. Crunch looked down at Desperate. The *Poseidon* turned south in Biscayne Bay and proceeded at an increased speed. Mr. McLaen watched a pelican. "Bonefish," he said. "Any relation to a shark?"

Desperate merely shook his head.

The bonefish is not so much a fish as it is a cult. An eight-pounder is a big one. A ten-pounder is enormous. It is an all-silver fish which reflects so much sunlight that snapshots of proud catches often show only a blurred glitter. It feeds on the flats as the tide comes in, nosing along the bottom in search of small crustacea. It is taken on shrimp, live or dead, or small crabs. It will, on occasion, seize other baits.

Muddy clouds in the water mark its searching progress and quite often it swims in such shallows that its dorsal may be seen. The bonefish angler baits up, casts, and sits in a small boat waiting. If he feels a nibble—or sees one, because the tropic ocean is gin-limpid—he allows the fish to swallow the bait and then strikes.

What happens after that can be fully understood only through experience. The antics of the trout are usually confined to small areas. The bonefish has the whole sea to move through. Trout leap. Bonefish merely run. But they are regarded as the fastest thing with fins. They smash reels. They break rods. They circumnavigate boats so swiftly that lines are wound around unwilling necks. Strong men go mad because of such fireworks. They rave and curse and weep—and come back to the old Spanish Main every year for the rest of their lives to get another shot. Inland anglers are unfamiliar with this fish—as they are in general with the power and stamina of all marine species.

A dyed-in-the-wool trout fisherman—a McLaen—who ties his own flies from hand-picked bird breasts—will smile superciliously at a black-bass fisherman. A brawny catcher of marlin will turn away from a man who describes the zest and glamour of fresh water. But a bonefish addict never discusses any sort of fishing save with another bonefisherman. Then the colloquy is obsessive, even paranoid. Bonefish break up homes, unless the wives go along. Then they cement marriages with a tie that is like fused quartz.

In the full knowledge of those facts, Desperate rowed Mr. McLaen away from the *Poseidon*, which lay at anchor in the middle of a tidal wash or "creek." He smiled beatifically at Crunch as he rowed, and the *Poseidon*'s skipper smiled back; then he lay down on the starboard day bed and opened a magazine. He had fallen asleep before Des stopped rowing an eighth of a mile away.

Mr. McLaen looked over the side. "Must be a good foot deep here," he said with marked scorn. "Maybe we'll hook a crawdad."

Desperate took an oar from its lock and planted it deep in the softly matted sea bottom. "Crawdad?"

"We used to call 'em that when we were kids. Crayfish. You find them in brooks. Some of them grow as long as six inches."

"If you see any crawdads here," Des replied, "and you might, they may measure three feet from whisker to tail. Here's your rod." He unwrapped the shrimp and put one on a hook. "Just cast over toward that little white patch of coral, and then take it easy."

Mr. McLaen examined the rod. "Nice," he said.

"I made it," Desperate answered.

"The devil you did! Why, Parsons himself—"

"Parsons makes good tackle too."

Mr. McLaen stood up. Desperate, from habit, ducked. But the Michigan trout fisherman knew one thing. He knew how to cast. He felt out the reel by allowing the bait to fall free. Then he wound up again and slung, putting his wrist in it. The bait sailed like a well-driven golf ball across the coral patch and it fell lightly a good fifty feet beyond it. Mr. McLaen grunted. "I sure do hate to cast bait! Now, if I had a good fly rod I could at least amuse myself."

The mate made no answer. He settled himself in the middle of the dinghy. His customer also settled down. Presently he squirmed. Without saying anything, Desperate produced two cushions. Mr. McLaen's grunt was more or less appreciative.

Time began to pass. The sun warmed them. Far to southward the Keys stretched in a dull green arc. Around them the bay sparkled. Along the northern horizon, in the mist, Miami hung half miraged, like a ghost city or a city that floated above the ground through an enchantment. Nearer by, on an island, palms leaned over the water and an old lighthouse stood red and rigid against the bluer water of the sea outside. Birds passed. Boats moved along by power and by sail, well beyond hailing distance, but near enough to be visible in detail. A plane took off from Dinner Key and floated south toward Havana like a dragon fly pinned on a blue blotter.

"Pleasant," said Mr. McLaen.

"If you feel a nibble let him take it," said Desperate.

More time passed.

"The sun gets into your bones. Makes you feel kind of good."

Des nodded.

The guy had called the *Poseidon* a power launch. Said they were trawlers. But he'd been plenty seasick. That was a good first lesson. Now, with a little luck—

"I feel a nibble," said Mr. McLaen.

Des looked. The lie was running slowly off the reel, in little jerks. "All right. Now push on the thumb-stall and hit him."

Mr. McLaen did so.

Something tore the reel limb from limb. Crunch heard the sound across the water, woke instantly, and looked with fascination. Trying to control the take-off of a hooked bonefish is like toying with a handful of lightning. The fish unwound a hundred yards of line in zero seconds. Mr. McLaen stood up. His eyes bulged out from beneath his beetling brows. He touched the reel, and regretted it with passionate profanity. The fish stopped and charged back. In his astonishment, Mr. McLaen tried to strip his line, peeling it from the rod and dropping it on the bottom of the boat. By that method he achieved nothing. The bonefish was within fifteen feet of the boat in an instant. It made a fast circle.

Mr. McLaen saw it: A silvery thing that went past like light from a mirror flicked a mile away. An unearthly thing. A glittering fragment of the sea itself, alive and incandescent. He saw it brake to an impossible stop, hold still for a fragment of time, and then disappear. His line snapped across his chest.

"Little fellow," Des said, though it was actually medium-sized. "Can't strip off your line on these fish. They aren't trout. Gotta wind."

Desperate's voice had been calm. But Mr. McLaen gave tongue. He called the fish a multitude of names, and, toward the end, he even included himself. At last he just stared raggedly at the mate. "It isn't possible," he said, panting. "It can't be! Why, he covered a hundred yards in—I—I don't know what to say. I was helpless. Clumsy!"

"Aw, said Des, "you were all right. I saw a guy fall overboard once and sit smack on a sea urchin. We took eleven spines out of him."

"But—the fish! Why, man, if they saw that in Michigan . . ."

Desperate shrugged. He repaired the damage and baited. "Try again," he said.

An hour went by. Mr. McLaen had waited at the beginning with inattention; now he kept his eyes glued on the water. The sun was overhead and hot then.

"A bottle of cold beer would go good," Des ventured.

Mr. McLaen glowered at him. "Don't torment yourself—or me!"

The mate lifted one of the dinghy seats. Underneath was a nest of cracked ice. In the ice were four bottles of beer. Mr. McLaen gasped. Not loudly, but earnestly. Desperate opened a bottle on the seat edge and passed it up. The eyes of the man from Michigan were expressive.

He had finished his beer when Des saw him quiver. "Look! Astern!"

Des raised himself and yawned. "Leopard ray."

"But, man, it's beautiful! A magnificent thing! And it's got grace! Look at it! By George! Amazing!"

Desperate had admired leopard rays many times. But he allowed himself only another yawn. "Plentiful," he said.

A while later Mr. McLaen had another start. "There! Something shot through the water like a torpedo! Greenish—and a yard long."

"Barracuda."

"Good Lord! Like a big pike, eh? Only quicker. And—what's that?"

"Another bonefish," Desperate answered placidly. "Sit tight. Maybe he'll mosey up to your shrimp."

Mr. McLaen sat tight. His knuckles blanched around the butt of his rod. He was breathing hard when the bonefish picked up his bait. He struck. And it happened all over; though, on the second occasion, Mr. McLaen endeavored to reel. The bonefish made a half dozen mile-a-minute runs at various angles. Mr. McLaen managed them skillfully. Then the fish went under the boat. He followed that too. But the last sweeping arc confounded him. He yanked too hard, and Desperate's rod snapped.

Mr. McLaen sat down, a saddened man. "I guess you've got something here," he said slowly, as he wound in the segment of the tip.

"I think we have. You're pretty good."

"Do you believe I could learn to nail one of those cannon balls?"

"Yep. Ought to get the next, if the tide's not too high."

But the next wasn't a bonefish. Mr. McLaen just thought it was: a strong fish that swam less swiftly than the two others, but fought like a bulldog. He was soaked with sweat when Des gaffed it. And he stared bug-eyed again. A diamond-shaped fish, bluish and silver, with fins that turned into long spines. A fish the like of which he had never dreamed of catching.

"Permit," said Desperate laconically. "Fair scrapper. Fair." That, too, was classic understatement.

"How many more kinds of fish do you have around here?" Mr. McLaen inquired, after a pause.

The mate's next words seemed like a poor effect at humor until he looked at the mate's face. Des said. "Six hundred."

"Six hundred, man!"

"Yeah. You can catch—I mean 'take'—thirty or forty kinds at different times right over on that dark patch near where the *Poseidon's* anchored." Des pulled up the oar to which the dinghy was moored. "Of course, the real fishing, in my mind, is outside."

Mr. McLaen allowed himself to be rowed back to the cruiser. When Crunch helped him aboard he said in a businesslike manner, "I'd like to charter you boys for a week of bonefishing. Just to get the hang."

Crunch shook his head. "Why? You can hire a kicker for a couple of bucks and fish all you want. You don't need us."

"You mean I can just come out myself and fish?"

"And fish," Crunch said. "No sense paying out thirty-five a day for that. Too bad you lost those bonefish. Perhaps sometime you'd like to try it outside. On a calm day."

"Maybe I would," said Mr. McLaen. "Yes, I think I would."

They ate lunch. Then they tried for snappers. Mr. McLaen caught one. Desperate caught eleven. There is a knack in snapper fishing, too, as any Florida cracker will readily testify.

The Owenses, *père, mère, fils et fille*, were waiting apprehensively at the dock when the *Poseidon* came in. Mr. McLaen bounded ashore. He had the permit in his hand. "Look, Evelyn," he bellowed. "I got this thing! I forget what you call it."

Evelyn nudged her husband. "Dad is in better spirits," she said.

Mr. McLaen was waving the permit at the crowd that had quickly gathered—not for him this time, but from custom—to inspect the catch of a returning fishing boat. "This is the doggonedest fishing hole on earth," he said loudly. "I took this fellow on six-thread line, they tell me. A beauty, eh?"

Evelyn's husband helped his father-in-law ashore. "Glad you had a good day, dad. If we were staying down here any longer you could get in a lot of them. But Ev and I . . ."

Mr. McLaen put down the permit. His grandchildren began dancing around it and chanting, "Grandpa caught a whale!" He smiled at them with tacit agreement.

"What is this nonsense?" he asked gruffly. "About not staying?"

"If I can't start that sugar-cane enterprise —"

"Who said you couldn't! Tomorrow we'll hire a smaller boat and go out on the flats and talk the whole thing over. It's my hunch cane is a comer down here. Now, about getting fish mounted as trophies . . ."

A couple of days later, Desperate was tenderly examining two of the finest casting rods he had ever seen. He then scrutinized the aluminum butts which went with them and the two reels. Presently he took the end of the six-thread line from a spool and knotted it onto a spindle. He was winding carefully when Crunch came aboard the *Poseidon*.

"Old man McLaen," Crunch said, "wants to take a shot at it outside this afternoon. It's a flat calm day." Idly he reread the card that had come with the rods. "From an old Crawdad," it said, "to a pair of anglers."

Desperate chewed gum slowly and nodded. "Yeah. Emery had seven sails up this morning. I think if we get Mac a sailfish, he'll plant sugar cane clear to Jacksonville. You know, it's funny. At first, I didn't like that guy."

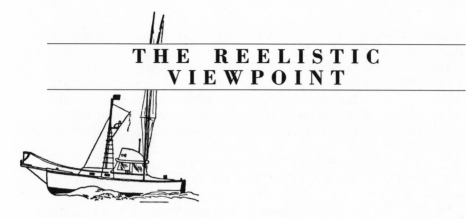

THE REELISTIC
VIEWPOINT

CRUNCH BLEW three lusty blasts for the Venetian Causeway drawbridge and three more to halt traffic on the county highway. The *Poseidon* slid past upended streets and grinding machinery into the steamer basin. A pelican dropped down on the balmy air and took a position off the bow.

"Look!" Crunch said delightedly to his mate. "That guy knows we haven't seen a pelican in months. He's piloting a couple of Miami boatmen home! Gaze at those old whipped-cream clouds! New Jersey is all right, but it somehow just isn't Florida!"

The fact was obvious to Des. He made ready the bowlines in case their old ones weren't on their hooks, and his lips broke into a gradual grin as he began to recognize people on the Gulf Stream Dock. A few minutes later they were ashore. Crunch was kissing Sari and socking young Bill lightly with his right. Bill was caroling and kicking back. There were swift words: How was the trip down? How's the apartment? How did Bill behave on the train? How's the boat? Going to haul her this afternoon for a few days and fix her in A-1 shape.

Desperate, not having a wife, mingled with the other skippers and mates. He answered questions with an unusual garrulity. "Sure, we had a good summer. . . . Yeah, got plenty of bluefins—biggest was six-seventy. . . . The Jersey mosquitoes ain't any worse than the ones from the Glades— but, boy! do those Jersey fishermen take their hunting seriously! . . . Hello, Jess. How are you, Mr. Williams?"

Crunch had finished the familiar preliminaries. He turned to the committee of welcome. "Hey! All you guys! Come on across the street! I'm buying everybody a beer!"

They drank and presently Crunch was ready to join his family. He instructed Des in the matter of hauling out the *Poseidon*. But Captain

Gwin Scully caught his arm as he was going. "There's been a little trouble while you were away," he said.

"Yeah?" Crunch's eyes flickered. "What kind?"

"Too bad the *Oriental Moon* isn't here now. She's in the Keys—with a party."

"*Oriental Moon?* Never heard of her."

Gwin gave the furtive glance-around of the gossipy male. It is the same glance used by females of that predisposition. "I didn't want to throw no monkey wrench into your home-coming—" it was evident that throwing the monkey wrench was a pleasure to him—"but we got some real competition, now. Fellow by the name of Henry Purvis owns her. Came in about a month after you and Des left Miami. He's rich. Inherited dough from an uncle, or somebody. Went into the charter-boat business just for the kick of it. He bought stock in the Dock Corporation so as to be sure of a berth here. What do you think of that?"

Crunch laughed. "Playboy stuff, hunh? Say, Gwin. I'll take any one of those millionaire charter-boat men, fish him nine thread to twenty-four, and catch enough stuff to sink his boat while he's trying to raise a houndfish!"

"You ain't seen his boat," Gwin answered. "It looks like a floatin' circus. Got more chrome platin' than the Empire State Building. Painted white and a kind of color he calls mauve. The dames go nuts about it. Why, even his gaffs is practically pearl-handled—and he's got controls in five different places."

Crunch was still amused. "Listen," he said. "I haven't seen Sari and Bill since I put them on the train in New York. I got important things to think about in this world—"

Gwin caught his sleeve. "Two engines," he continued, "and *what* engines! She'll do forty-five! Makes the rest of us look like a bunch of scows. And—he's a party grabber. Not only that—but he's been fishin' for fifteen bucks a day all summer—and says he'll fish for twenty this winter. It costs him money to do it, but he has plenty. What he likes—is to meet people and fish 'em. What he also likes—though he doesn't say so—is to see us workin' men eat dirt."

Crunch's mirth went away, then, like the print in a sharply closed book. "How about Mr. Williams? Doesn't he stop it?"

"He can't. This Purvis guy is in the corporation, like I said."

After dinner that evening, Crunch strolled from his apartment to the dock. Not half the regular boats were there. Some were still in Brielle. Some were out on Montauk. Some were up in Nova Scotia. Some were off Virginia, and Cape Hatteras, fishing experimentally. One was at that moment in a crate on the deck of a Pacific liner, homeward bound from a trip to the Fiji Islands with a skipper who itched to get back to the Gulf Stream Dock and tell them about the big ones that nobody could identify—not even the museum people. Miami fishing guides are famous, peripatetic, and responsible for many astonishing contributions to the science of marine biology. Crunch thought about that with a romantic tingle and spotted a face he had missed at his reception.

Old "Doc" Willis was sitting in the stern of the *Wanderer VII*, staring into space. Doc was a favorite on the pier—not only among anglers but also among the guides, where abiding affection is not exactly rare but subject to quick change in the competition for business and the hard rivalry over the quarry.

But nobody envied Doc his parties—or his catches. He was eighty-six, bald, cherubic, ruddy, and as tough as a football. He looked sixty—a virile sixty. His high spirits and the twinkle in his eye always sustained morale when the weather was so bad the boats couldn't go out. He was a roguish Buddha of a man; wise, witty when he wanted to be, and a staunch defender of justice. The oldest inhabitant could not rightly remember when Doc had anchored a battered Seabright dory in the bay and put a sign on her saying: "*Wanderer I*—Fishing Charters Accepted." It was long before Miami Beach was more than a mangrove swamp. But the intervening years had put no mark on Doc, while they had revolutionized "The Beach."

Doc's attitude surprised Crunch. He wasn't a space gazer. He loved to talk and he loved to read; he never sulked. The skipper of the *Poseidon* watched him for a minute and then said, "Hi!"

Doc looked up. His face broke into a venerable pattern of little wrinkles; the wrinkles that came from watching the sea and those that had originated in laughter. He laughed now—with a chuckle that was like the expanding puff of the first breeze across a glassy calm. "Crunch Adams! Well, well, well! Glad to see you back, son! Hear you had a good summer! Hop aboard!"

Crunch stepped down lightly. "What's eatin' you, Doc?"

"Oh . . . nothin'. Nothin'. Gettin' old, I guess. Old and gloomy."

"Hell, Doc! You'll be draggin' baits when you're a hundred!" Crunch watched the octogenarian's cheerfulness fade. "Aren't sick?"

"Sick? Don't know what the word means!"

The young man had another idea. In the empty slip beside the *Wanderer* was the slot reserved for the boat Gwin Scully had described. "That—*Oriental Moon*—been giving you any trouble, Doc? Is that it?"

"Oh . . . a little. A little."

"Let's have it," Crunch said tersely.

Doc sighed. "Well—I don't like to run folks down, Crunch. But this

Purvis *has* hurt me a lot. It's not just that he's cut his prices down to where I can't compete and make a living. It's . . . well—he's told a couple of my old summer customers I can't see good any more. A darned lie! Went to an optician myself to make sure. Don't even need specs. He's told other people—in my hearing—the planks in the *Wanderer* are rotten. Hell, son. *You* know you can't drive nails in that mahogany. He says to prospects I'm an old drunk. Well—I *did* get drunk—night I caught that big white marlin. It's a seafaring man's privilege, isn't it? Made me boil. Yep. He's swiped at least ten parties off me this month."

Crunch doubled his fist and looked at it. "No kidding?"

But Doc shook his head. "Won't do any good, son. Jake beat the devil out of him—and did thirty days for it. This Purvis is rich. He has pull. Threatened me with a suit for slander—and I guess he'd of taken it to court, too, if I hadn't piped down. Everybody's mad—and helpless. He's mean, Crunch. Real mean. You gotta watch him—out in the Stream. He's cut off more than one sailfish—and come in grinning and apologizing. You know, some people are just born to make trouble. Guess it must be they hate themselves. And this Purvis is tops at it."

It was after eleven when Crunch went home. Sari was waiting up, and Des had come over to report the condition of the *Poseidon*'s hull. Both of them knew immediately that the skiper was sore. Sari poured a glass of cold lemonade and said, "O.K. What is it?"

So he told them. He finished with a sentence that was cold and measured. "I'm going to get that guy."

He expected instant remonstrance from his wife; Sari hated fights. But he was mistaken. "Yes, Crunch," she said. "You're going to get him—and get him good!"

He stared. "You mean that? You mean—you're *with* me?"

"*With* you!" Sari was quite pale and very tense. "Listen. Who bought Bill his first sweater? Doc. Who sent those blocks over? Doc. Who got you that lumber for your engine bed when we couldn't afford butter on our bread? Old Doc. He's one of the sweetest guys on earth—and you two can't let anybody walk on him. I'd hate you if you did!"

Crunch was smiling by that time. He walked over to his wife's chair and reversed the svelte direction of her hair so that it curled over her eyes. "I *like* women like you," he said. "Now. What are we going to do? It won't be a cinch."

"We had one of those rich amateur guides down at Bandbox Key a few years ago," Des said. "A nice fellow. Only—he didn't realize every time he cut our prices with his flashy boat he was hitting us where we live. Business was lousy and more than one of us was on a straight diet of fish." He smiled at Crunch and Sari. "You know none of us is angels, and plenty is tough, and we don't mind any amount of honest competition. But some rat cut this guy's boat loose—and she sank. Can you imagine sinkin' a man's boat? They kicked every last one of us off the club pier— and I didn't blame 'em."

Sari spoke. "That's just what'll happen to Purvis, too. There's guides on the Gulf Stream Dock mean and shortsighted enough to do it. And then—you'll all have a black name. If you charter-boat men had a union— you could fix him. But I'm glad you haven't. It's about the only business left where you own your soul!"

Crunch had been thinking. "We ought to give him some kind of warning," he said. "Not just make him know he isn't liked; evidently he's too conceited to mind that—and even enjoys being unpopular. We ought to take him down a peg. Play a practical joke on him that'll make people snicker when they see him. Guys like that can't stand being on the short end of a joke. Now I got an idea. It's on the rough and tough side—but it might work."

He explained. Before he finished, Des was wiping his eyes. He conquered his mirth long enough to say, "In other words, just concentrate a whole season of natural accidents in a day, hunh?"

Crunch nodded. "Yeah. It's a dirty trick—but—"

"Dirty trick!" Sari's indignation was surprising. "After what he did to Doc! It's letting him off darned easy! He has plenty of money. He can afford to take a small loss! I think it's a good idea!"

Her husband look bemusedly at his wife and thought to himself that the man who had called the female of the species deadly was right.

On a morning soon after his return from the keys, Henry Purvis, owner of the *Oriental Moon,* was sitting in one of his *de luxe* fishing chairs looking at the rest of the fleet with condescension. He was a tall man— thin except for a paunch—with a bony, inhospitable face and small, beetle-brown eyes. He spied two gentlemen on the dock, wealthy-looking gentlemen, one of whom carried a walking stick, and he watched closely while they stopped to talk to the captain of the *Firefly.* Eventually they approached the lavish stern of the *Oriental Moon.* Mr. Purvis gave than an ingratiating greeting.

Crunch, who had practiced with the cane, and Desperate, who was wearing a stiff collar for the first time in years—returned the salute jauntily. If there was a certain clandestine attention on the part of other boatmen, it was well-hidden.

"My name's Adley," Crunch said, as he accepted the invitation to come aboard. "This is Mr. Wharton. Possibly you've heard of his father? L. M. Wharton of Consolidated United?"

Mr. Purvis was pleased and impressed. "Naturally."

Crunch was a good mimic and he knew his role perfectly. A hundred customers had educated him in it: Snobs, millionaires, Park Avenue Americans, Britishers, sportsmen good and bad, men who had fished before and men who had not. "Wharton and I have read of your fishing here. We don't know a thing about it. Polo's our game—" he laughed deprecatorily— "but we thought we might try a cast or two. A sort of warm up here in Miami. Then—if we like it—a month in Bimini. Something of the sort—eh? We're picking out a boat. Yours is rather—er—smart-looking, what?"

Even the bloodless Mr. Purvis was startled. A month in Bimini with a pair of wealthy American polo players would be a plum, indeed. Not from the financial viewpoint—which would have appealed almost pathetically to some of the business-hungry boatmen on the pier—but from the point of view of prestige and business triumph.

"We're utter neophytes," Crunch went on, with a look at Des. "Probably act like dubs of the worst sort. But we might improve—after a few weeks in Bimini. Think so?"

Purvis nodded eagerly and put on a bit of top spin on his own account. "Gentlemen," he said, "you've come to the right guide! Most of the captains here are really—day laborers." Crunch did not bat an eye. "The *Oriental Moon* is the only *safe* boat on the dock." He began to tick off his equipment. He mentioned his lower rates: "*I* fish for the fun of it. For the love of it. I'm no sordid commercial bumpkin. I, myself, have—er—complete economic independence, so I am in a position to make the sport what it should be!"

Desperate had not spoken. Now he nodded and looked vague. "I thought there was a—er—standard rate?"

"There *was*," the skipper replied. "I'm going to end that. I'm going to drive a lot of these chaps out of business!"

"I see." Des ruminated. "We heard—from a friend in New York named Wiggam—Stock Market—that a boat due here named the—hmmmm—*Poseidon*—was pretty good."

Mr. Purvis swelled with pomp and irritation. "The *Poseidon!* A home-made wreck run by a couple of brainless boys! She's been lucky—but let me tell you gentlemen—some fine afternoon that ship will founder! I haven't seen her yet, but I assure you she's worthless—and dangerous. Dirty, too, beyond any doubt!"

Crunch raised one eyebrow and pointed with his cane. "What do you call those sticks?"

Their host explained the function of outriggers. He also noted in passing that his were made of duraluminum at a cost of five hundred dollars. There was more palaver. A warm-up trip was arranged for the next day. If it proved successful—Bimini would be considered: A month in Bimini. Crunch and Desperate walked away in the company of Purvis, taking their time, asking a few idiotic questions of the other captains, and proudly stating that they had chartered the *Oriental Moon* for the following day. A few snorts followed their progress—but their true identity was guarded.

They appeared at nine. In their role of novitiate dudes they wore gaudy clothes—borrowed from the wardrobes of the entire fleet. Doe-skin trousers and shirts with stocks. When they passed the *Wanderer VII*, Doc waved impersonally. "Good luck, gentlemen," he said. "I may see you out there!"

Crunch tipped back his solar topee and answered, "Righto!" He boarded the *Oriental Moon* with an air.

There was no doubt about her speed. She flew along the ship channel, nearly upsetting two boys in a rowboat, and she was out on the edge of the Stream almost before Mr. Purvis's sullen mate had the baits ready. They were, Des observed, badly made baits. He lifted a finger at the mate: "By the way, son. What's your name?"

"Edgar."

"Ah. Well, Edgar. You'll have to show us everything. We hold these poles in our laps, I suppose?"

Edgar smiled with unpleasant superiority. "*Rods*. We call them rods. Yes. I'll show you." He put the baits overboard, pinched the lines into clothespins, hauled them up on the outrigger halyards, watched the baits bob along for a moment, and gave his instructions in a truculent tone: "If I holler, reel. If it's a sailfish, I'll take the rod and hook it for you."

Des winked imperceptibly at Crunch. Hooking a customer's sailfish is the height of unsportsmanlike procedure—although occasionally a man who cares more about a fish than his own self-respect will request that service. "We can manage," Des said.

It was a breezy morning. Crunch and Des had anticipated as much. The Stream was rough. Edgar watched for signs of seasickness, and was visibly irritated that there were none. A seasick customer meant, for him, pay without work. The two elegant anglers knew that the fishing was good; there would be ample opportunity to carry out their scheme. They held their rods loosely and lounged back with supercilious disinterest—a kind of behavior which had vexed them countless times in their own customers.

Purvis was steering—and looking back from time to time with smug satisfaction. A month in Bimini. Once, Crunch addressed him. "I suppose you break off line out here sometimes—and maybe even bust a pole? Do we pay for that?"

The skipper of the glittering *Oriental Moon* laughed magnanimously. "Certainly not! My equipment is the best. If it fails—I pay!"

"Dashed sporting of you," Des murmured.

A half hour passed without any sign of a fish. Mr. Purvis apologized. "Just be patient," he said over and over. "Part of the game!"

Crunch's patience, however, came to an end. He had already ascertained that there was on his reel about a hundred yards of new thirty-nine thread line spliced on twice as much twenty-four. They were fishing for sails. To let people fish for that delicate and dextrous creature with such heavy gear was, in his mind, a heresy comparable to hunting deer with machine guns.

Unobtrusively, while the mate was making a fresh bait and the skipper was avoiding a freighter, Crunch slipped off the drag. Line bellied down from the outrigger, hit the water, and slid rapidly astern as the reel spun silently. In a few minutes the weight of wet line pulled itself loose from the clothespin. But the angler gave no sign that anything had happened. He waited until all the line had payed out and then—feeling a jerk on the reel spindle—he struck so mightily that the whole business broke off and vanished astern.

Desperate, who had been watching from the corner of his eye, said in the blankest of voices, "Get a strike, pal?"

"I think I did," Crunch answered perplexedly. "Blooming fish took all my line!"

"What!" It was Purvis who spoke. He deserted the wheel and hurried astern. He perceived that the ignorance of his customer had cost fifteen dollars worth of line. "Sing out when anything like that happens!" he said heatedly. Then he remembered the value of his clients. "Never mind! Forget it! I should have told you—when the line drops—yell. You must have accidentally knocked off the drag. I'll give you a new rod and reel."

"Fine," said Crunch. "Splendid. Quite a thrill—eh?"

Desperate bit his lip and stared at the churning wake.

That happened at ten. At eleven, or shortly afterward, Desperate saw a brownish blur underneath his dancing bait. A sailfish. He saw it for a considerable time before it was noticed by Edgar or by Mr. Purvis—time enough to toy absently with the slack line between his rod tip and the outrigger. In the process, he managed to throw a half hitch over the top of his rod. Des was a little afraid the mate might notice and repair the situation before the moment came to strike the sail; so he took to jiggling his rod, and humming.

Crunch, who had also been watching the purple-brown blur, smirked and nodded in rhythm. Suddenly Mr. Purvis screamed. "Edgar! Sail—on the left bait! Where's your eyes, man!"

Edgar, who had been sitting on the fish box gazing at the contents of his soul, leaped to action. That is, he tried to snatch the rod from Des. But the erstwhile mate of the *Poseidon* hung on. Meanwhile, the sailfish stuck a foot of his bill out of the water, followed it with the upper half of his indigo dorsal fin—and charged. It then became obvious that Mr. Purvis was no soft skipper. A man, rather, of the old school, who ran his boat with iron discipline. He bawled at Desperate, "Mr. Wharton! Let go! The mate will do it for you!"

So Des let go. All eyes were focussed on the sailfish, which just then succeeded in batting the bait so hard the line dropped from the clothespin on the outrigger. Edgar waited tensely for it to come taut. Des murmured a prayer that the sail would pick up the bait. It did. The line tightened. Several things seemed to happen at once: Edgar struck violently—too violently, the passengers thought—the sailfish broke into the air with a mighty leap, and the line parted with such force that the broken end whizzed back into the cockpit. The sailfish fell with a splash and was no more to be seen.

For a second, there was silence. Then Mr. Purvis' round oaths marred it. He addressed his mate. "How could you pop thirty-nine thread, you fool!"

Edgar saw the half hitch. He showed it to Mr. Purvis. The skipper peered—and took time to gather his spiritual resources. "All right," he murmured in an embittered voice. "Put on a new leader. Let's go fishing!" He took more time before saying, "Gentlemen, somehow there was a turn taken around the rod tip. Otherwise—we would have a sailfish in the boat right now!"

Crunch could have debated that point. Instead, he said, "Very exciting! Awfully exciting! Reminds me of the time I skied down the—the . . . " he couldn't think of anything to have skied down.

"Matterhorn," Des murmured.

"Right. Matterhorn."

Mr. Purvis looked steadily ahead. His lips were moving. Crunch knew how he felt. Both those gems of outrageous behavior had been revealed to Crunch by niggle-headed anglers aboard the *Poseidon*. Crunch had learned others, too. But, for the moment, he was content. He lay back and listened to the purr of the engines. He looked at the distant sky line of Miami.

"Boat ever been bitten by a shark?" he asked pleasantly, after a time.

Mr. Purvis flinched, and gripped himself. "No. Can't say it has."

"Or sawed on by a sawfish?"

The owner-skipper was succinct. "No."

"Funny. Suppose you never got a look at a sea serpent, either?"

"No," said Mr. Purvis steadily, "I never did."

"This ought to be the right place for 'em. Well—maybe we'll see one today. What do you call that bird up there?"

Mr. Purvis squinted through the window under the canopy. He swallowed. "That's a Coast Guard plane."

"Huh! Looks like a bird. Think so, Wharton?"

Des did not reply. There was a bonita lunging at his bait. A good-sized one. Edgar was busy removing a weed from Crunch's hook.

The captain yelled. "Bonita! Take it easy, Mr. Wharton! When your line drops, wind up! When you feel the fish—strike firmly! A couple of quick jerks."

Des nodded. He straightened up in his chair. He assumed the fierce and frantic expression he had seen on the faces of other people in that same crisis. He gripped the rod like a drowning man. There was another splashing boil and slack drifted down from the outrigger. Des wound. When he felt the fish, he struck. He pivoted his rod back in the gimble on his chair seat with a quick, ferocious lunge. There was enough force in the movement to harpoon a whale. Both the skipper and the mate saw what was going to happen—and were powerless to prevent it. The tapered end of the rod came in shattering contact with the edge of the canopy overhead. There was a splintering sound—and the rod broke.

Purvis went white. The mate stared angrily. But Desperate was also having a mood: The bonita was still on; the reel spun; the broken end of the rod slid down the taut line and disappeared in the sea. "I got him!" Des yelled delightedly. "I got him! What do I do now?"

"Give him slack!" Crunch advised, remembering a similar insane bit of advice offered by a young man who had never fished before. "Plenty of slack!"

Des threw off the drag. The reel squealed, raced, and backlashed, before Mr. Purvis or the mate could get to it. Desperate's swift attempt to untangle the backlash made it worse. The bonita was stopped dead in its tracks for an instant. Then it tried again to run. But the snarl in the reel held fast, and—once more—the line broke.

Captain Purvis was standing behind Des, sweating. "That rod cost twenty bucks," he said hoarsely. "Twenty bucks! *Twenty!*"

But Des, having lost the fish, was serene again. He waggled his head. "Mighty sporting of you fellows to take risks like this! I suppose the damage is even greater—in Bimini?" He turned innocently to his companion. "Hot stuff, this fishing. Isn't it, Adley?"

"Bully," said Crunch. He smirked a little.

Mr. Purvis had no words left in him. At least, none for his customers.

He strode back to the wheel. He expended a certain amount of animus on the mate. "You fool," he said feelingly. "You idiot! Keep *near* those gentlemen! They don't know what to do. *Show* them! Incidentally, *you're* paying for that rod!"

Edgar did not reply. He looked machetes into his employer's back—and hoisted the outrigger halyard again. Not, however, before Crunch had tampered with it. Borrowing a leaf from Des, he had made two half hitches of line around the clothespin. Two half hitches form what is known as a clove hitch, and it is a firm knot. Any fish taking Crunch's bait would be affixed by strong line to the end of an outrigger fifty feet long. Crunch hoped his next strike would be something big—the outrigger, even with the leverage of fifty feet, would undoubtedly tow a small one. He kept his eyes open, and struck up a little conversation with Des on the subject of waistcoats.

The *Oriental Moon* was passing the whistling buoy when a small hammerhead shark—a mere hundred pounder—made a lazy pass at the bait. Mr. Purvis saw it, because he was watching everything closely. Crunch wheeled in his chair. "Fish!" he yelled. "I saw one! Maybe it was a marlin! A *big* fish!"

The captain was stony. "Shark."

"Couldn't we hook it—somehow?"

"They aren't any sport. No fight."

"But—it would be good practice! And we'd have *something* to take in. We don't seem to be doing so well on sailfish."

Perhaps Purvis was still thinking of the month-long charter. Perhaps he was considering his passengers' undeniably immense need of practice. He cut the motors. The shark, which was still languidly pursuing the bait, overtook it and swallowed it. "He's got it!" Crunch shouted with glee. Purvis instantly gunned the motors again—in the hope that he might hook the shark by the boat's speed in spite of any error his customer could make.

It was a mistake. The clothespin did not release the line. Instead, as the *Oriental Moon* shot forward, the long duraluminum outrigger bent like a yew bow. There was a second in which Crunch thought the thing was going to be strong enough to break thirty-nine-thread line; or even to yank the shark clear out of water. Then . . . it snapped with an alarming reverberation. Crunch ducked. Desperate ducked. Mr. Purvis screamed. Edgar ran under the canopy. The duraluminum pole dropped majestically toward the cockpit—and missed by inches.

What followed had not been on the program of Crunch's object lesson. There was a splash. And, after it, a grinding bang underneath the stern. The outrigger had been sucked into the propeller; it was methodically chewed up. In the process, the propeller itself was gouged and twisted. The shaft which drove it bent under the strain and the stern of the *Oriental Moon* began to shudder. It happened in a second—and Mr. Purvis cut the port motor.

He also cut the starboard motor. The vessel drifted. There was silence, save for a gibbering sound emitted by the captain.

"Golly," said Crunch in an awed tone. "This deep-sea fishing is kind of dangerous, isn't it? I mean—" he smiled reassuringly at Purvis— "nothing as bad as polo. I'm not scared. But you sure do run certain risks."

"Risks," panted Mr. Purvis. "Risks!" He could say no more.

Desperate's shoulders were shaking. He was forced to dissemble. "Startled me," he managed to murmur. His eyes were on the sea. He saw the *Wanderer VII* loom up in the near distance. Doc was at the wheel and his eyes were fixed on the stump of the outrigger. His face was a study in repressions. Aboard Doc's boat were four of the captains from the Gulf Stream Dock—also garbed as tourists. They were behaving strangely— hugging and pounding each other. Doc spun the wheel to cut them from Purvis' view. He picked up a little megaphone.

"In trouble?" he shouted.

"*Trouble!*" Purvis needed no instrument to amplify his voice. "We've lost about six hundred yards of line, a new rod, a wheel, and an outrigger! Our shaft's bent—and we can't use the port motor. *Trouble!*"

"Want a tow?"

"No!"

Doc nodded sympathetically and veered off.

Purvis sat down. With vibrating hands, he lighted a cigarette. "What happened?" he muttered to himself. "That thing was fouled, too!" He started viciously toward his passengers. "Listen! Are you wise guys—or what?" The hurt innocence of their eyes arrested that move. "I'm sorry," he muttered unconvincingly. "I'm . . . upset. Never had so much bad luck in my whole life put together. What do you say we knock off fishing—and eat lunch? Then we can troll afterward." He blotted his brow.

It was a silent meal insofar as the captain and his mate were concerned. But "Mr. Adley" and "Mr. Wharton" raved about fishing. It did not seem to endear them to their host.

At three, they resumed trolling. The captain supervised every move that was made. He was so attentive that Des whispered privately to Crunch, "If we aren't darn careful, we'll catch something!"

Even as he spoke, the day's third sailfish appeared behind his skittering balao. It rushed the bait and swallowed it. Both Mr. Purvis and the mate were upon Des before he could budge. They held him in his chair. They held his rod. They cranked his reel. They fought the sailfish—a middle-sized one—with the fury of men who were going to succeed or die.

They almost succeeded.

The fish, on thirty-nine-thread line, was soon hauled by main force close to the boat. It was still full of life—but no match for the powerful tackle and three men. Crunch had watched the process with increasing dismay. When he saw the mate reach for the swivel on the leader wire, he acted.

There is one way to boat a sailfish: Put on gloves and grab him by the bill—lift him across the gunwale—conk him with a billy—and it's all over. If you try to gaff him, he may be galvanized into a last spasm that is dangerous to anyone within his range. Crunch, during the splash and hurly-burly, helpfully picked up the gaff and walked over to the scene of action. The mate had the leader wire and Mr. Purvis was grabbing for the bill. Crunch made a leaping reach between them—and pulled home the gaff. The sailfish rose into the air, wrenching the gaff from Crunch's hands with ease. There was a brief tableau of gyrating fish and dodging men. The sail broke the leader wire, scraped paint from the hull, and was gone.

"Wowie!" said Des. "That was pretty good! Maybe we'll *catch* the next one!"

He seemed not to notice that the skipper had seated himself on the deck, and was apparently crying. He did not appear to see the homicidal expression in Edgar's eyes. He did, however, observe that the *Wanderer VII* was passing near by—and he waved cheerily. The figures aboard the *Wanderer* waved back. Des yelled, "Did you see that? We're getting warm!"

Behind him, Mr. Purvis spoke unevenly. "I ought to go in, gentlemen. I ought to see how much damage there is. I'm a broken man. . . ."

Des was on the verge of assenting. But Crunch shook his head. He remembered how he had suffered from amateur know-it-alls—and he remembered what Purvis had done to Doc. "The damage will keep," he said with assurance and good humor. "We still have one motor, and we're both just getting the hang of this! It's quite exciting! No wonder Wiggam and all those other chaps were keen about it!"

Purvis staggered back to the wheel. He knew doom when he saw it face to face.

Doom proved to be forthcoming. Doom—or the last straw.

Since he no longer had an outrigger, Crunch was trolling straight back from the stern. Before many minutes had passed, the fourth sailfish appeared—behind his bait. Crunch saw it, and his lips tightened. Edgar saw it and cringed. Purvis saw it—and with the resurgence of a final fanatical hope yelled, "Sail!"

Crunch turned helplessly. "What do I do?" The fish was striking the bait by that time, and the rod was nodding.

"Let him have it," Mr. Purvis bellowed. *"Let him have it!"*

He meant that Crunch should let the fish have slack line—an opportunity to pick up the bait. But Crunch displayed a peculiar hysteria—pardonable in a man on his initial fishing trip and after such a day. The second time the skipper bawled, "Let him have it!" Crunch stood up with a mad look in his eye, and threw everything into the sea—rod, reel, and line. He turned bewilderedly. "Well . . . I let him have it," he said in a calm tone. . . .

Mr. Purvis learned the identity of his "passengers" that night. Crunch was served with legal papers the following day. It frightened him—but not Sari.

"He'll never collect a dime," she said. "Not a dime!"

And Mr. Purvis did not collect a dime.

Three days after his disastrous encounter with "Mr. Adley" and "Mr. Wharton," Purvis warped the *Oriental Moon* from her moorings and headed north. He claimed that he was going to fish out of Palm Beach. Miami, he said, was a hellhole. And he was never again seen at the Gulf Stream Docks.

His departure was not entirely due to the fact that every time a captain or a mate saw Mr. Purvis he was thrown into uncontrollable paroxysms. It was not wholly due, either, to the nickname abruptly fixed upon him: "Let-him-have-it Purvis." It was due more to a hint which had reached his ears: A hint that when and if he sued Crunch Adams for damages, the courtroom would be packed with hilarious boatmen, and there would be ample testimony concerning Crunch's motives for reducing the elegant *Oriental Moon* to a shambles.

Sari had originated that hint. She was, she explained, a realist about such matters.

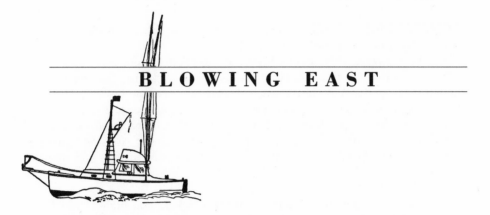

BLOWING EAST

"What is Bill going to do when he grows up?" Sari Adams said one night, in response to the question: "Well, he's going to be a doctor."

The people on the Gulf Stream Dock laughed at the year-old boy—about whom there was no suggestion of medical dignity, since he was sucking his thumb—and the wife of one of the skippers said, "Yeah? On what? When Bill's sixteen, Crunch'll take him out on his boat, and that'll be the end of the M.D. It costs money, besides."

"We'll get it," Sari said. "We've got time!" Because they were amused at her determined manner, she added a fiction: "I've started a bank account for him already."

Crunch came up in time to hear his wife's statement. He blushed darkly, so Mellie Mellish, who was scraping a sailfish bill into a paper cutter for the nine-year-old kid who had landed it on the preceding day, knew perfectly well the Adamses didn't have a dime in the bank that week. November had been slow and December disastrous, not because there were no prospective anglers but because the prevailing wind, which belongs to the trades, had been blowing from the east for twenty-six days, and hardly a wheel had turned.

In January, February and March the white marlin swim north past the coast of Florida. The Allison's tunas go about the same time—perhaps a little later. Then, in May, across the Gulf Stream, the blue fins start passing—hundreds of thousands of them, the size of horses. The largest may weigh a ton. They find the marlin again off Virginia in the summer, and they go after the tuna all the way up to the winter limit of pack ice. Sportsmen and commercial men, fishing for fun and for food.

Even the Gulf Stream runs north, like a river of violet ink. It doesn't mix well with other water; you can see the edge as clearly as if it were made by land and water, not just two different kinds of water. It goes at three or four or even five miles an hour, making a bow wave on buoys anchored in it and leaving a slick behind them. They can tell you what starts that gigantic river on its mill of thousands of miles and they can tell you where it goes; it's Bermuda's hot-water bottle and the warm embrace that keeps England from being like Labrador. But they can't tell you where the fish come from or what makes them migrate or where they end up. They'll guess: At Bimini the tunas are lean and hungry and on the move; in Newfoundland they're fat and full; but nobody knows very much about it.

That's one reason charter-boat fishing is difficult. But there are plenty of other tribulations and imponderables besides the sea ways of fishes. There's the high cost of keeping up a boat; there are lines that break and leaders that kink; there are days when the fish "won't bite a golden hook"; there are the customers, ignorant of fishing and fanatically sophisticated, kind, mean, good, wicked—all sorts of people—and there's the concealed, incessant competition between the guides for fishing parties and for a good catch, which means more parties, as well as for the sheer personal kudos of bringing in whoppers.

Charter-boat fishing has starved out hundreds of would-be guides. It has lost men their homes and their boats and their wives. It has driven more than one man mad. To engage in it takes stamina and nerve and human understanding. More than that, it takes a love of fishing and the sea so deep and intense that all other ways of living and of earning a living seem boresome and drab. You may be your guide's favorite angler; you may hook, battle and help boat a monstrous fish, but in his mind it will always be his fish—caught by him.

Such matters were everlastingly discussed by the personnel at the Gulf Stream Dock. Sometimes customers joined in, but mostly they listened— to men who were there when it happened. Often the conversation was loaded with complaint—and for good reason. Often a mate borrowed half a dollar to get his only meal of the day, or a hard-pressed skipper asked for help to pay up on his balance at the ship chandler's. Sari always defended the sport, or obsession, or whatever it is, not so much because she had fishing in her blood as because she had Crunch. And Crunch was as wedded to the sea as she to him.

Now, times were bad because of the weather. Sari worried. So did Crunch—and the whole dock.

You could go out all right, if you had a good boat and knew how to handle it. The swells were maybe fifteen or twenty feet high, and combing. Sometimes you might think one was going to lift your bows so steeply that you'd turn over on your back, and sometimes one would sink sickeningly out from under and you'd smack the surface as if you'd been dropped from the air. White water broke regularly over the canopy if you tried it, and the outrigger lines sang like violin strings in the wind.

There were plenty of fish—sails that poured right out of the steep walls of the waves to grab your skittering balao, kings, mackerel, dolphin, bonito—the works—but who wanted to sit on a fishing chair when it rode like the first dips on a roller coaster? And who, sitting there, could manage to fish and hang on at the same time? That kid had done it, whooping and hollering and having the thrill of his life while his old man lay sick below. But there weren't many people.

"Going to be quite a few boats turned back for the payments if this keeps up," Mellie said, and went on scraping.

"Not the *Poseidon*," Sari replied.

That was true. Every cent had been paid for the boat. They didn't owe money on the 16/0 reel, either, and half the rent for their winter apartment was in the landlord's pocket. But babies can't tighten their belts the way adults can, and babies can't live on fish for a week straight. They have a habit of growing out of their clothes too.

That was why Crunch, when he looked up and saw a man listening to the talk and carefully appraising the *Firefly*, detached himself from the group and set out to swipe the customer, if he could. The *Firefly*'s master wasn't raising any potential doctors, or even married. It was getting dark and it had been cold all day—cold for Miami—sixty, perhaps. The man was buttoned up in a topcoat and he had white hair.

He didn't look very strong or adventuresome. But Crunch—who'd been surly and silent for days, full of some unmatured thought—was determined.

"It's a nice boat," the man said, before Crunch had decided how to start a conversation. "Yours?"

"No," Crunch pointed at the *Poseidon*. Des was aboard her, listening to radio music over the ship-to-shore set and rubbing his hands to keep warm. "That's mine."

The man stared critically first at the *Poseidon* and then at Crunch. He seemed to like what he saw. "Nice lines," he said.

"She's a good sea boat. One of the best."

"Yeah. I can tell that." The man walked along the dock. By then, the people clustered around Bill realized that there was a prospect among them. Skippers and mates went back aboard their vessels and pretended to be busy, turning on lights and polishing their most impressive tackle.

The man was looking at Crunch again. "Where'd you get that build? Fighting?"

Crunch's eyes were usually direct. Now he looked away. Most people didn't notice his nose. It wasn't bad. They'd made it straight again every time, and only a little flatness on the bridge remained. He'd never had an ear messed enough to stay marked. And still fewer people put together the nose and his shoulder development.

He said, after quite a long pause, "Yeah." Just "Yeah." Nothing else.

The man's eyes twinkled. "My name's Grey." He read the sign behind the *Poseidon*. "And yours is Adams. That your kid yonder?"

"Yes."

"Husky. Nice girl." He had not paid much attention to Des, but it was enough. "Mate's a squarehead, isn't he? Great sailors. Great fellows, if you get to know 'em."

"Like to come aboard?" Crunch had a feeling, faint but growing, that he was going to like Mr. Grey. He was oldish—probably sixty-five. But he knew something, and he used his eyes, which was more than most people did. He stepped down into the *Poseidon* as if he'd been on boats before.

"Sloppy out, isn't it?"

"It's just plain rough," Crunch said.

"Any fish?"

"Plenty."

"Busy tomorrow?"

"No."

"I'll be down about ten. No use batting our brains out for any longer time. Let me see that kid, will you? I like 'em."

So Crunch introduced Mr. Grey to Sari—who was gracious as always, but did not let one iota of her relief show in her manner—and to Bill—who waved jerkily and grinned.

Mr. Grey brought oilskins for himself and a hot lunch for all three, packed by his hotel in vacuum jars. By daylight he looked even less fit for what was in store. He was pale and thin. You could see corded veins in the backs of his hands and there were narrow deep lines around his mouth corners.

Des noticed it, and was so worried that he tried to discourage Mr. Grey from going. "It's pretty rough out there," he said. "Scares quite a lot of people and makes even some of the captains sick."

That took the fun out of the man's eyes. "If you'd rather not go," he said, "I'll get somebody else."

Des was scared. He didn't have the social nimbleness for things like that. All he could think of to say was, "Oh, no! No."

But it brought back Mr. Grey's good humor. He seemed to perceive it was fear for him, and not for the boat or its crew, which had prompted the mate.

His face broke into a grin and he yelled up to Crunch, "Cast off, Skipper! Let's give 'em the devil!"

It took a whole hour to get out to the Stream. An hour in the teeth of a wind that felt semisolid. There weren't six boats on the ragged horizon and the *Sea Otter* passed them going in. But there were plenty of flying fish zooming and jittering over the monstrous waves, and once Crunch saw, from the gyrating top controls, a sail jump clean and high, as if the vast perturbation of its native element amused it.

Des didn't bother to lower the outriggers; the swing and heave of the *Poseidon* might snap them off. Mr. Grey would have to troll straight back. But he didn't seem to mind. He adjusted the footboard of the center fishing chair so that he could wedge himself against it; he sat in his oilskins, gripping a rod, and chuckling when they rode over an especially bad one.

They swung and wallowed for about an hour before anything happened. Then Mr. Grey's line went tight. Nobody saw the strike because it was made on the other side of a towering roller, but Des watched the reel whirl and said, "Wahoo!"

Mr. Grey thrust the rod in its socket and hung on. "Wahoo, eh?" he repeated excitedly. "Never hung one of them before! Goes like sin, doesn't it?"

It went fast and far. On the reel were three hundred and fifty yards of line. The fish peeled off two thirds in a few seconds and stopped. Crunch cut down the speed until the boat barely kept its head. It was a lot of line to have out when the waves were jerking the fisherman around every which way. Mr. Grey began to pump back the fish—and he knew his stuff, because he used the rise and fall of the boat to gather in slack for him, instead of trying to heave on the rod.

He had in about half when the wahoo took off at right angles. They're members of the mackerel family—the fastest of a fast breed—not common, but not rare, and they grow up to a hundred pounds. Mr. Grey's fish rocketed through those big swells and put a belly in the line. He straightened that out. In the course of twenty minutes he had the fish close to the boat for the third or fourth time. Des looked up at Crunch and winked. He hadn't found it necessary to give a word of advice.

Crunch winked back and looked for the fish, following the line with his eye down to the tumbling water. He saw it, by and by—a monster of a wahoo—its striped sides zebra-plain in the depths, its head yanking in an effort to turn against the pull that was inching it toward death. Crunch had never seen a bigger wahoo, and he yelled at Des to use a gaff—which was unnecessary; Des already had it in one hand. He was hanging on with the other and gazing over the stern, popeyed.

The swivel on the leader wire lifted out of the water an instant later and Des grabbed for it. But just then a big, curling sea slung the boat around sidewise and heeled it over. It threw an extra strain on the line and that strain pulled the hook from the wahoo's jaw.

Crunch could see the whole thing. Some oceans turn milky when they writhe with big waves, but the Gulf Stream stays as clear as the air. He saw the hook pop out of the wahoo's mouth. He saw the wahoo stiffen in dull surprise, hold still for a second, and charge back to freedom with what looked like a single whip of its tail. He shut his teeth together and gently pushed up the throttle of the motor they were trolling on. He fixed his eyes on the perfervid wilderness ahead as if he hated it.

Down below, Mr. Grey had sagged back in his seat. Des didn't notice, at first. He had pulled the leader and was trimming a new bait. But when he turned he saw that his passenger was pale and very near to fainting. He thought he'd been taken sick.

He reached over and seized his arm. "You'll feel better if you lie down!"

Mr. Grey shook himself and the grin he'd had when they started came back. It was a peculiar grin—challenging, or devil-may-care, or something else more than just pleased. "I'll be O.K. in a second. Boy! What a scrap!"

"Yeah. Might have been a record. Biggest wahoo I ever saw."

"Was it? Look. In the lunch box there's a pint of rye. Would you put about two fingers in a glass with some water?"

Des demurred. "I wouldn't drink anything. If you feel kind of queasy, I can fix up some blankets."

Mr. Grey's voice rose with indignation and authority: "Let's have this thing settled once and for all! I don't feel seasick! I won't feel seasick! Now will you get me that drink, or do I have to get it myself?"

"Sorry, sir."

Crunch was cursing at the sea then, as he had been for twenty-six days. First it had kept him from even a chance to earn a living, and now it had robbed a plucky old guy of a prize wahoo. That was the sea. Fierce and indecent and unjust. He knew he shouldn't try to associate justice and luck. It was permissible, when you had a bad day, to say you "weren't living right" or you "ought to go to church." But the man who began to believe that the deserving should get the sea's bounty, and the mean and the stupid its infinite misfortunes; the man who tried to act as if he, and not the ocean, were arbiter of such things, was riding for trouble. You had to take it, like it or not. And if a day came that you couldn't take— well, it was time to think about quitting the fishing business. He shut his teeth still harder and deliberately took a nasty one bow-on. It gave him some satisfaction to hear the *Poseidon's* bottom smack on the water. Some screwball king in ancient times had ordered his army to whip the sea for revenge. Sari had told him. He thought of the story, and laughed. You felt like that, often.

Half an hour later, Des came up on the sluing, soaked canopy top where Crunch was facing the wind. "I'll take a turn," he said. "I think that guy just about got sick after we lost the wahoo."

Crunch went down and looked over his customer. He'd buried his neck in his oilskin collar and was staring implacably astern at his bait.

"Feel all right?" Crunch said.

Mr. Grey turned."You, too, hunh? See here, young man. Did you ever hear of the splinter fleet?"

Crunch wished he hadn't asked Mr. Grey about his well-being. "Yes, sir."

"Well, I commanded one of those floating coffins. I sailed her to Bermuda and I sailed her to the Azores. I sailed her in the Mediterranean. We had a crew of school kids from the Middle West, and they used to lie on the deck and be sick till they couldn't stand up. Not unless you commanded them to." His eyes were on distant things, and the fact that he had mentioned that part of his past acted as a catalyst: "When you commanded 'em to, they did. My own particular death trap was ninety-six feet long and she had three engines in her—none of 'em worth a hoot! We dropped depth bombs in worse weather than this! One day out in the Atlantic off The Rock, a sub came up and shelled us to smithereens. We got into boats and it began to blow. The sub didn't pick us up." He spoke with a smile again, and less vehemence. "You see, Captain Adams, I've rowed through worse weather than this!"

"Yeah. I see. I'm sorry, sir."

"Don't be sorry! Lord, man! I've been running a wholesale-hardware business in Kansas City for eighteen years! Never a day on the sea. I came down here for my health. This is my first trip on blue water since the convoy brought me home. I'm having more fun than you'll ever be able to dream of! Let her blow! Let her blow a blithering hurricane! I used to fish in California when my dad lived there. Long time ago, that was. And I've read about it ever since. Last week the doctor told me I had to go up to New York or Baltimore and get a little something carved out of me. So I decided, before I went . . . well—see how it is?"

Crunch could smile. He did. "I wish we'd boated that wahoo."

His passenger chuckled. "Yeah. So do I. I never caught anything over twenty pounds. Always wanted a crack at this. I—"

He broke off.

But Crunch could fill in the blanks. He was going to say that he had nearly missed. They were planning to carve "a little something" out of him. That was why he was so pale. That explained the fine lines—pain. Crunch hung onto a cleat and unconsciously tried to twist it to pieces. It was guys like that—just ordinary, undersized, gray-headed little guys— who had rowed in worse weather than this. Who had dropped depth bombs in worse weather. Who had taken a bunch of "school kids from the Middle West" off the decks of a subchaser with the enemy's shrapnel breaking around them and pulled away into a harder blow than this. The muscles in Crunch's cheeks were stone-hard and he looked at Mr. Grey's back without speaking. His eye finally traveled to the sea again.

It was becoming more boisterous. The sky was thick with low clouds that went by like the balloon spinnakers of racing yachts. Des was quartering her into the seas and it wasn't comfortable, but if Mr. Grey wanted to fish, they'd stay out there and fish him until the whole ocean stood vertical.

"I got a strike," Mr. Grey said. "A little one."

Crunch spun around. The bait, as before, was hidden by a wall of water. But the wall rode under their stern and they could see it, then, diagonally down below them, with a sailfish chasing along behind, his purple dorsal spread and every sinew of his body concentrated on getting the balao. He rushed and struck before a welter of foam poured down on him, and Mr. Grey, who had been staring with an openmouthed ecstacy of appreciation, remembered it was his bait and threw the bolt that released the drag.

When he hit the sail, it took off in an instant. They could see it jump high above their heads, out of a crest. It poised there and was gone, and they watched the reel again. Crunch had an idea. He ducked below and banged his head on a corner of the wheelhousing without noticing it. He came up with a belt in which there was a round leather socket.

"If you want," he yelled above the wind, "you can fight that sail standing!"

Mr. Grey got the idea. "Buckle it on," he said.

A moment later he was poised at the gunwale with his knee jammed under it. He'd found his sea legs after all those years, and he was proud of it. You could tell it was what he'd wanted: The same wild ocean in the same swift shapes; the same feel of a deck that slid and teetered under your feet; the same concentration of effort. There weren't any shells bursting now, and it wasn't a matter of life and death—just fun—but it was doing things to the old man's memory and his imagination. His grin bared his teeth and he bellowed jubilantly at the fish, fighting it with every bit of energy he had, as if he had lived that long time just to get it aboard as fast as the job could be done. But maybe his luck had run out.

That particular sailfish went crazy with fear and with anger. Some sails come quietly, like beaten prisoners in the hands of the police. Some jump once or twice, as if to make an assay of the situation, and then dive deep, where they fight with a dogged hopelessness. Most dance flashily for a while, rush hither and thither on the deceptively innocent blue surface of the tropical water, and concede at last, like gentlemen in a duel. But there are a few, tough and primordial, to whom even temporary capture must be an intolerable affront. They are the memorable ones—not necessarily the biggest, but violent fish that set the sea boiling, fling themselves twenty feet across the surface, twist, shake, somersault, walk on their tails, in a paroxysm of aerial effort, until they rip themselves free or are brought to the boat's side exhausted and dying.

Mr. Grey had such a fish. In three minutes it performed a shocking repertoire of acrobatics, and at the end, with a fierce toss of its head, it threw bait and hook out of its mouth. For a split second it stood in the air as if plastered there, and the shining wire leader whipped around it. The hook bit again—in its back near its tail—and again Mr. Grey's reel squealed as line was torn from it.

Crunch knew what the end would be. He didn't say so, because there was always a chance. But only a slim chance, and this time it wasn't to be. The sail bored down under the *Poseidon's* stern, fifty feet, a hundred, two hundred, three. It got to the rocks on the bottom, held only by a piece of its tough skin. Tough, but not tough enough. The fish pulled the hook through after a while.

Mr. Grey reeled in. He went pale again and Crunch brought another two fingers of rye whisky in a glass; without water.

Later, Crunch went back to relieve Des. He addressed the sea silently. *You gotta give us a fish,* he said. It was profane—and impassioned— prayer at its most fervent. But the sea, whoever he is, did not listen.

Sari was rocking Bill's carriage when the *Poseidon* came down the Cut. She'd been pretty sure about things. Rebley had brought in two sails, and Johnson had a big wahoo. He'd lost a white—first he'd seen that year. And he had six dolphins. It stunned her when there wasn't a small triangular white flag on the *Posideon's* outrigger. That meant no sailfish. But maybe they'd caught something else. It wasn't important, anyhow. She tried to make herself believe that, but she knew she was lying and she knew they hadn't caught much by the very way in which Crunch swung the bow and reversed the motors and charged into wind and tide to dock.

Mr. Grey came ashore. He had to try twice before he could make the big step. He walked over to the baby carriage, and she noticed that he staggered. He was landsick.

He'd been all right out on the ocean, but now the memory of the tumult was strong in his brain. The dock seemed to heave and slide under his feet.

"Hello, son," he said smiling to Bill.

The baby chuckled and grabbed his finger.

He looked at Sari. "I think your husband feels pretty badly about not getting a fish," he said. "I wish you'd tell him I don't mind. I fought two beauties, and about licked both of them. I wouldn't have cared, really, if we'd never seen a fish. It was a wonderful day. Wonderful!"

He broke away from Bill's tenacious grip, made a pass at him with his fist, laughed, and went on down the dock. Then Crunch came. He didn't say anything. He was sore, and still thinking whatever he'd thought for days.

Sari could see his arm tremble when he began to push the baby carriage along the dock. It took a lot to make Crunch that tired.

"I got stew," she said. "Lamb. First time we've had anything but fish in quite a while."

Still he said nothing. So she was quiet.

The next morning Crunch told Des what he had on his mind. They were sitting on the dock together in windbreakers, and it was all cloudy. Cold. Most of the captains had given up hope, covered the sterns of their boats with canvas and stayed home.

Crunch broke his news without preamble, as Des had expected he would when the time came: "How'd you like to run the *Poseidon*?"

Des sat there for half a minute. "What's up?"

"Mac. Offered me seventy-five a week and ten per cent of the profits to manage the boat yard on the Beach."

Des said, "Is that a fact?" He was sick deep inside and he didn't know what line to take, what argument to make. He just sat there, watching Crunch squint at the boat the wrong way through a pair of binoculars, as if he wanted to see how it felt to push the *Poseidon* off into the distance. "It's a lot of money," he said finally.

"Sure, it's a lot, for steady dough. I ought to make five-six thousand dollars a year, and no boat to keep up. But do you think I want to sit on shore fixing up other guys? Do you think I want to quit watching baits and taking out new people and finding new ways of getting the fish up? I'd feel like a whippet if you amputated his legs!"

Des nodded. He was seeking his way in the morass of shock and fright that was engendered by this possibility. He watched an American flag on a steamer. It indicated a hard easterly, by streaming flat and edgewise into the west. That was no news.

"I could pay you out your share in the *Poseidon* little by little," he suggested. "Beejie'd be glad to mate for me."

"Beejie!" Crunch spat slantwise across the wind. "Beejie! That bow-legged, dim-witted, crawfishin' Cracker couldn't cut a bait that would interest a starving barracuda! He gets his parties from hotel bellhops and he's about as fit to work for you on our boat as he is to dock the Queen Mary! Beejie! Holy cow!"

"Sari wants Bill to be a doctor," Des said laconically.

"Sure! What do you think I'm working this idea over for? A doctor! Can you imagine me running a boat yard? Kicking around all day in a lot of paint and engine oil? Telling people I'll have the little outboard ready in an hour? Trying to sell Mac's lousy runabouts to a lot of dopes who don't know a propeller from a whistling buoy? I'll probably get TB myself and need a doctor before Bill's out of the first grade."

"Shore work's pretty healthy," Des answered, and added, "I guess." The session was long and not very conclusive.

That evening Crunch took Des to his apartment for dinner. He wanted reinforcement, but exactly what sort he did not know himself. He waited until the dishes were washed and Bill was asleep. Sari had expected it for a long time, and she listened without interrupting while he talked. He finished on a tense and interrogatory note: "So you see, there just isn't any other side to it, is there?"

Sari said, "I guess not." She spoke much too coolly for Crunch, and she looked at Desperate. "Reliable fellows are hard to find, these days. Mac knows Crunch is worth it. He'll probably bring a good deal of business to the place."

Desperate felt hollowed out again. "You know he can't accept that job, Sari." His voice rose: "Why, it isn't even healthy! He'd probably get TB or something!"

"Crunch?" Sari chuckled.

"Maybe he'd simply go nuts! You can't haul a saltwater man off the sea. Look at that poor old guy we fished yesterday. Come back after eighteen years! Now, you take a boat yard. It's chancy. May fail any minute, and the receivers move in, and then where's your seventy-five-plus a week? But you get a good fishing boat, and wherever there's water you got a living." He looked earnestly at Crunch.

Crunch said nothing. It seemed to him that his partner had been on the other side of the argument earlier in the day. Besides, he was disappointed in Sari's reaction. He'd expected possible relief, but not such immediate and apparently calculating acceptance of the offer.

At the moment she was smiling. "Oh, yes, Des! A boat is a wonderful living! Take tonight. Did you enjoy what was left of yesterday's stew? Do you approve of Crunch's slack suit? Four ninety-eight, and two years old. Compared to a shipyard, a charter boat is a mint!"

"What's the use of talking about it?" Crunch said bitterly. "I told Mac I'd let him know tomorrow afternoon. I'll tell him O.K."

By and by Desperate went home, feeling all the turbulence implied by his nickname. But there wasn't anything he could do. Crunch, in moods like his present one, was as tough and ornery as any man living. You had to let him fight it out. Des was disappointed in Sari too. But you couldn't blame her.

The Adamses went to bed early, and silently.

About midnight, Crunch woke up. He listened for a minute, and then propped up his head on his elbow. "I'll be . . ." he whispered.

The palm fronds outside his window were not plunging and slashing any longer. Instead, they quivered in the lightest of breezes. The wind was gone—twenty-seven days of it! In his mind's eye, he could see the nocturnal ocean. Over it the clouds would be breaking apart and regimenting themselves into peaceful squadrons of cumulus puffs. The moon, a day past full, would be out again, spangling the sea from the horizon to wherever you were. The combers wouldn't be combing any more, but, slick and gigantic, they would roll as ground swells. Riding them wouldn't be a process involving frantic vigilance and an exhausting expenditure of strength. You'd hardly know you were being lifted and lowered, whether you ran into the sea, or away from it, or in the trough. The after cockpit would be a sun parlor all day long. And the fish, hungry from difficult foraging in the long blow, would be out by the million. the million.

He sighed and tried to go to sleep. But he couldn't. The harder he tried, the more vividly his brain worked, recalling other such days as the next one would be—tarpon exploding on a bait as you came in past the jetty; blues that belonged in Bimini attaching themselves to sailfish baits; a grouper that jumped when he was hooked, against all natural precedent; a thresher shark that snapped at a bonefish bait and nearly killed one of the huskiest members of the Miami Angling Club before he got away. Those big smooth swells, cobalt blue, fifteen feet high and seventy feet apart, that always followed a hard easterly. There was fishing weather!

He got up, finally, and made some coffee and caught an early car down to the dock. Des was already up and shining the brightwork with an unwontedly possessive manner. Crunch picked up a rag and started in. "Might as well lend a hand. Can't see Mac till afternoon anyhow."

"Sure. Notice the wind's dropped?"

The *Poseidon*'s captain chose a look of contempt as an adequate response to that question. He polished.

"Johnson had a white marlin on yesterday," Des said after a while. "I wonder if it was a stray, or if they're maybe beginning to run?"

"Run's on, I bet. I bet, too, if you hung around Number Two buoy in weather like this, especially down south and inside, with a couple of big feathers trolled straight back—"

"Yeah," Des said. "Allison's, I bet."

Other boats were waking to life. The first party arrived—a man and his wife, who had reserved the *Firefly* for the first calm day. The *Widget* took off a minute later.

Mr. Williams called across the water to the expectant anglers, "Don't catch so many you sink the boat!"

Then the bait boy came up. "Cap'n Adams," he said, "look what I got! I was saving them for you—two bits apiece."

Crunch looked. Small bonefish—very small. Beauties. He could see them skipping along those big blue swells. See a white marlin rising behind them, trailing them. . . .

"Got no charter," he said, after swallowing.

"Sure. Not now. But people will be coming down later." The boy tipped back the battered officer's cap which he wore to show that he had to do with the sea. "Besides, they'll keep if you ice 'em. What's the matter? Losing your enterprise?"

"I'll buy 'em," Des said quietly.

So Crunch whipped out his purse. "How many you got? . . . Six? O.K. Here's a dollar fifty."

It left him with ten cents. The boy put aboard the regular quota of balao. There were already a dozen strips of bonito belly in the box. Des had cadged them from somebody. They lay there, red on one side and silver on the other. They looked tempting—in a figurative way, even delicious—to Crunch. He slammed down the lid.

"Guess I'll go below and pack up my stuff. Your captain's papers on board?"

"Yeah."

Crunch was packing when Des came down. "There's three guys up on the dock want to know can we take 'em out. They thought they had a reserve on the *Swordfish*, but she's gone. Look like good men. They got their own rods in leather cases, and lunch—"

"I gotta see Mac! You take 'em!"

Des' face was blank. "O.K. I'll run down the line and find out if Beejie can go."

"Wait a minute!"

The *Poseidon* went out at 8:30 that day.

In the evening, Sari and Bill were again on the dock. She was waiting. Her mouth was pursed in a sort of postponed smile. Her eyes were very bright, and when the *Poseidon* came around the turn, fast and jaunty, with two white flags and a blue one flying on her outriggers, she gulped down a lump in her throat and spoke to Bill.

"See," she said shakily. "Here comes your daddy! He's got a white marlin. It's the first one this year! We're both happy, Bill, because he'd be so miserable if he worked on shore! Only, you have to take the opposite side when you want him to do the right thing, sometimes. He's terrible stubborn! But he's a fishing man, Bill. He's a fishing man!"

The *Poseidon* came in smoothly, expertly. Crunch waved at Bill and Sari. Des tied up. He looked serene.

Sari blew her nose and whispered again, "You'll have to work your way through medical school, son. But if you work half as hard as your daddy, you'll be all right."

The men were paying Crunch. "How about tomorrow?" they asked. "Sure!"

"What a day!" they said. "What a day!" and "Get a photographer, Skipper! And we want that white mounted!"

Crunch was looking at Sari then, expecting to see fierce disappointment. All the way in, he'd been trying to frame an explanation. You couldn't tell a woman about—how it was to go out there in the sea, fair weather or foul, dragging baits and just hoping. He saw, in a moment, that it wouldn't be necessary to explain.

Yeah, he thought, *that's why I married her—her, in particular.*

They'd almost forgotten about Mr. Grey when they heard from him. A long thick letter that came one morning while Crunch was out on the Stream. Sari read it and handed it to him when he stepped off the boat.

Dear Captain Adams: This may strike you as the whim of an old fool. You may resent it. I hope not. In my life I've done a great many things I didn't want to, and few I've liked. I've learned from the doctor here in New York that I'm going to strike out soon now, no matter what. I've been lying up here for a good while now, and things keep going through my mind—things I believe in and things I enjoyed. Every time I recollect a certain wahoo and a certain sailfish, I grin for an hour. I liked you and Des, your wife and your kid. I heard Mrs. Adams talking about medical school for the youngster. So I've had my lawyers put aside a little nest egg. It'll draw interest till young Bill's ready, and if he does get ready he can have it. I didn't explain things very well to you the day we fished together. There wasn't any use telling you that I went out because I was determined to have a deck under me one more day before I had to stand the Big Gaff myself. Perhaps you don't know about the sea getting into a man's blood. If you don't, I can never tell you, and if you do, I don't have to.

Good luck to young Bill, and to you and Des. Tight lines!

Yours sincerely,

ARLEY M. GREY.

P.S.: The way things are, I'm mighty glad we didn't kill those fish.

"There's a letter from a bank," Sari said slowly, when she saw that Crunch wasn't reading any more. "He died—last week. If Bill ever gets prepared for medical school, there'll be two thousand dollars and its interest for him. Otherwise, the money goes to charity. I guess he felt the way you do—about the water."

Crunch handed the letter to Des and walked over to the edge of the dock. He made it look as if he were watching the mullet jump. But Sari knew he couldn't see anything, because she couldn't either.

LIGHT TACKLE

Miss Jones reached her favorite "spot" on the Country Causeway after supper but before all the color had gone from the sky. The tide was coming in, which was good, and the breeze was dropping. Unmindful of the trucks, the squealing trolleys and the horde of automobiles which streamed from Miami to Miami Beach and from the beach to the mainland, she unwrapped a paper bundle, took out a neatly wound hand line which was equipped with a sinker, a short wire leader, and a hook, and she carefully pressed the hook into the body of a dead, rather overdead, shrimp. She threw the assemblage into the flowing salt water, watched it drift out from the masonry that supported the bridge, and felt the lead touch bottom. She began her wait.

The sky flamed and bleached itself. The drawbridge lifted and settled ponderously many times—to the impatient accompaniment of the horns and voices of motorists. Ranged along the cement railing beside Miss Jones were scores of other fishermen—old men and young, women and children; some with rods and reels and pails of live bait, but most with less ostentatious gear: hand lines, or bamboo poles innocent of reels. Miss Jones fished hopefully, but without success.

It was dark and the distant beach had turned on the full glamour of its neon skyline when she noticed that the man nearest her was catching quite a few fish. Grunts and sand perch and an occasional snapper. He, too, was using a hand line, but he threw it farther than she could and in a diagonal direction. His bait was different. His manner of waiting after a nibble, and striking hard, was not the technique she had used. At last, though the act was unprecedented for her, she decided to speak to him; he was not well-dressed, but he looked nice.

"I guess," she said, "you're having the luck for the whole causeway." She smiled while she spoke—a little ruefully.

Crunch Adams had not even noticed his neighbor. Now, in the light of the street lamp, he could see a pretty girl, maybe twenty-three or -four, a bit thin; a girl with a mighty nice voice—sincere and curiously vibrant. Miss Jones was further illuminated by the headlight of a passing car. A blonde, Crunch perceived; one of the maple-fudge kind, and with gray eyes. No man—not even a happily married man—wantonly rebuffs the Miss Joneses of this world.

"The people," Crunch began, "who fish the causeways hardly ever bother to think about the bottom. But it's the bottom that determines where the fish are. If you come up here at slack tide on a calm day you can see that right where I'm throwing my rig there's a mess of rock. A barge sank there during the '26 blow. Here!"

The word meant that he had reached out for her line. She yielded it without a word and let him throw. He handed it back to her. She thanked him—and waited—and presently she felt a jiggle.

"Let him run with it a second," Crunch said, watching critically. "Now! Yank!"

The girl yanked. A yank answered her. The fish ran through the careening tide and the line slid through her fingers. She caught it up and pulled in, hand over hand. There was a white splash far below. She felt the fish wriggling in the air. Then Crunch reached down and tossed it onto the sidewalk, where it began to spring into the air. "Snapper," he said. "Nice one, too. Ought to go a pound and a half."

Miss Jones looked at the fish with shining eyes. "Would you . . . would you . . . kill it for me? Before it gets under somebody's car?"

Crunch picked up the fish, carefully avoiding its clicking teeth, and he dispatched it. He regarded Miss Jones' excitement with understanding, and threw his own line.

"Snappers are so darned good to eat," she said, wrapping the fish in paper.

"You bet they are. And people leave 'em lying around here to rot, sometimes." Crunch jerked his line, brought up a grunt, and dropped it—alive—into a pail of water.

"Once, right here," Miss Jones continued, "I got a grouper. Quite a big one." Success seemed to have made her talkative. "Two pounds, the man at the bait place said. I made chowder out of him—and it was simply delicious! Tasted like cinnamon." She began winding up her line. "And once I caught a jack—but he wasn't very good."

Crunch baited again—with a cubical chunk of purple meat cut from a bonita. It occurred to him that the young lady was more interested in her catch from the gastronomic standpoint than from the aspect of sport. He peered throught the night. She was pretty thin—although not that thin.

"You better keep right on fishing," he said. "We ought be able to get you a dozen of those."

She shook her head. "I haven't got any place to keep 'em. I—well—I sort of get 'em as I need 'em. *If* I'm lucky, that is." She looked into his bucket, where six or eight fish were swimming and panting. "They wouldn't keep—like that—I mean for days, would they?"

He was thinking about her—a pretty girl, a nice one, who fished for food and didn't even have an icebox to preserve her catch. He answered rather absently. "In a pail? I'm afraid not. Dic in an hour or two. My mate'll be along to get these soon—and put 'em in our live well. They're for bait. We've got an open party slated to fish amberjack tomorrow." His line tugged, and that kept him from seeing her face.

But her voice turned him around. It was stunned. "You mean—you're a charter-boat captain?"

"Uh-uh."

"Which one?"

"The *Poseidon*."

"Then—" she swallowed—"then . . . you're Crunch Adams! Last winter I used to go down to buy fish from the boatmen. Mackerel—and pieces of kingfish—and dolphin—and I've often seen your boat come in!"

Crunch knew what it was like to be poor. He also knew what it was like to be proud. But he took a chance. "You're—you're kind of—stranded down here—Miss—?"

The girl supplied her name quietly. She finished wrapping her fish and her line in newspaper before she continued. She had been thinking it over. It was all right for her to tell him. Everybody knew that Crunch Adams was a perfectly swell person. And you had to talk to somebody—sometimes. "Not exactly," she said at last. "I—I've got my rent paid for all summer. And a little money—if I stretch it. I've been looking for a job, but things kind of drop off here in the spring. I've got one promised—if I can wait till fall. You see . . . I'm a librarian. That is, I was—up north. I got arthritis and came down here for two months. I was fine—but when I went back, I got sick again. So . . . "

Desperate came along the causeway with a fresh pail of water. Not realizing that his skipper was engaged in conversation, he broached the only subject on his mind at the moment: "I got one more guy for tomorrow. That makes three. And guess who? Thornton Denby, no less! Wanted to weasel in for five bucks, as usual, but I made him pay six. He also wanted to fish the stream—but I said it was the reef or no dice."

Somewhat to Desperate's surprise, a response came from a lady standing beside Crunch. "You mean—you mean people can actually go out in a charter boat for as little as six dollars?"

Scenting a customer, Desperate lost no time. "Sure! When business is slack we split the summer price four ways and get four people to go. Twenty-five bucks divided by four is six and a quarter—and we knock off the two bits for luck."

"Could I be the fourth? Do you take—women? I've been absolutely out of my mind to go fishing on one of those boats ever since I got here!"

Crunch, upon seeing Miss Jones about to spend six dollars she couldn't conceivably afford, tried to think of something. The best idea—which he voiced—was hardly polite: "We can't take a dame—a woman. We don't know the first two guys very well—and this Denby is the stickiest fishing man in Florida. Besides—"

"We took that Mrs. Hoag with three men," Des countered, "and she caught a tuna!" His only alert instinct at the moment was the instinct for trade and commerce. "Crunch and I can look out for you. If you've got six bucks handy? . . . "

The *Poseidon's* skipper was stammering. Miss Jones hesitated and then produced a small pocketbook. Crunch heard her murmur, "I shouldn't do it! But I've just got to!" He didn't interfere, because his mate, with a smirk of triumph, was reaching for the money. Instead, he began to think of how he could return the six dollars to the girl.

Des glanced at the fish in the pail and said, "We'll need that many more, easy." He started off with them, giving Crunch a wink to indicate it took a go-getter to nail down the business. "Be at the dock at eight," he said to Miss Jones. "This Denby likes to start early."

Crunch and Miss Jones were left alone—except for the noisily passing thousands. "You shouldn't have done that," he said.

She nodded. "I know it. But a time comes in your life when you've got to do at least something rash!" She began to unwrap her line. "I might as well help, now, hadn't I, since I'm going to use some of that live bait? Golly! Can you imagine *me* in a charter boat!"

The morning was halcyon—soft as the spring always is in south Florida; sun-drenched, cloud-shaded, perfumed. A light breeze shattered the water outside the jetties into millions of bright facets; the sharp bow of the *Poseidon* divided a moving pattern of foam that was like etching on glass.

Miss Jones—she had been reticent about her first name—lay on the warm canvas deck forward, where Crunch put her so that the men could get acquainted, tell their jokes, and pass around an eye opener if they wished. She watched the changing blues of the bottom under the ship's keel—the light blue made by the sand and the dark patches where the rocks were. She watched the hawks tower and the gulls dive and the pelicans volplane. Inside her mind, she talked to herself.

I shouldn't have come, she thought. Those two men—Mr. Porter and Mr. Welch—didn't want me much. And Mr. Denby didn't want me at all! I never saw such a fussy person! A bachelor, I'll bet! All that tackle! And all that talk! You'd think fishing was as important and as difficult as a surgical operation! Mr. Porter and Mr. Welch didn't seem to like him much. Which makes things just lovely! And I can afford six bucks about as well as I can afford platinum shoes!

Crunch came and sat down beside her. She was wearing the same slacks—pink—purchased, no doubt, when she'd still had that librarian's job. Her pink and blue scarf fluttered in the air. Her eyes were dark gray; only, the water made them seem blue. And her hair, although of a maple-fudge blondness, had lemon-colored glints in it. "I'm sorry my mate hooked you for that money," Crunch began. "I'd have been darned glad—in your case—to take you out . . . "

Miss Jones flushed. "I wouldn't think of going any other way!"

"Yeah. I suppose not." He, also, flushed a little. "Those guys weren't rude to you when we started, were they? I had to be on top . . . "

The girl grimaced a little. "They weren't overjoyed at the prospect of a woman being along."

Crunch nodded. "Welch and Porter work in town—and have families. They can only afford to go out this way—once in a while—in the summer. They're both pretty good guys, really. As for Denby—he has plenty of dough. Stays here year around. Owns a house on the beach. He fishes light tackle—he's an expert at it—but he's stingy."

"A bachelor, I bet," she said.

Crunch chuckled. "For reasons too numerous to mention! Tell you what. He'll fish on top—always does. I'll put Porter up here, too. You and Mr. Welch can sit below. Ask him about his kids—he has five and he's proud of 'em all—and he'll be your friend."

"You're sweet," Miss Jones said gratefully. "I'll go through his kids from infant diseases to marks in arithmetic!"

So they began to fish. In the lazy morning, with Mr. Welch pouring out proud-parent anecdotes and beginning to think that the female passenger was not altogether a washout. Overhead, Mr. Porter was silent, sitting in a little chair on the edge of the canopy. Miss Jones held her rod tremblingly and watched the water. But Mr. Denby really provided the thematic monologue for the trip. He would have had a pleasant voice, she thought, if he had not kept it high and penetrating. He might have had pleasant manners, too—but fishing seemed to make manners inaccessible to him.

"Crunch," he said loudly, "you missed some rather good weeds about a hundred yards off the port quarter! . . . There's a rock bed just off the lighthouse that you completely overlooked! . . . Don't see how you fellows take any pleasure in fishing with that rope. . . . Look at my gear: a four-ounce tip—a six-thread line that breaks with a strain of eighteen or twenty pounds—and a hook with the barb filed off! Now—that's what I call fishing! Give the fish a chance! . . . Most men don't realize that even with reef fish there's often the problem of a drop back—very slight, mind you, but real. You do it with your rod, and everything depends on feel. Though I can't see why anybody wants to fish the reef. Let me show you, Porter. . . . Crunch! Don't you think we're going about half a knot too fast? And look at that bait! It turned over three times while I was letting it back! It'll unwind my whole line, if you don't trim it! I tell you, nobody knows how to cut a bait out here. . . . Now here's another thing, Porter. You fish a number ten hook and a 6/0 reel. It's a crime, actually! Take a squint at this 3/0 of mine. Had it built specially. Isn't geared up like that thing of yours. Winds in a ratio of I to I. The reason for that . . . "

"That guy," Mr. Welch murmured to Miss Jones, "knows all about fishing. *He* knows he knows it. And *we* know he knows. Why in hell doesn't he shut up?"

Miss Jones giggled. Then she had a strike.

For months she had watched them bring in the "big ones." Months of living alone in a one-room apartment with a bed that folded into the wall and an electric plate for cooking. Months of being lonely. Of going to "free" things—concerts and lectures and fishing docks. Months of being ill—and then better—but always poorer and more worried. Now—a "big one" had hit her line. She could see the welter in the ocean, feel the jerk in her arms, hear the reel's unforgettable sound as the fish ran—a harsh and heady whir. She had always imagined that it would be exciting; she had never guessed that it would have that particular quality of thrill—of wildness, violence, fury and fight.

She became aware of Crunch beside her. "Barracuda," he said quietly. Then she heard Mr. Denby's voice. It was an anxious staccato of advice. His heart was in it—and his whole nervous system—as if he were catching the fish by talk: "Keep the rod tip up, Miss Jones! But not too high! That's it! Now! Reel! He's going to broach! Bad! Very bad! You gave him slack! Better tighten the drag, Crunch. With a telegraph pole like that, she can stand more strain! Besides—she's keeping the rest of us from fishing! Come on! Wind, woman! Drop the tip and pick up what you gain that way! Then back—and do it over!"

Crunch cast toward his passenger a glance around which were invisible brass knuckles. Denby did not even notice. But Miss Jones was aware of his words, and, consciously or not, she began to follow each suggestion. Almost to her annoyance, she observed a change in his tone: "Fine! That's right! Never saw a man who could get the idea so quickly!"

In a few minutes, Crunch made a swoop with a big gaff—although Denby protested at gaffing a 'cuda—and brought aboard a silver fish about four feet long. It was mottled with black and Crunch spread its jaws with pliers for the girl to see. "Teeth like a wolf," he said. "Look!"

Miss Jones was panting delicately. Tendrils of her hair were stuck upon her brow. Her eyes were dilated. "Imagine," she whispered. "*Me!* I caught it! *Think of it!*"

Mr. Porter spoke rather petulantly: "Let's go fishing."

Des gunned the motors. The *Poseidon* moved along again. "On six-thread," Mr. Denby said good-humoredly, "that would have been quite a little scrap."

There are many sorts of fishing along the Florida coast. Trolling in the Gulf Stream is one. Trolling on the "reef" is another. The "reef" is a generic name for the shoal water along that edge of the Atlantic. It is clear water—green, sometimes, more often pale blue—and it varies in depth from coral emergences to more than a hundred feet. In that relatively shallow territory lie thousands of square miles of underwater wilderness—forests of coral, caverns, blind valleys, stone flowers and stone trees; and hundreds of square miles of submarine desert—regions of bare sand, rippled and duned, like the Sahara. There are lunar places in it—plains and abysses of raw rock—and places where colored vegetation grows in weird, uncouth jungles.

The reef is to fish what the primeval forest is to mammalian game. Not the streamlined, purple creatures of the gulf current live there—not sailfish and marlin and tunas and dolphins—but other fish which are strong, more numerous, and also, perhaps, hungrier. Jacks inhabit that fantastic land, and the groupers, which are bass, the many snappers, parrots, yellowtail, ordinary mackerel, triggers, countless small fish that travel in butterfly-bright schools, 'cudas, and, of course, all the rays together with a large variety of sharks. More fist are caught, as a rule, on a given day on the reef than are caught in a day on the Stream.

The *Posideon's* mixed party began to catch fish. Mr. Porter boated a twenty-pound grouper. Mr. Welch hung and lost a hard-running fish of uncertain identity. Miss Jones caught another barracuda. Mr. Denby managed to bring to gaff a small jack after a battle; he stood on his feet, with his light rod bowed in a "U," and kept his line taut with a skill that was admired even by Crunch.

Then Miss Jones hung a small mackerel and when she had it close to the boat, something tore it from her hook. For a moment line ripped from the reel. Then it went slack in the water.

Crunch, who had been at her side, acted swiftly. "An amberjack took that fish," he said. "Let's go!" He lifted the cover from the live bait well.

With a dip net, he took out one of the fish he had caught on the night before. Quickly he fixed it to a hook—with string. He chose the handiest hook—which was Mr. Welch's. He threw the fish overboard. "Watch it," he said to Miss Jones. "Watch it as long as you can."

So she stood up and leaned over the stern. The *Poseidon* was drifting, her motors stopped. She could see the little fish swim down in spirals, carrying the shiny leader. Then she saw something else. Around it loomed shapes—big, tan-colored shapes—and one of them shot toward it. She could actually see the big fish grab the little one and she bit the back of her hand. "He's got it!" she said sharply. "There's a dozen of them down there!"

"Let him run till he swallows it!" Crunch advised Mr. Welch. "All right! Sock him!"

Mr. Welch "socked." His reel wailed. Miss Jones sat back in her chair. She watched him hang on while the fish ran, watched him pump and perspire when the amberjack paused to consider, listened to him swear when the fish took off again, and looked at the expression on his face—an expression of concentration, jubilation, and anxiety which would have been funny if she had not shared every second of that mood. After fifteen minutes the fish was close to the boat. She saw that Crunch had gone to the bait well. He had another grunt in his hand. He peered up to the canopy. "Mr. Denby! Like to try one on light tackle? They're pretty big in this school."

Miss Jones hadn't guessed that there would be another chance. But now, looking into the water, she could see Mr. Welch's fish being hoisted to the surface, inch by inch, and around it was the school to which it had belonged. Big, shooting shapes following along beside their hooked companion, trying from time to time to make a grab at whatever it had in its mouth.

The small fish on Mr. Denby's line swam down toward what would obviously be a horrid reception, and, while Miss Jones still looked, she saw one of the big fish spot the new arrival, wheel, and torpedo toward it. Then she heard Mr. Denby's reel purr interminably. She wondered how such a thin line could hold so huge a fish.

For a while she forgot Mr. Denby. They boated Mr. Welch's fish. "Go sixty, easy," Des said, grinning. But Miss Jones just stared. She'd only seen dead big fish until then. It was a beautiful thing alive: opalescent, silver, bronze—from that color came its name—and full of dazzling, almost tangible vitality.

Mr. Denby called attention to himself, presently: "Crunch! This devil's got nearly all my line! Guess you better head around!"

So Crunch ran to the controls and started the boat. He chased the amberjack while the angler gathered back line on his little reel. That was the beginning of a long session. Very long, as Mr. Porter and Mr. Welch began to hint. A half hour; then an hour. And it was Denby, they said in guarded tones, who had complained that Miss Jones was taking so long to get in her fish!

When an hour and a half passed and Mr. Denby was still battling—still reeling with rapid endurance—still bracing himself against the hurtling runs of his quarry, Mr. Porter's patience snapped. "Really, man," he said in a tone of suppressed anger, "you're taking up our day! You shouldn't have used that light rig! It's not fair!"

But Denby fished on as if he had not heard.

Miss Jones began to look, but not at the water and the thin line cutting through it, but at the man on the canopy. He wasn't exactly selfish, consciously. He was just determined. Terribly determined. He fought his fish as if he were fighting something much more important. She wondered about that. And when, after nearly two hours, Denby's line broke, she did not feel furious, like the other two men. She felt sad. She looked at Denby to see how he was taking it. For a minute—a short part of a minute—she thought he was going to cry. But, then, he smiled. He smiled distinctly. "Part of the game," he said quietly. "Must have been a whopper. Sorry I held you up so long, fellows."

That was all he did say. Miss Jones felt like crying herself. She caught Crunch staring up at his finicky passenger and in Crunch's startlingly blue eyes there was a gleam; the kind of gleam anybody would like to be responsible for. But Mr. Denby didn't seem to see that, either.

They came in, late that afternoon, when the sun was shooting bars of radiance halfway to the zenith. Miss Jones was on the forward deck again. She had been there ever since the fish had been lost. She'd protested that she was tired—though she wasn't. And Crunch had supplied her with an abundant lunch, having suspected that she would not know it was the duty of the passengers to bring lunch for the ship's crew. Somehow, she hadn't wanted to fish any more that day—partly for fear that she would hang a big one and annoy the others by taking too long, and partly for some inner reason she couldn't analyze.

By and by—to her surprise—Mr. Denby came up and sat beside her. "I never quit until we get in past the bell buoy," he said. "Sorry I wasn't more sociable today. Your first trip? Thought so. You did well."

She thanked him. At close range, he looked different. He had direct, hazel eyes and a high forehead. His skin was sunburned a rather silly pink but, near to, that didn't matter. And his voice, when he lowered it, was shy. "It's too bad," she said, "you lost that big amberjack. I saw him take the bait, and he surely was a monster."

The two men in the cockpit invited them to have a drink, but Miss Jones' companion said he never touched the stuff, and, evidently, he assumed that she didn't, either.

"I . . . " he began presently—and was not satisfied with whatever opener he had in mind. "You see, Miss Jones—I'm a fanatic about fishing. I wasn't athletic in school or college. Quite the reverse. Kind of a—a coward. But after I grew up I got the idea that someday I could hang up a light-tackle record fishing—if I stuck to it. I love to fish, you know. I release most of the ones I get. Hate a meat hog."

She understood the look in his eye—then. The frantic determination. He had been fighting—not a fish, but himself. Old wounds, old feelings of inferiority. "Did you ever break a record?" she asked.

He smiled, a crinkly smile, as if he were looking into the future and seeing himself with the record broken. "Not yet. But—of course—I've only been after one for twelve years."

Then they were nearing the dock. Mr. Denby tried to seem offhand. "Well . . . another time! I hope you'll be a member of some party that I'm in one of these days?" He was earnest and worried, as if he wanted to say more and did not know how.

Miss Jones looked at him and smiled. "Thanks. I'm afraid not, though. It's a bit too expensive for me. I'm stricly a causeway Waltonian, and this was just a . . ."

"A binge?" He was chuckling sympathetically.

"Yes. For me—a binge. But I did enjoy it. And I think you're a terribly good sport."

They were throwing the stern lines aboard the *Poseidon* then. People on the dock crowded through the vermilion sunlight to see what wonders had been wrenched from the sea that day. Miss Jones made ready to go ashore. And Crunch came up to her. He was uncomfortable. "Look," he said. "One thing—I mean . . . Well . . . " He tried to thrust six dollars into her hand. But she stepped lightly on the fish box, laughed at him, smiled at Mr. Denby, and was gone.

Some nights later, just as Miss Jones was on the point of throwing her rig into the running tide, Crunch came along the luminous, thunderous causeway. He had a rod in his hand—a rod with a shiny reel and agate-lined guides. "Hello," he said.

Miss Jones grinned. "After more bait? You know, I still dream about my day at sea! It was just gorgeous! And I was probably an awful nuisance!"

"Not to one man," Crunch answered. "You made quite a hit with Denby, I guess. He's been hanging around for days—and I didn't know why until this afternoon. He came down with this rod. For you. He said it was an old one that he didn't use any more."

She was embarrassed—and touched. "I couldn't think of taking it!"

"Why not? He can afford it. You're fishing for serious out here—and I know what that's like. This rod'll help you. You can cast a mile with it—after a little practice. Look."

Crunch whipped the rod in an arc. The reel sang. The bait went flying through the twilight like a driven golf ball. It splashed far out beyond the other lines that sagged down from the causeway. "He was afraid you'd refuse," Crunch continued. "So he made me take it to you." The old hundred percenter had a barbless hook and three-thread line on it. "I changed the three-thread to twelve—you can't handle that fine stuff on a rocky bottom. But it's a nice rig. I'd take it."

"He's kind of a cute guy," she said.

Crunch eyed her as he handed over the rod. "I'll bet you didn't talk that way in the library!"

"Even a librarian," she answered, with an assumption of mock dignity, "has access to the vernacular."

"Denby said—if you ever got anything good—to let him know."

"Oh?" She pursed her lips. "A string attached, hunh? Well—I must say—that if I were going to sell my soul—I think deep-sea fishing whenever you wanted to go, would be a fair price. I loved it!"

He stood beside her for a while. A hell of a nice girl, he thought; if she were only a boy, I could get her a job as a mate; she'd be a crackerjack, I'll bet. He knew how it was to want things and not have them. He could imagine her "efficiency" apartment, her regular diet of fish, and her feelings, when she watched the fishing fleet go out and come in.

She reeled in and was getting ready to cast. He showed her how to thumb the reel, how to use her wrist, and, a moment later, how to pick out a backlash when you did it wrong. After a dozen tries, she had grasped the fundamentals. Maybe, Crunch began thinking, Sari could do something about her.

His eyes were fixed on the dark water of the bay—somberly—because his thoughts made him unhappy. And then his eyes flickered and focused. There had been a roll—a shimmer, a silhouette of a fin—out on the inky surface. He knew what that was. If he could get it—or them—to hit, that would be another happy experience for Miss Jones. But he had no plug. They came through often—under the arches of the causeway—in the spring. Sometimes they wouldn't strike a diamond brooch, but sometimes they'd take anything.

At Miss Jones' feet was the newpaper that contained her shrimp, and the string that had been around it. The paper was white and it would stay white in the water for a while. He tore off several strips and picked up the string. "Wind in," he said. "Let me have that hook for a second!"

Puzzled, she obeyed. Crunch fixed the strips of paper around the hook as much as possible in imitation of a feather lure. Then he scanned the water again. "Now," he said. "Yonder—just in line with the bow of that yacht! Cast as far as you can and don't let it sink! Instead, reel in slowly and jerk your rod a bit. If anything hits, hit back as hard as you can—and fast!"

She caught the excitement in his voice. "But—did you see something?"

"Go ahead! Cast! Exactly the way I said!"

Doubtfully, she cast the impromptu bait. It arced through the evening and hit the water. Crunch could see it there—a white dot. He saw it start to wriggle toward them. "That's it!" Then he saw the heavy surge under the paper lure.

Miss Jones struck. She pressed on the thumbstall hard. But something—something like lightning—was on that line. It ran as if she had hooked into a passing automobile. Then it stopped. "Wind!" Crunch yelled. "Wind as you never did in your life! It's going to jump!"

"But what *is* it?" she gasped.

"Look!"

She was barely able to manage her rod and to look. Out in the light of the electric signs and the buildings and the radiance from the causeway she saw a silverish-white fish crash up into the air, hang for a second, somersault completely, and vanish. "Oh, my," she murmured.

"Tarpon!" he yelled. "A beauty! If you get him—you'll really have something!" He raced along the sidewalk past the other fishermen. He bawled at the top of his lungs. "Pull in your lines, everybody, please! We've hung a big tarpon here! Hey! You with the big stomach! Pull in that line! The lady'll foul you if you don't!" His voice changed to an ominous roar: "And if you don't think I can make you, wise guy! . . . Well . . . that's better!"

He ran back to Miss Jones. "Keep the line tight! After we wear him down, we'll lead him along the Causeway to shore and beach him! Boy! That's it!" He ran off to warn more distant anglers.

Miss Jones was thinking. Thinking of the fish she had promised to bring to her neighbors the day she had gone out to sea. Fish she had not provided because she had caught only two barracudas. She was thinking of the size of the tarpon, and of poor old Mrs. Wilmot, and of Mr. Treelman who was out of work, and the Berkimer kids. She also thought, for a flash, of Mr. Denby and his tragic desire to break a record. Then she had no more time for thinking. The tarpon ran under the causeway and shot out—miraculously without cutting the line—and it began to leap and pinwheel in the air.

Around Miss Jones the other causeway fishermen gathered, but she did not notice them. She did not hear their shouts of advice. Behind her, a car stopped and a man in a white dinner jacket hopped out to look. He hurried back to a woman in the car and said rather dazedly, "Some girl has hung a walloping big tarpon on a casting outfit! Let's watch!" He helped from the car a woman in evening clothes. Behind them, another car stopped. A truck driver headed for the beach peered, slowed, and pulled up his brake. Horns began to blow. The crowd bulged out on the street. From Miami, a motorcycle policeman cut through the snarl with a braying siren and began to yell questions: What's going on? Where's the accident? Did some half-wit go through the railing?

Then he, too, saw the great silver king plunging in the night, and because many—perhaps most—of the people of Miami are fishermen, he forgot his duty, pushed to the rail, and bellowed, "Lady, you better watch out on those jumps! Come back farther with the rod!"

Miss Jones didn't notice him. But she did notice that the thumbstall— rotten by long sitting in Mr. Denby's tackle closet—was wearing thin. Her finger became hot. A chunk of leather tore away. He bare thumb hit the wet and racing spool. She shut her jaws. When pain shot into her arms, she used the other thumb, although it was awkward. Then she found that by pressing against the metal side of the spinning spool, less heat was generated. When her left thumb grew slippery, she knew it was bleeding. But she did not care. The tarpon was not leaping quite as high or quite as often. Crunch had cleared away all the dangling lines and was beside her again.

The fish sank below the surface and she could feel the slow, steady beat of its tail.

"Sulking," Crunch said. "Let's start leading him. Every time you come to a post, get all set and pass the rod around it from your left hand to your right. If he starts to leap or run—stop and fight him!"

So they began to move along the causeway. Miss Jones passed the rod around obstructions. Crunch followed, coaching. And the crowd followed, too, yelling, encouraging and voicing envy. Traffic behind them was a hopeless tangle and traffic was piling up ahead. From one of the stalled cars came a man with a camera to which was attached a bulb. Its soundless light broke over the mob.

Miss Jones found that by pulling steadily, she could tow the tarpon in the desired direction. Her fingers bled. Her wrists ached. Her shoulder joints felt separated. But she kept on. When they came around the end of the causeway, she was groggy. She tripped on some weeds and stumbled over a pile of rubble. The crowd stayed above her, looking down, and the man with the camera kept shooting pictures. But Crunch was at her side.

"Just get out there on that bare spot—and pump," he said. "The way you did the 'cudas."

So she pumped. She was out of breath and wet with perspiration. But she kept pulling. And suddenly, to her vague amazement, Crunch waded into the water. He bent over. He groped. Then he half threw up on the land a prodigious, glittering fish which flopped heavily in the red glare of a big electric sign. "Got it," Crunch said.

Miss Jones didn't exactly faint, but her knees gave way and she sat down.

Twenty minutes later she was ensconced in the stern of the *Poseidon*. Traffic had been restored on the causeway. There was only a small crowd on the Gulf Stream Dock—perhaps a couple of hundred people—and out of it came the fishing editor of the *Dispatch* to interview her. The tarpon was hanging on the rack. He stopped to look at it. He whistled. Then he said, "You're Miss Jones?"

She was about to reply. But another person broke through the awed spectators. It was Mr. Denby—without a hat—with staring eyes. He charged up to the fishing editor. "On three-thread!" he yelled. "Three-thread, old man! A *world's record!*"

Miss Jones, who had felt her heart bounce at the sight of Mr. Denby, now felt that same organ wither and grow ashamed. "On twelve-thread," she said quietly. "Crunch changed it. I'm afraid, Mr. Denby, we're still as far from that record as ever."

The skipper came up from below in dry shoes and trousers. He heard her words and took in the disappointment on the expert's face. "Yeah," he said slowly. "She couldn't handle three-thread on that bottom, Denby. Another thing—your thumbstall wore out and she's torn her fingers all up. Maybe it wasn't a world's record—but it's a new high for grit!"

Mr. Denby still seemed bogged in disappointment.

"Anyway," Miss Jones said sorrowfully, "It'll make up for the meal I promised the Wilmots and the Treelmans and the Berkimers. Not to mention myself. I've got the use of an icebox now."

Crunch gulped.

Mr. Denby stared.

"But," the fishing editor said, "tarpon are no good to eat! They're muddy."

Denby grabbed Crunch's arm and pulled him aside. "You mean to say—a lovely girl like that—fishes because she needs food?"

"Lot of people do," Crunch replied laconically. "Nice people."

Denby gulped.

"Our cameraman happened to be going over the causeway—" the fishing editor felt compelled to lighten a pall he could not fathom—"and he says he got some elegant stuff! We'll give you a spread on the sports page! . . ."

He went on talking. But the situation was not relieved then. Not wholly relieved later—when Mr. Denby insisted that as soon as Miss Jones' hands were healed she should be his guest for a day "outside."

It was that day which changed everything.

A day like all the other days of spring on the Florida coast. The *Poseidon* was moving smoothly out toward the purple edge of the Gulf Stream. Desperate was at the controls. Crunch was rigging up Mr. Denby's four-six outfit. And Mr. Denby detached himself from an animated conversation with Miss Jones. "Not the light outfit, Crunch!" he said in a low voice. "Give me the heaviest stuff you have. Thirty-nine thread, if you've got it. And tell Des not to head for the Stream. I want to fish the reef."

Crunch was startled. "Thought you hated the reef?"

Mr. Denby's mouth was firm. "We're fishing for groupers, today. Groupers for the Wilmots and the Treelmans and those other people. Big, delicious groupers. Dozens of them! I don't want to take a chance on losing anything we hang."

Crunch put down the light outfit. There was written on his face a masterpiece of mixed moods. Surely, he reflected, Denby has changed. Maybe Miss Jones was right. Maybe he was at bottom a good egg. "Head for Fowey Rock," he yelled to Des. He fixed two big rigs.

Mr. Denby had returned to the cockpit with a pillow. "This," he said, "will make you more comfortable—ah—Miss Jones. I wish I knew your first name?"

"If I told you, you'd be shocked. My mother had imagination, she was practically reckless."

There was amusement in his eyes—and affection. "I'll find out," he said. "You only gave your initials in the newspaper story. But I'm a determined man. Very determined!"

"Yes. I know." She said that earnestly.

"My own," he continued, "is Thornton. Does that give you courage?"

Miss Jones blushed. "You won't believe it—but it's Scheherazade."

Mr. Denby peered at the radiant sea. "It's beautiful," he murmured.

Crunch gazed at Mr. Denby and at Miss Jones. Then he ducked out through a window and joined Desperate.

The mate started below to replace him, but Crunch caught his arm. "As much as possible," he said, "I think we'll both stay up on top today. We may get some fish—but mostly, we're just a gondola."

Des thought that over—and understood. "I hope she'll teach him not to tell everybody how to fish," he finally said.

At that instant, Mr. Denby called, "I've got a strike! Nope! Missed him!"
Crunch leaned over the canopy edge.
"You hit too hard," Scheherazade said sweetly but firmly.
There was utter devotion in Thorton's response.
"So I did! *Much* too hard."

SPARE THE ROD

THE EYES of Dexter Heath were the most remarkable feature in a rather dashing ensemble—gray eyes, round, penetrating and vigilant. Next was his hair, which was dark and curly, but curly without pattern, and incredibly unkempt; his hair was like a distant view of some irregular object foundering in a stormy sea. The rest of him was normal for a boy of eleven—snub nose, a voice that was invariably an exclamation, although sometimes hushed, and, under his sun-tanned skin, young muscles of which he was proud to the point of racy braggadocio.

On a late summer afternoon, Crunch Adams, coming down the Gulf Stream Dock to minister to his fishing cruiser, was struck by the posture and attitude of Dexter. Balanced on a rail at the end of the dock, with his chin in his hand, the young man was staring ferociously at the universe, not seeing it, but not liking it, either. Crunch pondered the spectacle of fury in equilibrium for a moment, and then, with a grin, interrupted it.

"What's eating you, Dexter?"

The young man budged a little, put down a tentative foot, and looked at the captain. All traces of wrath had been erased by those slight movements. He seemed calm—even bored. "Nothing," he replied. "Nothing."

Crunch persisted. "Don't kid me. If there had been a nail between your teeth, you'd have ground it into filings."

"I was just thinkin'," Dexter responded lazily. And, indeed, he began thinking. Hard. His broken reverie was not a subject he could discuss. There had been sadness in it, and frenzy at the injustice of the world. His mind had been clamorous with ideas which were antisocial, hostile, and, even, illegal. Dexter did not wish to have any of his secret thoughts heckled out of him. It was therefore necessary to dissemble. Earlier in the afternoon he had indulged in a different sort of daydream. He recalled it and drew on it for material: "I was just thinkin' what if a brontosorassus came steamin' up the bay."

"A what?"

"Brontosorassus. Swimmin' like a submarine! Neck out. Fangs drippin' ooze! You couldn't hang him on any fifty-four-thread. But maybe you could hold him on three-hundred-thread. With a fifty-ought reel. You'd have to fight him night and day—for maybe a couple of weeks!"

"Oh," said Crunch. "A dinosaur." He was still grinning, but he fell in with Dexter's mood. He felt that he now understood the savagery which had been on the young man's face. "I guess you could never hang one. And you certainly couldn't boat an eighty-footer in a forty-foot cruiser."

"You could beach him," Dexter said, pleased at this attention from a great man, and yielding his inner sorrow to imagination. "Maybe, if they were still plentiful, you'd have to keep a swassy-cans on the dock."

"Swassy-cans?"

"That's French," said the boy with some small condescension. "My father taught it to me. My father knows most languages, I guess. It's the French word for a seventy-five. A gun. You could have one right here—if you put some cement posts under the dock. Then—Wham! Whang! Zowie! Boy! You'd have to mount her like a antiaircraft gun, too, in case any of those big old peterodackles flew by. Wham! Whacko! Blow a wing off one and steam out and polish her off with a lance! Wham! Boom!"

Crunch chuckled. "Guess you're right. Too bad we didn't live in those days. There'd have been some real fishing, hunh?"

"Fishin'," said Dexter, "and huntin'!"

"Like to wet a line now? I mean—I've got a hand line on the *Poseidon*. And some bait. I'd be glad to rig it for you."

Dexter was grateful, but negative. "No, thanks. I don't care much for this old hand-line stuff. But if I ever had a harpoon in any big old brontosorassus . . ."

Crunch nodded and stepped aboard his boat. He had no precise recollection of his own age of dinosaur hunting, but he felt an indefinite kindred-ship for it. "Maybe," he said as he picked up a square of sandpaper and tore it into suitable sizes, "you'd like to go out with Des and me some day?"

Dexter's head moved forward from his shoulders and his brow puckered. "You mean you'd really take me out?"

Crunch set up a rasp and sizzle on the varnish. "Sure. Sometime. If I get a couple of nice customers who don't mind."

The young man gasped. Then he controlled himself. Life had taught him not to count too many unhatched chickens. "How soon—how soon—do you think you might possibly run across a couple of people like that?"

"Oh . . . soon," Crunch answered. "Any day."

Dexter had put in frequent appearances at the Gulf Stream Dock before Crunch had made that astonishing offer. But, thereafter, he was the most regular of all the juvenile buffs—boys who wistfully watched the boats go out and who, when the boats came in, identified various fish for less knowing adults, with a marked air of superiority. Dexter scrutinized every party that chartered the *Poseidon*. Sometimes he knew at a glance that the customers were not the sort who would care for an eleven-year-old supercargo. Sometimes he had great hopes. But no invitation was forthcoming.

The truth was that Crunch had forgotten the conversation. Small boys were ubiquitous, indistinguishable, and, on a busy fishing dock, often in the way. The *Poseidon*'s skipper had noticed Dexter closely enough to like him—to be amused by him—and to make a suggestion which had dropped back into his unconscious mind. Dexter, however, was that rather common but always astounding combination of the dreamer and the man of action. His father, who knew all languages, had told him that one of the cardinal virtues was "initiative." He had explained the word. Dexter eventually enlarged upon its meaning.

In consequence, on one blue and golden morning when the *Poseidon*'s outriggers were trailing balaos down the enameled sea, Crunch went below and was startled by the sight of two medium-sized shoes protruding from beneath a pile of pillows, blankets, canvas and gear on the starboard bunk. He grabbed one of the shoes and pulled forth Dexter.

The young man was alarmed, but in control of himself. "I had to do it!" he said. "You invited me! Besides—Mr. and Mrs. Winton fishing out there are two of the nicest people in Miami. My father said so. I heard them charter you last night—so I sneaked here early . . ."

Crunch remembered his offer, then. His first feeling for his stowaway was one of intense sympathy. Mr. and Mrs. Winton would be amused and pleased by the event. There was no doubt of that. But, on the other hand, it had been presumptive of the boy to steal a trip. Crunch had been rather harshly brought up; he felt that contemporary children were less disciplined and respectful than they should be. His father would have given him a good licking for behavior like young Mr. Heath's. Crunch weighed the situation. The corners of his mouth twitched. He hid that reflex with his hand. Sternly, he eyed the boy. "I suppose you realize that what you've done is a crime on the high seas?"

"I just thought—since you'd asked me already—"

"If I had a brig," Crunch went on, "as captain, I could throw you in it. All stowaways are condemned to hard labor. And bread and water—"

"I got my own lunch—right here!" Dexter produced from his blouse a large and messy-looking sandwich which was inadequately wrapped in newspaper. "And I'll be only too glad to work . . ."

Crunch nodded and cast his eye about. The *Poseidon* was spic and span. "You'll go aloft," he said finally, "where my mate can keep his eye on you. Here's a rag and a can of polish. You can shine all the brass till it's too bright to look at. And you can also keep your eye on the baits. If you see anything—don't scream. Just tell Des."

"Gee!" said Dexter. "Golly!" he added. "I was afraid you'd keep me down here!"

Crunch motioned the boy up the companionway and into the cockpit, where the two Wintons regarded his appearance with moderate surprise.

"This," said the captain, "is Dexter Heath. A stowaway. I'm putting him to work polishing brass."

Mr. Winton, who was a big man with white hair and a white mustache, burst into hearty laughter. His wife only smiled, and she regarded the boy's struggle of jubilance and discomfiture with a certain tenderness. "I'm sure he didn't mean any harm, Crunch. How old are you, son?"

"Eleven," Dexter replied.

"Do you like fishing?"

"My father," Dexter said uncompromisingly, "is the greatest fisherman in the world! Sometimes, he takes me. I will be nearly as good when I get that old."

"Your father's a great fisherman," Mr. Winton mused. "Heath. I don't think I've heard about him."

"You would," the boy said, "if—" He broke off. "You can stand a hundred feet from my father and he can cast a plug into your pocket! I guess he knows mostly where every fish lives in every canal in the Glades. He hooked a water moccasin on a plug, once, and reeled it up and killed it with a stick!"

Mr. Winton whistled and shook his head in awe. Crunch turned away his face. "Go and polish that brass," he said.

Desperate received the newcomer placidly. Crunch had yelled up his name and the conditions of tolerance to be applied to him. The *Poseidon* sailed along. Dexter put elbow grease in his work and the results began to show. His eye attention, however, was largely for the baits. He labored for perhaps half an hour before he ventured any conversation. Des had been wondering just how long he would keep that humble silence.

"This is the Gulf Stream, isn't it?" the boy inquired.

Des nodded. "Right here, in this dark-blue water, it is. Over yonder, where the water is paler blue, it isn't. You can see the edge."

"Yeah," Dexter murmured. "Like two kinds of tile in a first-class bathroom."

Des pursed his lips, squinted judiciously at the boy, and nodded again. "If you look at that turning buoy out there, you'll see it has a wake behind it. Just as if it was being hauled through the water. But it's anchored. It's the Stream that makes the wake."

"Sure," the boy assented. "I can see it plain." And then, with every atom of his energy, every possible vibration of his vocal chords, he bellowed, "Marlin!"

Crunch dropped a bait and stared. Des whirled from the top controls. Mr. Winton sat up straight. His wife said, "Goodness! Where?"

Dexter was pointing with his polishing rag—pointing palely. His knees were knocking together a little. "Right out there!"

Some fifty feet behind Mr. Winton's bait there was, indeed, a fish. Its length lay yellow under the water. A fin stuck darkly from its back into the air. It was obviously following the bait—following it with a speed not greatly in excess of the *Poseidon*'s and with a peculiar wobbling motion, as if it swam in zigzags.

Crunch stepped toward the canopy and peered at his prisoner with annoyance. "I told you not to yell, Dexter. That's no marlin. It's a lousy hammerhead shark. Speed her up, Des, and we'll get away."

Dexter was not dashed. Instead, he seemed rather more interested. "A hammerhead shark!" he repeated. "A real, live one! Boy, look at her cut around that old bait!"

Des notched up the throttles. The shark began to lose the race.

"A real shark," Dexter went on excitedly. "A maneater! And I saw it first!"

Then Mr. Winton spoke. Perhaps his words contained the whole truth. But perhaps he understood and shared the feelings of the boy. "What do you say we slow down and let him get the bait? The fishing's slow today, anyhow, and I need a workout. Helen's always telling me to take more exercise."

"Boy!" murmured Dexter, in a low tone, but one that held audible hope.

"If you want to do it . . ." said Crunch, who was not much on fighting hammerheads. Mako sharks, or whites, or threshers, were different. He waved Des to slow down.

Out beyond the *Poseidon*'s wake, the shark was plunging back and forth in an effort to pick up the scent of the bait. When Des slowed the boat, the shark got it, and came boiling through the sea. His ugly, scimitar-shaped foreface broke water as he engulfed the small fish. The line drifted down from the clothespin at the outrigger tip. Mr. Winton reeled until it was taut and he struck hard several times. The shark gradually became aware that there was a thorn in its jaws and a hampering line hitched to the thorn. First he swam off in a logy manner. Then he essayed a short run. After that, he went fast and far.

"I saw him swallow it!" Dexter kept saying.

Mr. Winton screwed up the drag on the side of his reel. The extra tension bent the rod in a bow. The reel kept humming.

"Like a big amberjack," Mrs. Winton said. "Only—not so fast."

"He's got about three hundred and fifty yards," her husband finally muttered. "That's a good deal."

Crunch grinned. "You asked for it."

Presently the run stopped. Hammerheads, as a rule, make one exciting and fairly fast run. After that they merely resist—lunging lazily, throwing their weight around, bracing dead against the angler's pull. They are not sporty fish. They do not jump. They lack flash and fire and heart. But any fish that weighs three or four hundred pounds provides a tussle on twenty-four-thread line.

Mr. Winton worked hard. It was a warm day. Perspiration ran from him. He called for a glass of water. He called for his sun helmet. He dried his slippery hands on his trousers. He rocked back in the fighting chair and winked up at Dexter, who was standing on the edge of the canopy with, as Mr. Winton later said, "his eyes popping and his tongue hanging out."

"I can see him!" the boy presently yelled. "He's turning over on his side!"

And so he was. A moment later, the shark quit. He came in without a struggle—so much dead weight pulled through the water like a boat on a painter. Crunch went to the stern. He picked up a long knife. Dexter was panting—as if he had manipulated the tackle through the whole fight. He saw Crunch grab the leader and shorten it. He saw him reach down to the water. Dexter held his breath. The skipper actually grabbed one of the hideous eye stalks in his bare hand. Then the muscles in his arms and the muscles along his back bulged, and hardened like rocks. He pulled the great fish—a fish which in that instant seemed bigger to Dexter than any "brontosorassus"—at least a third of its length out of the water. He hooked one eye stalk over the gunwale and held the other while he plunged the knife deep into the white bellyside. "I hate sharks," he said coldly.

Dexter gasped. The shark trembled as the knife point found its heart. Blood poured from it. But, still calmly, Crunch put down the knife, picked up a pair of pliers, and went after the hook. The curved jaws snapped convulsively inches from the captain's hand. Nevertheless, he got the hook out with a quick, hard wrench, and he let the hammerhead slide back into the water. It sank, trailing crimson, stone dead.

Mr. Winton fanned himself with his helmet. "How'd you like it, son?"

Dexter swallowed. "Gee!" he murmured. "Imagine! Barehanded! I guess that's about the bravest thing I ever heard of."

Crunch laughed. "Nothing to it—if you know how to handle 'em."

"And," Mrs. Winton added, "if you're as strong as a derrick."

It had been a day for Dexter. A champion day. The fishing had not

And Crunch nodded. "Guess not. And that's a relief!"

Mrs. Graymond found the "extra" mate shy and rather uncommunicative. She was a dark-haired, dark-eyed girl and she had a way with boys. A most successful way, as a rule. She simply treated them as if they were twice their age. But Dexter did not seem to have an opinion about the outcome of the World's Series, he was not expecting to play football in the fall, he had no dog, and he was willing to admit that he liked fishing—but not with any emphasis or detail.

Indeed, after a quarter of an hour of lopsided conversation, Dexter embarrassedly asked Crunch if he could go "up topside" and shine a little brass. Crunch sent him up. And Desperate respected the boy's vast quietude.

It was a very tragic quietude. The one thing Dexter had wanted in his whole life more than the friendship of two such dramatic, important persons as Crunch and his mate, was that rod. He had taken it. Stolen it so craftily that even though he had been spotted on the night of the theft, he was positive nobody could testify he had been carrying away the precious tackle. Indeed, when the skipper of the *Firefly* had called to him, the rod, line and reel had been hidden underneath the dock in a spot from which Dexter had later retrieved it by means of a temporarily borrowed dinghy.

Now—they had taken him fishing. As he polished brass—and glanced up occasionally with sadness at the broad back of the best mate on the Gulf Stream—Dexter reflected that he had sort of hoped they might vaguely suspect him and would in consequence merely become negative toward him. They couldn't prove anything. And he would never tell. He would go on lying, even if they tortured him worse than the Indians. But the fact that they had invited him to go out—and even to fish—was an almost unendurable kindness. It showed they trusted him.

If he had known their true anxiety over the suspicion of his deed, Dexter would probably have tried to slip overboard unnoticed. On the other hand, when his conscience smote him with the epithet of "thief," he did not flinch. He merely stuck out his chin and squinted back any dampness in his eyes. Maybe he was a thief, but there are things worse than robbery.

It was in the company of such fierce feelings that he watched them cut the *Poseidon*'s speed, make ready the anchor, pick an exact spot over a favorite patch of rocks after much searching through a glass-bottomed bucket, and come to an easy rest. In the distance were the V-shaped outriggers of boats trolling the Stream, the spindly legs of Fowey Rock Light, a few sails, and the smoke-plumed hulls of a pair of tankers beating south inside the current. Under the *Poseidon*'s keel were the irregular blurs of a coral bottom—lumps and caverns, miniature mountains and dark valleys of a size to hide groupers, jewfish, sharks.

The baits went overboard and Dexter was summoned from the comparative obscurity of his place aloft. He was given a hand line by Crunch, who said, "Now, son, hang a whopper!" Desperate grinned at him. He wondered how he could stand it all day long.

They fished with dead shrimp and chunks of balao. Mrs. Graymond used a rod like the one Dexter had stolen. Its twin. Her husband chose a larger rig with a bigger hook, a heavier hunk of bait, and a reel that buzzed instead of clicked. The three lines soaked up salt water.

"Just about like perch fishing, isn't it?" Mrs. Graymond said.

Dexter smiled back at her smile. "Perch?"

"We catch them in Tennessee. And catfish. And bass, sometimes. Quite big ones. Two pounds—even three."

Her husband nodded. "I was thinking the same thing. I'd expected, somehow, that salt-water fishing would be different."

Then—it was different. His rod jerked. His reel whirred. His arms shot up and down. "Whoa!" he shouted. "Must be loose from that anchor! I've got bottom, captain!"

"You've got a fish," Crunch said.

Mr. Graymond opened his mouth as if to make a denial. Then—the grouper really ran. If he'd had bottom, the *Poseidon* would have to have been going at its top speed; even Mr. Graymond could reason that far, although his reasoning processes were seriously compromised by the situation. Crunch set him in the fighting chair and helped to thrust the bucking ferrule of the rod into the gimbal.

It was a pretty fight, though clumsy, and marred by a mild profanity of amazement. Even Dexter almost forgot his burden of trouble. Until Crunch reached over with a gaff and scooped in the fish.

Just an old grouper, Dexter said to himself at that point. His reason was the violent behavior of the Graymonds. *You'd think,* Dexter went on thinking, *it was a blue marlin. Or some kind of swordfish, or something.*

"But it's a monster!" Mrs. Graymond gasped. "A perfect giant! How much does he weigh!"

"Oh," Crunch murmured, "around, say, twenty pounds."

"Why, darling, it's a whale!" She kissed her husband.

Perhaps Mr. Graymond caught sight of Dexter's eyes. "Well, dear . . . it may not be so big for here. You've got to remember, we're pond and stream anglers." He stared, however, into the fishbox, where the grouper displayed its tweedy pattern of browns and its brilliant fins, spread taut. "Still," he said, "it's a doggoned big fish! Doggoned big." He glanced at Dexter defiantly.

But Dexter had lost his cynical expression. Something had hit his line. He was pulling it up, hand over hand, with an expert continuum of effort which gave the fish no slack, no chance to escape. He flipped his fish deftly into the box, without benefit of gaff. The enthralled Tennesseans bumped heads lightly in their eagerness to look. Dexter had caught a pork fish—a vivid yellow chap, eight or nine inches long, with a flat face and black, vertical stripes.

"It's the most gorgeous thing I ever saw!" exclaimed Mrs. Graymond.

"And good to eat," said Dexter.

She turned toward him with surprise. "But—it's *much* too beautiful for that! It ought to be in an aquarium!"

Dexter went to the box for bait.

And the fishing continued. Every fish, it appeared, was too beautiful for Mrs. Graymond to think of eating. Even Dexter, who was a practical individual, began to see the quarry through the lady's eyes. And they were kind of pretty—mighty bright-colored—when you thought of it. Right down to grunts.

The accident happened in the only way it could have happened. And in a place where even the most nervous boatman would hardly expect anything serious to occur. Dexter, liking the Graymonds almost against his will, and passionately eager to do anything to aid Crunch and Des, had undertaken to remove fish from the hooks and to put on baits for the customers. He was perfectly competent for the chore. He had weeks of dock fishing behind him.

Relieved of the duty, Crunch had gone below to prepare a special chowder from the grouper. Desperate had already occupied himself with the rearrangement of gear on the foredeck. Thus the two novices and the youngster were left alone. Mrs. Graymond hooked a fish. Dexter went to her side to give advice. It was a pretty good-sized fish—a snapper, he hoped—and his attention was entirely focussed, on the lady.

Mr. Graymond also hooked a fish. Not wishing to disturb his thrilling wife, and imagining himself by then a fairly proficient fisherman, he fought the creature in silence. It ran and it shook and it bent his rod but he dragged it to the surface. Then, seeing that Dexter was still busy, he undertook to copy the boy's trick of flicking his quarry aboard. He wound the line up to the swivel, blocked the reel spool with his thumb, braced his feet, and gave a tremendous heave. His fish was yanked out of the water. It rose into the air, writhing. It landed in the cockpit. It spat out the hook. And Mr. Graymond yelled.

Crunch and Des, separately, interpreted the yell as evidence of another triumph. It was not. It was a yell of sheer horror.

For the thing in the boat was horrible. A thing like a fat snake, five feet long, a sickly rich green, with a sharp, reptilian mouth, terrible teeth, and brilliant, evil eyes. Even as Mr. Graymond yelled, it slithered into a knot and struck like a rattlesnake, at the support of a chair. It bounced from that and struck again, biting fiercely on a glove. Dexter wheeled and saw it and turned ash-pale. Mrs. Graymond also saw, and she tried to scream and could not. She tried to move, but her legs would not budge.

"Keep away from it!" Dexter said hoarsely. "It'll bite! It's deadly poison!"

That it would bite was obvious. It was, even then, striking a pail. That the green moray is poisonous is a technical problem, since the toxicology of slimes and fish poisons is an unfinished science. Certainly morays make bad wounds that are slow to heal. Certainly men have suffered fearful infections from their bites, or from bacteria that entered the bites. Certainly all the boatmen in Florida waters would be hard put to choose between a big moray and a rattlesnake, if one had to be let loose in a cockpit.

Dexter's husky advice was heeded by the terrified man. He jumped backwards mechanically and found himself, somehow, standing on one of the couches. But his wife was still transfixed. The moray saw her—and started for her.

Dexter had been standing behind her. He came around in front. In coming, he grabbed the only thing handy—a gaff. The moray turned toward him. As it struck, Dexter clipped it with the gaff. Savagely, the green, repugnant monster plunged again and the boy hit it again, knocking it back. His gaff was too short for such work, and he knew it. He knew that if he missed, the moray would not. But he struck a third time. Mrs. Graymond came to galvanic life. She realized the boy had made a place which would permit her to jump to the side of her husband. She jumped. And, at last, she screamed.

Seeing that the lady was clear, Dexter lost no time in leaping up on one of the fishing chairs.

Then Crunch came, fast. He had recognized the scream as one not of exultation. He snatched up the long-handled gaff—which Dexter hadn't been able to reach—and he broke the moray's back with it.

It took two hours and a half, together with one of the tastiest dishes in all the experience of the Graymonds, to start the fishing again. They called Dexter a hero and the bravest kid they had ever seen and Mr. Graymond patted his back and Mrs. Graymond kissed him. There were long discussions of the venomousness of the big eels, and there was a brief but tense altercation between husband and wife over the uncourageous behavior of the former. Dexter noted a look in Crunch's eye which eased away a full half of his sadness. Then the lines were wet again, no more morays were caught, and Mr. Graymond made no further attempts to fling fish aboard unaided.

It turned out to be a good day, with a fine catch of panfish, and two more groupers. A day marked by An Adventure to Tell People Back Home. The Graymonds began to refer to the battle in that fashion. Dexter slipped back into his melancholy. The sun moved down. The anchor went up. And, in the purpling evening, the *Poseidon* hummed paint-slick down the Government Cut toward home.

Dexter was sitting alone on the canopy top when Mr. Graymond came up beside him. He didn't say anything. He just shook Dexter's hand, and his own head, and went away. But he had left something in Dexer's palm. The boy looked at it. And—for him—the sun shone brightly, the sea was perfumed, there were flowers on every tree. It was a five-dollar bill.

His first impulse was to shout for Crunch. Five dollars was a fortune. It would pay for the rod. But Dexter was a youth accustomed to consideration. Maybe four dollars would foot the bill. Or even three. His ideas about money, in sums larger than ten or fifteen cents, were not merely vague. They scarcely existed. If three were enough . . . what he could do with the other two would be! . . . But he sturdily thrust back temptation. He leaned over the cockpit.

"Captain Adams," he said in a low tone, "would you come here a minute? It's important."

Crunch recognized the tone. He had been hoping to hear it all day. "Take over," he said quickly to his mate. "I'll see the kid."

He climbed up on the canopy. He sat down beside the boy. He was smiling. "O.K., Dexter. What's important?"

Dexter handed him the five dollars. "That's for the rod I stole."

Crunch took the money. "Oh," he said somewhat numbly. "Where'd you?—"

"Mr. Graymond gave it to me. A reward, I guess, for saving that Mrs. Graymond's life, or maybe her leg."

"I see. Yeah. Look, Dex. About swiping the rod. Why?"

Dexter was crying a little, then. Things had broken too well for a man to bear. But he started to talk. Every sentence made the going tougher. Crunch didn't interrupt. He just sat there, watching the causeway slide past, watching the boat swing as Des prepared to back her in.

"I had to," the youngster began. "You gotta believe I had to! If you didn't, I'd about die!" He swallowed. "Look. You know about 'business reverses'? Pop's been having what he calls that. It really means we don't have any money. Until they started, we had enough. We had a wonderful time! We'd get up together, and I'd help get breakfast, and eat lunch at school, and evenings, we'd cook at home and sometimes we'd go out for dinner to a real restaurant! Then . . . when Saturdays came . . ."

Dexter had to pull himself together. "When—Saturdays came—he'd take me out in the Glades—fishing in the canal! We'd drive in our car, and I'd fish a jack pole and he'd cast plugs. I—I—I told you he could put one in your pocket a hundred feet away. It's true! Then—when we had to sell the car—we couldn't go so far and we had to fish in places that weren't so good—but we hardly ever missed a Saturday! He's—he knows all the birds—and how to catch snakes—and we saw deer and 'coons and possums! And then . . ."

The boy's voice went lower—close to inaudibility. His words ran fast. "School was coming. I had to have shoes and knickers and books and things—and Pop sold his rod and his reel and his tackle box and he had about a million plugs and he sold them and said he didn't care to fish with an old jack pole so we didn't go out together any more. He didn't tell me he sold those things to get my school stuff ready—but I found out from the man that bought them. Pop had a chance to sell—and he knew he'd have to buy all my stuff in a few weeks. I found that out. So I knew."

He didn't get any further than that. He couldn't. But there was no need of it.

The *Poseidon* was edging toward dock. Crunch jumped to the top controls while Des made fast the bow lines. Crunch didn't particularly want Dexter to see him at that instant, anyway. His jaw was set like steel. When the *Poseidon* was snug, Crunch looked at the hunched back of the boy. Then his eye traveled ashore, and he saw a man standing there. A medium-sized man, an unimportant-looking man, with a good face, full of worry. The man's eyes were hurt, and in his hand was the rod Des had made—the one his son had stolen.

Des helped the passengers ashore. Immediately afterward, the man— Mr. Heath—accosted the mate. He spoke rapidly, nervously. "My boy must have stolen this. He left it in my room a few days ago with a note saying he had found it. As soon as I had time—I traced it—through the tackle shops. Somebody recognized your work . . ."

Des just stood.

But the boy heard his father's voice. He leaped up with a tearing, ecstatic cry. "It's all right, Pop! It's yours! I just paid five bucks for it!"

The man, gray, embarrassed, gazed at his son. He spoke the first words that came into his head—spoke them bitterly. "Five bucks—when it's worth twenty-five! See here, son! . . ."

Dexter slid down into the cockpit. He was not breathing, or even seeing. He was sick. Sicker, perhaps, than he would ever be again in his life. He leaped ashore, and eluded Desperate's panicky effort to catch him. He ran away down the dock—to be alone.

Crunch dropped down, also, and came ashore. The Graymonds were waiting for their catch to be put on the fish rack. They realized something was wrong. They stood by, puzzled and unhappy.

Crunch took the gray-faced man by the arm. It was quivering. "Look," he began urgently. "I can't explain now. But you've got to believe me, Mr. Heath! This is a mighty important moment in your kid's life! He's a fine kid, Mr. Heath! I only hope mine grows up half that swell! But I want you to let me handle this my way. I want you to keep that rod—"

"I couldn't, Captain! I—I'm kind of broken up about it. I came home that night to tell my son I had found a job—a good one—and there was the stolen rod and the lying note! I've tried to teach him—about stealing—lying—and it half killed me! I decided not to say a thing about the job, till my boy confessed the theft. He—" Mr. Heath stammered. "He did it—for me. That is—for motives which were decent. If you . . ."

Crunch squeezed the father's arm hard. He also swallowed. "Look, Mr. Heath. I know all that! You keep the rod. Do you hear me? You've gotta! You've got to trust my judgment!" His blistering blue gaze held on the gray eyes of the other man.

"All right," said Mr. Heath, sighing. "All right. I'll trust you. I'm sort of mixed up—anyway . . ."

Crunch raced away—butting into people on the dock. He found Dexter hiding, on the ground, under the truck that took away fish carcasses. Dexter was racked by crying. Crunch seized his foot, pulled him out, and stood him up.

"Go away!" Dexter said in near strangulation. "I don't want any favors! I thought that five bucks was plenty."

Crunch shook him. "Listen!" His own voice was wild and tight. "Listen, Dex! I want you to get square with me! You gave that rod to your dad. He's gotta keep it. You got to pay for all of it. That's what I'm here to tell you."

"How can I? Twenty-five!—"

"I told you to shut up! Now, shut up! I'm doing the talking! You owe me twenty bucks. All right. There's just about twenty days before school begins. From now on—every day—you're working for me all day. A dollar a day. And lunches," Crunch added hastily. "A dollar a day and lunches. If you don't earn all of it—if you're a couple of days short—then you can go out a few Saturdays! You shine brass, and watch baits . . ."

Dexter shook his head miserably. "I—I ain't no good! You know that! I steal, and I think hammerheads are marlins . . ."

"No good?" The man's voice was incredulous. "No good! Son, you got bait eyes like a hawk's! You can see a fin before even the fish knows he's coming up! You're the rarin'est, tearin'est moray fighter I ever saw mill-ing in a cockpit! No good! Why—you're worth any three eighteen-year-old mates on the Gulf Stream Dock! Now! You working for me—or not?"

Dexter had listened. He wiped a wet sleeve wetter. "Gee!—" He hesitated, and dared it—"Gee, *Crunch*, you're a swell guy!"

Crunch slapped his shoulder and caught up his arm.

They went back along the dock together in a swift, easy lope, taking care not to butt into anybody.

FIFTY-FOUR, FORTY
AND FIGHT

"REEL IN!"

"Drop back to him!"

Those earnest cries, issuing separately from the lips of two of the best deep-sea fishing guides on the South Florida coast, expressed diametric contradictions. The effect on their customer was to paralyze all action. He stood in the *Poseidon*'s stern, his eye fastened on a sailfish that sculled along behind his bait. His face became embossed with doubt. "Which?" he finally yelled.

"Reel!" Crunch repeated.

"Drop back!" Des bellowed.

The man tried to do both; but, since a bait is a solid object, that maneuver is a physical impossibility. He threw the drag lever on his reel, freeing the spool and causing the line to run out. He also yanked his rod through an arc of about a hundred degrees, which spun the reel so rapidly it backlashed. The result was first, to allow the bait to stop and begin settling in the sea, and second, as the backlash snubbed up, to start it trolling again at the speed of the *Poseidon*'s forward motion, which was four or five knots.

"Not like that!" Crunch called.

"Hey!" said Des.

The man coughed nervously and froze.

The end product of such gross mismanagement was to reduce the sailfish's interest to a minimum. A minimum for such a creature is zero. The sail rolled his round blue eye at the strip of bonita belly, glanced, perhaps, toward the disagreement aboard the cruiser, and sank like a submarine—with dignity, purpose, and on a slant.

Crunch walked to the edge of the canopy—deserting the wheel in the full majesty of his annoyance—and looked down into the cockpit with disgust. "What's the idea?" he asked of his mate, in a prologue that has

111

long augured wrathy oration. "That fish was dopey! Slow! Bored! If Mr. Kaveny had given the bait a little action, you'd have seen the fish come after it again. But—drop back—he realizes the bait is phony, and goes away. No kidding, Des! I've got a niece—six years old—and she could get more fish out of an aquarium blindfolded with greased tweezers that you can nail in the whole ocean!"

Mr. Kaveny had been mildly disappointed by missing the fish. But he was a man of patience and philosophy. He could wait for another. Meanwhile, he turned his eyes toward the arc of a horizon as blue as willow-ware, and prepared himself for one-man audition of a kind of argument renowned in those parts. There was a minor smile on his face.

Des had listened to the indictment. He peered up at his skipper, squinting his eyes against the sun. "I suppose," he replied, with sarcasm like a slow avalanche, "you saw that sail finning on the surface? I suppose you saw that his dorsal had been spread so long it was as dry as newspaper? I suppose you've been out here on other trips? Fished before? You know that when a sail lies on top he's hungry, and charges, and keeps charging till he gets the bait? You noticed—maybe—that he knocked it out of the outrigger, and then hit it again? I have a cousin—" this was a strain on Desperate's brain, which was slow and durable rather than fecund—"who has learned more about the habits of fish from playing with celluloid toys in his tub than you'll!—"

Mr. Kaveny's lips stretched wider.

Crunch spat into the water and interrupted. "What you know about the fine points of hanging sails I taught you! You don't learn easy, either! And you forget, the way dishwater goes down the drain! Maybe you thought it was a turtle! Look. You run the boat. I'll do the coaching down below."

Des spoke hastily, then, but his voice was still ash-dry. "Maybe I better had run the boat, at that! Looks like you're going to ram the *Firefly*."

His skipper whirled, rushed to the helm, and spun it in time to avert danger—but not soon enough to escape an indignant jeer from the *Firefly's* mate.

Mr. Kaveny chuckled and rearranged himself for a spell of bait watching. As he sank into the eternal psychic state of the fisherman—a condition of languor, of fantasy concerning what might happen, and of hair-trigger vigilance—he reflected that all the Miami guides were probably on edge these days. Sailfish were scarce around Miami. They had been scarce for almost a week. But reports came in every evening from the Palm Beach region, of exceptionally large catches. Six or eight hung in a few hours from a single boat. Those reports were printed in the Miami newspapers, and unsophisticated customers probably complained about them. "Why," they probably said, "can they get dozens of sails eighty miles up the coast, and none here? Are the guides better up there?" Crunch and Des wouldn't like such comment. And yet, there was no way to bring back the sailfish to the Miami area. They'd either migrated for a while, or quit feeding. And fish don't gather around decoys, like ducks. You simply have to wait for them to swim back or to start feeding again.

Mr. Kaveny knew his maritime comrades felt themselves under a certain amount of pressure. They had, in fact, carefully explained the dearth of sailfish before accepting his charter—an ethical act which a great many boatmen would have honored in the breach. It was as if they were personally responsible for the antics of all the fish in the sea, and a trifle embarrassed by their present behavior.

Not long after he had diagnosed the situation, Mr. Kaveny was set into violent activity by an albacore which nailed the bait from underneath—violently. Because albacores are fighters, and because he was exceptionally fond of salad made of cold, boiled albacore, onions, chopped celery, capers and mayonnaise, he forgot the altercation, and was not reminded of it until they were on the way in that evening. Then he overheard Des say, irritatedly, "Just the same, Crunch, I was right! He'd ought to have dropped back to that guy!"

"Like hell! He should have reeled!"

"Listen!—"

"Oh, shut up!"

It wasn't like the two young men to become embroiled over so trivial a point. Mr. Kaveny felt distressed. He said so when he paid them: "I wish you'd stop arguing. We didn't get a sail, but we got that little tuna—or albacore, if you insist—and plenty of dolphins. It was a great day. See you again soon!"

They grinned in agreement and he walked away. Then they returned to the argument. . . .

Shortly after six o'clock, Sari, accompanied by Bill Adams, drove the family car into the parking yard and surveyed the Gulf Stream Dock. The *Poseidon* was at her moorings, but neither her husband nor his mate were aboard. Bill, who was something more than two years old, sighted a pile of bonitas which were being carried to a fish rack for a photograph. "Fiss!" he cried, and hurried forward. He joined in the work—grabbing a bonita by the tail and sliding it along the planks to the foot of the rack. The mates and captains urged him on; Bill was a sort of universal nephew to the fishing fleet. The crowd on the dock smiled.

Mr. Williams, the dockmaster, ambled to Sari's side and peered at the general scene. "Like a postcard, isn't it? The boats—outriggers against the sky—the fish—the people—"

"Where's Crunch?"

"That's what I was going to tell you. Your hubby and his mate are sore at each other. Crunch stamped off here like a bruised hornet. And Des came along a few minutes later. Couldn't get a 'Good evening' out of him. Zipper on his mouth."

"What are they sore about?" she asked quietly.

"Funny thing. They got arguing about who can fish the best."

"Mmm. Guess I'll hunt 'em up."

"I wouldn't. Let 'em cool off. They nearly came to blows. I understand they did—once—up in New Jersey. And it was all right afterward. But with the fishing bad—and two guys as easy to short circuit as they are—I'd lay off."

"I can handle them," Sari replied. "I've got an idea."

He looked at her. She was almost smiling. Not quite. Thinking about smiling, maybe. The evening breeze, whispering above the changing tide, stirred Sari's dark curls and replaced them. Her eyes had a quality that could not be seen, but was nonetheless perceptible; a rhythm, a chord from some serenade written by nature. Mr. Williams' attitude was subtly revised. "Yeah," he murmured, "you can handle 'em, I reckon."

There was a big steak snapping under the broiler flames. Sari had tied a purple kerchief around her head, and a purple apron over her yellow dress. She stuck a fork in Bill's baked potato and lifted the other potatoes, which were cut in strips, from the deep-frying basket. She glanced at the cauliflower. The front door banged.

"Smells good," Crunch called.

"Mmm. Hungry?"

He barged into the kitchen and poked Bill. "Not especially."

"Where's Des?"

"Search me. He's not coming for dinner, though."

She turned to be kissed. "What's the matter?"

"Who said anything about anything the matter?"

"The tone of a certain guy's voice."

"O.K. We had a fight. So what? He tried to tell me how to get a fish—"

Sari laughed. At the same time, she popped open the oven door so he would have to notice the steak, whether he was hungry or not. "I heard about it, as a matter of fact. Silliest thing in the world! You and Des arguing over who's the better fisherman!"

"What's silly about it?"

"Get washed. Everything's ready. What is? Well—for one thing—you're both about as good as people can get—"

He thrust his hard hands under the faucet. "Buttering me up isn't going to do any good. I'm peeved at that squarehead!"

"And—for another—why don't you find out?"

"Find out? How?"

"Fish."

Crunch was busy with the roller towel. He arrested his energetic effort. "Des and me? Doggone! The way you work and figure to save dough! . . . And now—all of a sudden—you want us to go out on the *Poseidon* and troll all day just to settle an argument! If a man lives that can dope out a woman's brain—he's in an asylum somewhere!"

"Who said anything about the *Poseidon?*" She was lifting the steak onto a platter. He was watching tensely: It might slip and drop on the floor. "You've always told me that catching little fish on light tackle was the best test of fishing skill. Why don't you and Des go out on a party boat and have a tournament? Trolling a day on your own boat might not settle anything—anyway. Neither of you might get a strike. But the party boats bring in gobs of fish. Some not so little, either. Of course, when men get debating a thing like that, they like to stand around and holler. Maybe even fight. My idea would be—prove it. Settle it. Once and for all. But— as you say—women are screwy . . ."

Crunch sat down at the kitchen table. He looked like a person who is about to snort. "I could spot that squarehead ten snappers and a 'cuda and fish him chin deep before he had a bite!"

"Could you?" It was an innocent query. Innocent—and rhetorical.

"You think not?"

"I didn't say that. I just—"

"You really think Des would have a better day bottom fishing than me? That guy? With ten thumbs and no more sense'n a turbot?"

"I just think that instead of getting a blister on my soul, I'd take a day off and prove it. On the *Minerva Collins,* say."

Crunch absent-mindedly hoisted Bill into his highchair and seated Sari. He began to carve the steak. "Sometimes," he murmured, "you don't really know you've got an appetite till the grub's in front of you! Darned if I haven't half a mind to do it! I could stand a day off. And if that squarehead would go for it! . . ." He ate. "The *Minerva Collins.* Sure. Old Cap'n Collins is a swell gent—and I haven't seen him in months."

It was hard to tell what the *Minerva Collins* had been. She would have baffled a man possessed of even considerable sea lore. Under a hundred feet, with two decks, a clanking Diesel, a stick capable of carrying one scrap of cloth of no known rig, a big cargo port where, nowadays, a skiff hung on davits, a candy and drink counter amidships, rusty anchors, bait barrels, a hose running into the sea through a scupper, and a coin phonograph with the volume of a theater organ. She put out to sea every decent day from Miami with a supercargo of fishermen who had paid two dollars for the trip, a lunch, and bait. Tackle was a dime extra and came in the form of hand lines. A ship to make a true salt shudder. But seaworthy enough, if you looked her over with care. Actually, the *Minerva Collins* had been built long since, for insular trade in the Bahamas. The trade had fallen off but not the *Minerva;* there was nothing in her but mahogany; instead of retiring to disgraceful decay, she had joined the fishing fleet as a "party boat."

On the day after Sari had planted her suggestion, there were aboard her, besides the two grim fishing guides, some fifty people of varying ages and both sexes. The *Minerva Collins* carried them sedately out toward the reef two miles offshore: Old men with placid eyes and treasured tackle boxes, middle-aged women with expressions of determination—determination to catch fish and determination not to get sick—city folks, kids, fellows with their girls, four school teachers from Montana who had decided to skip the included-trip-to-points-of-early-Spanish-association-and-various-other-historical-landmarks, as well as a sprinkling of persons of obvious substance who preferred this form of fishing, or who preferred to keep their pleasures within a closely held budget.

A nice crowd. The usual crowd. They oiled reels and ate candy and worried about it. They chatted and made friends—in a miniature replica of social conduct on longer sea voyages. There was a chilly breeze blowing. There was a warming sun in the sky. Men in the shade put on sweaters. Men across the deck took off their shirts. Somebody opened a bottle of beer. Somebody put a nickel in the phonograph. Old Cap'n Collins, making more of a show of his nautical voice than he'd dared while he'd run in rum from Bimini during Prohibition, cupped his hands and bellowed, "Let go to the starboard anchor!" A young man clad in slacks and engine oil let it go. The *Minerva* hauled up, swung in the tide a bit, and sat down to her day-long lift and roll on the moderate swells.

The barefooted young man went amidships and lifted the cover from a tub of chopped fish. He put a scoopful into a bucket of salt water which immediately began to dribble a raw-fish potage into the sea by way of the hose than ran through the scupper. The bucket was covered and the exposure of chopped fish had been brief. Nevertheless, one of the middle-aged ladies forthwith lost her determination to catch anything and also her determination not to be ill. She was escorted into the *Minvera's* cabin and put on a couch. The man who had escorted her was pleasant to look at, young, and polite. He brought in two other persons ultimately, and instituted a game of hearts.

Meanwhile, on the deck of the old trader, lines of all sizes and sorts had been tossed into the water. On some there were sinkers and on others there were bobbers. Some were held in hands. Some were tied to bamboo poles. Some were affixed to expensive reels which sat on fine steel and laminated wood rods. Most of the lines had been inexpertly tossed out from the side of the ship; a few had been adroitly cast. But all the faces which lined the rails were hopeful.

Cap'n Collins abandoned the bridge and strolled among the passengers. He returned greetings cheerfully. He helped put live shrimps on hooks. He gave advice. And when he'd finished half his tour, he stopped dead. Amidships were Crunch and Des. They held light casting rods—identical rods, with identical reels and six-thread line. Beside each was a box in which all the gear of the other was duplicated—plugs, feathers, sinkers, extra lines, fancy lures and chunks of bonita. Between them was a pail in which shrimp swam. The captain took in those facts.

"Doggone," he finally said. "Didn't know you were aboard, Crunch. Hi, Des! What the deuce you doin'? Never heard of you guys goin' out on a party boat! An' you look like somebody'd just worked over the *Poseidon* with a augur!"

Crunch said nothing.

Desperate said nothing.

The captain's eyes twinkled. On his chin was a little white beard. He tugged it. "Same equipment! Fishin' the same spot! What you got—a bet on?"

"Mebbe," said Crunch. One of the Montana school teachers was listening interestedly. She was a pretty Montana school teacher. Crunch flushed. "I got the space from Sammy—by phone—last night. Any objections?"

"A bet, I bet," the captain said. "An' for blood! O.K. If you need a referee—call me in. Ought to be good today. Soon as that chum gets carried down stream apiece there'll be some action." He chuckled and walked away.

Peace descended. Silence—broken by wave sounds and the jubilant discovery of the chum slick by some gulls. Des, who had not even bothered to look at old Cap'n Collins, undertook a covert survey of his skipper's line.

It was not covert enough: "No," said Crunch coldly, "I haven't got a strike."

There was more silence. More concentration. The *Minerva* rose and nodded and dipped again. The sun levered itself higher and turned up its thermostat. The school teacher began to whistle softly. She was good at it. She stole a more successfully covert glance at Crunch than Desperate's had been. She decided that he was married. She wished he wasn't. She wished she'd get a bite.

Then a child's voice burst out in wild excitment: "I got one! I got one! I can feel him wiggle! Help me, somebody! Tell the men to get the boat ready to gaff it! He's pullin' like a mule! It's a whale! I got one!"

Faces turned—and broke into smiles. The boy was hauling in line hand over hand—making a tangle around his feet. On the surface of the sea there was an aquatic flurry. A bright creature flashed in the air and smacked on the deck. The fish was about nine inches long. It began to do nip-ups. The boy did not seem to be abashed by the fact that he'd yelled for the gaffing boat. "A peacherino!" he said. He was panting. He thought—and most of the people aboard would have agreed with him— that he'd done a pretty hard job.

Cap'n Collins was there. He nodded with grave approval. "Yep, son. That's a mighty fine grunt!"

Then there was another sound. The whizz of a reel and the mutter of a busy man. "Little jack, I guess! See that son of a gun go! Yeah. Jack. Get me that long-handled net, will you, somebody!"

He wound—his reel whizzed—and it was still.

"Broke off," he said disappointedly.

Two other voices came from invisible owners. "Say! Captain! Commere! I got a purple fish. What is it?" And the other, "Pull your line up, will you, dope? You're going to foul me!"

Crunch felt a hard hit. He'd been looking at the people. He struck back. His light rod wouldn't sink the hook deep enough to suit him, so he pointed it toward the water and yanked; with the line straight from fish to reel. His quarry ran. He turned to Des—with sardonic eyes. "'Cuda. Go about six-eight pounds." Des ignored it. Crunch faced the sea again. "Breakin' out there."

It was, too. An explosion of white and silver, flame-fast, flame-bright. People called encouragement. Crunch kept busy. The barracuda shot out clean two or three times—somersaulting. Then it sounded and scurried back and forth. Crunch addressed the fish. "Come on, mister! No use trying to get loose from Uncle Adams. In close, now. Easy." Somebody handed him the net. He held the rod high in one hand. It made a half circle—and it shook. The net plunged down and emerged with the fish in it.

Crunch pulled it up to the rail. He spoke to the school teacher. "If you'll just step aside a little? . . . They got teeth." He dispatched the fish. Then he harried his mate again: "Eight pounds, easy! That's ten points for first fish—one point for a 'cuda—and a point a pound."

Des said nothing. He had an idea—and then he was sure of it. In his turn, he struck. "Grouper," he said, as the line poured into the water. He tested the thrust of the fish by thumbing his reel. "Go twenty, I bet. Good-sized."

Crunch sniffed. He rebaited. He was about to cast. But the teacher's line began to jerk her hand. She'd wound it round and round her palm. "Please!" she implored. "It's cutting me!"

Crunch was a gentleman by instinct, and a guide by profession. He looked ruefully at Desperate's melting reel spool—and gave his aid to the lady. It proved to be only a little shark. He was disappointed—but she was not. "It's the first one I ever saw in my life," she said. When that did not erase his expression of disappointment she added helpfully, "You see, there aren't any sharks in Montana."

Time passed.

Toward eleven o'clock, both Crunch and Des had done a good deal of fishing. A good deal of accomplished fishing. People had noticed their technique. Indeed, when either of them hooked anything, there was an instantaneous gallery around them. Each had also done considerable surreptitious peeking; each had made various calculations. Crunch had the 'cuda, four grunts, seven snappers, a parrot fish, one sand perch, and a mackerel. Des had the grouper, three blue runners, seven snappers, a grunt and a moray—which latter, by previously arranged common consent, would cost him five points. It was pretty even. Just about exactly even, they believed.

And it was about eleven when Mr. Beeson appeared. Mr. Beeson was dark-eyed, unprepossessing, not very well dressed, and extremely jovial. He had a still more nondescript friend named Mr. Burley whom he introduced to Crunch, to Des, and to the four school teachers—as well as to everyone else within earshot.

He said it was a nice day. A lovely day. A lucky day. He said fishing was a great sport.

Crunch said, "Uh."

Mr. Beeson helped a little girl untangle her line. He assisted an elderly man in the removal of an angelfish from his hook. Crunch felt a little more kindly disposed toward him.

"Maybe," said Mr. Beeson, "you chaps would like to get in our pool?" He put his hand on Desperate's shoulder as he said that.

Des shrugged off the hand. He said, "What pool?"

Mr. Beeson gazed at the various fish lying around Desperate's feet. He pressed his unimportant mustache against his upper lip. He tapped the rail with his line—he was "circulating" rather than fishing—and it wasn't much of a line. A dime-store variety, wound round a small board. "Well," Mr. Beeson began, with seeming uncertainty, "you two chaps seem to be way out in front. Don't know as I ought to let you in on it, now that I see you're hot today. But—" he laughed—"why not? All in fun! Why, it's like this. I met Mr. Burley this morning, and he's a pretty sporting fellow. Not much of a fisherman—but a good egg. Suggested a little bet that he'd beat me out—and I thought, why not make up a pool? Get everybody in. Good idea, don't you think? I mean, a pool with the winner whoever catches the biggest fish? Any kind. I just thought that for a buck—"

"No," Crunch said.

Inasmuch as Des was feeling the heat of a great hostility toward Crunch, and inasmuch as they were already engaged in a tourney, the mate was of a mind to be contrary. "Sure," he said. "I'll go in." He brought a rather sordid assemblage of small bills from his pocket and extricated a dollar.

Mr. Beeson was tickled to death. He said so. He looked rather deprecatorily toward Crunch. Crunch looked angrily at his mate. He took out a billfold. He handed a dollar to Mr. Beeson. Then he turned his back and went fishing. He was aware of the fact that Mr. Beeson was accepting dollars from the school teachers, from the old man, and from the father of the boy who had caught the grunt. Then he had another nibble. Snapper. He let it run the exact second and a quarter, struck, and brought in the fish.

At noon, Des spoke for the first time directly to his skipper. "Twelve," he said.

Crunch checked with his watch. He nodded. They wound in their lines and had lunch. Precisely twenty minutes were employed in the consumption of the meal, which Sari had prepared. The pretty school teacher from Montana watched them eat. Enough, she thought, for six cow hands. She wasn't hungry. Not sick—but just not taking any chances. While Crunch and Des sat in deck chairs and ate, she hooked a redfish. They helped her with it. That is, through mouthfuls of sandwich, they gave advice— which conflicted—but the girl caught the fish anyway, and Des grabbed her line while Crunch dipped the long-handled net. That much was done with perfect co-operation, from long habit. But, while the girl exulted over the size, beauty and power of her catch, they failed to exchange their usual contented glances.

"I'm so grateful to you!" she said. "I'd never have done it alone! You're both dreadfully good at fishing, aren't you?"

"Crunch is," Des said acidly.

"Only my pal really knows anything about it," Crunch maintained.

His mate wandered away. "Stretch my legs," he said. "Be back soon. Don't wet a line, either, while I'm gone."

Crunch muttered.

For a considerable time, he listened to the rhapsodies of the Montana girl. He was introduced to her companions. He explained his business. He did not explain, however, his presence on the *Minerva*. Probably the girl—whose name was Alice—thought it was a busman's holiday. Then

Des returned, and the business of catching fish was fiercely resumed.

There was, however, a change in Des. His dark and ordinarily impassive countenance was restive. Two or three times he opened his mouth to speak. But each time, he clamped it shut. A school of dolphin swam up to investigate the *Minerva*. Both men switched from bonita chunks to feathers. They could see, in the dazzling indigo swarm below, a big bull—and they vied to hook him. Alice, however, succeeded. She fought him and lost him. And she said it was "like having a strip of the rainbow on a leash," which satisfied both Crunch and Des, separately.

They caught three female dolphin each.

Then the *Minerva's* anchor was lifted and she was permitted to drift over the reefs. The wind had fallen. The seas were broad and smooth. The ship was carried slowly over the shadowy bottom visible some forty feet beneath the surface. The anglers gathered on one side of the decks and "trolled" at the gentle rate of about a knot. Those among them who were experienced, jigged their lines by yanking and slacking off.

Music was playing. People were drinking beer. One couple had abandoned fishing and was dancing on the top deck. Somebody hung an amberjack and lost it after a few minutes of struggle which was attended by cheers from the crowd. Des kept worrying. He continued to glance at his skipper. A psychologist would have seen that, inevitably, sooner or later, he was going to speak.

He did. "Say, Crunch?"

"Yeah?"

"While I was walking around—"

"What?"

"That Beeson. When he got us into the pool—he was carrying a lousy dime-store line. Right?"

"So what?"

"He's fishing fifty-four-thread, now. Wearing gloves. Got the line down on bottom with a big lead. Using a whole snapper for bait. Live. Long wire leader."

Crunch turned. He stared at his mate. He stared at the sea. A rocky bottom—forty feet of water—fifty-four-thread line—a big bait. It meant that Mr. Beeson, after cajoling the passengers into a friendly pool, was angling for something big; angling the way commercial fishermen do— which is not sporting. Nobody else was using a bait that size. Nobody on board had line that heavy. Mr. Beeson intended to get a big fish. Grouper, amberjack, shark. He intended to haul any such fish out of the sea bodily. He intended to win—and he wasn't fishing fair—and he'd stuck about forty or maybe even fifty people for a dollar each. Crunch's face darkened too.

"The other guy, Burley," Des added, "is doing the same."

The *Poseidon's* master wound up his line. He leaned his rod against the rail. He went in search of Cap'n Collins. He found the old man sitting in a chair on the bridge, almost asleep. He asked about Beeson.

Cap'n Collins looked carefully around before answering. When he spoke, his goatee quivered and his voice was low. "It's been goin' on for a month, now, Crunch! I'm sick about it. There's three pairs of 'em, an' they take turns working the party boats. It's a good racket. Instead of havin' two chances in fifty of winning the day's pool—this Beeson and Burley got about five to one in their favor. They win—them fellows—five days a week, easy."

"Why don't you toss 'em overboard?"

Cap'n Collin's anxiety became intense. "Yeah! Leave 'em ashore! Why don't I? I'll tell you. There's six of those fellers workin' together. Cap'n Lum on the *Salulah* gets a cut. They offered me a cut. I cussed 'em out good—first I heard of it. So what? So I had a fire on the *Minerva* next night. Then somebody threw a hundred dollars worth of tackle overboard. Then somebody busted the windows in the cottage I own. Then I got a letter threatenin' to turn me in for—for—" the old man halted. A grin wrinkled his face. "Well, Crunch, before I reformed and went into the party-boat business—I did used to see to it that a few guns got carried down to Cuba. These eggs know that. So—I had to let 'em fish. After all—it's perfectly legal—as they point out. Anybody that wants to, can fish fifty-four-thread. . . ."

Crunch spoke softly. "Yeah. But it's not sporting. It isn't much fun to haul maybe a hammerhead out of these rocks by hand on fifty-four-thread. But anybody that wanted to could. You got any?"

"Any what?"

"Fifty-four-thread? Or thirty-nine? Sash cord? Anything heavy?"

"I wouldn't tangle with those guys, Crunch! They're bad news!"

Crunch ignored that. "Taking fifty bucks a day out of a crowd of nice, decent, friendly people like these! Poor people, mostly! Makes a man burn. These folks love fishin'—an' they're good sports enough to go into a pool—and—"

"Come to think of it, I got some hand line. Test about two hundred. . . ."

What Alice and the three other school teachers saw that afternoon, they never forgot. Crunch returned to his place at the rail; he had a hank of dark green line under his arm. He untied it. He cut it in two lengths. He attached a long wire leader to each. He fastened the leaders to hooks. Gigantic hooks. Des began to help. He didn't say a word. They looked over their catch for the day and each baited up with a big snapper. They put on gloves. They fixed fist-sized sinkers on the lines. And they began to fish.

The four girls quit their own activity to watch.

Des got the first strike. A heaving wrench that almost yanked him overboard. Crunch grabbed his belt—and for a minute Des was a living part of the gear stretched taut between the ship and some unidentified, fearfully swimming monster. Then the strain slacked off. Des pulled in. His thick hook had been straightened out. "Big jewfish," he said. Crunch nodded. Des put on a new hook and a new bait.

They lost another hook, broke a leader, and snapped off fifty feet of a line. The teachers' eyes were popping.

"Sharks," Crunch said.

Cap'n Collins drifted by. "Be goin' in soon," he said.

Another man passed them. He slapped Crunch's back. "Might as well quit, pal! That Beeson—fellow who started the pool—has a sixty-two-pound grouper. Warsaw. We just weighed it. Next biggest fish today only goes twenty-nine. Beeson must of had a hunch he was lucky today when he roped us all in, hunh?"

Crunch nodded. The disappointed angler went away. Des swore—softly, so the teachers wouldn't hear.

Then something straightened out Crunch's right arm. That took a lot of force. Crunch struck back—half a dozen jerks that were the opposite of a prizefighter's jabs. His line pulled so tight that it twanged like a bowstring. Des peered into the water and laughed.

"I'll hop in that dory and gaff it personally," he said. "We don't want to lose this baby!"

Crunch pulled in line, wiped off sweat, and afterward let the line slide in surges through his gloved hands. Alice ventured to murmur, "Another shark?"

"Kind of," Crunch said.

Then they could see it. A thing like a rug. Slicing sidewise in the water, the way a paper plate does when it falls through air. Des was out in the dory with the barefooted youth from the *Minerva's* crew. Des did the gaffing. Both men heaved the creature aboard. And both dodged violently when its long tail began to flick at the seats and the gunwales.

"It's—hideous!" Alice said. "What is it?"

"Stingaree," Crunch answered. "Sting ray. Big one. Go a hundred. Got a spine that sticks up about a foot out from the base of its tail. Barbed spine. It can drive through, say, the calf of your leg. Breaks off there, and the spine has poison in it. That's why Des is hopping around so." He caught sight of Cap'n Collins—who was passing by—and not sharing the pleased excitement of the passengers. Cap'n Collins looked frightened.

Crunch grabbed his elbow. "Start in now, Cap'n. We don't want to be beat again by those chumps!" He turned to the lady and explained more about the nature and habits of stingarees—which are shark-relatives: Compressed sharks, with winglike fins.

They were weighing the ray when the *Minerva* chugged into Government Cut. Des read the steelyard. "A hundred and seven and a quarter pounds."

The passengers gasped and crowded around the animal.

Beeson came up—pushing through them. He looked amiable—unless one looked carefully. "I got the pool here," he said. "Forty-six bucks! Too bad you lost!"

Crunch gazed at him. "Lost? We won. That is, I did."

Mr. Beeson shook his head. "Sorry, my friend. That's not a fish. Not eligible. It's a stingaree. Now—my warsaw grouper is a fish. So I keep the dough."

"A ray," said Crunch, "is a skate. A skate is a shark. A shark—is a fish. I won."

Mr. Beeson laughed and shook his head. Des moved in behind him. The passengers began to mutter. A few of them—ignorant of ocean lore and aware, only, that the stingaree didn't look much like a normal fish—argued in behalf of the grouper. But Crunch was firm. He leveled his blowtorch eyes at Beeson. "Just hand over that dough," he said.

Mr. Beeson coughed, asked for the captain, found him not in evidence, glanced briefly at Crunch's eyes, and passed over the bills. The crowd dissolved.

The *Minerva* was moored at her own pier—a ramshackle projection some half mile from the Gulf Stream Dock. The people thanked the captain for a marvelous day. The teachers prolonged grateful good-byes. Even the ladies who had been sick at the beginning were well and pleased. The anglers had packed their tackle and their fish. They streamed ashore, where friends and relatives waited to be dumbfounded. Crunch and Des were about the last to go. Cap'n Collins was down in the engine room. Crunch wanted to talk to him—but the old guy had locked himself in. So Crunch and his mate, with their fish wrapped in newspaper, started along the pier.

At the shore end was a dockhouse made of unpainted boards—open on the water side—with a door that gave on the pier. Cap'n Collins liked to snooze there, with a line out for grunts on the open façade. As Crunch passed that untidy building, its door yawned.

Mr. Beeson stepped partly out. Mr. Burley was behind him. So were four other men. "We'd like to talk to you," Mr. Beeson said. He set himself in front of Crunch, as if he expected the skipper would try to slip past.

Crunch didn't. "Like to talk to you," he said. He wheeled, and entered the dockhouse. Des followed. The door closed.

It was rather dim inside the little building. Beeson, Burley, and four other men. The rest of the party boats were in, Crunch thought. Somebody turned a key in the door behind Des.

"It's like this," Mr. Beeson said. "We don't enjoy being robbed. We think we won. And we don't like to have wise guys come aboard the party boats and try to bust up—something that's our business."

"Hunh," said Crunch. He was in the middle of them. Each one, he saw, had a marlin billy. A marlin billy is a club used for killing marlins. It's like a short baseball bat. Generally, it's weighted with lead. Crunch pursed his lips and thought a moment. He looked meditatively from face to face. "This . . . racket of yours . . . hurts fishing," he finally said. "It's not sporting. Cap'n Collins is an old friend of mine, too. I just want all you six eggs to realize that I'm against it—and what happens now is going to happen every day till you lay off." His voice was still conversational— which is why they didn't understand what was to come. "They got billies, Des," he continued sweetly.

But that was all Crunch said.

Beeson never knew what hit him. Neither did Burley, who was standing nearest to Des. A big man named Gullen waded in, swinging. Crunch ducked—and the billy whispered past his ear. Gullen flew backwards through the open side of the shed—into the water. Des caught the wrist of the first man who managed to swing at him. He put on the pressure. The man dropped the billy and screamed. He wore that arm in a sling for some weeks after Des let go. At the same time, Des planted a foot in the midriff of another man and shoved. That passed the man along toward Crunch—who hit him and who also hit the last man standing, a split second later. Then there wasn't anybody left to fight. They walked to the edge of the water to see if Gullen could swim. He could—enough.

Half an hour later, Crunch and Des were sitting together on the stern of the *Poseidon*, waiting for Sari. Getting on toward suppertime, Crunch thought. He turned his head. Des was staring into space—smiling raptly, goofily. Crunch found himself donning the same sort of smile. "You know," he said, "about this business of who can fish better . . ."

Des pivoted and seemed surprised. "I'd forgot about that. Hell! I concede. You won anyway."

"Well . . . catching rays don't count, really. Your grouper was the biggest honest fish. And you handle snappers better than I do . . ."

Des snorted. "I do like! You can outfish me seven days a week!"

"You know I can't!"

For a minute, each argued that the other was the better man. Then they realized the absurdity of such debate. Co-operation, they decided, was the thing. They began to laugh. Their minds reverted to another topic.

"Those poor old party-boat skippers!" Crunch exclaimed. "Knifed by a lot of lampreys like that! Boy! How that big lug squealed when you bent his wrist!"

"And that Gullen!" Des was chortling. "Sailed like a clay pigeon!"

When Sari came, leading Bill by the hand, their mirth was the dominant note on the dock. Bill heard, recognized the voices, and laughed, too. Then he saw a sail lying astern of the *Firefly*. "Fiss!" he cried.

Crunch caught the sound. He saw Sari. He beamed and waved. Quite suddenly, however, his expression changed to one of suspicion. "Say, Des," he said softly, "do you think Sari knew about those lice on the *Minerva?* Think she sent us there on purpose? I wouldn't put it past! . . ."

Sari was standing in the sunset, smiling, knowing that all was well. Des whispered to his skipper from a deep intuition: "Even if she did—don't ask her! Women like to think they get away with those little schemes! Like to think they can handle men. And Sari's a girl in a billion."

THE EXPERT

CRUNCH ADAMS walked up Miami's Flagler Street with an expression like the weather. His eye was beaming and his lips were slightly pursed, as if he were on the verge of whistling. Equal-sized, evenly spaced clouds alternated sun and shadow on the thoroughfare; and the people, in fur jackets, in shorts and blouses, without neckties and with them, were individually engrossed in the thought that nobody else on earth would imagine this was January. Crunch could not frown, even when a lady from New Jersey drove down the street in a fender-sniping manner—obviously annoyed that a city dedicated to pleasure was so rude as to have traffic regulations. Indeed, when she caromed lightly from a laundry truck and began to berate its luckless driver, Crunch merely grinned.

His errand was a sort that is rare in this world—an errand of potential good to several people and of likely harm to none. Sari, his wife, had devised it out of various bits of information. Crunch turned from the human confetti in the avenue to a side-street, and entered a store. Its dim interior was an aromatic refutation of the dullness of the word describing it: hardware. The place smelled of oil and iron and turpentine, of oakum and varnish and rope. Crunch walked perceivingly between counters to the tackle department, where there was a crowd. These persons—men and women and children—were inspecting and endeavoring to purchase everything from bamboo jack poles to sixteen/ought reels. Overhead was a sign that read, "Selling Out—Tackle Bargains," and under the sign was a beleaguered man.

A man neither young nor old, blond nor dark, short nor tall—a man with mild blue eyes, clipped wavy hair, a shy voice, and an amused but rather stubborn mouth. He was talking to several persons at the same time; it could be noticed that he gave the most consideration to youngsters—a fact which irritated several wealthy gentlemen who held big reels and big bills. The man saw Crunch and waved a handful of red-headed

127

plugs. "Hi, Skipper! In for the slaughter, eh?"

Crunch laughed. "I could use a couple of six/oughts. But I want to talk to you, Hank, if you can get a chance."

The clerk glanced at his wrist watch and peered across the crowd. "Okay. It's fifty minutes past my lunch hour and Jim's supposed to spell me here. Hey, Jim!" A man left the relatively deserted area of anchors and binnacle lights and pushed through the people. "You take over here while I eat with Crunch. And don't forget—these kids grow up to be as good customers as the tourists!"

Ten minutes later Crunch and Hank sat facing each other in the restaurant of a drug store. Hank's features had relaxed; gone was the enthusiasm with which he had discussed baits and grass beds with the bargain-hunters; in its place had come worry, and paleness—as if he had not slept very well, and as if he was unsure of himself.

"Too bad," Crunch said, "that old man Hembley's selling out the tackle department."

Hank nodded. "Yeah. Crazy. It's made a nice profit all these years. He just—doesn't like to handle fishing gear."

"You got anything lined up?"

"No. Not yet. Vi thinks I ought to try a new racket. You know how it is. Your gal always thinks you should be the president of a bank." He smiled a little. "If she's any good, that is. But when you've been selling tackle ever since you quit high school—and fishing in all your spare time—you sort of get in a groove. I don't know anything, really, except tackle. I've approached the other stores in town and on the Beach—and nobody seems to need a clerk. Maybe I can find a spot in Lauderdale or Palm Beach—"

The little wrinkles around Crunch's lips and eyes deepened. "Hank, how would you like to go on the road for FabSteel?"

Hank held a spoonful of vegetable soup in mid-air. "Me? On the road? Who'd put me on the road? I bet that's Sari's idea!"

Crunch was unabashed. "Sure, it's Sari's idea. She said—"

He was interrupted by a quiet torrent. "It's nuts, and you know it! I'm not the type. I'd miss the trains and go to the wrong towns. I'm rotten at meeting people. There's not a drop of go-getter blood in my veins. I just like to stand around in some little old store and yarn about fishing with a lot of mokes like myself. I—"

"Pipe down! You've been retailing FabSteel rods and reels and baits for years. Fishing with their stuff, mostly. You know it thoroughly—"

"That's not the point, Crunch! I'm a clerk—not a traveling salesman—"

"—and the kind of drummer a big manufacturing company needs is a guy who'll yarn all day with store owners. Look, Hank. You're the state bait-casting champ. All right. You've caught blues, and blue fins. You darn near have fins yourself. Born fishing. On a commission, salary and expenses, you and Vi and your kids could live like rich people—"

"I tell you," Hank said desperately, "I haven't got that kind of character! I got no personality at all—!"

"Then how come half the best fishing men in South Florida like to trade with you?"

"That's what I'm trying to say! I'm oke with the anglers. But business men take one look at me and start laughing! Walking into a strange city with a line of samples, I'd lose my nerve before I hit Main Street! I gotta find another clerking job, Crunch! Soon, too! And besides, how the deuce would I go about even getting a shot at representing FabSteel? They're a big plant—in Cleveland—"

"If you'll just stop sweating out loud," Crunch answered, "I'll tell you. Why do you think I'm buying you a lunch?"

"I'm buying you a lunch!"

"We'll skip that. Listen. A week or so ago I got a letter from a guy named Thurston. He's a vice-president of FabSteel but he doesn't know anything about their tackle at all. He's coming down here to do the race tracks and the night clubs and stay out of the sun, like half the other tourists. All right. His company, the letter says, has its eye out for a good new man to push their stuff. Could I recommend anybody? He got my name from a mutual friend—an oil man who fishes the *Poseidon*." Crunch eyed Hank earnestly. "See? I read the letter and couldn't think of anybody, so I tossed it in the wastebasket. Sari fished it out because she remembered your department was closing and she wrote to Mr. Thurston. He's chartered the *Poseidon* for tomorrow and he's going out with you to see an expert in action. It's all set."

Hank looked hunted. Then relief crossed his features. "I'd like to do it, Crunch. But you forget. I gotta work. I need every dime I can raise—"

"Ever hear of Robert E. Lee?" Crunch asked. "It's his birthday tomorrow. I guess you've been so worried you sort of overlooked that."

Regimented Caribbean clouds were still sailing along next morning on a light southeast breeze. The pale blue water between the Gulf Stream and the green transparency over the shoals was the color of new larkspur blossoms and people in the windows of offices and hotels looked at it with wonderment. The blimp that lives noisily in Miami's sky stood out to sea; small yellow training planes made ceaseless, ragged repetitions of the same take-offs and turns; a gray destroyer wheeled at the whistling buoy and came down the Government Cut with a cargo of sailors bemused by the prospect of tropical shore leave. It was an ordinary day.

And Hank Ferguson, an ordinary man, walked reluctantly down the dock to the place where the *Poseidon* lay. He boarded her with a nod at Desperate, the mate, and a muffled, "Hello, Crunch," for her skipper. He put down carefully on the day bed the tackle he had brought: a casting rod, a level-wind reel, a five-ounce rod, a reel for that—loaded with nine-thread line, a box, and a heavy rig. These things he arranged with the care of an artist getting ready his paints and brushes. Then he lighted his pipe; its stem clicked a little between his teeth before he could set them on it.

"What kind of a guy is this Thurston, Crunch?" he asked.

And Crunch, who had finished filing some hooks needle-sharp, said, "I dunno, Hank. Never saw him. But he's late."

"I'll bet," the clerk-expert went on, "that there won't be a bonita in the ocean. Is he going to fish—or just watch me?"

"He didn't say. He never has fished though. He said that. I guess—this is him."

The guess was hypothecated on a limousine, larger and glossier than most, which drew up at the dock house. A tall man came out of it and he was followed by a uniformed chauffeur who carried a fancy lunch basket. Mr. Thurston bore down upon them with long strides. Iron-gray, frowning, tight-lipped. Like a British general in mufti. He saw the boat's name and he saw Crunch. "Adams?" he asked.

"Right. Good morning, Mr. Thurston. Come aboard."

Mr. Thurston had already come aboard. The chauffeur followed with the basket, tripped, and nearly toppled into the cockpit. Hank caught him. Mr. Thurston did not berate the man for clumsiness: he just looked at him—and, somehow, that was worse.

"This is Hank Ferguson," Crunch said. "The chap I told you about."

The vice-president of FabSteel examined the candidate. "Expected somebody bigger," he said. "Stronger. Mean to say, how can a bird like that wrestle a tuna to death?"

Hank stammered that he'd been lucky, on several occasions. Crunch nodded to Des, who started the motors. Mr. Thurston sat down in the center fishing chair to see what would happen next. And Hank, looking off into space with unhappy eyes, suddenly called, "Hey, Crunch! There's Vi! Getting off the bus! Hold it a minute, will you?"

Mr. Thurston said, "Vi? Who's Vi?"

And Hank, although embarrassed, replied with dignity. "My wife. Something must be the matter."

Vi came running down the dock. She was wearing slacks, and more than a little untidy, as are most women who have just started a spouse off on a fishing trip and three youngsters out for a day's play, made beds, washed dishes, and commenced to clean the living room. She was carrying a small carton. She stopped breathlessly at the stern of the *Poseidon*—a girl with nice brown hair, and bright brown eyes. "Hankie," she said, using an endearing diminutive because she was nervous, "after you left, I found you'd forgotten your favorite reel! So I grabbed it and hopped the bus—"

Hank was standing in the cockpit, isolated from the others. His face turned so red that they noticed—and wondered what was wrong. "Oh," he answered. "Thanks, Vi. Thanks an awful lot!" He seemed to be appreciative, in spite of his flush.

Vi smiled almost maternally. "I knew you wouldn't dream of wetting a line in the Stream without your old Super-Seaway—!" Then Vi, also, grew crimson and abrupt tears filled her eyes. The reason Hank had left his favorite reel at home was that his favorite was not a FabSteel product. And she had ruined that bit of tact. By bringing it on the bus she'd made it completely evident to Mr. Thurston that her husband preferred another sort of reel to the one Mr. Thurston made. Her voice slewed and thickened: "But maybe, today, you won't be wanting it!" she said. Then she dipped her head at the man who resembled a British general. After that, keeping the reel in the box, she ran away like a deer.

Mr. Thurston stared stonily at Hank.

Crunch gunned both motors and Des slapped the hawsers over the nails on the piles. The *Poseidon* took off like a speedboat—and a man on an oil barge moored nearby shook his fist and cursed at the approaching swells.

When they were about halfway out to the edge of the Gulf Stream, Mr. Thurston clambered clumsily up on the canopy and stood beside Crunch in silence for some time. He surveyed the sparkle of the water and the beige panoply of the Beach skyline; he watched a porpoise roll and wallow; he squinted with interest at a Portuguese man-o'-war. "Chance of getting a sailfish?" he finally asked.

Crunch nodded. "Good one. They were running yesterday. And Hank's about the snappiest man at it in these parts."

"I mean—me."

"You bet. Good chance—though it's always only a chance."

"I'll fish, then. Not on that spider-web Ferguson is getting ready to use. Something sturdy."

Crunch thumped the canopy with his foot and when Desperate's head showed above it, he gave directions. Mr. Thurston would take a balao on a medium outfit on the starboard outrigger. A whole mullet would be "hung up" in the port outrigger. Hank would watch that—and also fish a small cut bait straight astern. *The Poseidon* nosed into the larkspur-colored water and slowed. Baits went overboard and began to move on the water—the mullet leaping and splashing, the balao sliding like a tiny hydroplane, and the cut bait flashing under the surface in the wake.

Mr. Thurston looked at everything and said not a word. Hank said nothing, either. He was even more uneasy than he had expected to be. And he was inscrutably sore, too. Mr. Thurston might have had the decency to laugh off Vi's error, instead of making it tougher by just staring.

As for Desperate, he often said nothing for hours on end, even under the best conditions for conversation. He simply stood still behind the two anglers with his eyes shooting from bait to bait and out across the sea and back to the fishes again. Without knowing it, he observed many things: the freighter sliding down on the rim of the Stream, the sailboat out practicing, the other cruisers—two with flags up already, a school of flying fish, the yellow blur of a shark going under their keel, some gulls gathering over a likely patch of Sargasso weed, the Firefly doing business with a good-sized dolphin—a female, Des saw—and the Ambernoon hung on a bonita. Or possibly an albacore.

Then Hank said, with a tremble he did not want in his voice, "Say Des! Isn't that—?"

Mr. Thurston followed Hank's gaze. "Something back there under your bait, man!" he exclaimed.

Des said, "It's a sail."

Crunch, on the canopy, with better visibility from the high angle, looked down on the eight-foot fish, purple-brown and rapier-nosed, and he thrust his tongue hard against his lower lip as if to feel the grin coming there. This was something Hank knew all about—a chance to get square with his humiliation.

Hank rose. He held his rod a trifle higher. The gesture brought his bait to the surface, where it splashed and yawed. That act seemed to excite the big fish. Its snout broached like a ram on a submarine. Mr. Thurston came to his feet and bent over the stern to see better. Hank reeled a little, teasing the fish. It made a left-right slap with its bill, like a boxer finishing a blow with an illegal backhand. But it struck too far behind the bait. Hank reeled again. The precisely cut strip of fish belly was not twenty feet astern of the *Poseidon*. It trolled along. Every breath was held. The sail came out high—head, upper and lower bill—its great dorsal fin spread purple, hissing in the sea. It opened its mouth wide. Its tail bit like a propeller and it charged on the bait.

Everyone clearly saw the two bills clamp on the bait. Crunch and Des smiled wider. Hank would release the drag on his reel and let the sailfish swim off long enough to swallow. Then Hank would strike. Only—Hank didn't. When the bills closed, Hank gathered himself and hit with as much force as his light tackle would stand. His rod bent. The line went taut to the sailfish. Its pectoral fins stiffened. It seemed, almost, surprised. It opened its mouth. The bait came skittering back on the surface and the hook hit the boat's stern at the water line.

Thurston said, "Damn it, man! You yanked too quick!"

Hank just nodded.

Thurston said, "He's going away, man! Can't you do anything?"

Hank shook his head. "Nope. Muffed it. Pricked him with the hook. I should have let him have it."

"But—why'd you do it?"

"I dunno," Hank replied. "Startled me."

Mr. Thurston stood staring at him, holding his medium-weight rod awkwardly, shaking his head. And, even as he stood, his arms jerked away from his body and his reel began to sizzle. "Hey!" he bellowed. "Something's got at this!"

"Hit it!" Crunch called. "Strike it!"

Mr. Thurston struck savagely. A big sailfish went into the air, landed flat, and came out again, shaking its dorsal like wet laundry in a wind.

"That's the one Hank missed," Des said.

Mr. Thurston spoke violently: "Don't stand speculating on what it is! Do something about me!" The reason for his frenzy was manifest. He was holding his rod with both hands on the upper grip and the butt jammed into his abdomen. Each rush of the sailfish unbalanced him and caused him to bang himself variously against the gunwale, the fighting chair and the partition amidships. But as he spoke, Des began conducting him to the center chair. He sat down and braced his legs. He panted. He stared with incredulity at the hysterical fish.

It settled down into a regulation fight. Mr. Thurston got the sail up within view four times. Each time, the fish took off in a new direction. Once, it made a series of vaults close to the boat. Twice, it sprang into the air at a considerable distance. And through it all, Hank sat still—a numb but hopeful spectator. If Thurston caught a fish, it might change his mood. In fact, Hank felt it was a cosmic neccessity for Thurston to catch that fish. The more sharply he perceived the fact, the more closely he watched every incident of the battle.

Fifteen minutes passed. The steel man was sweating profusely—and saying nothing—if inarticulate rumbles were excepted. It occurred to Hank, who was a light tackle fisherman, that quite possibly the tension on Mr. Thurston's rather hefty line might eventually straighten out the hook or pull it from the place where it was fixed. The thought expanded into such a horror that presently he heard himself say, "You ought to let up on the drag, Des! There's too much strain on that line! It'll erode the hook out! No kidding!"

Des was more panicky than his contenance showed. He looked at the reel, at the set of the rod, and at the spot where the line was cutting through the waves. "Think so?"

"I'm positive!" Hank said frenetically. "Positive!"

Des worried a moment, no doubt weighing the likelihood that Hank's opinion on the matter was even better than his own. At last he leaned over and unscrewed that drag a quarter turn. Immediately the sailfish, taking advantage of a reduction of pressure, shot up to the surface and ran out in a loopy curve. Des then said, "Wind, Mr. Thurston! You've got a belly in your line! Wind fast—or he'll use that slack to—!"

There was no need explaining how the fish would use the slack. The problem was illustrated. Before Mr. Thurston could recover enough line to regain control of the fish, it sprang into the air, high and clear, tossed its head, and flung from its jaws the hook and the remains of the balao.

Mr. Thurston sat perfectly still for a considerable time. Then, slowly, because it pained him to use his muscles now that excitement no longer masked their condition, he reeled in. "Mr. Ferguson," he said, when Des took hold of the leader wire, "I feel reasonably sure that if you hadn't ordered my drag cut down, we'd have had that fish."

Hank's face was tormented. "Yeah. You would. Bad judgment on my part."

"I was given to believe that you were an expert."

Hank didn't reply.

Des put a fresh bait on both lines.

There were no more strikes that morning, and lunch, when it came, was not a festive meal. Crunch set up the bridge table—it was calm enough for that—but Mr. Thurston stayed in his chair. He was restive—bored, perhaps—but he was understandably reluctant to move away from his rod. He wanted another crack at a sailfish. As for Hank—Mr. Thurston seemed to have made a pact with himself to act as if Hank weren't on board at all.

In the middle of the afternoon, Des joined Crunch briefly at the top controls. "Your pal," he said rather grimly, "looks as if he'd burst into tears any minute. And the rotten thing is, he quite possibly could have been right both times. You can never be sure about such things till they're all over."

Crunch was gazing out over the glittering blue sea. "Mmm. That Thurston guy is sure a prime sourpuss!"

"Yeah. I guess so. For a minute, when that sail rose, I thought he was going to turn out human. But he's sitting there like a crab in a hole."

Crunch pointed. "See that big bank of weed?" His hand indicated a floating island, tawny gold, the size of a tennis court; it undulated with the gentle ground swell; in it were packing crates, cartons, cans, boards and other flotsam. "There ought to be dolphin under that grass. Look. Rig up Hank's casting outfit and haul his bait out of the water on some pretext. If Thurston gets a hit, Hank can maybe redeem himself by showing off on the little rod. It's a FabSteel." Crunch winked.

The idea was sound. Schools of dolphin often lie under islands of weed. They rush at trolled baits from that sanctuary, jumping like jack-rabbits as they come. And often, when one is hooked, his comrades will follow him to the boat and hang around hard by—vivid shapes—indigo, lavender, yellow, green, brass, azure, silver—ready to snatch at any morsel of fish or any artificial bait that touches the water.

It worked that way. Crunch cut the *Poseidon* in a tight circle around the weed island. Des took out Hank's bait because he "thought it was spinning." Mr. Thurston's line dropped from the outrigger. He battled and brought in a dolphin of about ten pounds. When Des grabbed the leader he saw an incandescent school below and yelled at Hank to cast a feather to them. A light of understanding broke on Hank's face. He flashed a smile at Crunch, snatched his casting rod, stared down once at the fish, and tossed a feather among them.

But Hank was rattled that day. It was his unlucky day. The fish that snatched his feather was not one of the females in the scintillating school, but a big, flat-faced bull—a twenty-five or thirty pounder. There is no hope of catching such a fish on such tackle. It jumped twice, causing Mr. Thurston's eyes to bug out, and rushed away, taking all of the light line. Hank rushed to the daybed, broke open a new box of line, and refilled his reel. Mr. Thurston took another fish. But when Hank was ready again, the dolphin had vanished and Crunch was unable to get them up. Mr. Thurston stared for a long time at the dolphin in the box. He seemed fascinated by their beauty, but not necessarily pleased.

Another hour of trolling failed to yield another strike. Crunch began working back down the hotel-bordered shore toward the turning buoy and home. The day's last action occurred when they reached the buoy. A bunch of grass had been caught by Mr. Thurston's hook and its weight had knocked the line from the outrigger. He had jumped into action, thinking it was a strike, and then disappointedly undertook to reel in the weed. As he reeled, it came off, leaving his bait clean. He kept reeling. A snout rose behind Hank's strip. Mr. Thurston did not see it and continued to bring in his bait. The fish abandoned the strip offered by the breathless Hank for the faster-moving lure of the steel man. Then, instead of stunning its quarry with a blow and circling to devour it, the sail simply raced up and gulped. Thus Mr. Thurston "stole" the expert's fish.

Mr. Thurston was too excited, by that time, to have dropped back. He merely hung on to his rod. He hung on for some twenty minutes, unaware of the boats around, of the nearby passage of a steamer, of the Nassau plane coming in, or of anything else except the lunging, leaping fish. He did not even observe that Hank, to prevent himself from prompting, had gone all the way forward to the harpoon pulpit, where he stood with his eyes shut, praying for luck for the dour Mr. Thurston.

At the end of twenty minutes, Des had his hands on the leader wire. He bent over the gunwale with what seemed like shocking unconcern to the magnate, and he boated a small sailfish. A fish of about twenty-five pounds. Afterward he looked at his customer, concealing any sign of triumph, and said, "Congratulations. That puts you in the league."

Mr. Thurston nodded and mopped his face and squinted his eyes and replied, "I wonder if you'd mind—heading in, now?"

That was all he said until they reached the Gulf Stream Dock. The *Poseidon* tied up against the usual backdrop of tall buildings and flamboyant sunset. Mr. Thurston paid Crunch and thanked Des. His eye roved momentarily to Hank and his lips jerked somewhat satirically. "I really hate to have topped an expert," he said, "especially since I've never been fishing before in my life—for anything." He inspected his wrist watch. He stared off. "My car's here. It's only five-fifteen. Is there a phone booth up there? I'd like to put in a call to Cleveland."

Crunch said there was a booth and Mr. Thurston hurried away without the trouble of a formal good-by. His chauffeur came down for his things— the empty lunch basket, his pith helmet, his sweater and sunburn cream. Crunch sat down on the fish box, watching Hank dismantle his gear. Finally he sighed and spoke softly. "I'm sorry about all this—fellow! Somehow—I had a different picture."

Hank grinned. He seemed almost glad that he hadn't made good with the manufacturer. Almost—but not quite. "Well—we tried. I flubbed— just as I knew I would. I told you I didn't have the personality—or whatever it is—to fool around with people like that. They—intimidate me." He stretched and smiled ruefully. "Vi'll be mighty disappointed, though." His brow knit. "What's that?"

"What's what?"

Hank was staring overboard, at a spot in the water where the tide ran swiftly toward the Gulf Stream Dock. The sky colors were fading like the red in a switched-off electric heater and it was getting hard to see. "That! A big boil. Something rose and grabbed a shrimp, I think."

"That'd be one of those big snook."

"One of what big snook."

"Oh—a lot of big ones live under the dock. Record-breakers. But they're too darned smart to take a bait. We've tried it for years. Everything in the world. Never hung one."

Hank's interest was academic, but fairly concentrated. "I didn't know you had snook lying here. Funny." He searched the sky and the shore, studying the wind and the light and the temperature. "Ever try a Mulligan Madcap plug on 'em?"

"Never heard of one."

"Oh? I bet they'd hit it." He started to unship the reel on his casting rod and it gave him an idea. "I'll show you."

He affixed to his line what Crunch afterward described as "a plug that looked like a cross between a radish and a cockroach" and he stepped up on the dock. He was smiling. "I'm insane!" he said gently. "A minute ago I'd sworn I'd give up fishing and fish tackle for good. Sell coal or roller skates. And then I see a boil—and right away—!" He cast. It was a lovely cast—a cast with a shell trajectory, smooth and long, and it ended with a circular splash exactly where the boil had been. The Mulligan Madcap popped, hopped and dived down. The reel suddenly whistled. "See!" said Hank, gently still, "he's hit it!"

Crunch's words were not so pacific. He permitted himself something in the nature of a sailor's oath and his tone brought running feet. "Hey, fellows!" he yelled. "Hank's hung one of those snook!"

Up in the telephone booth, Mr. Thurston had made his connection with Cleveland. In a large, mahogany-paneled office, a secretary was going through a door marked, "President." To a man something like Mr. Thurston, she said, "It's Mr. Jim—calling from Miami." The President snatched one of his nine phones.

Mr. Thurston, fifteen hundred miles away, was no longer the man that Crunch, Des and Hank had seen all day. Not the imperturbable executive. He was shaking from head to foot. He was pale. His eyes were moist. He heard a familiar voice. His response was boyish: "Biff! It's me—Jim! I win that bet! Just write a check for a thousand, will you? . . . Yep—sail! . . . No . . . little one . . . but it's got a sail and a bill, and I got two dolphin beside. . . . Nope . . . not a bit. . . . I was scared out of my wits all day that I'd be sicker'n a mackerel any minute—but I didn't have a qualm—except for worrying. . . . Yeah . . . No . . . I'm staying down here for two more weeks . . . going to try for a white marlin next. . . . Ferguson? . . . well . . . I'm afraid he won't do for us . . . nice little guy, but no spirit—no stamina—nothing competitive about him. . . . Yeah—I'll keep looking." He laughed. "I'm hanging up now—to charter those boys for tomorrow before anybody else gets 'em. . . . Say! I like this! Want to lay another hundred to a grand on a white marlin? Unh-hunh. I thought you wouldn't! How about fifty cents to five bucks, you lousy piker? Okay?"

He came out of the booth and started toward the *Poseidon*—a new man with a new interest in life. Through the precipitating murk, he saw the crowd of people. He hurried. He pushed rather rudely into the middle of the throng.

A sight met his eyes. Hank was fishing. Hank the meek, Hank the man without a fighting heart, was standing on the edge of the pier, holding a delicate rod in his left hand and one handle of a tiny reel in his right. The rod was bent like a croquet wicket. Hank's eyes were rapt. His body was congealed in single purpose and his movements, when he made any at all, were so swift and cat-like that they were hard to follow.

"What is it?" Mr. Thurston asked excitedly.

Red, one of the boatmen, answered without moving his eyes. "A snook, mister. One of the big guys that lives under this dock, getting fat on the stuff we throw overboard every night. Nobody ever hooked one." There was a boil and gurgle on the darkling sea. A tail showed. "Looka that! Thirty pounds—maybe more."

"Has he got a chance?" Mr. Thurston enquired in an anxious tone.

Red snorted. "A snook like that on a bait-casting rig, and all these boats and piles? Mister—that bird hasn't got no more chance than a pinch of gunpowder in the fires of hell! Just the same, he happens to be the best light tackle man in South Florida—and it's mighty exciting to see how long he can hold her!"

Crunch, who was standing behind Hank, glanced around and saw Mr. Thurston. He saw the blazing interest on the big man's face. A little late, Crunch thought. Then he saw Vi—and she lifted her eyebrows in an ardent question about the day. Crunch thought that perhaps it would make life easier if he, and not Hank, broke the news, so he gave the girl a "thumbs down" signal and watched anticipation die from her eyes. Then he heard Hank's voice, grim and game and sardonic: "He's heading under the dock, Crunch! It's only a matter of seconds, now! But I sure gave that snook a run for his money!"

Crunch looked. Swimming easily along the bottom, the snook was surging toward the piles that supported the pier. With each surge, Hank lost five or six feet of his precious line. Crunch laid his hand on the clerk's back. "You did good, boy! I'd have sworn nobody could hang one—and it's about impossible to hold one even this long."

Hank bent with his bending rod. "He's under!"

"Mmm. You'd have to be a fish to follow him now!"

Maybe he lost his balance. He said so, afterward. But Crunch said he saw him dive. Saw the day's disappointment and disgrace ferment into a look of abandonment and saw him set his toes so he'd turn right in the air. Anyway, there was a splash and a murmuring yell from the crowd on the dock and Hank hit the water. He went down in it and the tide caught him. Somebody switched on the dock lights. For a second they could see him in the middle of a billion bubbles, holding his rod in one hand and swimming with the other. Swimming up. Then he was pulled under the dock in the wake of his big fish.

Crunch was on board the *Poseidon* in a flash. So was Des. So—to their amazement—was Mr. Thurston. He and Crunch unlashed the dory and Des lowered it toward the running tide. Crunch took the center seat and Mr. Thurston got in up forward, as the dory spun around. He pushed clear of the *Firefly* in the next berth. The crowd watched that maneuver for a moment and then ran to the other edge of the dock to spot the emergence of Hank. Crunch pulled on the oars and the dory walked water—east, north, and west, around the dock.

Thurston said, "Can he swim?"

Crunch answered, "If he doesn't get caught under there."

Then the people began to yell, "There he is! There he is! Farther out, Crunch!"

So Crunch bent his back. Mr. Thurston swung around and straddled the bow, as if it were a saddle. His feet were in the water—but he didn't notice. Hank came up, kicking hard, stroking with one hand, keeping his face out. Moreover, the arced rod came up with him. Mr. Thurston bellowed, "By George, he's still got the pole!" and then he leaned forward. He caught Hank by the collar and next by the belt. With a heave that shipped water, he lifted Hank up in front of himself and slid back, so that they were like two men astride the same saddle. And Hank did not let go of the rod.

Crunch had to drop the oars and hop back to the stern to keep the dory from nosing under. Somebody on one of the boats switched a searchlight on them. The mob on the dock began to cheer. Mr. Thurston asked a feverish question of Hank, who was wheezing and sputtering, "Is he still on, boy? Is he on?"

"You bet he's still on," Hank said.

"Are you okay?"

"Reasonably," said Hank.

"Good," said Mr. Thurston. And then he added worriedly, "Don't you think, old man, you ought to ease up a bit on him?"

"Yeah," Hank coughed. "I believe you're right!" He eased up, but the snook's jaw was full of hooks and he couldn't escape.

Crunch, meanwhile, was sitting on the stern seat. For a man in the midst of a dilemma, he was behaving oddly. He was laughing. Not loudly, but with every fibre in his body. He was laughing in paroxysms. In convulsions. In eye-wetting, debilitating waves of mirth. For amusement— and also in great relief. When Hank brought the fish alongside, it was all

Crunch could do to reach down, thrust his hand into the rasping gills, and bring it aboard.

Crunch was late in getting home that night. Sari had supper waiting. She called to the sound of his feet on the porch, "Any luck?"

"Well—we got a snook. Big one. Nearly a record. It'll knock off Strikes Caldway for first place in the Tournament."

"Snook! I thought you were sailfishing!" He had come in and she held up her lips. After the kiss, she said, "Your feet are wet! Why not break down and tell all? Did Hank get the job?"

"The dory," Crunch answered somewhat inscrutably, as husbands will, "had inches of water in her! I'll say he did! He and Vi are having dinner with Mr. Thurston over at the Beach-Paradise Hotel. And Mr. Thurston chartered me for two weeks—fishing with Hank. Yep. He got the job!"

"He deserves it," Sari replied delightedly. "A swell person—and such an expert fisherman! He is terribly good, isn't he?"

Crunch pondered. At last he said, "An expert angler, Sari, isn't necessarily a guy who always does the right thing at the right second. But—one thing he necessarily is—and that's a fishing man! A man who'll fish on banks and beaches, in creeks and puddles, from rowboats and cruisers, deep down and on the surface—a man who just can't quit fishing no matter how low he feels—a man, so help me, who'll fish *under* water, in a pinch!" Then, to Sari's wonderment, he laughed until he was too feeble to explain himself.

THE MAN WHO
HAD BEEN AROUND

FRIENDSHIPS ARE often regarded as odd, but enmities are taken for granted. Crunch developed an enmity, once, and it taught him a lesson, besides nearly costing his life. The object of a mere acorn of umbrage that grew in him to an oak was a person named Cornwell Humbert. The moment of inception was a late summer afternoon on board the *Poseidon* while Mr. Humbert was fighting a large dolphin.

There did not seem to be anything the matter with the charterboat's passenger. He was tall and lean and full of charm. He had paid his fare in advance. If he had a pseudo-British accent of the sort often discovered in second-generation New Yorkers, he was also rugged. The dolphin did not seem to be tiring him. In fact, after it had come out of the water a half dozen times as high as a man's head and as violently as a trapped panther, Mr. Humbert removed his right hand from the reel, which was shedding line, and delicately patted his semi-visible moustache with a steady finger. "Magnificent," he said. "Really—superlative."

"As good as we've got." The skipper's pride was restrained. The dolphin would go well over forty. If they boated it, they would be tops for the species in the summer tournament. "You better be ready to wind fast, though. If he comes toward us, he'll come like a fireball."

Mr. Humbert nodded and continued to pat his moustache. "Never fished in the Humbolt Current, I suppose?"

"No," said Crunch. "He's turning."

The passenger glanced at the sea. "Mmmmm. Possibly. Or the Great Barrier Reef? Went out there with a chap a few times. An Australian. Name of Purdy. Picked up a hundred and twelve thousand dollars' worth of nuggets—barehanded—made a cairn, flew in a plane, copped a fortune. Purdy did. Had a marvelous boat—Purdy. I hung a fish there—leaped like this one—a bigger, salmon and purple—never did get the name right. Bit me when I got it aboard and I spent four

141

weeks in ship's bay with a nasty infection—"

Crunch was, by then, telling himself that he was too old a guide to be anguished by the behavior of passengers. Mr. Humbert's dolphin made another leap—a full front somersault with a half twist—and came around in an arc, two hundred yards from the boat and going like lightning—on nine-thread-line, which is a light line. "You better watch him," Crunch murmured.

"Hmmm? Oh." Mr. Humbert lowered his rod tip six inches, tried turning the reel, decided apparently, that the tension was still too great, and returned to the business of investigating his moustache. "I've had a lot of fun with sharks on rod and reel. Tigers. Not game fish, you'd say, but did you ever try to hold one—a fifteen-hundred-pounder—when you were treading water?"

Crunch said, "No."

"I did. Off Mazatlan. Foolish thing to do. I went overboard because I was standing up when the fish hit and he pulled me off balance. I was standing up because another shark had attacked a dinghy—actually was shaking it in its teeth, about a quarter of a mile away—and I wanted to see the excitement. In I went. Hung on convulsively—at first. Aquaplaned along. Then the shark came around to see what was aquaplaning in his wake. The two Mexicanos got me with a boathook about then—or maybe I wouldn't be having this fun right now."

Crunch said nothing. The dolphin came racing toward the boat and passed it on the port side. Crunch could see it, like a barrel of strewn jewelry under the clear sea. Des was turning the boat and Mr. Humbert had actually condescended to reel. In fact he was reeling with considerable speed and competency.

He was also still talking. "The shark that attacked the dinghy shook it in its jaws three or four times and gave up. We harpooned ours, after I'd been on it four hours. Sun too much for me. Must have been a hundred and thirty—out in it—that day. Funny thing. I've kept, and had kept, the records of the stomach contents of thousands of sharks and not a sign of a person in one."

It was at about that point that Crunch felt in his soul the burn of dislike for Mr. Humbert. Des couldn't swing the boat fast enough. The dolphin was threatening to cross her bows. Mr. Humbert was standing, with his rod far out over the gunwale. His pale blue eyes were sparkling with amusement—but whether at the dolphin or at his memories, Crunch could not say. "I owned a shark factory," the passenger explained. "Lost in it every dime I made out of a bunch of radium shares I had. Man's an idiot to trade good radium stock for a shark business he never saw."

Crunch prepared to run forward to hold the line clear of the *Poseidon's* bows until Mr. Humbert and his rod could be brought up by Des. At that instant, however, the dolphin changed its course. It came about fast, throwing a vast belly in the line. Mr. Humbert wound, silent, for the moment. The dolphin jumped, fought doggedly sidewise against the pull of the line for a few moments, and gave up. Mr. Humbert reeled steadily the while. In due time, Crunch leaned over the side with a long-handled gaff, stabbed the fish cleanly amidships, and brought it aboard. His passengers viewed it with interest. "Nice fish. Nice work, skipper. Your mate handled the boat marvelously. Funny things—fish. Beautiful, and as coldly blood-thirsty as juramentados."

"As what?"

It was late. Crunch started in. Mr. Humbert went up topside while Crunch piloted toward the sunset and the Miami landscape beneath it, and told him about juramentados—who are fanatics sworn to die killing Christians. Mr. Humbert, it seemed, was a Christian who had killed a juramentado—by a narrow margin. "But that crease wound," he said, "made me gimpy for months."

The passenger went his way down the Gulf Stream Dock in due course. Mr. Williams had attested to the weight of the dolphin—forty-four and a quarter pounds—and it was tops for its kind on the list, with every chance of staying tops, as the 1941 Summer Contest had only a few days more to run. But Crunch went back to the *Poseidon* and sat on the stern tightening a cleat until the screwdriver marred the bronze.

"What's the matter?" Des asked, at last.

"That clown. Got my goat."

Des was honestly surprised. "I thought he was a nice guy. Everybody likes him. He only just came to Miami—but he already knows more people than most."

Crunch's eyes narrowed. "One of those, hunh? Is he trying to sell anybody anything?"

"He's got dough. Plenty. Rented the Bogart place till fall."

"A high-toned con man, then hunh?"

"Valerie Jones doesn't think he's a con man."

Crunch almost jumped. That is, his muscles contracted and his face took on the expression of someone on the point of performing a physically violent act. "Valerie! Does she know this monkey?"

"She's crazy about him. Look, Crunch. He talked a lot, but he was fishing all right, too—if you noticed. He's an angler—that guy—!"

"I didn't notice," Crunch answered. "I was too busy listening." He frowned for a moment and shook his head. "Why does Sari have to be away whenever anything like this happens? I ask you?"

Des could be stubborn. "I bet Sari would like Mr. Humbert!"

"I bet she'd snatch Valerie out of his reach before you could strike a grunt on a handline! Sari likes Valerie."

Crunch went ashore. He drove to his cottage, which was empty and desolate. He scrambled eggs, fried potatoes, made coffee and dined. Then he called up Valerie. Her mother said she'd gone to the Purple Palmettoes with a friend. Crunch unlocked the cedar chest and took out his white flannels and his light blue flannel coat. Sari had folded them away and they were ready to wear. He decided his black and white shoes would do without a fresh polish. He took a shower and dressed.

He felt hot and damp and uncertain. It was the kind of weather that produces such feelings; it had been, for many days. Each morning was steely grey and teeming with heat; the peak of every noon was a torment of sun, and the afternoons were brassy and listless. Thunder showers perpetually muttered and flashed on the horizon but rarely moved overhead to bring the brief relief of rain and wind. The Gulf Stream ran tiredly north, flat as satin and as impenetrably penetrable as the edge of plate glass. A sailboat on the Bay would not have moved a mile in a week, except for the even push and pull of the tides. Sometimes, at this season, Floridians pay the price for having June in January. They pay it in the sweat and haunted megrims that assail all people during tropical hot seasons.

Night was like warm, damp furs that had been too heavily perfumed. The breeze stirred up by the car was not refreshing, but suffocating. Crunch found himself wishing for the hundredth time that he had gone to Jersey for the summer and early fall and he wished with a depressed, passionate uselessness that he was not engaged in trying to interfere with a girl who was twenty years old and as independent as if she were fifty.

When he entered the Purple Palmettoes the band was playing and most of the customers were dancing. It was a patio night club; it had a central outdoor terrace which could be quickly covered by a sliding roof in the event of rain. The walls were painted blue and the lights were rose and blue. Dried palm leaves and trunks gave the proper atmosphere— which was, of course, improper. That is to say, it was in a lurid and artificial way, the atmosphere of a low-grade South Sea Island dive. The people drank beverages which had the names of ports in the Far East and the lady guests wore leis around their necks. In spite of this effort to be declassé, the club was in good repute, patronized by Miami's best people, and managed by a man who often fished with Crunch.

Crunch spotted Valerie at a table with Mr. Cornwell Humbert. He nodded to the headwaiter that he had found his party and proceeded slowly through the palms. He was not in the least surprised to hear Mr. Humbert say, as he approached, "—there I was, lava down the mountain, and a new flow from that last blast cutting me off up ahead. What to do? Trees were bursting into flame as if the tops of them were match-heads—"

Valerie glanced up, looking pleased and then faintly startled; she blushed. She said, "Why—Crunch—!"

Mr. Humbert turned. Crunch had prepared several speeches, to meet various imagined reactions to his appearance. If Mr. Humbert were cold, Crunch would be insistent. If he were insulting—fine; Crunch could be. If he tried any slick stuff—Crunch would sit there and act as if he were too tight to know enough to go home. Above all, if Mr. Humbert threatened to toss him out on his ear—that would be delightful. But Mr. Humbert did none of these things. He leaped to his feet and said with what seemed vast pleasure, "This is great! Simply perfect! I was just boasting to Val about the day we had! She said she knew you very well! I've been in seven heavens all at once ever since I met her!" Crunch was being forced into a chair. "Look at her, man! How many times do you see that particular creamy complexion with that dark, smooth red hair—and grey eyes? How many? Twice—three times—in your life? And how often is a girl with a personality like Val's attached to the composition? Once? Only if the gods are all working on your side. Man—I'm batty about her! Sit down! Have a drink! Have a dozen!"

"I'll have one, anyhow," Crunch said. He made his face amiable. He was very fond of Valerie—which helped. But a small sound track inside him was pouring out epithets against Cornwell Humbert. A super-cad, if there ever was one. Not only sweeping Val off her feet—but also Crunch, or a restaurantful of people, or all Miami. Crunch had noted the starry look in Valerie's eyes before it had changed to mild dismay upon seeing him. Val—like Des—was sold on this clattering oaf.

Mr. Humbert beamingly beckoned for the headwaiter.

Val said, "I never heard of you—prowling—" She sounded hurt.

Crunch flushed. "Me?" He grinned. "It's a mild prowl, Val. In my bungalow there is nothing but heat and emptiness. I came here because the guy who owns the place is my friend."

"A man like Captain Adams," said Humbert, "never prowls, Val. Those are the strong and silent ones. I knew a guy looked very much like Adams, as a matter of fact. Met him in Rio. Half Irish and half Russian. Had a combination name, too, like Dmitri O'Hara, or Tim Shovlevsky. Made a lot of dough in meat. Meat and river pearls. Ten thousand miles from home, every senorita in the bistro crazy about him, a dozen absinthe frappes under his belt—and what? He gets out his wife's picture and tells me about her for two hours and a half. That's the type. I'm only half of it. Strong—but not silent."

Valerie smiled. Crunch ordered a drink. The girl said, "You were in the middle of the lava, Hum—remember?"

Mr. Humbert patted his moustache; it seemed to stand out more clearly at night. "Oh, that. Nothing—really." But he told her. He, and another adventurer named "Cal" found a cave—deep, with an icy spring in it, and holed in until the lava was cool enough to run across. When that one was finished, Crunch was tempted to say, "I suppose the sulphur fumes made you hoarse for months afterward?" But he didn't. Valerie was drinking it in.

They sat there for three hours—and Mr. Humbert talked. Crunch fermented, but he concealed every sign of it. The girl had a bad case of Mr. H. Every quiet movement she made, every look, every gesture, was in a soft, malleable awareness of the tall blond man who talked to her. When you see a girl doing that with a man you like and respect, Crunch thought, there are few sights on earth that give you more pleasure. But when a girl you like and respect behaves in those small outgiving and gracious ways for the benefit of a dope who is probably wanted by the police in several states, or perhaps several nations—it makes you angry at women.

It was not necessary for Crunch to talk. Furthermore, he could not think of anything to say. If Mr. Humbert had been alone, he would have said plenty. If Valerie had been alone, he would have said a different plenty. As it was, Valerie finally exclaimed, "It's after twelve!"

Crunch suggested quickly and without much hope, "I'll run you home."

To his surprise, Mr. Humbert said, "Fine, old boy! I've ordered two cars—and they haven't been delivered. We came in a cab."

Crunch drove to Valerie's house. Mr Humbert escorted her under an arch of stephanotis and said, "Some night, Val, I'm going to ask you to kiss me. That will be a very important night for me—and I hope—for you." Crunch heard him say it; Mr. Humbert made no effort to keep Crunch from hearing. Valerie answered, "All right," in her quiet voice. Mr. Humbert came back to the car whistling something off-key. "Chinese love ballad," he confided idly. Then he fell silent. And Crunch chauffeured him home without launching into the monologue that began, "Listen, you silver-tongued silver fish, if you do anything to hurt that gal, I'll take you apart one vertebra at a time." He decided he was too sore to begin it just then.

At the Spanish gateway of the Bogart villa Mr. Humbert said, "How about tomorrow? Booked? I had much fun."

Crunch said, "Business is slow—these days."

"It's a date. 'Night, skipper!"

Fishing, on the next metal-hot afternoon, was very slow. Eventually, they ran alongside the *Astra*. She was anchored on the reef and Pete, her mate, was overboard, diving, with goggles. He wasn't using a spear—just going under bare-handed and bringing up sea fans, plumes, coral, and gorgonias for two enthralled lady customers. Des idled the *Poseidon*'s motors, because Mr. Humbert seemed interested. The sea was so flat that they could watch the mate almost as if he were swimming in air. He descended to the bottom and moved among the waving stone sea gardens slowly, scaring out schools of striped and banded fish and shaking his fist at a big grouper that loomed up in front of him and hurried off scene.

"Ever try it?" Mr. Humbert asked Crunch.

"Yeah. Fun. You?"

"In the Solomons," he answered readily. "With some pearl divers. I learned to get down about forty feet. They'd go twice that deep. Then, one day, a nice kid that I'd gotten quite attached to put his foot in one of those big clams. I went after him—and his father did—and then we went together and we got him up. He lost his foot."

Crunch looked bitterly at the sea. "There's plenty of goggles on the *Astra*—and I've got a bathing suit that would fit you—if you want to add to the ladies' collection."

Mr. Humbert shivered slightly. "Rather not. That clam—you know. Got me off the idea—hunh?"

Crunch spat where he was looking. Someday, he thought, I will break that guy up like kindling. They resumed fishing. Mr. Humbert took a sail—a beauty. He said it was his first. Crunch wanted to ask if there hadn't been a Siberian sail or two—five-hundred-pounders. But he didn't. The radio news broadcast got him off the idea. A storm was stirring, out beyond the Bahamas. That meant watchful waiting and work to do, if the storm started winding toward Florida. He said as much to his passenger on the way in.

Mr. Humbert seemed pleased with that, also. "Really, now! I've been in three, so far. One in the Caribbean. Took the deckhouse off a tramp I was aboard. Two in the Far East. Like to see the Florida version."

"Mmm. You better have Bogart's men board up his house."

"I will! Thanks for the tip. Join us tonight?"

"Maybe. Later."

"Lovely girl—Valerie. Been thinking about her all day. Been mildly in love—often enough. Never had the whole thing come up like—well—it's not stormy. Just a warm tide growing on you, eh?"

"That's a nice girl—" Crunch began.

"If anybody said she wasn't, I'd move his mouth around to the back of his head." Mr. Humbert announced that cheerily and touched his moustache. He repeated his invitation when he left the dock.

Crunch was uneasy that night, for several reasons. He woke up twice and turned on his radio. The storm was coming, all right. Early in the morning, he boarded up. He had built the shutters for his bungalow and the fixtures for the shutters. He knew where they went and they fitted accurately. It took an hour and a half to make his cottage proof against all but the legendary ones.

When he drove down to the dock it was still early but all the stores were open and Miami was bustling. People drove along with sheets of plywood and plasterboard tied to their cars. People emerged from hardware stores with nails, hammers, screws, wire, rope, flashlights, candles, solidified alcohol, and other hurricane sundries. People were carrying cartons of food from groceries and laying in supplies at drug stores. The streets rang with the sound of hammers. Facades of busy stores were already covered and lights burned inside them. Lumber piles were being nailed and wired to the earth. Earnest householders were climbing up in their trees to affix guy wires and heavy ropes. Up the harbor, a parade of boats moved toward sanctuary in the river and the canals.

Des had already taken down the *Poseidon*'s outriggers and lashed them to the dock. "House fixed?" he asked.

"All set. Let's go!"

They—and the others—had done it before, many times, usually for nothing, and they would do it again. Crunch and Des took their boat to the cove in which they had rebuilt her from a wreck to a first-class fishing cruiser. They covered her, battened everything down, lashed her fast enough to hang by her moorings, put on more lines because they loved the boat and she was their livelihood, and, between times, listened to the radio and smoked cigarettes. The storm was coming on in—toward Miami; not a tough one—but no zephyr, either. By the time they were doubly and triply sure of their job, it was mid-afternoon.

Des said, "Well, son, I got a date to sit this one out in a hotel with some people who throw hurricane parties. Want to come?"

Crunch grinned and said he thought he'd stay in his house, to make sure nothing got wet. Des urged him. And Crunch had another idea. "As a matter of fact, there's a monkey I'd like to be with—if this one hits."

"Humbert?"

"Yes, sir—Mr. Humbug! I'm going to phone Sari down at Key West— looks like they're safe enough—and tell her we're all snug. Then I'm going to look up this Humbug mug and stick to him and I hope it blows a thousand miles an hour. I want to see how green he gets."

Crunch drove back to the Dock. All the boats were gone. Mr. Williams had, in the dockhouse, a chart that represented the progress of the hurricane. Crunch studied it attentively and nodded. "On the nose, hunh?"

"On the nose," said Mr. Williams.

The captain changed a bill and called Key West. Sari had been looking at the map, too: her voice showed it. If the blow had been headed in her direction, she would have kidded Crunch. Now, she only tried to kid. She said they were all shut up and anchored down and okay. Key West had been getting ready for them for a couple of centuries. Some of its houses were even furnished with cables, attachable by turnbuckles at the corners. Crunch made his report about the bungalow and the boat. He thought of explaining the matter of Valerie and Mr. Humbert, but he didn't. Nothing Sari could do. He just said, "Call you after, gal. Give Bill a kiss or a cuff for me—whatever he deserves. So long."

Then he went in search of Mr. Humbert.

The afternoon was wearing away and the blueness had eroded out of the sky leaving not clouds, but an ever-thickening greyness. The wind blew, occasionally, in whirling fits that spun newspapers and pushed up tree branches. Miami's citizens, like good troops at the approach of battle, were a little quicker in their movements—and a little more careful to be humorous and languid in their greetings. The hammering, where belated preparations were still in progress, went faster than it had in the morning. The last of many huge metal shutters were clanging into place along the street floors of big buildings. Out over the bay, Crunch noticed a couple of birds circling nervously, and the fact that only a couple were visible in a vast reach of air impressed itself on him.

Mr. Humbert was at home, supervising the work on his rented premises; he seemed to take a personal interest in every fastening of every board. "Tighter," he would say to the perspiring colored boys who were working for him. "Another turn! Wind might get under it and rip it off! Then where would we be?" From time to time he glanced intently at the sky. From time to time, also, he took a sip from a highball which he was carrying around the yard and bent over a portable radio. The sight pleased Crunch.

When Mr. Humbert saw him, he smiled rather perfunctorily. "Think it'll amount to much?"

Crunch shook his head gravely. "Look like a bizzmaroon to me." It didn't—but Crunch said so. He added, "See Val last night?"

"No. We had a date. For some reason—she broke it."

The skipper sat down on a pile of shutters. "Really? Tough!" He thought that probably Val was coming to her senses. He accepted a highball and acted as if he had nowhere to go and nothing to do, which was true. "Bad—these blows."

"You're telling me," said the man who had known adventure. "I get nervous—just thinking about the ones I've been in! I—say. Do you think it would be better if we moved to a hotel? If I did?"

Crunch shrugged. "Search me. They stood up in 1926. Uncomfortable, though. I mean—windows smashed, sea raging right into the lobbies, big ships, barges, tugs, schooners—crashing against them like battering rams on every wave. Dangerous—kind of."

Mr. Humbert stared. "You don't say!"

"It's a gamble—whatever you pick." Tossing palms seemed to hold Crunch's attention.

"You doing anything particular tonight?" Mr. Humbert asked.

"Why—no. Trying to save my life is all."

"Care to join me?" The question was eager.

"Why not?" Crunch stared at the Bogart villa. "She ought to hold."

Mr. Humbert sighed unevenly and pushed his moustache the wrong way. He turned up the radio. The voice of the local announcer was steady: "Storm advisory. When last reported to the weather bureau, half an hour ago, the storm was centered about a hundred and fifteen miles east of Miami and somewhat south. It was headed west northwest and is of hurricane intensity. All interests are urgently warned to take all precautions. The storm is expected to reach the Florida coast sometime after midnight. Special provision should be made for sick persons. People wishing advice will call 45-1000. Special warning has been given—" Mr. Humbert shut off the set. . . .

Crunch ate a good dinner. Mr. Humbert ate practically nothing. After dinner, for an hour or two, Crunch played the automatic phonograph. He played it loudly, sitting on a red damask divan in the Bogart living room. Finally Mr. Humbert asked him to turn it off. It made him, he said, definitely uneasy; music in large doses always upset him; he had inherited the quality from his mother. Crunch snapped the switch. Then they heard the wind. It was blowing about a half gale, Crunch thought, gusty and rising. Trees were wheezing in it and vines were scratching the house. They sat and listened to it—Mr. Humbert with a highball, in an iron and leather chair.

At eleven, they turned on the radio again. No music was playing. Local stations were devoting themselves entirely to the subject of the storm. It had slowed down but it had not turned. The announcers were busy giving lists of the addresses of refuge places, first aid stations, and the like. They left the radio on.

At midnight, Mr. Humbert said, "Guess I'll phone Valerie and see how she's getting along. I called this afternoon and asked her to come here with her mother—but she said she always stayed at home."

Crunch thought it was a pity Valerie had not accepted the invitation. Mr. Humbert was well on his way toward first-class heebie-jeebies.

He returned from the library looking pale. "Phone doesn't work."

Crunch said. "Tchk, tchk! Doesn't sound that bad—does it?" He cross-ed the living room and before his host could prevent it, he turned the door knob. The wind did the rest. It came into the room like a soft fist, overturned a chair, blew the afternoon paper into separate sheets, and spun a lampshade. Crunch calmly walked out on the loggia. The night was dark but not black. It had a greyish tinge that made it possible to see the down-bent, hammering tree tops, the streaming vines, and the litter accumulating in the yard. Rain was moving horizontally; it tasted salty on Crunch's lips. Down the street there was a lavender flash as a short took out a big fuse. Crunch looked at the tempest calmly and became aware of Humbert at his side. Humbert raised a thin voice and yelled, "Better come in, old top! You'll get hurt!"

So Crunch went in. He and Mr. Humbert began to play gin rummy. Time passed. Out over the ocean, in a stretch where Crunch knew every wave, a fantastically low pressure area with a spinning wall of wind wrapped around it was pushing and pushing toward Miami, lightning-streaked and roofed with night, on a sea that ran high, white, and hid-eous. The thought made Crunch's scalp creep. As he settled back to the game he noted that his opponent was an indifferent player.

Hours went by. They sat there—two men in a room, playing cards—listening to a voice that talked firmly about the weather gone insane. And listening to the wind. It neared the time when it should have been dawn. Crunch felt the gale tighten up and the gusts hammer harder. His own muscles stiffened a little. Water began to stream under the door. They piled towels on it for a while and then gave up, moving the rug and the furniture out of its reach. The radio said, with a touch of excitement, "The weather bureau reports that the center can be expected on the Florida coast at any time now." Crunch looked at Mr. Humbert. He was white and shaky; his eyes were opaque; but he was still holding on—play-ing his cards and sipping, not whisky, any longer, but iced coffee which he had made.

The house trembled steadily. It made a grinding sound, like a train passing in the distance. The water now gushed under the door and they sat with their feet up. Every few seconds, from outside, came a horrible whine, a note on Satan's bull fiddle, as the wind bent a tree far enough to draw its guy wire taut and vibrate it. The sound, Crunch thought, would unnerve almost anybody. Things hit the house—branches, cocoanuts, metal cans, anonymous gobbets that thumped and were lost in the tumult. A tree outside split with a protracted crash that sounded, in the roar of the wind, like the crushing of a strawberry box. The radio commenced reporting addresses of distress calls—and it also reported that the wind at a lighthouse had passed a hundred miles an hour.

"Breezy," Crunch said.

Mr. Humbert merely gasped.

Then they heard a mention of their street: "Fire reported . . . neighborhood of five hundred, Upper Bougainvillea Terrace. Reporter unable to offer aid . . . sick in bed. Anybody in the vicinity . . ."

"That's right around here," Crunch said steadily, and he looked up at his companion.

Mr. Humbert had risen. It had been hot indoors and he had loosened his tie. He was now adjusting it. He donned his light jacket. His face was alight and composed. He patted his moustache with his forefinger. "Let's go, pal," he said peacefully.

They took a flashlight. That was all. The wind in the loggia staggered them. They caught their balance and plunged into the yard like halfbacks bucking the line. There was light, now—a jaundiced greyness. The stripped shrubbery flickered in the wind. Trees bent to the ground and pounded it as if they were trying to thresh something from the debris that rolled and scuttled upon it. A wall protected them for half the distance to the five hundred block. For the other half, they plunged with their clothes slapping and ten thousand leaves and little branches stinging them and piling against them. As they went, the thin, racing sheet of water on the sidewalk grew deeper, until they were up to their knees in it and it tore at them like a rapids. It was difficult to see. At one point, Crunch felt Humbert seize him and pull him backward. Crunch stumbled and sat down backward in the water. Very slowly, it seemed to Crunch, a tall palm crashed to earth precisely where he would have been if Humbert had not seen it coming.

Crunch bellowed, "Thanks!"

Humbert was grinning. He put his mouth to Crunch's ear. "Watch where you're going, pal! These falling trees can give you a nasty scalp wound."

Crunch got up and shut his jaws. One possible answer: Humbert had gone crazy from fear. Only—that wasn't the right answer—because, a moment later, Humbert pointed calmly and Crunch saw a fire-lighted window. They went around to the lee, where they could stand up. The house was shivering and grumblimg. They yelled and beat on the back door with branches. Nobody responded. The house was boarded up. In the end, they broke in, first through a screen and then through a glass door on a sheltered porch. There was no one at home. But somebody had left lights burning and the wet wires had shorted. The short had started a small fire in the woodwork of the front hall.

The interior of the place was smoky. They found a fire extinguisher—and finished off with buckets of water. Crunch went out to the garage, battered through a weak lock, and pulled the main switch. Then they noticed that the wind was falling. It fell fast and switched. "Lull," Crunch said. "Shall we beat it back—or stay here?"

"Scrambola," said Humbert. "Fire's out."

They ran back, two blocks, through a yellow-grey and almost windless carnage that dripped and gurgled and lay flat all about—uprooted shrubbery, fallen palms, boards, branches, cocoanuts, cement shingles, garden furniture, cans, flower pots, a hundred nameless objects upended by the wind and shedding a lake of water. Indoors, the radio was still talking: " . . . center has passed . . . no damage reported except minor property loss and injury to vegetation . . . hospital has received no casualties due to storm . . . mild intensity . . . main force exerted about ten miles south of Miami . . . wind expected after lull will not reach hurricane pitch in Miami area. . . . "

Both men were panting and grinning. "I thought," said Humbert, "that you said it was going to be a bizzmaroon."

"Mistake," Crunch answered. "You realize you've lost one pantleg and half your shirt, don't you?"

"You've lost your whole shirt, pal. Well, we had a little fun, anyhow! You know, I'm always running into messes like this—or worse. A mining engineer bats around a lot. But I'm a weird guy for trouble. And I always get the jitters when I see it coming. Not during. Before. What's the matter?"

Crunch had been staring. He said in a low voice, "Nasty scar on your leg, there."

"That? That's the crease-mark that juramentado put on me." Mr. Humbert rolled up his sodden sleeve. "Here's where that fish bit me. Even nastier—after they operated for the poison, hunh?"

The next night, when Crunch joined them at the Purple Palmetto, Valerie was listening rapturously—and Humbert, as usual, was talking. Crunch approached through the music and the blue gloom with deliberate inconspicuousness. He felt fine; Sari and Bill were safe; so was the house—and the *Poseidon*. Humbert seemed to be at the climax of a story: "The wind was hitting over a hundred! A hundred and fifty, I'd say. Old Crunch was slogging on ahead of me! The stuff in the air was whipping us to death! He couldn't see. But I've been in four of these things. I had my hand over my eyes and was peering through a slit. Saw a big palm topple just as Old Crunch was pushing on into it and got him by the belt! If I hadn't—by jiminy—old Crunch would never drag another sailfish out of the sea!"

Crunch oozed away until that one was finished. When he came back, Humbert was discussing tornadoes. He'd been a boy in Kansas, it seemed.

"Sit down," he said jovially. "According to the papers, it was hardly a hurricane at all. Say! You've got to do me a favor!"

Crunch smiled. "I owe you one."

"Know why Val wouldn't see me night before last and last night? She thought you didn't approve of me. Not that I blame you. I'm a damned magpie, I know. But she says she likes that. Says she doesn't talk and loves to listen."

Valerie flushed. "I didn't say that! I just said—I wondered if Crunch liked you—that was all."

The skipper gazed at the man from everywhere. "Think you'll ever run out of yarns?"

"Dunno. I've asked Val to marry me. Want to take her out to an island in the Coral Sea. Hear there's vanadium on it. Vanadium and volcanoes. If we run out of yarns—we can dig up some new ones, can't we? Sh seems to be waiting for the word from you. What are you—her uncle. '

"He's all right," Crunch said gravely to the girl. "Strong—even if non-silent."

He was all right, too. That was what Valerie proclaimed when she came back from their wedding trip—with a half interest in a vanadium mine, a pet monkey, and the minor scar of a python bite on her shapely left calf.

THE WAY OF ALL FISH

CRUNCH ADAMS was present in the dining room of the Salt Water Anglers' Club of Miami on the night "Gatsie" Simmonds hit Horace Boyle with the custard pie. Gatsie did not actually throw the delicacy in the conventional way; rather he whammed it.

The thing began, or, more accurately, continued, in an argument that is without a beginning among fishermen. It grew loud at the point where Horace said, "I tell you, Gatsie, a bonita — a second-degree cousin of a lousy mackerel — tied tail-to-tail with a bonefish of the same weight, would tow it backwards and drown it in five minutes!"

This is heresy to a man who spends myriads of his waking hours out on the lavender flats in quest of the bonefish, or *Albula vulpes*. Mr. Simmonds shuddered. "Bonita!" he said, and his scorn made the chandeliers dance. "Bonita, indeed! A bonefish would tear the tail right off a bonita!"

The riposte won the attention of all twelve men at that table, and half of those at the next. Horace gazed dreamily at his antagonist, patted his greying forelock, and murmured, "People go after bonefish because they get seasick on the ocean. The bonefish is a torpid creature that wouldn't live to swim through eight waves in the Gulf Stream. A sort of shiny mud-puppy. You catch him in six inches of water, and you get the illusion he's fast because he barges around so close to you."

Mr. Simmonds thrust a finger between his expanding neck and his contracting collar. "Did you ever hook a bonefish?" he shouted. "Ever boat one?"

Horace was still bland. He nodded in a meditative way "Yes," he said, "and I recall foul-hooking a turtle, once. A six pounder. The way he waddled off toward his hole was singularly reminiscent —"

"Turtle!" thundered Simmonds. "I leave it to Captain Adams, here! Crunch! Tell this skinny idiot the truth!"

Crunch smiled in a mollifying way. He had his own reasoned opinion, but Mr. Simmonds did not seem to be in a reasonable frame of mind.

Furthermore, Crunch was the guest of Horace Boyle, and Horace was one of his regular customers. He liked Horace. He did not know Mr. Simmonds. He said, "Well, since nobody will ever be able to tie a fresh, live bonita to a bonefish, there's no way to find out. Bonita are strong. Bonefish are fast—"

Horace, seeing the waiter approach with a whole cut pie and the silver for serving it, moved his coffee to the side of his place and said in his vague voice, "A bonefish is a sort of shad, I believe. Anyhow, it looks like one. No teeth. Grinds up clams and crabs, like a cobia—instead of chasing something racy. You paunchy, deluded sissies, who can't sail the high seas in a boat, or hang onto anything heavier than a casting rod, have *got* to go on believing bonefish are red-hot, or you'd lose your self-respect. If you're willing to take off about forty pounds, Gatsie, I'll ferry you free of charge to the Gulf Stream some calm afternoon and hang you onto a dolphin. One medium dolphin would convince you that bonefishing is like hunting in a hen yard with field dogs—"

"Some pie, Mr. Simmonds?" said the waiter.

"Yes," Simmonds replied. He rose abruptly. He scooped the pie, tin and all, from the dish in which it sat, using both hands. He inverted it over his head and kept it intact by the force of his down-swing. Horace, although grey-haired, was agile as a bat. He dodged. The pie caught him a glancing blow on the side of the head, ricocheted, poured upon his shoulder, and splashed Crunch. The tin clattered to the floor.

There was a moment of quiet. Fully a third of the ninety-odd men in the room had witnessed the incident. They, together with the other two-thirds, stood up. Crunch, with great presence of mind, commenced to remove gobbets of custard from his host, using a napkin much as a plasterer uses a trowel on excess mortar. The waiter thawed from a condition resembling rigor mortis and started to daub at Crunch.

Mr. Simmonds sat down slowly, his face aghast. That the dignified, retired president of Simmonds Sweet Shops should do such a thing was incredible. The Chairman of the Casting Committee, as well! He found himself wondering what his wife would think—as a man does, in such circumstances. He thought of trying to maintain his attitude of righteous fury; after all, bonefish are bonefish; to insult them is the first form of sacrilege among shallow-water anglers. But there was no wrath left in Mr. Simmonds.

As Horace swabbed at moraines of custard and plucked away fragments of crust, he began to laugh. His laughter was soft but merry—and when he came upon an unusually sizeable chunk of the pie, he handed it to Gatsie. "Here," he said. "Make you a nice bait. A bonefish would probably mistake it for a scallop."

Then he rose and left the dining room. Mr. Simmonds also departed.

Crunch, much embarrassed, sat still. He drank his coffee and waited for the denouement. The men gradually stopped laughing. A fellow with red hair, who was standing at the end of the table, said, "Boy! Was *that* something! Old Horace was right, too, in spite of getting the worst of it!"

A very fat man dropped his cup in a way that menaced its saucer. "Right? What do you mean, right? Son, bonefish are the smartest, fastest, wickedest finned lightning — !"

"Phooie!" said a third man — a man with broad shoulders and grey, assertive eyes. "There's nothing on the flats that can turn the drag of a deep water reel! Eh, Crunch?"

The Poseidon's skipper realized that a shot had been fired which would be heard around the club for weeks to come. "Well," he answered, "there's permit — "

A fist banged. "Permit!" exclaimed a wiry gentleman beside Crunch. "Pompanos, really! Do they jump? Break water? Do bonefish? Bank fishing is washtub fishing!"

Somebody said to the waiter, "Hey! Herman! Bring a few more pies!"

Crunch presently wandered from the dining room through the bar and thence into the trophy room, where a number of men were preparing to play poker, with every intention of attending the meeting later, and every likelihood of missing it. Near a corner of that room, ignored or unseen by the others, sat Mr. Simmonds, in a black leather chair, stroking his jowls and scowling unconvincingly. Crunch halted when he saw him and smiled with an effort.

To the candy manufacturer, even a mechanical smile was a relief. He rose, seized Crunch's arm, and walked with him to the staircase. They went down, through what had been the drawing and living rooms of a vast, Victorian resort residence. One of the Founding Members had presented his grandmother's mansion to the club when he had discovered that living in it alone gave him the jim-jams. Its main chambers were now filled with rows of folding chairs. Mounted fish, awesome even in such a rococo demesne, adorned the paneled walls.

"I suppose," Mr. Simmonds was saying, as he pressed Crunch along, "I'll have to offer my resignation. Golly! What if they accept it?"

"They won't. That wasn't — anything. Half the guys are on your side."

Mr. Simmonds pointed a still wobbly finger to one of the smaller fish. "That. I caught it. Ten pounds and one ounce. A record bonefish, in its way. This club means a lot to me. I've been a member for seventeen years. I had a good business — in the far west. Candy. I came here and they took me in. Gave me a nickname. Gatsie. My first name's really Gatterson. I'd never had time to go in for things like nicknames. Worked my way up from the wrapping room. I—I never did anything like throwing a pie before. Maybe I'm sort of—losing my grip."

"You aren't the first Bay fisherman that tangled with a Stream man!"

Mr. Simmonds walked on out to a cool corner of the verandah. The view of the harbor from that point was luminous and dramatic. "I wish," he sighed, "I could think of something to do to—fix this. Horace Boyle probably will. He's clever. Educated. Harvard. By the way. I didn't catch your name?"

"Adams. Crunch Adams. I'm a charterboat captain." The statement gave Crunch an idea. "If you really feel that rotten, why don't you go out and sailfish—or something? On the quiet? If you bring in a sail, you can tell Horace what a kick you got out of it—and that'll more than square him. He's crazy about blue water fishing—and he's a swell guy."

The big man chuckled. "I've always been afraid of the sea. Scared to pieces. A—a phobia—I guess. I know about you. Would you take me—on the quiet, sort of?"

"You've made a reservation!" Crunch answered. By and by he left the man—to his phobia, and his new feeling of relief.

He went back through the club, hunting for his host and finally spotted the pinpoint of a single cigarette on the club dock.

"Sit," Horace said. His tone was unusually sharp and his saturnine face was pale, even allowing for the effect of murk and distant neon lights. Crunch sat on a piling. "I'm sore," Horace continued, after a while. "That big egg made me mad!"

Crunch was surprised. "He lost his temper. Went kind of nuts. Seems like a good fellow. You laughed it off—"

"A person goes out to sea," Boyle went on, "in a forty foot boat. It's winter. The wind's blowing forty miles an hour and the waves are damned near forty feet high. It's cold, cloudy, and it rains. You freeze to death. You eat a lot of water-soaked sandwiches. You catch flu. But no fish. You ride that confounded ocean in the summer when it's so bloody hot your lips burst. Once in a while you manage to bring in some sort of fish that weighs a quarter of a ton. And then a big, chuffing glug like Simmonds has the infinite gall to tell you that a minnow caught from a rowboat stacks up with what you've been doing. Maybe he's right. Maybe I'm the jackass. Maybe I'm getting too darned old for Bimini and the Keys and Liverpool. I'm sixty."

Crunch felt a distinct anxiety. He did not like to see one of his best customers going stale and getting angry. He thought of his suggestion to Mr. Simmonds about fishing in the Stream. The reverse might be effective for Boyle. "What you ought to do," he said in his most engaging manner, "is to sit on the flats for a day, pick up a nice string of bonefish, if possible, and present them to Simmonds here one night. Tell him you caught 'em on one-thread—with a one-ounce rod."

"I never caught a bonefish," the other man answered shortly.

Crunch was astonished—and silent.

"Maybe that's why I'm mad. I've lived here so long—fished so much—that everybody assumes I've caught every kind of fish. I do myself, sort of. But it happens I never did fish on the banks. Don't even have the tackle for it. Hate the idea. I lied tonight because these darned shallow water oafs burn me up."

"Maybe," said Crunch, "you ought to catch one."

"I will," Horace answered, "if I get rheumatism, heart trouble, ulcers, high blood pressure, and lose an arm. Otherwise, you can keep fishing me on deep water!" Inside the clubhouse, the bell for the meeting sounded. "I'm going home. In a bad mood, I guess. Go on and have fun. The chorus line from the Sand Dunes is dancing here later on."

But Crunch did not return to the club. Instead, when Horace Boyle had driven out of sight, he walked unhappily to his own car and drove through the violet-colored night to the cottage where Sari, his wife, was waiting for him. He told her the story of the custard pie and its divergent aftermaths.

Sari lighted a cigarette. "You shouldn't have popped up with those bright ideas," she said finally. "Mr. Simmonds will surely get sick if you take him out. And Mr. Boyle will be sore at you now, because he admitted to you he's never caught a bonefish. He's terribly temperamental. I've heard that—often. A good lawyer, and very funny, but a prima donna. I wish you hadn't gone to the club tonight."

"So do I," he answered. "A lot of those fellows are going to be peeved about this business. But Horace Boyle—well—I've always thought of him as one of those fishing men who puts into it a—a little something extra you can't describe."

Sari asked, after a pause, "Which *is* better, Crunch, a bonefish—or a bonita?"

Crunch thought for a full minute. His final, considered reply was, "Hunh!"

"I see," Sari said. But she didn't.

The war waged on the topic of which fish is gamest is as frantic as the war over which southpaw is the best pitcher, or which pro has the best form with woods, and as hypothetical as a discussion of what sort of fighter it will take to rout Joe Louis.

In the days that followed, various items and rumors anent the struggle came to the attention of Crunch Adams. Bob Breastedt, fishing editor of the Miami *Dispatch*, wrote a gleeful account of the Boyle-Simmonds affair, naming no names, and citing bonefish as the top species. Dan Dorset, of the *Press*, replied that no fish could stack up, pound for pound, with the white marlin. Flick Halkenberg, President of the Dade County Pelican Club, bought a half mile of line that was dyed a different color every hundred feet, together with a stop-watch, and tried to time various fishes pulling against a one-pound drag. His reports were garbled and inconclusive. Strap Malloy popped Kite Whittier on the nose because he said a round pompano, for which Strap held a world record, was a kind of "vertical flounder."

Crunch felt a certain responsibility for the thing. He believed that he could have arrested the entire quarrel by saying that a broadbill swordfish was strongest and fastest: almost nobody caught broadbills. Or he could have said, with considerable scientific defensibility, that each powerhouse among fish is supreme in its proper environment and inadequate outside it. But he hadn't, and Sari, his conscientious spouse, periodically rebuked him for his inept participation: "Mr. Boyle hasn't called you since that night, and neither has Mr. Simmonds. You've succeeded in making both of them feel inferior and foolish."

Mr. Simmonds did call, however, some ten days after his attack on Boyle. He phoned Crunch at his home and arranged to be taken out by the *Poseidon* "on the first calm day," and from a private dock, so that his junket would be kept secret in case of fizzle. It happened that the very next day was calm, and at about ten o'clock, the *Poseidon* went outside via the Government Cut, carrying a lone passenger who remained out of sight below decks.

When Crunch leaned down from the canopy and said, "Okay! You can come up!" Mr. Simmonds appeared in the cockpit with the long, leather tube. He peered at the sea with suspicion—as if he expected a serpent to swarm out of it. He said, "Mighty far off shore, aren't we?" He opened his rod case and withdrew a five-and-a-half-foot tip which weighed something more than two ounces, a butt to match, and from his tackle-box, a level-wind reel the size of a demi-tasse. On it were wound one hundred and fifty yards of fifteen-pound test line.

Crunch frowned a little. "That stuff," he said, "isn't any use out here I mean, if we hang it from the outriggers, nearly a third of it will be overboard when your fish hits. And even if we don't—a—a—a mere kingfish could strip it off." He had been on the point of saying "bonita."

Mr. Simmonds' tolerant mouth became firm. The chin of a man who had made his way from the wrapping department to the president's desk, was thrust out full. "I wouldn't prove a thing—catching a deep water fish on any but a bonefish rod, would I? I mean to say—*I* was the one who insisted bay fish were stronger—!"

"That's not the point. Suppose a twenty-five pounder—?"

"I caught a nineteen pound permit on it," the old man said with meas-ured pride. "Let's get going!"

Crunch fastened a small strip, cut from an albacore, on the delicate line. He let it float some forty feet astern. He climbed back on the canopy and said to his impassive mate, "Well, Des, there's one thing about fishing guys. They got to be the stubbornest men on earth."

"That's because they nearly always lose," Des said. "Lookie!"

Crunch pivoted. Under the fluttering, silvery bait—which was the size of an ordinary shoehorn—was a dim, chocolate-purple blur, about the size of a stepladder. The bait had been in the water less than three minutes. "This," said Crunch, "is murder."

It was murder. The sailfish submarined upward and put out the peri-scope of its bill. Mr. Simmonds saw, for the first time, the ungodly emergence of this particular form of marine voracity. He did not think to drop back. He did not need to. The sailfish, unduly hungry or unusually bold, simply gulped the bait. Mr. Simmonds struck, instinctively. He shouted. "Say! Whoa! No kidding! Hey, fellows! Come down here, somebody!"

Crunch saw the level wind on the tiny reel shoot back and forth like the bobbin on a sewing machine. The line did not melt away; it vanished. When it came to an end, it broke. The sailfish, four hundred-odd feet astern, jumped once and indignantly flung the small hook from its jaws.

Mr. Simmonds sucked his hot left thumb. "Blue marlin?"

"Sailfish."

"Must have been a whopper!"

Crunch shrugged. "Maybe forty pounds. I'll get you a new outfit. I've got a rig with eighteen-pound test line on it—five hundred yards. You can catch a sail with that—"

"I'm fishing casting tackle," Mr. Simmonds answered and he produced several spools of new line.

For an hour after that he sat alertly in the stern, watching his bait, making tentative jerks, and adding to the adhesive plaster which he had wrapped protectingly around his thumb. He was fiddling with the plaster when his next strike came. Nobody saw the fish approach—it did so from under the water, at express-train speed. There was a splash at the bait such as might be caused by pitching a brick overboard. Mr. Simmonds, accustomed to letting his reel yield a foot or two of line while his quarry mouthed a live shrimp or crab, was not prepared for this dynamic assault. He lifted his thumb. His reel backlashed and the light line snapped.

"Was it another sailfish?"

"No. It was small. Ten pounds. Maybe fifteen."

"But—what could it have been? You must have some idea?"

Crunch, anxious to dissuade the man from the folly of using so delicate an outfit, ticked off an alarming list. "It could have been a lot of things, Mr. Simmonds. A bonita. An arctic bonita. An albacore. Barracuda, dolphin, cobia, amberjack, African pompano, baby Allison tuna, mackerel, kingfish, wahoo, almaco jack, mutton snapper—plenty more."

Mr. Simmonds put on a new line. He kept putting on new lines.

At three in the afternoon, he gave up. He had succeeded in getting three jumps out of a sailfish before it broke away. He had lost six anonymous fishes. He had caught a mackerel of about four pounds, a barracuda of about nine, and a seven pound bonita—after a battle. He had almost caught a fair-sized dolphin. A nine or ten pounder, Crunch said. Mr. Simmonds was stunned—and also, he was out of fifteen-pound test line.

"We'll go in now," he said to Crunch. "I'm going to write a full letter of apology to Horace Boyle. He was right, of course. I can't even get to first base with this gear out here! What happened scares me. I'm through—licked—stuck with my own story. I'll resign from the club. I'll write a letter to Bob Breastedt, too, and tell him he's crazy!" He noticed a subdued sparkle in the captain's eyes. "Okay?"

"No," Crunch replied. "Not okay. Look here, Mr. Simmonds. You fished that tackle all day. You nailed a seven pound bonita. We had to chase it with the boat—but I bet you had to pole after that ten pound bonefish on the club wall? I imagine you've hooked some forty or fifty pound tarpon with that rig, in the Bay? You didn't get them, did you? I thought not. So far, you're even-Steven with Horace. Another thing. These fish out here have room to go deep. In the Bay, they don't. Wouldn't you like me to put over a regular sailfish rod, now, and see what you can do with it?"

Mr. Simmonds shook his head. "I'm cured," he said. "I was always nervous about the sea. Now—I know what the reason is. Someday, you or Des is going to get pulled overboard and eaten alive!"

Crunch drove home from the Gulf Stream Dock in a preoccupied mood. He gave his young son a lusty spank and he answered Sari's look of enquiry succinctly: "Maybe I thought I'd make a convert today! If I did, I was nuts. Gatsie's a whale of a good blue-water fisherman—but he'll never find it out."

Sari didn't say, "I told you so." She merely looked it—which, Crunch felt, was worse.

The days dribbled into months. Crunch made a trip to Cat Cay. He took a party to Bimini. He spent two weeks down on the edge of the Gulf of Mexico. Young Bill Adams got the measles and recovered. The Salt

Water Anglers' Club went on having Wednesday dinner and entertainment in its baroque mansion on the bay front. Mr. Simmonds' resignation was not accepted and his experiment remained a secret. The Stream vs. Bay debate settled back to normal. But not once, that winter, did the welcome voice of Horace come over the phone to the ears of the skipper.

"You should have defended him that night," Sari said. "A custard pie was a joke that he just couldn't bear. And then—he lied. He lost face—with you."

"I feel sorry for him, too," Crunch answered. "And darned disappointed. He's quit on me! I'd have bet a month's dough—"

"Don't you *ever* bet even a *day's* dough," Sari said firmly.

One afternoon when the Miami *Dispatch* and the Miami *Press* were busy trying to alibi an "abnormal" spell of cold weather—and while Crunch was occupied with the blue-fingered business of skinning and slicing a day's catch—Mr. Boyle sauntered down on the Gulf Stream Dock with his usual air of sinister cheerfulness. Unseen, he regarded Crunch for some moments and then said, "Captain, I have heard a good deal about this deep-sea fishing business. Are you free tomorrow? I would like to go out and harpoon some mackerels."

Crunch grinned. His insides warmed. But he did not turn his head. "Sorry," he replied in a formal tone. "Mackerel aren't running. Maybe you'd be interested, though, in dynamiting some cod?"

Horace, a stooped and stringy man with innocent brown eyes and a look of constitutional debility, clouted Crunch on the back so hard that he inadvertently cut a kingfish steak in two. "Register pleasure, you ape!" he said. "I've come back!"

"Back?"

"Didn't you know I was away? I've been in a byzantine bedlam called Washington. My clients wanted a few cards dealt the New Deal off the bottom of the deck. I demurred. I went to the OPM, and even the RPM, and I arranged a compromise. I rolled an egg on the White House lawn. An egg in the RFC. If I'd been old Herring-bone Simmonds, I'd have wet a line in the Potomac. Hung the Tuscaloosa, no doubt. How *is* that shrimp-catcher, anyway?"

It was a cold late afternoon. Crunch would not have minded a small blizzard, at the moment.

In the morning, the thermometer was rising as the blood pressure of the local press agents went down. Des steered the *Poseidon* between rows of pelicans annoyedly discussing migration to Panama. Horace Boyle polished his glasses with a silk handkerchief, and said, "I called on Simmonds last night."

Crunch was wrapping dental tape around the juncture of a double line.

He cocked an eyebrow. On the canopy, Des steered past a channel marker with one hand. The tide was ebbing. A large tarpon rolled on the slick surface. Des casually shied a soft drink bottle at it—and missed.

"Yeah," said Horace. "Called to tell him I'd lied about catching bonefish. Been on my conscience. He told me he'd taken a day with you—"

"Unh-hunh," Crunch said.

"—and if that stranded sea elephant can fish silk line in the Gulf Stream, I can lower myself to a day's effort on the banks! Tell Desperate to head her in, south of the pines. I've got my four-ounce, six-thread outfit along—and you've seen me kill marlin with it. I'm going to hang a couple of those bonefish today—and jerk 'em out of the water into the dinghy before they know they're hooked. *Nobody* can make a liar out of me! Except myself!" He smirked. "And a couple of guys in the SEC."

The *Poseidon* presently lay at anchor in a channel. Crunch pushed her dinghy along a tangle of mangrove with easy strokes of a stob pole. His eyes searched the almost indistinguishable edge of the crystal water for a small variety of conch shell—a shell in which the original owner was no more, and the present tenant might be a hermit crab. He found eight or nine and put them in the bait well under the center seat.

Horace regarded everything with interest. The dinghy turned from the shore toward a broad reach of bay and moved up on a limitless bank. The water over the bank was less than a foot deep. A brownish grass covered it like an uncut lawn—a grass that looked lavender from a distance—a grass as sharply visible at close range as flower stems in a glass vase.

As Horace's gaze became accustomed to the Lilliputian version of the big reef out at sea, his concentration increased. Schools of gaudy, minute fish moved in the grass. Small crabs scurried out of sight. The dinghy traversed a "pothole"—deep as a man's neck; in it were shells, a conch moving slowly, and snappers that lay stiff and vigilant, looking up at them.

"Kind of fascinating," Horace said. "Had an idea it was just muck."

"There's as much life in it," Crunch answered, pushing his stob into the ooze under the grass, "as there is in the Stream. Smaller scale, that's all. And not always small, either. I've seen tarpon that would go over a hundred pounds coming across these flats with their backs out. Ten foot sharks. Thirty pound permit—"

He fixed a hook on a light leader and attached the leader to the line with which Horace had "killed" marlin. There was a small sinker on the line. He cast—awkwardly, because the tackle was not designed for casting. He handed the rod to Horace.

"What do we do? Wait for a bite, like the barefoot boy?"

Crunch grinned and scanned the immediate sea pasturage. "Maybe. Maybe we see a bonefish coming, and sneak toward him, and drop a bait in his path."

There was a silence. Horace lighted a pipe. "Cosy," he said. "Peaceful. And you don't have to be afraid you'll soon hang somebody too big for you, hunh?" He leaned back in the dinghy's bows. "What's that!"

Crunch winked, pulled up the stob, and began poling toward a caudal fin, or a dorsal—Horace wasn't sure—that was fluttering on the surface. Crunch took the rod; the sinker shot through the air in a parabola, with the crab circling underneath it. There was a splash, and another splash, followed by a grey-white streak that manufactured itself racily. Crunch grunted. "Landed too close. Scared him away."

Horace stared at the roily trail which hung in the wake of the fish like the glow of a meteor after its blistering passage. "I was the fellow," he murmured, "who said a bonita could drown one of them! What I wonder now is—how does the bonita catch 'em?"

More time passed. Crunch sighted a second bonefish. He cast again. He gave Horace the rod. This time, there was no white-wash streak of alarmed flight. The fin on the surface turned and moved gradually toward the center of the ripples. Horace began to whisper feverishly, "Come on, bonefish! Nice fresh hermit crab! This stalking your fish is fun, hunh, Crunch?"

The bonefish caught the scent of the crab. It shot forward. Its tail quivered over the place where the bait lay.

Horace whispered, "This isn't any strike I'm getting—but I imagine it's what these flat fishermen call a nibble."

"Yeah," said Crunch. "Hit it."

Horace hit the bonefish as he would have hit a white marlin. He was good at that. The bonefish weighed, however, some four pounds. The presumptive marlin might easily have weighed fifty. The result of the marlin tactic astonished Crunch, because he had never seen anything like it in his life. The strike literally turned the bonefish upside-down in a half somersault that broke him out of water. He made a large splash and for a second lay still—dazed and no doubt baffled.

This did not surprise Horace. "Just as I thought," he murmured. "Cold turkey."

At that point, the bonefish recovered his sensibilities and hurried away, against the drag of Mr. Boyle's reel. Mr. Boyle stood up in the boat with a grimace of wonder, and watched line leave his reel. He stopped the run at a distance of four hundred feet. The bonefish came back. Horace wound violently, and kept a reasonably tight line. The fish swung around, then, and ran in surges. Presently the line went dead.

"Rubbed the hook out on the bottom," Crunch said. "Keep your rod tip higher, if you can, on the next one."

Horace sat down, looked at the flats, and forgot to light his pipe. The next fish cut the line on one of the sharp shells scattered on the grassy bottom. The third one got under a ledge at the edge of a small, blind channel; in trying to pull him out, Horace pulled out only the hook.

The fourth and last one, Horace caught. He weighed it on Crunch's scales. Six pounds, one ounce. He held it up. "Shimmery thing!" he said. "And imagine finding a devil like this, where there's hardly liquid enough to baste a leg of lamb!"

The tide had come in high. Crunch rowed back to the *Poseidon* and took Horace out to the Stream for a couple of hours of "real fishing." Horace's eyes were abstracted; he kept looking back toward the shore, where the flats were turning purple in the waning afternoon. He missed a sailfish, without seeming to notice that there had been one behind his bait. When the *Poseidon* was at last moored, he started home in a singularly vacant-minded manner. "Swell day," he said. "Educational."

Crunch did not hear from Horace for more than a week. Then the meeting was accidental. The *Poseidon* came down the Miami River from the boat yard, where she had been scraped and painted. She turned into the bay and was confronted by a brand new outboard boat which cut across her bows. The boat bristled with casting tackle. On its bottom, two bonefish glittered. In its stern, alone, was Horace Boyle. He cut his motor and came alongside.

"*Poseidon*, ahoy!" he called, grinning. "How do you like the *Nemesis*? Bought her a few days ago. Been on the flats every afternoon since! Nights, I've been over at the club, practising up my casting. Made a whole new slew of friends. And can I cast!" He reached, stood, and swung; a sinker arced into the *Poseidon*'s cockpit. He reeled himself slowly toward the *Poseidon*'s stern and fended off with his hand. "You've lost a customer, Crunch! I'm nuts about this stuff! I was getting a little old for the big ones, anyhow. I hate to do it to you—but I'm as happy as a kid! Crunch, never take a Stream man on the shoals!"

He waved. His motor snarled. He foamed down the bay. Crunch waved back—cheerfully. But neither he nor Des spoke, all the way to the dock. They were low. Not at losing a customer—but at the off-hand way in which that customer had quit them.

The dandified *Poseidon* tugged at her lines. Evening came. Crunch and Des were still aboard; seldom did that pleasure seem so small to them. Crunch read a magazine. Des watched the crowd on the dock, hoping, perhaps, to spot a prospect for the morrow. He finally spoke. "Here comes that fellow that threw the pie."

Mr. Simmonds came briskly, importantly. He hopped down into the cockpit with a crash that made the teak deck creak. "Glad I caught you fellows before you left! I've been buying tackle. A raft of it. Some is new—and some isn't. Since I saw you guys last, I've been out on three other boats. Didn't like the skippers as well. Now—I'm going to have a shot at Bimini."

Mate and Captain stared. Neither said a word: nothing adequate came to mind.

Mr. Simmonds squinted down the pier. "My chauffeur's bringing a load of the stuff now. The dockmaster said you were free for a couple of weeks. Make a nice starter. I caught a sail Wednesday. It was in Breastedt's column." He looked at them. "Guess you didn't see it. Now—I'm taking dead aim at marlin."

Crunch said, "That's great!" He rose to help Mr. Simmonds' colored chauffeur aboard. The man was heavily encumbered with reels of every size and rods of every sort known to the heavier forms of angling. Crunch began to unload the man. And his blank amazement changed to understanding.

Among the rods were three well remembered ones. Rods famous at the Salt Water Anglers' Club. Registered rods—which had once been the property of Horace Boyle. Mr. Boyle had, indeed, quit big fish fishing. But he had furnished the *Poseidon* with a substitute. He had sold his tackle—but he had not sold out his long-time fealty to Crunch and to Desperate.

The new proxy was speaking again. "Can you imagine," he said buoyantly, "a guy like Boyle giving up the big stuff, and going after minnows—at his age! Why! I'm sixty-six—and I expect to catch some too big to boat! The *sissy!*"

Thus began a train of events which led to the appearance, in many newspapers, of photographs of a retired candy merchant standing in the shadow of fishes far larger than his ample self. Thus a ten pound three ounce bonefish replaced the old one on the club walls. Thus, too, the club was provided with a classical antidote for the blue water-shallow water quarrel. But Crunch felt he'd had little enough to do with it. The *dei ex machina*—for there were two of them—were, first, the ways of fishes, and second, the ways of those fishing men who put into the sport "a little something extra you can't quite describe."

THE SHIPWRECK OF
CRUNCH AND DES

THE ARGUMENT began in New York City—if so mild a term as "argument" may be used to describe an altercation which came fairly near costing three people their lives. It happened on a March afternoon in 1942, when the local weather was threatening everybody with pneumonia by an assortment of changes from rainy warmth to frigoric drizzle and back again to tepid. The subject was the relative efficiency, as a fish-catching device, of those small artificial lures known as plugs, and that other category of single-hooked bait which includes feathers and squids.

Eight persons pored over this matter in the board room of the brokerage firm of Smith, Gladwyl, Chevvy and Kitteridge. The room had windows on four sides because it occupied one floor of a tower. A decorator had used thick gray carpeting, pink velvet drapery and chrome furniture to turn it into a chamber that was not an office at all, but resembled the boudoir of a merchant princess. Even the upper strata of Wall Street regarded it as ultra.

Chauncey C. S. Smith, senior partner of the firm, had called the meeting at the behest of various Government officials and military personages, to study, modernize and improve the fishing tackle used on lifeboats and life rafts. The men summoned by Smith, who was a world-renowned big game angler, were experts all—an ichthyologist, two tackle manufacturers, a writer of books on fish and fishing, and three guides, hand-picked by Florida's association of charter boatmen. These three had flown from Florida to New York—Crunch Adams, Desperate Smith and Captain Bill.

They sat in session around a huge table in the center of the office. Ranged on the table were samples of the tackle which had been aboard lifeboats and life rafts at the commencement of the war; some of it so primitive and inadequate that, as Captain Bill said, "it hadn't been improved or changed since the old Moby Dick days." Also on the table was a glittering collection of other baits, hooks, lures, nets, lines, sinkers,

168

leaders and other impedimenta used by the most up-to-date commercial anglers and sportsmen.

"Our tasks," Mr. Smith had said as he opened the meeting, "will be to discard outmoded gear, to winnow the new material, and to devise from it a simple kit, light, strong, durable, which will give a fighting chance— maybe I should say a fishing chance—to every man adrift in a lifeboat or an airplane's rubber boat or on a raft." Mr. Smith had spoken with a broad *a*, while elegantly fingering his gaudy foulard tie and removing two or three flecks of lint from his hand-stitched gray woolen suit.

Mr. Smith was a shock to Crunch and Des. They had known about him—his New Zealand marlin, his Chilean broadbill, his Nova Scotia tuna—but they had never seen him. Indeed, save for old Bill, they were acquainted with none of the gentlemen at the conference. Their eyes, meeting humorously at the outset of the discussion, had at once classified Mr. Smith—the fisherman elegant, the deep-water dandy, the rich sportsman whose angling consists of taking the fighting chair when the gamester strikes, whipping it with heavy, expensive tackle, dusting gen- teel hands lightly afterward, and turning the fifty-thousand-dollar cruiser toward shore for cocktails and the applause of thrilled dowagers.

Now Crunch and Des were locked in argument with Smith. "I think," Crunch said, his sunburned face dark among the pale countenances of the broker, the writer, the scientist and the manufacturers, "that we ought to have a couple of plugs in every one of these emergency kits. A man on a raft can fasten a sinker above a plug, twirl it, throw, and yank back the plug so that it gets a lot of action. That'll attract fish—and fish mean staying alive to him."

"Plugs," Mr. Smith answered, rising, pouring water from a silver vac- uum bottle and sipping it like vintage wine, "are a bit too chi-chi for our need, Crunch. The squid"—he picked one up as if it were a jewel—"is the thing. A mere lead thickening of the shaft of a hook. Scrape the lead with a knife, and it glitters. It is simple. Rugged." The word seemed inappropriate on his lips. "Yes, Crunch, old boy, the squid and the feather are our meat. The feather is a simple bait. But the plug! Too complicated, old man. Breaks easily. Tangles. Picks up weed everywhere. Rather a gadget, you know."

Des was embarrassed, but he spoke, "Why can't we have all three in every fishing set? Plugs, feathers and squids too?"

Mr. Smith sipped again. "My dear Des! For many reasons. Space must be saved; it's vital. Weight and bulk, old boy. This gear must consist of the absolute minimum. Essentials only. Besides, the men adrift won't be anglers, mostly. Few plug casters among 'em. Can't employ anything that's tricky or needs practice. Your plug—"

The plug was not Desperate's invention and he resented the word "your." He flushed. "Any fool can learn to use a plug on a hand line in ten minutes. These guys are adrift for months sometimes. And we're going to have instructions in every kit, aren't we?" He looked at the writer.

Mr. George Calden, author of *Game Fish the World Over*, was pained that anybody should disagree with Mr. Smith. "I am afraid," he said, "that I, too, hold against the plug."

"We," Crunch said, "are talking as practical men. Not theorists."

Mr. Smith smiled. That is, his thin mouth curved up. He shrugged his thick but obviously padded shoulders, "I think, gentlemen, that I may be considered as a 'practical' fisherman also."

"Hear, hear," said one of the tackle-makers pompously, and with a needling look at Crunch and Des.

Crunch came back into the argument. "All I mean is, if I were adrift in the Pacific, north or south, or the Atlantic, either one, I'd want a couple of small plugs—white with red heads and a good wiggle—in my kit. They're light and they don't take much room. Feathers and squids are good—I don't deny that—but—"

"We'll go on," Mr. Smith interrupted. "After all, gentlemen, there's a war. We're in a hurry about this business."

"Not too much of a hurry to get it right," Crunch said vigorously.

Smith—Chauncey C. S. Smith, III—turned his narrow, indolent-looking face. "You Florida boatmen are stubborn lads, I must say! Look here. I'll let you in on a confidential matter. We're going to give whatever we select a field test under Navy and Coast Guard auspices. I'll have you demonstrate the plug at that time."

Crunch was mollified. So was Des. A field test was more to their taste than bickering in a plush Manhattan office.

"The C. S. in the middle of Smith's name," Crunch said later to Des at their hotel, "stands for Café Society. Why the Government picked that vanilla custard to head this committee is one of those things not even a New Dealer can explain with graphs! Spends his nights in hot spots and his days in Turkish baths."

"Hot spot to hot spot," Des agreed. "But we'll prove what a plug can do, if we ever get a chance."

The chance eventually came. On a warm spring morning, partly overcast and lightly breezy, a Coast Guard patrol boat with no name and a number put out toward the Gulf Stream after passing through a drawbridge on the Highway that Goes to Sea between Miami and Key West. The boat was painted blue-gray. She carried a heavy machine gun foward and depth charges aft. Aboard her, besides certain special officers and her crew, were Smith and the members of his committee, flown south on a special plane.

She proceeded some miles into the ocean. Her engines were then cut and she swung about, rocking in the moderate chop. No ship and no other small boat was to be seen anywhere in the vast sweep of purple water. Such traffic as passed the Keys moved at night, and in convoy whenever possible, for here, at this time, Hitler's submarines were trying to make good the Führer's boast.

"We want," said Mr. Smith, gathering the officers and his committee in a clear space amidships, "to dispose, first of all, of Crunch and Des' claims for the plug. I therefore suggest that we put them over in the rubber boat. We will keep them in view and allow them, say, eight hours of fishing with the plugs they have brought along. Meanwhile, we on this craft will experiment with the various trolling devices chosen for testing. . . . Is that satisfactory, Commander?"

Commander Evans nodded. "You're the boss, Mr. Smith."

"Crunch?"

The skipper eyed the New Yorker. No hand-sewn gray woolens adorned him now, but a costume just as ostentatious—pearl-gray corduroy shorts, a light doeskin shirt, also gray, sandals and a pith helmet.

Crunch grinned. "Suits Des and me."

"Later," said Mr. Smith, "we'll try squids and plugs under the same conditions."

Neither Crunch nor Des bothered to argue that the "same conditions" might not arise for weeks at this season. They did not protest that eight hours was too short a period for a fair test. They had become accustomed, by then, to the arbitrary manner of Mr. Smith. They merely hoped that they would be lucky enough to nail some fish from the rubber boat before sundown.

The boat was inflated by turning a valve in a cylinder attached to its peak, or forward end. It filled with a hiss, like a child's balloon. It had a cushiony, air-packed seat in its middle, a rubberized canvas seat forward, oarlocks, a pair of aluminum oars that came in sections, zipper pockets for holding equipment, and a life line around the edge. It was bright yellow, so that it could be spotted on the blank sea. The crew dropped it overboard. The ship's cook brought some sandwiches and a canteen of water. Crunch and Des put their tackle aboard and stepped into the craft with care.

"Just like standing on a hot-water bottle," Des said. He took the oars. Crunch lounged astern. A few strokes separated them from the Coast Guard boat. Crunch waved.

"I doubt," Mr. Smith called, "if you get a single strike. We'll be around."

"Lovely guy," Crunch murmured, trailing his fingers in the warm Gulf Stream. "I betcha when he caught his big mako he had himself locked in his cabin below until somebody killed the fish."

Des chuckled and rowed. With every stroke, the life craft moved a length forward. It was very easy. Des kicked off his shoes. His bare feet on the fabric could feel the run of water beneath. "Thin," he murmured. "You'd hardly expect these things to stand up for months, but they seem to. Just the same, what an annoyed marlin or a shark could do to one in about ten seconds isn't anything you like to think about."

Crunch was already unpacking the gear. He looked back toward the Coast Guard boat. She was under way again; a trolling line was visible astern.

"Smitty," said the captain irreverently, "is sitting among those ash cans, dragging a spoon. Likes to take things easy. Probably he'll have one of the sailors hold an umbrella over him and somebody else fan him before long. It's hot out here."

"You said it."

By and by, Des stopped rowing. The lifeboat drifted, bobbing on little waves. The shore was a smoky pencil line to the west. A lighthouse stood above the horizon like a matchstick. The patrol boat dwindled. Waves splashed. The sun burned through more clouds. Gulls squeaked like rusty hinges. A man-of-war bird towered in the blue altitude.

Crunch sniffed and smiled. "Nice day."

"Nice day." Des reached for a rig. He inspected it. "Jumping Josephine," he said with approval. It was one of his favorite plugs. He coiled his line carefully on the round yellow bulge that formed the craft's side. He spun the plug in a widening circle and flung it, downwind, some twenty yards. Crunch, at the other end of the boat, followed suit with a Manitoba Bobber. Each man retrieved his bait with a series of quick yanks, re-coiling line carefully as it was brought in. A half hour passed and nothing happened.

"You'd get a sore arm," Des finally said, "if you had to do this forever."

"You gonna get a sore arm. We gotta have fish. Otherwise a few thousand guys are going fishing without plugs, and fishing for real, too, not for fun."

The sun rose higher and hung in the sky like a burning glass. They passed the canteen back and forth and patiently tossed their plugs out on the water.

"According to Pinchot," Crunch said, after a deep draft of the warming water, "we don't need this. All we need is fish. Cube the meat, squeeze it, and presto, drinking water. I wonder how thirsty you have to be to hanker after fish juice?"

"First catch your fish," Des answered.

But they didn't get a strike. Toward noon, the Coast Guard boat cruised close to them. Its motors slowed and Commander Evans hailed them, "You guys O.K.?"

"Oke!" Crunch yelled back.

"Any luck?"

"We're catching nothing but a sunburn!"

It was after four when they had a hit. Crunch had not been precisely kidding when he had spoken of sunburn. It penetrated their basic, year-round tan, heated their cheeks, dried their lips and scalded their bare shoulders. They were wearied by incessant casting. They were limp with the heat and stiff from the confinement of the boat. The continual splash of the small waves had repeatedly dampened them and the dampness had dried in fine crystals. Crunch threw for the five hundredth time. The instant his plug touched water there was a bluish swirl under it. The Manitoba Bobber vanished in such a splash as would be made by a thrown brick. Crunch yelled jubilantly. The line slid through his fingers and cut them; he had long since taken off his fishing gloves. Now, he wrapped the line in a handkerchief.

Des asked excitedly, "What is it?" and was answered by the emergence of a big dolphin—a bull—that came out shaking his head like a slugged boxer, twisted once completely, and hit the sea with a smack. It was a thirty-pounder at least.

Desperate's eyes narrowed and the corners of his mouth sank. He saw the fish shoot around in a circle some forty feet from the boat and a foot below the surface. It took off on a straightaway after that and Crunch's line snapped.

"Too big for us," Crunch said ruefully.

Des nodded. "I wonder how many guys have had that happen. Too big to hold with the tackle that can be carried in a small craft. If we'd tied the canteen or something for a float on the end of the line, we could have tossed it overboard. We'd have had a buoy on the fish then, and I could have chased it till it wore itself out."

"A point," Crunch nodded. He was already rigging a new line, unmindful of the cuts on his fingers. "Still, if we weren't just playing shipwreck, we wouldn't dare risk losing the canteen. A big dolphin like that might tow it miles—probably would steal it—and, anyway, if you were bushed from floating around the ocean, you couldn't row that much."

Des said, "Yeah," and they went on fishing.

Toward six, Crunch coiled his line on the yellow-rubber side of the boat, blinked his eyes tiredly, set the plug in the center of the coil and rose on his knees. He shaded his hand toward the lowering sun and saw nothing. He looked north and saw nothing. He looked south.

"Our ship's a doggone long way off down there," he reported. He kept on kneeling, his eyes squinted to azure slots. "She ought to be coming up here or it'll be so near dark we'll be hard to spot, but darned if it doesn't look as though she were heading straight out to sea!"

Des, in turn, coiled his line and stared. The distant speck seemed to gather speed as they viewed it, and it was presently evident that she was, indeed, making off toward the east at full throttle. Presently, she could be spotted only at intervals, and before long she disappeared.

"Now that," Des said, "looks like Smith's work."

"He wouldn't dare risk it," Crunch answered. "Not as a test or as a joke. Too much water out here. Weather too uncertain this time of year. After all, she can do twenty-five knots and she isn't too far away—"

They sat down then. They resumed fishing in a desultory manner. The sun slid behind the level bars of low stratus cloud which glowed scarlet and gold. The hues faded and the high clouds overhead took on the cosmetics of afterglow. Gulls banked, turned and winged west. The coast line dissolved into the seascape. Overhead, the vault grayed and twilight descended. The day-long variable breeze died and picked up again, coming more steadily from the northwest.

A faint false light, like a stage effect, gave them one more chance for a circular sweep of the sea. Then it was gone and night hurried over them, full of stars.

"Fine thing," Crunch said.

"We're a cinch," Des replied. "After all, they know about where we are. They know how fast the Stream is running north today. At least, if they're any good, they've estimated. They can calculate our drift. They can cruise around where they think we are, and we can hear the motors. There ought to be some kind of signaling gear in one of the pockets."

They looked. There wasn't.

"Anyway," Des said, "they'll cut their engines every so often, and we can holler when they get near where we are." He didn't believe it.

"Sure." Crunch picked up the canteen and shook it. "About a cupful. Smart guys, we are. Not a sandwich left. Going to be a long sit, pal."

"You said it." Without saying so, they were agreed that rescue would have to wait for morning.

"Think you could sleep? Now, I mean? We'll have to guess the watches. I'll take it for a few hours and wake you."

"Okay." Des stretched out, his knees bent up over the center seat. "Comfortable, with only two of us. Hate to have about six here. Better save the water for tomorrow, hunh?"

"Yo."

Crunch watched his mate relax and presently heard his regular breathing. The skipper's muscles were painful from throwing the light plug all day long, but he began again. If they were leaving the boat out on purpose—as a test—he might as well do his best.

Des slept. The stars rode up the sky. Crunch fished.

It was much later when Des sat up suddenly and shook himself. He looked up at the Dipper. "Say. It's past my turn, hunh? Must be one or two o'clock. You sleep now." He saw the white spot of the plug in the sea. "Still at it?"

"I was. After all, there's guys doing it tonight all over the world by the hundreds, and nobody coming for them in the morning. We might as well carry on with the experiment. But if I find out Smith ordered this little routine on purpose, he'd better talk fast or I'll hang a lamp he can show to café society for the next fortnight—and I do mean fortnight!"

Des took over. Crunch lay down.

When he woke, the rubber boat was tossing uncomfortably. The east exhaled a pallor that was not yet light, but it silhouetted the determined jaw of Desperate as he threw, once again, line, leader and lure. The wind carried it out of sight. A crisp wind, now, and cool. Nor'west. Crunch yawned and his lips felt as though they were cracking. He licked them. Salt. He leaned over the side and washed his face. The water was warm. He rinsed out his mouth and wanted to swallow, but spat instead. Thirsty already. It grew light. Des was watching him. He looked haggard and his beard had pricked through his skin during the night.

"Can you sleep some more?" Crunch asked.

The mate shook his head. "Naw. Blowing up. Going to get rough. I've been sitting here the last couple of hours thinking what I'd say to Mr. Smith. They better find us soon. Want some water?"

"I'll take a sip." Crunch took one. Then Des.

They judged the passing of time by the sun. The day was clear and the wind chilly. It brought aboard spray enough to dampen them every time they began to dry out. Crunch could feel the gritty powder of salt on his face when it was dry and the bite of the wind when it was wet. The sun burned them without providing warmth enough to relieve the shiver of their wet bodies.

"Wouldn't care much about this as a steady thing," Des said. "Wanna fish?"

Crunch started again. His arms hurt, but the exercise was restorative. He kept rising up and looking, but there wasn't anything to see—no land, no boats, no planes—zero.

"If the Gulf Stream happens to be really running," Des said toward noon, "we may be heading north from where we were at about six knots."

Crunch grunted. "And we've been at it a long time. Say twenty hours from when they last had a bead on us. That's maybe a hundred and twenty miles. Whither, so to speak, are we drifting? Of course, though, the Stream probably isn't running that fast and the wind's holding us back."

"But just the same, there's a lot of water to hunt in by now, and this isn't much of a thing to spot."

"No."

They kept talking. They ran out of cigarettes. After a while, they realized that their growing thirst made conversation a luxury. So they stopped talking and fished.

In the middle of the afternoon, Crunch got another hit. He yanked in his line, hand over hand, with great energy. A three-pound dolphin came aboard. Crunch picked up the flopping fish and looked at it. "I could kiss you," he said. "At least, we don't have to starve."

A second dolphin hit Desperate's line a moment later, and he boated his fish. Quickly, he produced the knife which was to accompany the fishing kit they were helping to design. He cut off the tail and fins of the dolphin and tossed them overboard. He handed the knife to Crunch. "There must be a school of these babies. Chum for them." They chummed, throwing in the entrails and the heads, cut in pieces. They saw the flash, several times, of other dolphin feeding on the gobbets, but they were able to hook no more. The school swam out of range.

When they were sure of that, they looked at the two fish they had on board. Des said, "Well?"

Crunch nodded. He stripped off his jersey—neither of them had worn a shirt when they had embarked the day before. He washed out as much of the dried salt as he could, and wrung it. He and Des carefully fileted the fish. They cut the slabs of meat into small cubes. They put a double handful of the cubes into the jersey. They next shared the balance of the water. After that, Crunch held the canteen between his knees and took one end of the jersey. Des took the other. They twisted, wringing out a trickle of clear liquid from the meat—perhaps a cupful and a half in all.

Crunch took a sip. He lifted an eyebrow. "By golly, it isn't salty, at that! Tastes like something familiar—like clam juice. Like unsalted clam juice!" He sipped again and passed to Des his share.

Afterward, they looked at the white fish meat that remained. Des tasted it. "Okay," he said.

But Crunch shook his head. "Me, I'm not that hungry yet."

They went back to fishing, relieved by the liquid. If they could keep getting fish, they could stave off severe thirst indefinitely. And they were beginning to think about the length of their sojourn as indefinite. They resumed casting.

In the late afternoon a plane crossed their area of vision, but it was many miles away. They didn't even bother to wave; as sailors, they knew the futility of that. They watched it and went on fishing. The sea piled up five or six feet high. The rubber boat rode with a combination of motions—a buoyant wallow. Dusk ultimately descended.

"If it weren't for the dim-out," Crunch said, "we might get some idea of where we are. We can't be so doggoned far off the coast yet. If it were peacetime, we'd catch the glow of Miami. And if there weren't so much west in the wind, I'd try rowing. Kind of useless, the way it is. With any kind of a sail we could go the other way, and hit into the Bahamas someplace."

"Yeah. Someplace. Before the Stream takes us north of them and the next points are in Europe."

They thought that over. Crunch laughed. "A fine bunch of sailors we are! Pile into this bath-mat dinghy without water enough or provision, a sea anchor, a sail, a compass! We deserve to spend a week out here!"

"Yeah. Get a free ride as far as maybe Charleston."

"Scared?" Crunch asked.

Des thought. "Yeah. You?"

Crunch shrugged. "Sure, I'm scared. If you hadn't been, I'd have given you a devil of an argument. Figured they'd find us today."

"Me too. If the wind hauls, of course, we'll be okay. We can lash the shirts and our pants on the oars and paddle with our shoe soles and start making in toward the Florida coast. If it doesn't, we better start thinking hard."

"But we better just drift tonight. Best way. They'll try to figure our position on the basis of drift. Tomorrow—"

Tomorrow was a long time coming. The wind blew harder. It pushed and whistled on the jagged sea, scouring salty crests into their faces. They bailed with their hands and with their jerseys, sopping up the water and wringing it out. In the blackest part of the night an extra-steep wave turned them over.

Crunch had been resting groggily, sitting on the boat's elastic bottom. He was thrown out into the warm sea. As he went, he grabbed the light Manila line that encircled the craft. When he came up, he was still holding on.

He bellowed. "Des!"

"O.K., pal! I'm right behind you! Let's flip her back!"

It was easier to say than to do. Every time they turned the craft up on edge, the wind shoved it back. They tried a half dozen times before they got the boat righted. They climbed in and kept low, with the water gushing around their chins. They bailed furiously, but they were exhausted by the time they had the boat empty.

When morning came, they sorted out their gear. They'd kept the canteen, the tackle and the knife tied to the boat. These articles floated around them now. They brought them back aboard and untangled the lines with stiff, shaky fingers. They coiled them and recommenced to fish.

"I don't know when I've enjoyed fishing less," Des said.

"And I can't remember wanting a fish more. I'm hungry enough for it now. Two days! Golly! You sure change your appetite fast!"

"Your lips are cracking pretty bad," Des said.

"Yours too. And my tongue feels big. Funny. I don't suppose we're thirsty, as thirsty really goes. But—"

"We may be yet."

"Yeah. We may be yet. Let's fish." The forenoon wore on. The wind grew fresher. A real sea began to build. Crunch's eyes, glazed, bloodshot, uncertain, kept watch. Within himself he struggled to decide whether to go on drifting, to try to row toward Florida or to attempt to sail southeast before the wind. It seemed to him that he had never been faced by a problem so difficult. But at last he made up his mind. "A northwester'll blow out in a day or two, Des, as a rule. She'll haul northeast or east, and shove us back across the Stream slantwise, so I say we save our strength and drift."

"Just about the answer I was getting myself. . . . Hey!" Des shouted the last word and pointed. They rose on another wave. Not far away was the Coast Guard boat—or another like it. They staggered to their knees on the unsteady bottom and waved and yelled. The boat saw them and plunged forward, with a sailor fanning his hat on the forward deck, and bow waves flying out like wings. Somebody threw a rope.

Commander Evans himself helped them on board. He was ghost white and the muscles in his cheeks showed. "Thank the Lord!" He pumped their hands. "You all right?"

"We could use a drink."

"Cook!" the commander bellowed. "Break into my private stock of bourbon—"

"Water," Crunch said somewhat thickly.

They gurgled it down and followed it with hot coffee and cigarettes.

Commander Evans was abjectly apologetic. "You see, late that first afternoon we got word from a plane south of us—out of sight of you, I guess—that a sub was running on the surface not more than a couple of miles from our position. Naturally, we ran for it. She must have dived—we never saw a thing. And right in the middle of the uproar both our engines cut out. We've been looking for all you guys ever since. We thought you'd lie doggo. Only thing to do. We figured the Gulf Stream drift as closely as we could. Of course, everybody available is out—

planes, blimps—but there's a lot of water here, and it seems that the Stream ran backward for about ten hours. It does, occasionally."

"Yeah. It does." Crunch looked at the red-rimmed eyes of the Coast Guard crew. He thought over the words he had just heard. "What do you mean—'all' you guys?"

"Smith," said the Commander. "We put him over too. In a Navy raft. An hour after we planted you. He's still unsighted."

Crunch murmured his opinion in whispered, knotty words. He had more coffee, eggs and some bacon. So did Des. Commander Evans went out on deck. A plane zoomed noisily. The radio operator kept talking near by. It seemed to Crunch that he said, "Roger," thousands of times.

Crunch was falling asleep when the man yelled through a window, "Commander! The blimp's sighted a raft! One man on it! Sounds like ours!"

The patrol boat put on her last ounce of speed and headed for the position of the raft. Crunch and Des roused themselves and went out on deck. The blimp could be seen hanging low in the sky some five miles off.

"Imagine." Des muttered it in Crunch's ear. "Navy raft! One with a slat deck that lets down, hunh? He has to stand waist-deep in the water. And he was out as long as we were! Doggone, I'll take bets he's dead, the screwball!"

Mr. Smith was not dead. When they came alongside, he waved placidly. He was, it is true, standing waist-deep in the water and he had been wet continuously during his sojourn. However, he seemed to be in good shape. A shark—a little one weighing perhaps a hundred pounds— was moored to the raft by its life rope. The shark was still alive, roped by the tail, and swimming feebly. Lashed to the top of the canvas-covered balsa ring that made the oval raft were slabs of fish meat—a dozen or more. On Mr. Smith's head was a broad, stiff contraption of fishskin and fishbones, tied under his chin with fishline. It was not a hat of any known pattern, but it shaded his face from the burning sun. As the patrol boat drew near, Mr. Smith took a small waterproof sack from the breast pocket of his doeskin shirt. He opened it and fumbled a moment. He closed it and returned it to his pocket. When he looked up, he was smoking a cigarette. And he came aboard unassisted.

His first words were, "What about the other chaps?" Then he saw them.

The cook hurried forward with water. Mr. Smith drank a little. Then he waved the pitcher aside.

"No real thirst. Used to it, anyway. Africa, you know. . . . Well, how'd you do, boys?"

They told him.

"Two dolphin, eh?" He yawned delicately. "Bit sleepy. Good. Maybe we'll include a plug, at that, if you nailed a couple of dolphin. I got eight. Two kingfish. Snagged three turbot yesterday. A tripletail—stole that. Got one mackerel and two bonitos, so I had plenty to eat and drink. And a meat bank, besides—that shark alive, in case it began to get tough. He attracted fish too. Chilly, though, wasn't it?"

Crunch understood Mr. Smith then. He grinned, although it hurt his mouth to do it. "I think I'll change my vote. Squids and feathers will do."

Mr. Smith tapped the ash from his cigarette and threw his fishskin hat overboard. "Suppose we get a little shut-eye and then try the trolling gear—what say?"

Crunch felt his insides rebel. He denied them. "Suits me."

Commander Evans spoke then. "I think, Mr. Smith, we'd better put in. That writer has been seasick for forty-eight solid hours. One of those other men—Mr. Stevens—is in the same shape. And provisions are low."

"Very well, Commander." Mr. Smith walked with Crunch and Des toward the staterooms below. Toward sleep.

"I owe you one terrific apology," Crunch said. "I thought—"

Mr. Smith lighted a fresh cigarette and stood on the companionway looking down at Crunch. "Yeah. It was written all over you in New York. You thought I was a phony. Fair weather sailor and pretty-boy angler. Well, you know, I am something of a meadow lark, at that, in my lighter moments. But I'll tell you one. I thought, from the way you and Des argued with me, that your reputations had gone to your heads. Wise guys. Just now, when you were willing to keep on going if I was, I changed my mind. Matter of fact, I'm falling apart from the knees down and the shins up. We've got a swell practical kit for the fellows at sea in this way. Afterward, when it's all over, I want to charter you two guys and take you clear to New Zealand."

"It's a go," Crunch said—and all three shook on it, widening the salted cracks in one another's hands and widening their grins to match.

TROPHY

ON A Sunday morning during the unforgettable hot spell in Miami's summer of 1942, Crunch, Sari and young Bill Adams arrived at the Gulf Stream Dock shortly after the early sun had highballed another scorcher. Mr. Williams, the dock manager, regretting each one of his scores of extra pounds, gazed at Sari ruefully. "It isn't human," he said, "for anybody to look so starched and cool!"

The skipper's dark-haired wife smiled. "It won't last. Bill wanted to see his father start out fishing. Then he wanted to fish from the dock. And I thought there might be a breeze down here."

"A breeze," said Mr. Williams bitterly. He glanced from the bald, blue sky to the waters of the bay, which were as flat and warm as standing tea. "There aren't any breezes any more! A mosquito with a lame wing could probably fly from here to Nassau without getting half a point off his course!"

Sari laughed and led Bill down onto the dock. It was already crowded with soldiers and civilians preparing for fishing in the Gulf Stream. Des was on board the *Poseidon* with three of the four sergeants who were to make up the day's party. Crunch had gone to the locker to rig a hand line for his son.

The young woman sat down on a bench. Bill leaned precariously over the oily tide and watched the dim forms of fish moving slowly, close to the bottom. The scene, except for the unusual temperature and the presence of many uniforms, was just as it had always been. The voices of the people had the same ring of expectancy, whether they were in uniform or not. Some were boasting of what they would catch. Some were betting on it. In the late afternoon, Sari reflected, most of the boastful ones wouldn't have much to say. A few would be even more excited than they were now, and trying hard not to show it.

Of course, it was really altogether different. Crunch and Des fished soldiers exclusively now, on Sundays, their one day off. Weekdays, the *Poseidon*'s charters were irregular. Sometimes she was occupied with a volunteer job for the Coast Guard Auxiliary. Sometimes she lay for days at anchor while her skipper and mate worked long hours in a shipyard, repairing small craft for the Navy. All different. It just sounded the same and had the same salty smell—which fishing would, forever.

As Sari sat there, a familiar character personified itself. She had seen men like him a thousand times, watching the goings and comings of the boats. Men with ardent, luminous eyes, with a knowing interest in every bit of gear and tackle that went aboard every boat, with an attention to the detail and a look, underneath, of ecstasy mingled with hopelessness. In this case, the man was in his thirties; everything about him was middle, Sari thought; middle-sized, medium brown hair, medium weight, hazel eyes—the kind of person you could look at in a crowd and lose sight of if he merely moved a few feet.

Little by little, as if the fishing cruisers were magnets, he moved toward them and peered more closely, more shiningly. The boldness inspired by his fascination finally brought him to within a few feet of Sari's bench. He had not even observed her existence—which most men noticed at once, and kept noticing. He was dressed in khaki pants and shirt, faded, not fitting well; probably planning a day of fishing from the bridge and just having a dream, like the thousand others, of what it would be like to go out over the abyssal pastures of the whoppers. It startled Sari to realize that the faded khaki was a uniform. The man was a private in the Air Forces.

She watched him watch until his concentration became part of her own feelings. And suddenly she heard her own voice. "Why don't you go out on one of the boats? Several of them are making up parties?"

The man turned, smiled brightly and shook his head. "I hadn't made any arrangements. This was my first chance to get over here. I'm just kind of looking."

"Fisherman?" Sari knew he was. But she knew, too, that you always asked.

"Well, fresh water. Crazy about it. Trout. Bass. I had a crack at muskies one year. Got six too." His voice wasn't much either. Not obsequious, but deferential, as if he had always talked to people who knew more than he, who had accomplished more, who impressed him. "I'd sure like—" His shoulders lifted. "Maybe someday before I get shipped out I can get in one of these parties." His amiable and unimportant face grew intense. "In fact, I've gotta!"

He said it with such emphasis that she repeated it. "Got to?"

The private nodded several times. He still had not noticed that Sari was young and beautiful. He realized only that she knew something about fishing and was sympathetic. "Yes. That's the way I feel about it. And I'm scared by the feeling, I guess. You see—"

He talked, keeping his eyes on the busy fishing boats.

When he finished, Sari stood up. "I think you do 'gotta.' What's your name?"

"Munn. Clarence Munn."

Sari walked over to the *Poseidon*. The fourth sergeant had arrived. Des was about to cast off. She looked down at the quartet of noncoms in the cockpit; they looked up at her—and kept looking. One of them made his mouth into the beginning of a whistle. She saw it and said quickly, cheerfully, "I'm Crunch's wife."

The man who had started to whistle said, "Oh-oh!"

Sergeants, she thought. *Well, they all look as if they could be tough when it was necessary. But they also look friendly.* "You fellows think you could stand it to take along a fifth man?"

"If it was you," one of the noncoms said, and they laughed.

So did Sari. "Not me. A private."

"Listen, Mrs. Crunch, a private among four sergeants!"

"He wouldn't bother you any."

"Bother *us!*"

"He's a nice little guy. If he goes it'll take a dollar and a half off the cost for each of you. I'd appreciate it." She saw Crunch approaching from the top controls and avoided his look of indignation. "Five men can fish almost as much as four. This one has a special reason for wanting to go. No kidding! He's practically frantic for a day outside! It would be mighty decent!"

One of the sergeants—the one with the fanciest chevrons—looked at the others and then said, "Throw him aboard, lady. If we run out of food we can eat him."

Private Clarence Munn found himself in the cockpit of the *Poseidon* as it was pulling away from shore. The thing had happened so suddenly— the young lady had just grabbed him and led him down the dock—that everything seemed blurred and a little crazy. His face was red and he was sweating. He started to salute and remembered you didn't have to. The men came forward. One by one, they clapped him mightily on the back. They shook his hand, bore down on it. "Glad to have you with us, Munn," they said, grinning. "Take a seat. Take that big seat in the center in the stern. We want you to be comfortable."

He just dropped his jaw and couldn't answer. But his back had withstood the hearty hand smacks and his hand was not crushed.

"Been down here long?" The man who asked that had red hair and blue eyes that were full of fooling.

"Four weeks, sir." He remembered you didn't have to say "sir."

"Where'd you come from?"

"New York."

"State or city?"

"City."

"Well, Munn, you're in pretty good shape for a city man. You have the Army to thank for that."

"Yes. I kind of like it. But I always kept fit."

"You did, eh? How? Pushing into subways?"

"I have a bar bell. Morning exercises."

The red-headed sergeant seized Munn's biceps. His eyebrows shot up. "Darned if he isn't telling the truth! What'd you do in New York? Shovel coal?"

"I was a clerk in a store."

"Well, for Pete's sake!"

The *Poseidon* entered Government Cut. Des, red-faced, suffering embarrassment with the unwanted and unexpected passenger, had been furiously working with leader wire, hooks and feathers. Now, carrying three rods, he hurried into the cockpit. "Ready to fish three lines," he said. "Mr. Smith, Schultz, Tollivan, you start."

The noncoms stared at Des, bridled a little, and accepted his authority. This was, after all, a ship. They didn't know anything about ships. They took the rods and sat where they were told, following Desperate's instructions about letting out line. That left only one sergeant to kid the miserable Munn—and, a second later, a jack hit. Munn was forgotten as the three noncoms undertook to counsel their companion, who was too occupied with the hard rushes of the jack to do more than swear back steadily.

While the jack was being subdued, gaffed and boated, Crunch got the attention of Munn and showed him how to climb out a window and up on the canopy. Munn sat on one of the little stern-facing seats with a quiet sigh of relief. As long as the four men below concentrated on fishing, he would be safely out of sight. The sun was scalding hot; the metalwork on the small fishing seat was untouchable; but he was content.

The *Poseidon* headed north at the turning buoy. Much of the charterboat fleet was already in evidence, outriggers lowered in their trolling V, baits skittering, and fish engaging the baits. Quite often, across the satiny blue sea, came the shout of an angler who had made contact. Plenty of fish and the fish were hungry. Once, in his first hour on top, Munn was convulsed by the tremendous sight of a hooked sailfish, leaping, a couple of hundred yards behind a cruiser. The boat was a quarter of a mile off, but Munn plainly saw the fish. Down in the cockpit during that time, the sergeants, taking turns on three lines, nailed two bonitos, three dolphin and a mackerel.

Crunch had resented Sari's last-minute intrusion of Private Munn. But as he watched the man drink in the fishing he began to feel an interest like Sari's. Finally he said, "Sari said you had a particular reason for wanting to fish?"

The soldier was a long time in answering. He seemed embarrassed. "Ever been in New York City?"

"Sure."

"Ever been in Sawtelle and Slater's?"

Crunch's eyes jumped up at the medium-sized man. They were surprised. Sawtelle and Slater was one of the largest sporting-goods firms in New York, and probably in the world. Its windows, filled with stuffed animals, fish, guns, tackle, safari equipment, tents, and all the paraphernalia of the outdoors, were a stopping place for thousands of nostalgic gentlemen walking on Fifth Avenue.

Crunch nodded.

"I work there," Munn said. "Fourteen years."

"But—"

The private smiled a little. "I'm thirty-four. Started when I was twenty. For the last eight years I've run the trout-fly department."

Crunch said, "Oh." He remembered the department.

"Mr. Gleason—he's my boss—has kept a place on the wall for me for five years, now. You know the fish floor?"

"Yeah. Like the palm of my hand. And I know Mr. Gleason too."

Munn swallowed, thinking of the distance and the difference between Air Force training in Miami Beach, and Sawtelle and Slater. "We've got several world-record fish mounted and displayed there."

Crunch cut the engines, but otherwise he ignored the whoop from below that had followed the hard hit of a bonito. "Des and I helped get the mako you have up over the elevator doors."

"I know that. I realized it a few minutes ago. Thinking of the names." Munn turned and watched the fight made by the red-headed sergeant to bring the bonito to boat. "Well, if I ever get a decent fish and have it mounted, Mr. Gleason has promised to put it up behind my counter. Helps, you know. The customers are impressed if the salesman can point to a good fish and say he took it. The salesmen's names go on plates under the fish too. Don—he's trout flies, my assistant—has a big salmon up. Smith in spoons and feathers, has a wahoo. I don't have my fish yet. I caught some muskies, but they were rather small. I was telling your wife about it—"

There was a flicker in Crunch's eyes. "I see." He frowned. "Would a sailfish do?"

"Would it!" Mr. Gleason has caught four and he talks about it for at least an hour every day!"

"Have to be a record breaker?"

"Lord, no! Any sailfish would do! If I had a sailfish behind my spot it would certainly make that wahoo and the salmon look cheesy!"

"There are quite a few around today," Crunch said quietly. He watched Des flip the bonito aboard. "We'll see what we can find."

Mistiness enveloped Private Munn, and what happened was never wholly clear to him afterward. Des gave him a rod. He fished straight back from his perch over the noncoms. Three other lines trailed in the water, but Munn watched one bait only. He had read about the matter; attention was half the game. His attention was continuous like that of an electric eye. His bait fluttered along, sometimes a foot under water, sometimes on the surface.

He did not see Crunch focus on a busy cruiser, far away. He did not observe two other cruisers slide up near the first and become equally busy. He did not see the slow smile that came and stayed on the captain's face. There was a school of sails—a big one—out there; and they were hitting everything.

Munn did hear shouts below. But, so concentrated was he upon his bait, that he did not realize they were different. No mere bonito had hit. A large sailfish was racing along behind one of the sergeant's lines. The shouting increased as a second sail came up behind the second outrigger. Munn ignored it all, and gasped only when he saw a vast, dark shadow leap out of the blue nothing and materialize as a colossal fish behind his own hook. He gulped and tried to remember the directions. The fish shot forward. Munn felt a very light jerk. He released the reel spool and let his line drop astern. At the same time, the two outrigger lines were falling. At the same time, also, Des was earnestly advising the sergeant on the fourth line to drop back. Crunch was just looking. He had seen the sight before, but not often. Everywhere around the *Poseidon*'s baits were sailfish, cutting across, racing one another to the strips, breaking water, plunging away with bait in their jaws. Twenty sails, at least, Crunch thought.

All four lines came taut at about the same time. The sailfish that had taken one outrigger bait stripped it off and went free. But three big ones were hooked simultaneously. Sergeants Shultz and Tollivan and Private Munn, above, found themselves hanging to bent rods on which were sizzling reels, while three fish hurtled away from the *Poseidon*. Presently, far away, as the boat slowed, first the Munn sailfish, then the Schultz specimen, and, last, the Tollivan fish, slammed into the air, high and twisting. Then all three fish disappeared and took separate paths. Lines began to cross under water. Even Crunch couldn't tell exactly what was happening.

Munn was standing up, bellowing louder than he ever had in his life. All he yelled was, "It's on!" but he sounded as if he were trying single-handedly to get out the engines for a ten-alarm fire. Crunch, Des and Sergeant Smith lowered Munn down to the cockpit, where the other two anglers were also roaring with excitment. Sailfish seemed to be everywhere, jumping, rolling, tail-walking, turning the placid sea into wet acres that resembled the basin at the foot of a waterfall.

Munn sweat and reeled. By and by he no longer felt the fish. "Gone," he said with flat despair. He sat down in a vacant chair. He reeled in his slack line mechanically and watched Sergeant Schultz perform the difficult task of carrying his rod under the rod of Sergeant Tollivan in order to uncross lines.Then his own suddenly and amazingly came taut once more and his personal sailfish did a couple of outside loops about fifty feet from the *Poseidon*. Private Munn resumed battle, and his shout.

The *Poseidon* tied up as the sun went down. Onto the Gulf Stream Dock, Des heaved one after the other, five sailfish. Five firsts. They had caught three more and released them. It had been a field day for all the boats. In a mild delirium, Munn posed for a picture with the four sergeants, who were treating him by then as a near equal. They barged off to celebrate the occasion. Munn stayed. Consciousness was beginning to return to him. In his mind's eye he could already see his trophy above the counter to which he would return after the war. A magnificent fish, eight feet and one inch, sixty-four pounds, gleaming bronze, pale silver and glowing violet, its polkadotted dorsal spread in splendor, and a small, conservative plate: CAUGHT BY CLARENCE MUNN OFF MIAMI, FLORIDA.

But a sane and practical question kept intruding into Munn's mind: How much? His capital was low. After he had accepted Sari's congratulations, thanked her overflowingly, and congratulated young Bill on his string of grunts, he took Crunch aside. "The mounting—it'll run to—?"

Crunch saw the look. "Well, Hal Flannagan—he's the best taxidermist—usually charges fifteen bucks a foot for the kind of mount you want. Special rate for service men is ten dollars. That'd be eighty."

Munn gulped slowly. "I see."

Crunch was about to make a further suggestion, but Mr. Williams' voice on the loud speaker called him to the phone. A mate, who had been standing by, sidled up to Private Munn. "If you can hold the fish till tomorrow I can get it done for fifty bucks."

To Private Munn fifty dollars was nearly as bad as eighty. This cost was an element for which he had in no way prepared. Indeed, being a shy and modest man, he had never actually expected to go sailfishing, let alone to catch one. He looked at the mate. "What do I do? Leave it here?"

"Can't do that." The mate pressed a card on him. "Call me tomorrow. Stache the fish away. If you leave it, it'll be carted off and ground up for fertilizer."

Munn had paid Crunch for his share of the charter. He stood alone on the busy dock with his fish. It was twilight. Mates and passengers, everywhere, were dragging sailfish by their bills to the racks for flashlight pictures and to the scales for weighing. Munn felt lost. He stared at the smooth, metalic grandeur of his fish. He had nine dollars in his pocket. A madness overtook him. He seized the sail by its bill, slid it along the murky dock and on to a place of hiding under a ficus tree beyond the parking yard. He phoned furtively for a cab.

Private Munn shared a ground-floor room in a small, luxurious beach hotel with three other privates. That night the three returned to their quarters together. Good fellows, Munn had thought. They came in noisily—and stopped cold.

"What is it?" one of them said.

Cold sweat broke out all over Munn. "What is what?" he asked vaguely.

"Fish," said the second roommate. "So help me!"

They stared angrily at Munn. He sat up. "It's a sailfish," he said finally, in a rather high tone. "I caught it."

"A sailfish! Go take a shower, man!"

"It's here. Under my bunk. It's dry and clean and wrapped in newspapers."

"Here! How in the name of—!" The trio expressed three separate forms of irritated incredulity.

Tenderly Munn slid the huge, wrapped parcel from under his bunk. He sketched the importance of his trophy to himself and told of his day at sea. His roommates listened, satisfied by the visible proof, but not at all satisfied with its presence. "How did you get it in here?"

"I slid it into a hedge in a private yard down the street. Then I kept an eye out for MP's and the guards. I sort of shifted it up to our window. It was open and dark. I dropped in the old fish. Then I came around and reported in and came up here and pulled the blackout curtains so I could wrap it."

"You can't have it here in the morning! Or even tonight," one of the three said.

"I gotta keep it and get it mounted," Munn replied desperately. "I gotta—that's all there is to it!"

"There's a wood box outside the house next door. The place is boarded up. We could sneak it out again and in there if we were quiet." It was the youngest of the roommates.

"Somebody might steal it!" Munn said.

Another of the men lighted a cigarette and lay down on his bunk. "Munn," he said, gazing at the ceiling. "I like you. You're a good little egg. But if you don't have that fish out of here in ten minutes, I'm going to call the guard, and I'm not kidding! We have to sleep here. Come on, toss her out. Duck the light, fellows!"

When Munn went to bed that night, his sailfish was in the empty wood box of the house next door to the hotel. He slept uneasily. He intended to ask for time off, on the following day, but he didn't have the nerve. Military duties made impossible even so much as a peep at the mighty treasure until late afternoon. Then, after retreat and before supper, he managed, by skulking and short, unobtrusive dashes, to get to the wood box. He opened the lid. His fish, indeed, was still there. He was gazing at it, trying to think of a plan, when somebody tapped him on the shoulder. Munn turned slowly because his muscles had petrified. An MP, no doubt. It would mean the guardhouse.

It was not an MP, however. It was a testy-looking man in an informal uniform with a revolver at his hip. "Whatcha doing, soldier?"

Munn tried to explain. The man looked. "Well, get it outta here. I'm the watchman for this place, see?"

"Yes, sir."

The watchman watched. Munn despairingly labored to lift out his wrapped fish. "If you'd just let me sort of store it here for another day, mister—"

"If it was here another day, there'd be posses tryin' to find out what and where it was. Take her down on the beach and bury her."

Munn felt sudden relief. "All right, I will. I'll—"

That night he slept better. The sail, wrapped in paper and several layers of burlap which he had rustled from the hotel disposal heap, lay carefully interred in sand. He could do something about it, perhaps, the next day.

He did not hear the wind gather and the thunder roll as a heavy squall blew in from the northeast sometime after midnight. Consequently he was as much at a loss as any of his fellows when the men in his detachment were lined up, next morning, in the bright sunshine in front of the hotel. A shavetail by the name of Roberts presently addressed them. He seemed good-humored, in a nasty way.

"The subject," he said dryly, "is sailfish."

Munn stiffened as he never had for the command, "Attention!"

"Very dead sailfish, the property of a member of this unit, according to our intelligences. Name unknown. Said sailfish has washed up in front of the hotel. Will the owner please step one pace forward?"

There was no motion in the somewhat uneven ranks.

The lieutenant's eye ranged up and down them.

"I believe that I could detect the owner of said fish, if necessary," he went on. "I do not need to point out that the matter is irregular. If—"

Munn stepped forward. "It's my fish." His voice wavered.

The shavetail walked up to him, followed by a sergeant. "Yours?"

"Yes. It's mine! I caught it. I wanted to get it mounted! I mean—yes, sir!"

"Can you drive a jeep, private?"

"Yes, sir. Munn, sir. Clarence T."

The lieutenant eyed his man. "Sergeant, see that he gets a jeep. The one we used last week on the emergency garbage detail. Private Munn, remove said fish in said jeep. Take it to the South Dock. Sergeant, see that this man has an order for a rowboat. Munn, you will row the fish no less than half a mile from shore and dispose of it. Return and thoroughly clean and police the jeep. Then report to Mess Sergeant James for duty until further notice. Your experience with deceased fish should make you invaluable around the company kitchen." He faced the men. "Detail, dis-missed!"

It was a signal for a general shout of laughter. Munn walked off feebly, trailing the sergeant.

"Said fish," when he had been shown it, proved not to be the shining miracle that had come aboard the Poseidon. The seas of the previous night had uncovered it, unwrapped it and carried it a few rods south to the beach in front of the hotel. True, its tough hide was unbroken. But its color was an all-over slaty gray. Its eyes had no luster. There was a puffiness about it.

After an initial blunder, Munn approached it from the windward side, rewrapped it in heavy paper and carried it to the jeep. He obtained his clearances and drove away. Halts for traffic made him uncomfortable. He was even less comfortable when the MP acting as checker at the entrance to South Dock waved him to a stop. "What you got there?"

"A dead fish."

"I'll examine it."

"Here is my order to get a rowboat," Munn said worriedly.

The MP stripped back the paper officiously. In a moment he stopped. He stepped clear. He merely scowled at the order. "Proceed! Why didn't you tell me how dead?"

Because the rowboat had been taken over by the Army, it was painted a funereal brown. Munn's spirit was also brown, although he did smile at the thought of how the Navy must feel when it saw land camouflage afloat. He rowed patiently into the bay, upwind, reflecting that the greatest asset he had ever possessed—a sailfish—had turned into his greatest liability.

When he was sure that he was a good half mile offshore he stepped to the stern and pushed the burden overboard. It floated and the wet paper spread out around it. He sighed with relief, sat down again, took the oars, turned and rowed sadly toward shore. He had covered a distance equivalent to a city block when a fast gray motorboat shot up behind him and made a circle around him. He rocked on its swells. The boat stopped. A man in a Coast Guard uniform with a chief's hat cupped his hands. "What was that you dumped in the bay?"

"A sailfish. A dead one." He remembered the MP. "Very dead."

"Soldier, don't you know you're not allowed to dump that sort of thing in the bay? Fouls it. Might damage a fast boat. Go back and pick it up and take it ashore."

"I had orders to dispose of it here."

The Coast Guardsman was emphatic. "So what. Now you got orders to take it back. Get going! We'll stand by until you prove it was a sailfish. We saw you jettison something big."

Munn rowed sluggishly while the Coast Guard followed. He tried, for a while, to make out that he had no idea where the fish could be found. The chief bawled into his hands again: "Quartering off your port bow!" Then, under the assumption that he was dealing with a landlubber, he added, "Up ahead of you about fifty strokes and to your right!"

The men on the motorboat watched while Munn undid the sodden papers, heaving up their contents by its bill to prove what it was, and gingerly took it back aboard. "What'll I do with it when I get on shore?" Munn asked bitterly.

"Why don't you have it mounted and present it to the general?" The Coast Guardsman and his crew laughed, not very touchingly, and tore south down the bay.

Private Munn dried his hands. He smoked a cigarette. He let the wind and the tide carry him along. He knew they wouldn't permit him to bring the fish back on South Dock. Finally, because he couldn't think of what to do, he started rowing again and presently he had an idea. It might mean being considered A.W.O.L. But the hell with it. He rowed on a diagonal, clear across Biscayne Bay. He wasn't on any precise schedule; the lieutenant had merely said, not less than half a mile.

He tied up at the far end of the Gulf Stream Dock. The *Poseidon* was there, but Crunch and Des were not aboard her. He walked to the dock-house. Mr. Williams supplied the Adams phone number. Munn put in a nickle. Sari answered. "Crunch Adams? He's working at the boat yards."

"Oh." There was a world of disappointment in the tone.

"Can I do anything?"

"This is Private Munn."

"Munn? Oh! Yes! How are you?"

"Fine. I wanted to find out how to get rid of my sailfish. The one I caught Sunday."

"You mean you've still got it? You iced it or something?"

"Well, I've still got it. But it wasn't iced. In fact—" He told her.

When he finally stopped, Sari's voice was peculiar. "Crunch tried to find out what happened to you and your fish. He wanted to ask you if Mr. Gleason would let a taxidermist put his name on the plate in Sawtelle and Slater's store."

Private Munn's voice was flat. "Probably would. But it's too late now."

"Crunch thought that since it would be such good advertising Hal Flannagan might—just might—mount the fish for—"

"Mrs. Adams! That has become a purely academic question! I'm simply trying to find how you dispose of such things around here."

"Oh." There was a pause. "Mr. Williams does that. Just put the fish on the dock. I'll talk to him, if you'll call him."

Infinitely relieved, Private Munn hailed Mr. Williams and departed in swift silence while that outsized gentleman was chatting cheerfully with Sari. He had abandoned the fish, freed himself of it, unloaded it at long last. He rowed sturdily. By and by he realized that there were blisters coming up on his hands. He got out a handkerchief to protect himself and returned it to his pocket. A hard shrewd look came into the eyes of the ordinarily timid private. He remembered another soldier who had been let off KP because of a bad case of blisters. The mess sergeant couldn't use men with blistered hands. Munn bent his back and rowed as never before.

The summer was gone, the autumn, and much of the winter. There was still sludge in the New York streets, however, and an acid rain dribbled between the skyscrapers from an oyster-colored sky. But to First Class Private Munn, as he walked up Fifth Avenue on furlough, the sun was shining and birds sang. He inspected the Sawtelle and Slater window. A scene from Guadalcanal. Terrific! He went in and took the elevator.

Mr. Gleason looked up from his desk, didn't recognize his quondam salesman, and then did. "Munn! Gad! You're a changed man! Great to have you here! On leave, eh?"

They walked together among the counters. Munn was talking. "Yes, sir! And when I return to my post—well—we may be alerted any day now. We've got a hot outfit, Mr. Gleason! Once we get over we'll be coming back before too long!" His eyes were seeing the familiar floor—the only place he had ever loved, until very recently. But there was no sadness in those eyes. Just quiet satisfaction. It would be good to come back and settle down. It was good to know your job was waiting. But the war and his outfit came first now.

Then he stopped dead. They had reached the trout flies. Old Don was waiting on a customer—a fusty gent who knew his stuff and was getting set for April. But Munn was staring at a sailfish between the salmon and the wahoo above the counter. He began to hear Mr. Gleason: ". . . and the biggest of the four sails I got only weighed forty-six! A fine fish, Munn. Such a surprise! I'm itching for the story!"

First Class Private Munn pushed forward and stared at the plate: "Caught by Clarence Munn, USA AF, Miami, Florida, 1942. Weight, 67 lbs.; length, 8 feet, 3¼ inches. Mounted by Hal Flannagan, Miami."

For a moment, Munn thought that his fish had somehow stretched. Then he thought of Sari Adams and Crunch Adams and a certain telephone conversation. Sari had been on the point of telling him that Crunch was going to get Hal Flannagan to mount the fish for nothing, as an advertisement of his skill. But this wasn't the real fish. This was probably one that had been left unclaimed at the taxidermist's—one somebody had ordered mounted and later refused to pay for or forgotten to send for. The nearest size to his own that they could find. He was going to have to lie all the rest of his life about a matter of two and a quarter inches and a matter of three pounds.

He hesitated. Then his chin came up. *Noblesse oblige,* he thought. The new Munn spoke out. "Quite a story, Mr. Gleason." He gestured toward the gigantic mako shark over the elevators. "I took my sail with the skipper and mate who got that guy."

"Crunch Adams? You don't say! Let's have lunch, Munn."

At lunch the ex-clerk recited the story of the capture of his sailfish. He told it exactly as it took place, leaving out nothing except the details of what happened after the demise of "said fish." In time, he thought, he would probably forget those details entirely. And after lunch he went nonchalantly back to the store to purchase, in the sports-jewelry department, a pin, which he caused to be mailed by Sawtelle and Slater, in a gift box, to Sari Adams.

It was a silver and enamel pin, very handsome. A sailfish, in fact.

ONCE ON A SUNDAY

SOMEWHERE UP the river a noon whistle blew; quiet came over the boat yard. The band saw stopped screaming first; mallets and hammers fell silent; old man Kane's handsaw was last. Crunch Adams, acting yard superintendent that day, picked up the box of lunch his wife, Sari, had prepared for him and walked over to the lean, gnarled shipwright. Crunch inspected the intricately worked chunk of madeira—looked his thoughts—and the old fellow nodded with satisfaction.

Crunch sat in the shade of a cabbage palm, out of the heat. Kane moved beside him and opened a pasteboard shoebox. The two men began to eat. Multiple riffles moved along the turgid river at their feet.

"Mullet," Crunch said.

"Mullet," the old man agreed.

The backdrop of Miami glittered in the sunlight and murmured with an abnormal springtime industry occasioned by the presence of thousands of soldiers and sailors. By and by Crunch's eyes traveled purposefully to the blue-grey sides of the hauled crash boat on which they were working. "Navy'd like to have her back in the water tomorrow night."

"No doubt," said the skillful old man. "But it's Sunday."

The *Poseidon*'s skipper nodded. "Yeah." He let time pass. They watched a brace of pelicans float up the river on stiff wings. "Enemy works on Sunday, though. Usually attacks then, if possible."

Mr. Kane spat. "Swine."

"Short-handed," Crunch went on. "We are. Everybody is. If we could get that piece fitted tomorrow morning, they could paint it later—"

"I'm a strict Presbyterian," the old man replied firmly. "At eleven tomorrow, I'll be in church, that's where I'll be."

"I know how it is." Crunch's expression was innocent. "I fished a Presbyterian minister once—on a Sunday."

"You don't *say!*"

Desperate, the *Poseidon's* mate, was swabbing down. The sun was a red disc—a stagy decoration; it emitted no glare but it dyed the line of boats at the Gulf Stream Dock a faint orange. Soon it would be gone. Crunch and Sari were up on the pier, laughing with the last customer. A tall stranger made his way past them, stared at the boats' names, and walked lithely to the stern of the *Poseidon*.

"Are you Crunch Adams?" he asked. His "r's" burred with a trace of Scotland and the voice that pronounced them had a slow sonority.

"I'm Des, the mate. Crunch is yonder."

The eyes of the stranger were cavernous. His nose was large and beak-like; above the six-foot level of his craggy head was a shock of iron-grey hair. Des wondered what sort of man he was and had a partial answer when the man saw young Bill Adams. Bill was three, then—proudly toting a suitcase for his father. The evening breeze stirred his blond curls. He tugged and grunted—a scale model of Hercules, in a blue sunsuit. A twinkle came in the man's recessed eyes and his broad mouth broke into a smile. "Likely lad!"

"Crunch's. The skipper's."

"I've been told he's the best. It shows—in the offspring."

Des began to like the guy. "Hey, Crunch!" he called.

"My problem," said the man, as he and the two charter-boatmen put their heads together, "is as difficult as it is simple. I'm a minister o' the gospel—a Presbyterian—though I wouldn't like it to be held against me."

Crunch and Des chuckled.

"When I went to school in Edinburgh—which was a considerable long while ago—I used to slip out as often as the opportunity afforded and cast a fly for trout and sometimes for salmon. I haven't wet a line since." He rubbed his chin. "My daughter spends her winters here with her husband, who's a man of means. I've joined them for a few days' vacation and my son-in-law insists I put in a few on the sea. He's footing the bill—and a man ought to keep in good with his son-in-law, don't you think?" He beamed.

"Very sound," Crunch said.

"But there's more to it than that," the man went on. "Do you mind if I light a pipe? It's safe on these gasoline boats?"

Crunch struck the match.

The prospective customer sat down with a sigh of composure. He sniffed the air. "Salty. I like it. Smells as good as the recollection of a frith. Unfortunately, for the past twenty-five years, I've hardly smelled it at all. I've been preaching the gospel inland. Not that it isn't as desperately needed there as on the coasts. I am simply explaining the rest of my predicament—an altogether happy one, as it chances. This vacation I'm on comes between my old church and a new one I'm to take direct-ly after Christmas. What's that yonder?" He pointed with the stem of his pipe.

Crunch looked in time to see the triangular top of a dark fin ease into the blue water. "Porpoise."

"You don't say! They come here in this Bay?"

"Some of 'em live in here."

"Well!" He watched the big mammal rise and blow. "Fine creature! But to get to the point. Where I'm taking the new pastorate, fishing is partly a business and largely a recreation, besides. It's in New Jersey, at a place called Antasquan—a big town or small city, whichever you will. Some of my new congregation are commercial fishermen, and some of the wealth-ier ones are boat-owners, like yourselves. They go out for big tunny, I understand. Then, there's something called 'blues' they're partial to—"

"We know a little about it," Crunch said appreciatively. "We've fished a few summers from the Manasquan nearby."

The minister smiled. "Which, no doubt, is one of the reasons my son-in-law stipulated you two! What can a man expect in a corporation lawyer, though, except guile? At any rate, I've got a congregation of fishermen—and golf players, to boot. Being a Scot, I can handle the golf, on week days, though it somewhat drains my congregations on the Sabbath, I hear. As fishing does, to an even greater degree, in the summer. But I like to know something of the pursuits of the men I preach to. So I'm doubly glad to be able to take advantage of this vacation to find out what I can of salt-water fishing. Have I made myself clear?"

"You sure have, Mr.—?"

"McGill. The Reverend Doctor Arthur McGill. And if, in the heat of the excitement in the three days I've got to fish, it should become neces-sary to use a shorter term, you'll find I respond to 'Mac'."

He shook hands with them to seal the bargain.

When he was gone, Des grinned at the descending twilight. "The trou-ble is, there aren't enough ministers like that. If there were, I'd go to church oftener, myself."

"Just what I was thinking," his skipper agreed.

The Reverend Doctor Arthur McGill appeared on the Gulf Stream Dock at seven o'clock the following morning—a green-visored hat flop-ping above his grey mane and a huge hamper carried lightly over his bony arm. He took the gap between dock and stern in an easy stride and deposited the basket.

It was a cool, breezy day—it would be choppy outside—but, if he knew it, he did not seem concerned. "Bracing weather," he said. "I hadn't expected it of the tropics. I rose before the servants and picked my own grapefruit from a tree in the yard. There was something burning out toward the Everglades and it recalled my autumn fire anywhere in the world. But the grapefruit was a distinctly pagan note; it made me understand a little why it is that north country men always have a sense of guilt in the south. It ought to be snowing and blowing—and here you are picking fruit!"

Des was already hanging the bow lines on the dolphins. The *Poseidon* pushed into the ship channel and started east. At the jetty-mouth, the outgoing tide, bulled by the easterly wind, threw up an unpredictable maelstrom of lumpy current; the *Poseidon* tossed, smashed hard and found her sea gait for the day. Three warm December weeks had changed, overnight, into the Floridian equivalent of a winter day—a day with a twelve-mile breeze and a temperature in the shade of sixty—a "cold" day, in the opinion of the natives.

Crunch cut baits. The minister wrapped an elbow around one of the canopy supports and watched, his eyes bright under his tangled brows. Once or twice, the skipper glanced at him covertly; he wasn't going to be seasick. He took in each detail, as the strip was sliced wafer-thin, tapered, pointed, beveled, and pierced for the hook. "It's an art, I can see that."

"The idea is to make it flutter in the water—like a fish with a busy tail." Crunch dropped over a bait on a leader and tested it to make sure it would not spin and wind up—or unwind—the line. He handed the rod to Reverend McGill and, under the same intense scrutiny, he arranged two balao on the outrigger lines. Then, because his passenger looked quizzical, he explained the operation of outriggers.

"You see," said the minister, "I'm a dub and a tyro and I have plenty of need to learn all this. A congregation of fishing enthusiasts will listen with a polite and patronizing interest if their domini discusses the fine points of netting fishes in the Sea of Galilee two thousand years ago. But if you can bring the matter up to date—put it in terms of outriggers, so to speak—and use it in an illustration, you may even wake up the habitual sleepers."

Crunch laughed. "I get the idea, parson. Now. About 'blues.' Being a part-time Jersey fisherman myself, I understand the Jersey attitude. It's cold today—and we may run along like this for hours without a strike—so I'll explain what they do off the 'Squan Inlet—and why. Their fishing is done this way—and other ways."

"I'd appreciate it." The minister snuggled into the fighting chair and pulled his muffler tighter.

Crunch was deep in a lucid description of the art of chumming for tuna—remembering to cite the fact that Jersey old-timers still call them "horse mackerel"—when there was a splash behind the center bait. Reverend McGill went taut as his reel warbled.

"Bonita!" Crunch said. "Just hang on till he gets that run out of his system."

Reverend McGill hung on—and hung on properly—with his rod high enough so that no sudden bend could snap it over the stern and low enough so that he had room to lift it and take in slack in the event the first turned suddenly. It did. The rod went higher and the minister began to reel. He brought the bonita to within a few yards of the boat and it sounded a good seventy-five feet. His rod tip shivered with the rapid tail action. He pumped the fish up, under Crunch's instruction. It sounded again—ran again—and came to gaff.

Crunch brought it aboard and the exhilarated minister looked. "Magnificent creature! Herringbone back—and the underside as white and sleek as alabaster! Funny thing! It's almost as big as any fish I ever caught in my life—and yet it pulled so hard I expected a fish my own size!"

"Bonitas are strong," Crunch said. He resumed his discussion of chumming. His back was turned to the water when Reverend McGill had his second strike. The minister handled the fish with considerable skill. "'Cuda," Crunch said, after a moment.

It proved to be a barracuda. Crunch flipped it over the gunwale, showed the ferocious teeth by clamping the fish's head under the lid of the box in the stern, and removed the hook with pliers in a gingerly fashion. The *Poseidon* ran steadily for some two hours after that. Then there was a bluish flash under one of the outrigger baits and its line drifted gently down to the water only to spring tight like the wire of a snare. Crunch eyed the line as it cut the surface—pointing, in a curve, to a fish that was barely under water. "Dolphin," he explained. "Get ready for him to jump. And when he does jump—watch him."

When the fish jumped, it was quite a sight. This particular dolphin at the particular instant was green and silver. Sometimes they are luminous cobalt and silver or gold—with pale blue spots. Sometimes they are almost pure gold or silver. Their rainbow patterns cannot be predicted—they change in seconds—and they range through all the natural colors save red and those with red in them, as well as through the spectra of precious metals.

"I know," the minister said quietly and between breaths, when Crunch gaffed the dolphin, "why people write poetry about them." He watched Crunch bait up again and went back to his vigil. "It's amazing," he continued, "what eyes you have. Now, in all three strikes, all I saw was a flicker and a lot of spray. But—each time—you saw the fish and named it correctly."

Crunch laughed. "I didn't see the fish, itself, any time. Except, as you say, an impression of a fish. I could tell what they were by the way your rod tip behaved—by the angle at which the fish fought—by a lot of little things."

"They must be fine points, for fair! I don't suppose you reveal them to the novitiate—the lucky novitiate, I might add?"

"Why not?" Crunch grinned benignly. "Take—the bonita. He was first. He hits hard and fast, usually at a sharp angle to the course of the bait. When he feels the hook he puts on every ounce of power he's got. He goes away, maybe for thirty yards or so, and then, still feeling the hook, he goes down. He'll bore straight down or go down in a spiral, like an auger. Now there's a fish out here that's related to the tuna, called an albacore. He does the same thing. But when the albacore swims, it's like a glide, all power and no wiggle. With a bonita there's the wiggle. A flutter. You see it in the rod tip. You feel it in your arms."

"You do that," the minister agreed.

"'Cuda's can sound—or run—or jump. In fact, they usually give a jump or two like a pike or a muskie. On the same tackle, they're even stronger, I believe. But they do one thing that's characteristic—they jerk. If you get one near the boat you can see him do it under water. He'll yank his head back and forth trying to get rid of the hook or to break the line, just the way a bulldog yanks."

"And the dolphin?"

"He always skims along at a terrific rate right below the surface. You can tell that because your line, instead of boring down into the sea, will be stretching out over it for a long way. Then the dolphin will circle, first one way and then the other, in big arcs. That is, he will unless he's foul-hooked. Hooked from the outside, in the back, say. Or hooked through the eye. In that case, he's very apt to sound—and if you haven't seen him when he hit, you'll be hard put to guess what you're fighting. Of course, you occasionally do see dolphins before they hit, because they sometimes make several bounds into the air to get to the bait, as if they were impatient with the resistance of the water."

"I see." The minister mused, "Funny, that. If you're fishing for sal-mon—you take salmon. You know what you've got when you have your rise. Trout, too, unless you happen to encounter a chub or dace. Here, though, the possibilities are vast."

"There are hundreds."

The minister thought that over. "And what would a sailfish be like? That is, if we were to have the fantastic good fortune—?"

So Crunch told him about the ways of sailfish. And in the end, he was, as usual, completely at a loss: "What I've said goes for the average sailfish. But you're continually running into the exception. The fellow who just gulps the bait and runs. The one who strikes like a bonita—with only a flash under the bait. And then, when you know it was a sail because you saw its high fin and its bill—and you hook it—it'll possibly turn out to be a white marlin."

"I presume, in the three days I have, there's no chance of that?"

"I dunno," Crunch answered. "There's always some chance. They're tailing today, though. I've seen a couple. They don't strike, as a rule, when they're running south from a cold snap."

The minister nodded. Crunch knew by his attitude during the discussion of sailfish that the Reverend Doctor McGill had a very definite dream about his three days of deep-sea angling and the dream was centered around that particular breed of fish. In his mind's eye, the minister wanted not only what knowledge of marine angling he could glean from the period, but a particular object, a mounted sail, to hang, probably, in his study, where the visiting members of his new congregation could observe it and admire. Reverend McGill did not say so. He was too humble a man. But Crunch knew.

While the skipper was contemplating that matter, the novice in the *Poseidon's* stern had another stike. The reel sang. The fish ran. Then it went deep. The rod tip fluttered. "A bonita!" the preacher cried with certainty.

"Well—it's not quite like a bonita. A little, just a shade, less powerful. Not quite so vicious. It might be a small bonita, at that. But I think it's a kingfish."

It was a kingfish. The minister chuckled. "You're not giving away all your trade secrets in one day!"

"Well, that one wasn't easy. I couldn't be sure myself. If we call three quarters of them correctly we're doing fine."

"I won't be so rash and conceited on the next," The minister promised. But there wasn't any "next." They ate the excellent lunch in the big hamper. They trolled the length of the island that is Miami Beach. Then they turned south and went as far as the old lighthouse. But there were no more strikes upon which the minister could test his fresh knowledge.

That evening the *Poseidon* came in as late as the winter sun would allow. "I've had a wonderful day," the minister said. "I've thought of at least six new sermons. I've settled in my head a minute point of ethics brought to me by one of my former flock which stuck me for a long time. I've caught four prime fish—whoppers, all—and two of 'em, you say, are superb eating. There's a good fifteen pounds of meat for the larders of myself and the friends of my son-in-law. And I'll never be able to thank you enough. The best part of it all is," his eyes crinkled, "we'll be at it again in the morning—and the day after, also. That's what they mean when they call this place a paradise on earth!"

Crunch stopped the recital and carefully poured a cup of coffee from his thermos. He raised his eyebrows enquiringly at old man Kane. The shipwright nodded and held out a cup from which he had been drinking milk. "Thanks, Crunch. So—what happened? Did he get a sail?"

"No," Crunch said. He peered reminiscently at the murky river and tossed a coral pebble to break the immaculate surface. "No. Doctor McGill never caught a sail, so far as I am aware."

"I'm disappointed."

"Maybe he wasn't! Des and I got fond of that gent. Whatever a good man is, he's it. And by that I mean he was both a man, and good. We fished Friday, from seven till dark, and got skunked. It was raw and windy with low clouds. Not a strike. But the old boy saw a whale, a finback, that came up close to the *Poseidon* and cruised along, blowing—and he insisted it made the day worth while.

"Then—Saturday came. His last day. He was going home Monday and he was planning to take in a couple of Miami preachers Sunday and Sunday night. So we started at six, in the dark, and we dragged a bait till night. He caught one grouper over the reef, and a rock hind, and he had one sailfish rise. I swear the old boy's hair stood on end. The sail came like an upside-down yacht with her keel out, and it followed the bait for a mile, but it never hit. Old Mac McGill stood up the whole time, muttering. First I thought he was praying and then I had a kind of shock because I thought he was swearing, but he wasn't doing either—he was just coaching the fish—like a quarterback on the bench when his team's in a spot. The fish never did hit, just eyed that bait, wallowed behind it, and finally swam away. And then it got dark and we came in and the domini's vacation was over. He said he'd be back some day when his pocketbook could stand it and he said he'd had more fun than ever before in his life. His eyes shot sparks and he meant every word of it. He was disappointed, I am certain, but not as much disappointed as pleased. Des and I, of course, tried to make up for the thin fishing by telling him as many stories as we could—and by giving him as much dope as we knew how."

"A good sport," Kane nodded.

"The real thing. Well, he shook our hands and thanked us and went away. Mr. Williams, the dock manager, had us down Sunday for a party—we didn't know the people—and we sat around Saturday evening feeling pretty low about the preacher. Sunday, we got down about seven and our party hadn't shown up. So we just sat around some more. Lots of people get a special kick out of deep-sea fishing for the main and simple reason that you don't have to get out at the crack of dawn. I mean, they'll hit at noon just as often as they'll hit at daybreak, which isn't like fresh-water stuff. Anyway—"

During the night the wind had hauled. The norther had blown itself out and the Trade Wind, dawdling back from the southeast, had taken its place, pushing the cold air aside, dissipating the lowering clouds, and substituting the regimented wool-balls of Caribbean cumulus. The thermometer, between midnight and sunrise, had gone up fifteen degrees and a balminess characteristic of Florida had supplanted the sharp chill. Even the first level bars of sunshine were warm and it was certain that by noon the temperature in the shade would be eighty. On such days, after a cold-weather famine, the sailfish are likely to be ravenous. Crunch knew it, and Des, and they wondered in their separate silences what Reverend McGill would think about it. Because he knew, too. They'd told him how, as a rule, the sailfish would come up fighting on these days when the weather broke.

By nine o'clock, they were getting restless. Their party hadn't appeared. All the other boats were out, with the exception of one, engine parts of which were strewn over its stern cockpit for repair. Des was commenting on the laggardliness of some people when Crunch said, "Look. There's Reverend McGill."

The minister stepped from a car. He was wearing a neat serge suit and a high, starched collar. He walked down the dock with a sheepish expression and said, "That was my son-in-law. Off to play golf—like too many in my own congregations! I went along with him this far—I can walk the balance of the way to the kirk." Then he realized that the boats had gone. "How does it happen you're still hanging to the pilings?"

"We were chartered," Des said bitterly, "by some slug-a-bed named Ellsworth Coates."

The minister turned pale. He swallowed. "That," he finally murmured, "is the name of my son-in-law—the heathen tempter!"

Crunch merely glanced up at the tall man on the dock. Then he squinted across the Bay. He neither smiled nor frowned—just squinted. "I guess he must have seen the weather prediction—and realized what it would probably be like out there today."

Reverend McGill sat down shakily. "It's like him! The lawyer's guile! Dropping me here to walk to church! And with you two boys waiting, steam up and bait in the box! What does he take me for—a weakling? Is some crafty second-rate, amoral attorney to be the first to make me break the Sabbath? Not that, in the proper cause, I mightn't! I'm none of your hardshell preachers! I've been known far and wide as a liberal man, these long years! But a precedent is a precedent and I've kept the Lord's day, in my own fashion, as an example. Fie to Ellsworth—the wretch!"

"This might turn out to be a good cause," Des said. "After all, it's a day in a hundred, and you wanted your future parish to feel you were one of them."

"It could be a day in a million!" the minister said scornfully.

Time passed—a good deal of time. Crunch began to repair a light rod which had lost a guide in an encounter with a wahoo. Up where the Gulf Stream Dock joined the Florida shore a school of big jack got under a walloping school of small mullet. The result was aquatic chaos: fish showered into the air as if they were being tossed up in barrelfuls by Davy Jones himself. The minister watched, goggle-eyed, and said something that Crunch thought was, "It's more than flesh can withstand!" But Crunch wasn't certain.

And then the *Clarissa B.* came in. She came in because one of her four passengers, a novice, had been taken ill—although the sea was smooth: only a vague ground swell kept it from being as calm as pavement. The *Clarissa*, as she approached, throwing two smart wings of water from her bows, was flying four sailfish flags.

"Four of them!" Reverend McGill whispered disconsolately. "I could have stood two—or possibly three—!"

The boat turned, backed in smartly, and deposited her shaky passenger with little ceremony: the other anglers were manifestly annoyed at the interruption and anxious to get back on the Gulf Stream. She pulled away from her slip again—showing four forked tails above her gunwales.

"Good fishing, eh?" Crunch called to the skipper.

"They'll jump in the boat!" he yelled back. "It's red-hot! We've already had a triple and two double-headers and a single!" He turned his wheel and purred into the blue distance.

Reverend McGill sighed and stood up. He shook out his full length of supple anatomy. He brushed back his iron-grey hair. "In any event," he said, grinning, "I'll not rationalize. I had it on the tip of my tongue to say that the Reverend Doctor Stone, whom I had intended to hear this morning, isn't so much of a preacher-man. We'll agree that he's the finest preacher in the south—and that by going fishing, I'm committing a mortal sin of the first magnitude. But—boys—let's get a lunch on board and make all the haste we can to violate the canon that has to do with this precious and altogether magnificent day!" He took off his collar as he came aboard.

By four o'clock in the afternoon, the lone passenger was stunned. In the interim, no less than seven sailfish had come up from the purple depths and done their best to be caught by the cleric. But in each instance that gentleman, through bad luck and inexperience, had failed to bring his fish to boat. In testament of his effort there was a broken rod. There were blisters on his fingers. There was a burn on his left arm where the running line had cut him. There was an empty reel from which the line had been stripped. And there was, on the deck, a leader to which was still attached the upper half of a broken hook. But no sailfish flag flew from the *Poseidon*'s outrigger.

The loquacious Reverend McGill was dour, and his accent had become more Scottish. "I will nae say it's injustice," he proclaimed morosely, "an' a' would not ha' missed this day for the worrld—it's a sterrn way to remind a mon of his evil intent!"

Crunch and Des exchanged glances. "There'll be more of 'em, parson," Des said encouragingly. "Just—take it easy."

And, even while he spoke, the outrigger line on the port side fell again and a big boil of water showed briefly where the bait had been. The line came tight and the minister struck to set the hook. The fish ran off rapidly for about forty yards and sounded. "It's no sailfish this time," he cried. "A bonita, I think. At least, perhaps we'll ha' one small fishie to show for our sins!"

Crunch looked critically at the bend in the rod. "If it's a bonita, it's the father of all bonitas," he said quietly.

"Very unlikely," Reverend McGill replied as he jockeyed to get in a few feet of slack. "Nothing sensational. The last two hours, I've realized I was predestined to have misfortune to the end of the day. But at least my face will be saved. I'll never have to exhibit a sailfish I caught on Sunday and acknowledge my guilt. The deed will be a secret between the two of us—and my son-in-law—who will use it, no doubt, for some blackmailing tomfoolery, one day. Now—he's coming toward us nicely!"

The fish swam toward the *Poseidon* for several yards. Then it turned, still deep under the water, and ran three hundred yards with the speed of an express train. The reel screamed. Crunch yelled. Des brought the *Poseidon* around in a fast arc. They chased the fish at full throttle for five hundred yards more before the minister stopped losing line from a spool that was by then no thicker than his thumb.

"It must be a sailfish, after all," Reverend McGill murmured.

"It's no sailfish," Crunch replied. His mouth was tight and he shot an enquiring glance at Des.

"What then?"

"I dunno. I dunno, Reverend. Maybe a marlin—"

"A marlin! It isn't possible—!"

"I think," Des called, "it's an Allison tuna. Better take it easy, Mac. You've got a long fight on your hands if it is."

"I'll gentle it like a baby," the angler promised. "I'm getting a bit of line, now." He tried tentatively and then with fury. "He's running to us—*to* us—faster than I can reel!"

Crunch waved—and waved again. The *Poseidon* leaped away from the fish but even at full gun she barely made enough speed so that the man on the rod could keep his line taut. Presently Crunch signalled again and the boat stood still. "Mac," as Des had called him in the stress of excitement, began to horse his fish toward the boat, lifting slowly until his bowed rod came high, dropping the tip swiftly, and winding in the slack thus gained. Two feet at a time, he brought the fish toward the place where the two guides leaned in tense concentration and where he labored sweatily. When the reel-spool was well filled with line, the fish turned and raced away again—a hundred yards, two, three. The process was repeated. The fish ran.

On the fifth struggle to the boat Reverend McGill gasped, "It's a new tribulation! I've hung a whale! Every joint in me is protesting—!"

"Stay with it," Crunch breathed fervently.

"Mon—I'm a *Scot*."

He stayed with it. Stayed with it until it tired and until, an hour and three quarters after he had hooked it, a head and jaws rolled out of water not forty feet from the Poseidon. Crunch felt himself grow weak. He just stood there. Des said in a small voice, "You see it?"

"Yeah."

"What is it?"

"I dunno." Crunch repeated the words as if they angered him. "I dunno. It was red—wasn't it?"

"Yeah. It was red."

"But it wasn't a snapper," Crunch continued. "Not a snapper—not a monster mangrove snapper. I never saw it before. Mac—take it mighty easy, now. It's something new you've got there."

"I couldn't put any strength on it if I had to," the minister said grittily. Then he did put on strength. The fish made a last flurry—a rush, a mighty splash—and Crunch got the leader in his gloved hand. Swiftly, skillfully, he rammed home the gaff. The tail hammered on the boat's hull like a piston. Des jumped clear down from the canopy without hanging and made a noose around the leader. He dropped the rope into the sea. The two men pulled, and the fish came aboard tail first.

It was red, scarlet, from mouth to caudal. Its underside was greenish-white. It had big fins and a square tail. It was toothed. Its eyes were green. It gasped like a grouper and flopped heavily. They guessed it weighed about a hundred and eighty.

The minister flexed his raging arms slowly, caught some of his wind, stirred his back a little as if he were afraid any further motion would shatter it, and he looked and looked at the fish. "You mean—this is one you boys can't give a name to?"

Crunch said slowly, "No, Mac. And I don't think anybody—any taxidermist, any ichthyologist—can give it a name either. I think it's a new one. Somebody comes in with a brand new one every year or so, around these parts. Tonight you're gonna, Mac."

"Whatever the name is," Des said with the voice of a man who had seen a miracle, "part of it will probably be McGill—forever."

Crunch walked stiffly to the radio telephone. He put in a call for Hal— and for Bob Breastedt—the two foremost piscatorial authorities on the coast. "It's built like an amberjack—something," he said into the transmitter. "Fought like one—more or less. But it has scales like a tarpon, almost, and fins like a bass, and the darned thing's red all over!"

The experts came to the dock to meet the *Poseidon*—and so did the reporters.

It was a new one. Part of its long scientific name eventually became McGillia.

Many weeks later, Crunch had a letter from the minister. It was postmarked "Antasquan, N.J." It said, in part:

". . . and the celebrated catch we made that memorable day has become a not unmixed blessing. It served the purpose of giving my new flock an advance notice that I'm a fisherman of distinction. Indeed, the reputation carried ahead of me by the national publicity was so great that I'm alarmed whenever I remember that next summer I'll have to go out and show my lack of proficiency on the blues and the school tuna—not to mention the great horse mackerel. However, I'll take my chances on that.

"The point is, the fact that I caught the fish on the Sabbath was one which the press associations did not glaze over. On the contrary, they prominently noted it, and my congregation here was quick to make the discovery. Some of them chided me. And all of those who fish, and those who play golf, are smugly planning to be absent from their pews as soon as the spring weather breaks. After all, their domini fishes on Sunday! This, however, has set me thinking—this—and the lesson in wiliness I learned from my son-in-law.

"Even now, war work is engaging the daytime hours of some of my people on Sunday—so I have stressed the evening service. It is already a feature in this city and the kirk is full every Sunday night though it was formerly sparsely attended at that hour. Come spring, my friends, and I expect to have most of the golfers and anglers in the evening habit and it'll be another bit of triumph I can credit to you and your fine ship! In short, I'm punished by the richly deserved lampoons of a fine group of people—and rewarded with an evening attendance that beats the old morning service average!

"The fish itself arrived in due course—splendidly mounted and a thing of wonder. In that, I lost out, also—because I still have no symbol of my dubious skill to hang on my study wall. One of my parishioners is on the board of the American Museum of Natural History—and there the creature hangs. Still—I think the day was well spent—for myself and my fellow men—don't you?"

Crunch rose and stretched. He looked at his watch. One o'clock. Presently, the sound of the band saw rent the air. The boat yard resumed work for the U.S. Navy. Crunch had been reading the letter—having taken it from his hip pocket at the proper moment. He handed it, now, to the old shipwright, who stared blankly.

"You mean—you brought this thing here this morning?"

"Sure," Crunch said.

"You knew I was going to tell you I wouldn't work tomorrow?"

Crunch nodded. "Yep. But we need you—if we're going to get that job back in the water on time for Uncle Sam."

Kane glanced down at the name of the church on the letterhead. He sucked his teeth. "Well," he said slowly, "if that preacher can go fishing—and have it turn out all right—I guess I can work."

"It was for a cause. So's this."

"I still don't get it! You planned to tell me this story—and brought the letter to prove it was the truth—"

"I'm like the preacher's son-in-law," Crunch said as he walked away. "Guileful."

FAIR-CAUGHT

THE SKIPPER and mate of the fishing cruiser *Poseidon*, happily ensconced in Bimini for a succession of charters, awaited the arrival of their next customer on the public dock. While they waited, they passed the time of day with the port doctor and with the natives on a conch-boat. It was nine in the morning—and a green-gold-blue Bimini day. The crew of the ramshackle ship with the sea-stained sail were chuckling over a mountain of conchs which they lazily unloaded into a "crawl"—a pen made of stakes driven in shallow water. Half a dozen dark, Nassau-talking kids looked on; one or two licked their lips; and there was conch chowder in the eyes of all.

Crunch said, "Nice haul."

The captain of the conch boat grinned. "Found an emigration center. They were amassed like snapper. And hastening all around."

Everybody laughed, then. Not because the language was elegant—the dark-skinned citizens of the British Bahamas learn English in a fashion that surprises American tourists—but at the idea that conchs could "hasten."

Curiosity showed in the doctor's eyes. "Who's coming, Crunch? Old customer?"

"Stranger. Fellow named Totten—A. B. Totten. In the furniture business in New York. Chartered us through the Chamber of Commerce in Miami."

"Jolly," said the doctor. From a little case perched on a piling he took one thermometer, read it, shook it—and was ready to function as quarantine officer.

One of the children called, "Plane's visible!"

It was a speck in the west and then a crimson, loud enormity that banked in over the roofs and palms and banana trees, split the water of the lagoon, sent up a shower of irritated needle-fish, and coasted to a stop near a buoy. The big passenger dory started out to pick up personnel and

208

luggage. Everything, Crunch thought, was routine—routine in the amiable, slightly exciting way which accompanies each new fishing trip.

And that, as so often happens on fishing trips, was the last occasion
Crunch had to think of "routine" in connection with the two weeks charter of the Poseidon by A. B. Totten.

The pilot climbed out and tied up to the buoy. He handed two suit-
cases to the doryman. He then handed down his passenger. Sharp-eyed
Des needed to see only one human foot before he whistled. "A dame!"

She stepped lightly from pontoon to a seat in the dory, stepped down
from the seat, and surveyed Bimini as she and the pilot were sculled
toward the dock. She wore a dark blue suit and a dark blue little hat and
she had a fur coat over her arm—which seemed strange in the eighty
degrees of Bimini morning until one remembered that it was winter and
that she had doubtless boarded a night plane for Miami not twelve hours
before, at La Guardia Airport, in New York City.

Crunch was thinking about the letters of inquiry and arrangement.
They had been business-like, masculine, without a hint. The check for
deposit had been signed by initials—which had suggested nothing
feminine. Maybe "A. B. Totten" had been delayed—and this was his
wife—or a secretary. Under the hat—black hair—curly, not long or short.
New York eyebrows, plucked and arched. Blue eyes—wide and nervously
uncertain as they moved from person to person while the oarsman drew
near. She stood up. The dory jarred against the dock and made her stag-
ger. *Not used to boats,* Crunch thought. *But she's well put together—not
weak—or too fat.*

That is a skipper's first observation of a potential new passenger when
he has been chartered for trolling in marlin waters. Sometimes they are
too fat or too feeble.

She was coming up the steps, now. A bright, "social" smile pushed the
dismay—was it repugnance?—from her face.

The skipper stepped forward. "I'm Crunch Adams. This is Des, my
mate. And Doctor Bevlington, the quarantine officer. You're—?"

"Annabelle Totten." It was a nice voice—not chi-chi, natural.

The worry—or distaste—couldn't quite be hidden. Crunch understood.
A quarantine officer ought to be wearing an official cap and a blue uniform and he should be found in an immaculate white office. Bimini—the
Mecca of anglers—ought to be glamorous. But Bimini was sun-blanched
and tatterdemalion. Its houses hadn't been painted since before the war.
And His Majesty's Quarantine official was a lean Englishman with lazy
brown eyes whose uniform consisted of one pair of sneakers, one pair of
shorts, one trifling moustache and a coat of tan. His "office" was a little
steel box somewhat rusted on the outside by the salty dampness of the

air. He thrust his thermometer in A. B. Totten's mouth. His fingers found her pulse. Des held the fur coat. It was a muskrat coat, rather worn.

The girl looked nervously at the watching natives, the heaped conches, the house on shore, and the three white men—all of whom were darker than some of the permanent residents. Obviously, she had never before submitted to a physical examination in public.

Finally, the doctor read the thermometer. "You'll do, Miss Totten."

"We'll have to check in at the Commissioner's," Crunch said. "Thanks, Bev."

"Right, Crunch old boy. Good fishin'."

The hotel seemed to reassure the girl considerably. It was bright, airy, clean and—except for louvers and fine screens on the windows, and for the bizarre nature of its potted plants—much like any hotel. Crunch and Des waited for her to unpack and to change. The *Poseidon* further relieved her anxiety. A well-eqipped fishing cruiser, even when moored at a dock that looks dangerously rickety, is a spectacle both very much of the modern world, and, in Miss Totten's own phrase, "out of this world."

Crunch went up topside, started the engines, and headed through the cobalt channel which leads from the Bimini lagoon into the Gulf Stream. Des rigged two bonefish busily, silently, and set them splashing astern. Once, the girl spoke.

"Hadn't they ought to be farther back?"

Desperate's eyes were vacant. "They work better short in calm weather."

Skipper and mate changed places. Crunch stood behind the girl, his natural reticence at war with his puzzlement. Her skin was creamy white—she'd have to be watched for sunburn. Her eyes were fixed on the baits. She'd at least read about deep sea fishing. Around her swirled the perfume she wore—very urban and sophisticated—very strange in the salty breath of the warm sea.

"You've fished before." He made it a statement.

"Not for marlin. Just—fresh water fish."

"How—?" He decided not to go on.

She turned around, then, and smiled at him. "Was it a very dirty trick? To make out I was a man?"

"No."

"I was so afraid you'd refuse to take a lone girl. Besides, I was just generally afraid. I wrote the Chamber of Commerce, as if I were a kind of timid old man. I asked for the names of boats with very dependable crews. Married men—with reputations of the very highest order. You have that, you know." She made a sound near to a giggle. "They were terrifically solemn about it. They sent me six names and said I could have the 'utmost confidence' in any of them."

"How'd you pick the *Poseidon?*"

"Eeny meenie minie mo."

Crunch laughed. "Lucky us."

"Unlucky you. If we raised a marlin, I wouldn't know what on earth to do. If I did hook it, and if I didn't faint right then, I would probably never last long enough to bring it to boat."

"I think so. You look as if—"

She stretched out a pair of long, sound limbs. "I dance a good deal. And ever since I chartered you last fall, I've been taking exercises. I can chin myself twenty-five times."

"Golly! I wonder if I can?" Crunch reached up and seized the monkey-rail. He began to count. At "twenty," he quit—not out of necessity but for moral effect. "You'll do, Miss Totten—as Bev said."

She glanced over her shoulder. "I was certainly—amazed—that he was a—doctor."

"It's informal around here."

"You really mean that!"

"Like a cola?"

"You bet. It's hot, isn't it?"

The morning passed. They had lunch. A. B. Totten put on anti-sunburn cream, then a big hat, then an old shirt, laundered thin, which Crunch provided. She seemed to be—just a darned nice New York business girl.

Along toward four o'clock Crunch felt well enough acquainted to ask, "How come you wanted to fish for marlin?"

"Oh—I belong to a family of anglers. I decided last year to take my two weeks vacation in the winter. Then I'd had a—a windfall. So I decided to try to—oh—to show up my male relations. This is kind of a secret expedition for me."

"I see." Crunch knew he didn't see—exactly.

Not long afterward Des called, "Starboard line!"

It wasn't a blue marlin. But it was a relatively big white marlin. It hit hard, after following with its pointed dorsal standing out of the water like a periscope. A. B. Totten leaped to the center chair. Crunch slammed the rod into the gimbal. The line came tight. She struck—four times—hard—and without any coaching because none was required. In the descending sun, on the calm sea, the marlin—white-bellied, blue-backed—its fins rigid and shivering—hurled itself high, splashed enormously, jumped again, re-entered the water bill first, hardly rippling it—and tore up the sea by greyhounding in a semicircle—head and body in the air, tail racing like the screw of a torpedo.

Crunch spoke when it was necessary. "Lower your rod-tip a bit! Good.

Reel as fast as you can—there's a curve in the line! Enough—he's taking it and you can't gain on him now. Good. Now reel again—and then lift—!"

Five minutes. Ten. Fifteen. The white marlin sulked—yanking brutally whenever she tried to turn him toward the boat. Then he really jumped—somersaulting, twisting, throwing head and bill against the leader wire in wild jerks while he was in the air, so that his balance was lost and he fell back recklessly—only to emerge again in an instant—spinning and twisting.

Suddenly the line went dead. Far off, the marlin broke into the sunshine—a sea-enamelled beauty, going away fast.

"What happened?" she asked.

Crunch quietly gave the probable explanations. "Maybe the line just broke. Maybe some little fish took a bite at the swivel and cut the line. Maybe it got cut on a submerged log, or a board in some weeds."

"What was it?"

He felt apologetic. "Why—a marlin—a white—a whopper."

For a long time she seemed just to be thinking. Then she said, in a curious tone, "I see—I see all about it. How wonderful!" And she burst into tears.

There wasn't any more action that day but—by going-in time, she seemed reconciled. "They sure are jet-propelled," she said, and she said of the sunset—with a half-humorous sadness that was not quite that of a disappointed angler, "I never saw so many colors! There are positively too many! It makes you want to go up there and sort them out. I can hardly bear it!"

The tropic night wore sables—warm, thickly sprinkled with rhinestone stars. Far up the palm-lined walk from the *Poseidon*, the Harmonizing Four chanted to the lush air about the Sweet Chariot, the Battle of Jericho, and the Lord who is so high you can't get over Him. Mate and skipper listened.

"You recall anybody who was ever chartered in Bimini by a lone, young gal?"

Des peered at his skipper. "She's okay." He realized he hadn't answered the question. "No."

Crunch's grin was in his voice. "Why you wearing a necktie, boy? Didn't know you brought one across from Miami."

"Same reason you made us late for dinner scrubbing your nails. Seen the doc?"

"Why?"

"White trousers," Des said indignantly. "Blue coat. Bow tie. White shoes with brown saddles—the polish-stuff wasn't dry on 'em when I saw him snaking up to the Angler's Inn. Looked mighty cute. After dinner, I happened to spot 'em both—"

"You trailing her, detective?"

Des answered with dignity, "I was just checking—to be sure she was all right. No need. She and Bev were in the patio doing a rumba to a Havana radio station. He can rumba to beat the band." There was a somber pause. "Those damn Englishmen sure get around. It's owning all that Empire, I guess."

She had a letter. Not one that arrived by the pilot boat or by plane or from Nassau. One she carried with her. They saw it on the third day of her charter. The second day, they'd fished on the reef to give her some fun and some practice. She'd caught groupers and amberjack—fifty pounders—big snappers and horse-eye jacks—and come in ecstatic. She'd insisted on learning to clean and filet the fish and she had personally distributed the meat.

But on the third day, she missed her initial shot at a blue marlin, and that was when they saw the letter. The blue followed the bouncing bonefish bait for half a mile—surging along ten feet below the surface like a one-man submarine—before he decided to rise and strike. When he came out, he came fast, with his bill raised and his lower jaw yawning whitely and he hit, as Des said, "like it was raining kitchen stoves."

A. B. Totten was all set. Set—nerved up by watching the deep and meditative pursuit of her bait—hardly breathing. The marlin shoulders broached, the jaws closed, the thirty-six-thread line drifted from the clothespin on the outrigger tip and came tight. Crunch said, "Sock him!" and the girl heaved back on the rod. There was no contact with the fish. "Wind up!" he said. "Wind to beat the devil!"

It was hard for her to reel the bonefish against the forward rush of the Poseidon. Des stepped on it; the bait popped out and raced in a zig-zag along the surface. The marlin came up again behind it—angered by missing—and hit. Crunch said, "Drop back," and the girl threw off the brake. Line poured from the big reel spool. He said, "Now!" and she struck without remembering to flick on the drag. This time, she hooked the fish. The reel raced, the line backlashed, the marlin jumped once and broke away because of the snarl on the reel. Like the white marlin, he came out again—the bait in his jaws, the leader trailing into the sea.

A. B. Totten started to weep again—quietly. By now, she possibly wondered if two weeks was enough time to assure the catching of a blue marlin. "I did wrong," she said—as if to herself, or to an imaginary audience. "I'm sorry."

Then she went below. She brought the letter from her citified handbag and stood in the stern cockpit while Crunch re-baited—watching over his shoulder—and she slowly read the letter. It was mussed and frayed. Blue stationery—six or seven sheets. When she finished, she put it back and returned to her side chair and said, "Let's go again." She wasn't weeping any more. She was tranquil—yet filled with some personal emotion, and she seemed unreachable. That was the way Crunch felt. Beautiful—full of fun—worldy, too—but dedicated to something not in, or on the sea, or anywhere near Bimini.

The *Poseidon's* skipper kept a log, a technical document, which might have annoyed a navigator because its course and compass data was perfunctory. An ichthyologist would have considered it a gold mine, however. For the daily condition of the sea was described carefully—currents, clarity or marliness, estimated temperature, and so on—along with details concerning every major fish taken by the boat; its species, condition, variations, the bait used, the manner of attack, visible presence of other specimens, schools of food fish in the vicinity, and other such facts.

Occasionally, when Crunch felt in the mood or thought it would be of value, he made notes about his passengers. And after A. B. Totten had been on board for a week—after he had described the various dolphin, kingfish, the single wahoo, and the big bonito she had taken, together with the second blue marlin she had had a chance at (and lost to a mako shark after an hour of deep and dogged tug-of-war), Crunch wrote, "She is one of the hardest-trying woman anglers we ever fished. She's nuts about small fish on light tackle. I'm not even sure she likes to go after the big ones. But for some *reason*, not just fun, she's determined to get one. She isn't used to Bimini, yet, or to the heat."

On the morning of the first day of her second week, she said, "I think I'll stay ashore and swim till afternoon. It might change my luck."

Crunch's blue eyes were brotherly—and amused. "Bev usually swims around eleven—down the beach in front of that little coral bluff."

She made a face at him. "He told me."

Crunch relented. "Des and I will perform some primitive rites to appease Old Man Poseidon and maybe get you a fish. Such as polishing brass."

Her poise—a careful, thoughtful quality—broke a little. "Crunch, who, exactly, is Bev? I asked him—and he told me fables."

It was meant seriously. He answered—slowly selecting his phrases. "Well—Bev's been around the islands for a lot of years. Loves 'em. He had a London practice, once. In fact, a big one—he was pretty famous. There was a girl—it didn't turn out right—and then, according to local talk—a lot of whisky and a nervous breakdown. Finally, he went to work for the Bahamas Government. He's gotten to be—part of the scenery. Is that what you wanted to know?"

"You mean—he'll never leave here."

"That's what I mean, Miss T."

"Annabelle."

"He's a nice guy, Annabelle. He does a lot of good for a lot of people on these islands. Not very important people. Except, of course, when some big shot fishing over here gets the crud."

She was standing on the wharf near the *Poseidon*—in a dress the same color as her skin, a rosy brown—so that, except for her hair and her eyes, she seemed to be a single-hued creature—firmly curved and at the same time tucked and fluttered by the morning breeze. She reminded Crunch of his wife—though he thought Sari even prettier. She had smiled at Crunch's words.

"Bev spoke about treating American visitors. He said they kept him comfortably fixed—but they often made him feel as if he was getting a tip, not a regular doctor's fee." The smile receded like a little wave and came back as a sigh. "It must get monotonous here, though."

"Monotony is something inside you, not outside. You can run into it anyplace."

"That sounds like some horrid maxim! I suppose you're right—he'll never leave."

Crunch shook his head. "Nope. He thinks people are meant to live like this. Naturally. Outdoors. He hates cities."

"Greg used to," she responded—and when she realized what she had said, she checked the question he was going to ask by adding, "A guy I loved."

About two o'clock, Crunch looked up from sorting out, for discard, some rusted leader wire that had been sold to him as rustproof, and saw Annabelle approaching with the island-woven hat and the straw handbag she had bought for fishing. Bev accompanied her—in a shirt and shorts and sneakers—a pith helmet and dark glasses.

"He's going along," the girl said.

An hour later Crunch stood on the canopy with his back to the bows, his eyes on the two big baits, and his mind in the sapphire reverie of trolling on a beautiful day—with nothing happening. Below, in the cockpit, the doctor and the girl talked in such low tones that the engines blurred their words and left only an affectionate sound for the ears. Far off to stern, Bimini lay along the horizon like a level fringe stretched upside-down. A mile or more away, dark spots appeared in unison at regular intervals and Crunch knew, not consciously but adequately, that a school of porpoises was busied there in a sporty search for food. Des wasn't visible at the moment: getting colas in the galley, probably.

A novice, noting the hypnagogic look in the skipper's eyes, the relaxation of his muscles, and the easy swing of his walnut-brown shoulders in the heat and the slow movements of the glittering sea, would have believed Crunch was inattentive, and almost asleep. But that novice might also have noticed, an instant later, that Crunch's muscles took a sudden shape. He bent forward slightly. There it was: a deep shadow sneaking along behind Annabelle's bait. Crunch tapped the deck. Feet mumbled on the galley steps and Des appeared—taut, questioning. Crunch nodded toward the bait; the mate spun and saw the shadow rising.

"Miss T! Center chair!"

She moved. The marlin surfaced, followed, lunged. The line fell down from the long, willowy outrigger. It came tight. "Now!" Des said.

Bev murmured, "Pray, fellas!"

But the marlin did not take the bait. It simply vanished. Crunch cut the helm. The *Poseidon* turned in a narrow circle—and then a widening circle—over the place. Presently there was a small splash where Annabelle's bonefish was bouncing as she reeled it in. She dropped it back again—but again, there was no response.

"'Cuda," Des said disgustedly. "Bring it in."

The bonefish bait had been spoiled by the flashing strike of the barracuda. The mate prepared to change it.

Up on the canopy, Crunch wondered why a marlin that had risen so avidly had failed to take the bait. There were, in the area, numerous small clumps of golden seaweed. Perhaps one of these had caught and briefly clung to Annabelle's hook—a circumstance which would have rightly seemed unnatural to the fish. Crunch turned the boat in a still wider circle: the doctor's bait was intact.

He went around once. Nothing happened. Annabelle, he saw, had taken the letter from her straw handbag and, once more, was reading it—standing at the gunwale, facing the sea, biting her lips to conquer the new disappointment.

Then he stopped looking at the girl because, without warning—without following the bait under water or on the surface—the marlin (or *a* marlin, Crunch thought) shot diagonally into the air with the bonefish clamped in its jaws. It clove the water and crashed back and tore away from the boat. Crunch had never seen the slack in an outrigger line come taut in less time. It seemed to snap straight. And the doctor, who had seized his rod from the gunwale socket, took the full force of the run before he could get to the fighting chair.

It twisted him around and yanked him off his feet. He crashed against the stern violently. But he was up again in no time, whirling to face the fish, and striking as if the heavy tackle were a bass rod.

Des was at his side, now, with the harness. Annabelle had turned and was staring. Bev sat, buckled on the harness, tested his drag, and struck four more times. The surging fish came out in a series of low, furious leaps.

The girl said, "Oh, wonderful! You've hooked him!"

Bev waited for the jumps to end. Then he looked at them, showing the excitement in his usually calm eyes. "First time I ever connected with one of the beggars," he said. There seemed to be no parallel excitement in his voice.

Annabelle put the letter on the gunwale, absently, and came closer to him. He was "working" on the fish—his coppery arms rigid, his lean back pulling, his reel-hand grinding. "The first time?" She seemed incredulous.

"Verily, ma'am."

"Have you—have you been out much?"

"Oh, lots. My—patients often take me. Dozen of trips. Look out, there! Thinks he can learn to fly!" His tone changed to alarm. "Lord! Porpoises!"

The girl was still watching intently while the marlin raged into the air—and while the school of porpoises rolled and sped forward toward a spot between the boat and the fish. In her mind was the definite realization that to hope to catch a marlin on a two weeks trip was to take a very absurd gamble. And, in her sudden glance at Crunch—painful, apologetic—was the further realization that he had done his best for her and that his best was very good. But Crunch didn't take long notice of her. His gaze was bleak and bitter. The porpoises, bearing down in a way that was probably gay and certainly innocent, would cross the line. And if one of them hit it—swimming at that speed—!

He shrugged and turned his eyes away. There was nothing—just nothing—anybody could do about it.

But Des was trying. He hopped up on the fish box and shook his fists and bellowed as if he were an indignant fan at a stadium game, "Get out of there—you're going the wrong way! Fools! Beat it! You'll cut our line! Turn around! Hey!" At his feet was the bitten bait, which he had not had time to cut from its hook and leader. He grabbed it—leader and all—spun it around his head two or three times—and let it fly in the course of the porpoises.

Crunch, unamused by this, for Des, very emotional exhibition, saw another movement out of the corner of his eye. Annabelle's letter, which she had left on the gunwale, was blowing into the water, page by page. There was nothing to do about that, either. You couldn't stop to hunt up and try to retrieve a letter from all over the sea when you were tied to a marlin. Des was yelling, "Yah! Yah! Yah!"

Crunch looked at the threatened line.

The blue pages of the letter, or the splash of the thrown bonefish, or the white streak of the line itself, apparently caused the porpoises to veer. He saw them make simultaneous turns under the surface—like minnows in a school rather than two-thousand-pounders. He saw them surge past the boat. And Bev's marlin began greyhounding in a big curve, so that it was necessary for Crunch to turn the boat and put on full speed.

The fight lasted an hour and twenty minutes and was, from that point onward, what an old hand at big game angling might have called "regular," or even "ordinary," and an artistically inclined spectator would have called, "classical." Into it, the doctor put his great strength and endurance. During it, he smoked cigarettes which Annabelle lighted and executed the difficult, contortionist maneuver of taking off his soaked shirt while in the harness. Toward the end, the marlin put up a display of lunges and half-jumps so close to the boat that they could see the fury with which it used its bill on the leader and the raging glare in its eyes.

Crunch took the fish, Des got a rope over him. They had no native assistants on board because they had recognized that there was no room in Annabelle's budget for unforeseen expenses. The marlin banged on deck. Des delivered the coup de grâce.

"Go about four hundred and a quarter," he said. "Nice one."

Annabelle was panting and big-eyed. "Anyway," she murmured, "I *saw* one caught! I was actually glad it wasn't me. I'd never have lasted! What a thing!" And she kissed the doctor.

His brown eyes were lazy again. "I stole my hostess' fish, you know," he said. "Rotten luck for her. Terrifically bad manners. But I got kissed for it, right? Women are beasts for punishment, I guess. Carry on, Annabelle. I'll watch."

"We will not," she said. "We'll go in and weigh that fish and clean up and have a drink. Oh—I'm so happy!" And, in that peak of excitement, she remembered. She looked at the gunwale. She looked in her handbag and drew out the empty envelope.

The doctor moved his eyes from the fish to the girl. "Lose something, my dear?"

Her voice was far away and strange. "It was just a letter. It blew overboard, I guess. It wasn't important—and anyway—I know what it said."

The Poseidon murmured contentedly by means of the ropes that held her to the dock. Bev's fish hung against the purpling sky—a four-hundred-and-forty-two-pound silhouette. Somewhere up the King's Highway, the Bimini Band was tuning up for an evening concert. Its musical jargon—its Calypso rhythm—was like a spirit of the island—like the voices of such dryads as would live in tropical trees.

Crunch relaxed in a stern chair and wondered whether to join Des at the dance or fish for snappers. Archibald Ovlen, known locally as "One-knife"—black, bright, and thirteen—came down the dock on quiet feet.

"Crunch," he said.

"Yes, boy?"

"I found a letter—part of one—behind the fish box when I was mopping up."

"Why didn't you bring it to me right away?"

"I am."

No use arguing about promptness in Bimini. "Did you read it?"

"Naturally not, sir. I tested my spelling on a few words."

Crunch took the blue page. Whatever it said, the boy would know; and so—if it said anything dramatic or revealing—would all Bimini. "Scram, Two-knife."

The skipper thought a while longer and then read the page: "—so I'm mighty glad you're training as a nurse. We need 'em over here—every one you civilians can spare. Italy was rugged. Where we are going, it may be ruggeder. The other night I got thinking. If it pans out for me that it *doesn't* pan out, do something, will you? You being all the family I got left, I made out some extra insurance to you. Two G's. You know how I like the sea—and fishing. We were born on the seacoast, after all. You know how Pop never even got a decent crack at fishing—though he dreamed about it—because of the store all the time. I decided I don't want dough—or an office job, if I get back. I want to catch me one big fish most of anything in this world—and maybe, I'll be a fisherman. Commercial—or run a charter boat. But if I don't—you take the extra insurance and nail one for me someday, will you, baby? All my love. Greg."

Crunch put the letter in his pocket. The big sunset went out. Stars appeared—one here, one there, then in showers. He walked up the King's Highway, after a while; to the hotel. The Bimini Band was playing on the verandah; among the dozen couples dancing were Bev and Annabelle. Crunch cut in. "Like to talk a sec," he said.

She looked closely to see what expression went with his tone. She said, "Sure, Crunch."

They found an unoccupied corner of the long porch and sat down. He handed the page from the letter to her. "Blew aboard. The kid that washes down the boat read it—probably others, too—so I did."

She folded the blue page on its frayed creases. "That was quite a while ago. It didn't 'pan out' for Greg. He was killed in Normandy. The second day."

The pause was filled with orchestral beat. "I thought you worked in the furniture business," he said.

"A girl friend does. She's the secretary of the boss. I borrowed the stationery. I thought A. B. Totten, furniture, would look better as a fishing customer, than a gal who lives in a nurses' dormitory."

"Who was Greg?"

"My twin brother. Nobody's left of the family but me, now."

"Were you as keen about the sea as he was?"

"We lived on it—in Maine. Sure." She shrugged. "We—Greg and I—worked our way through a co-ed university together. He went to war afterward. I went to New York. I was determined to make good. I wanted to be a city girl—and marry somebody with a penthouse. Even after I decided to change from business to being a nurse—"

Crunch sniffed the aromatic night.

"But now—" she had interrupted herself. "I haven't caught that fish for Greg. The chances aren't so good, with only a few days left. And I've spent his insurance. All I seemed to have caught, Crunch, is the man that caught the fish. I'm crazy about him. He could use a trained nurse here. Do you think Greg would settle for that? And could I?"

"You'll have to figure out yourself, for yourself," Crunch answered. "But as a fishing man, speaking for one who sure had the makings, we always settle—for what we git."

"That's another platitude," she said. "Thanks, though."

It was very early in the morning—dawn, and no more—when Doctor Bevlington walked down the dock, making his steps loud in the evident rude hope of waking the skipper. Crunch sat up, rubbed his face, threw off the bedclothes and joined the doctor. For about five minutes they silently watched the still-hidden sun announce itself on the Caribbean clouds. Then Bev said, "Four o'clock."

"It's about six, man!"

"I mean, this afternoon. Invitation. I'm marrying that Yankee of yours."

The upper edge of the sun was a sudden white scimitar that gleamed on the marlin. Crunch stared at the fish and thought about the Englishman's over-restrained announcement. He felt a Yankee riposte-in-kind was necessary.

"Really!" he said.

Then he reverted to type and nearly knocked Bev off the dock with a mighty whack on the back.

FISH BITES MAN

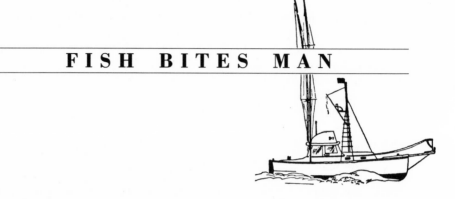

NOISY GROCERIES, unofficial mascot of the Gulf Stream boatmen, was racing in figure eights through Crunch Adams' back yard. The mongrel carried a small green cocoanut in his mouth. Behind him, with the fervor of a beagler, ran young Bill Adams, yelling. His mother looked without seeing; there was unhappiness in her expression. She did not hear the car roll to a stop in the drive. Crunch put his hands over her eyes and she made several deliberately preposterous guesses.

"It's Izaak Walton, Nimrod, the Old Man of the Sea," Crunch said. "*Your* old man, in short." He took his hands away, kissed her, yelled a loud "Hey!" at his son, and then asked, "What's the matter?"

Sari's reaction was a widening of the eyes. "What's the matter, yourself?"

Crunch felt the reddish spot on his check. "Barker. How that guy loves me! I was walking past his boat and he pulled up a rusty leader wire I couldn't see. I fell flat—and scraped a bench on the way down. It could have been accidental. He said it was. It could have been, that is, if captains were in the habit of fastening rusty leaders across the dock for no reason." He dismissed the deed. "Skip it. Point is—what's wrong with you?"

"Oh—nothing." Sari reached out from her deck chair, plucked the purple end of a bougainvillea vine, and held it under Crunch's chin. "You like grape juice," she said. She bespoke her trouble, indirectly. "Remember those people—the young ones—that caught the marlin?"

Crunch could never get accustomed to the vagueness of the feminine prelude. But he always tried. He rolled back his memory through hosts of fishermen, dozens of marlin, young couples, white and blue marlin. He drew a blank. "Which ones?"

"The poor ones," she answered. "I can't this minute think of their

221

names. He worked in a bank. He'd been an engineer—up north—and they came here for her health. You took them out for nothing, and I was sore about it."

Crunch's eye beamed with recognition; his head shook dolefully at the inadequacy of woman's brain. "Jeff and Janet James. Sure I remember 'em. Why? Something happen to 'em?"

"They're going to Cat Cay."

"That's dandy! I thought something was wrong! Don't you recall? Old Whitbie gave 'em a better job in his bank—after that marlin? I suppose Jeff's making enough to afford Cat Cay now—which is swell."

"That's the thing," Sari responded flatly. "They aren't making that kind of money. But they're going anyhow. They've saved up, and made arrangements. They can only afford a few days—and they're going with Captain Pinney, on the *Aurora*."

Crunch was visibly flabbergasted. That emotion became mirth. "So Lucius Pinney is going across at last!" His chuckle crescendoed into a shout of laughter.

Sari remained somber—almost bitterly so. "I don't see anything so funny about it! They're terribly nice kids and I'll bet if they knew at Cat Cay what kind of boat the *Aurora* was, they'd never let her anchor. It'll be dreadfully embarrassing for the Jameses! Honestly, Crunch, you've got to make 'em give up the idea!"

He was not laughing any longer. Noisy Groceries lay down on the grass beside him. Young Bill, more inexhaustible than the dog, began to throw the cocoanut for himself. "Yeah. I see what you mean. All those boats that go to Cat Cay—and the *Aurora*. It would be mighty humiliating. But, doggone it, Sari, the Jameses must realize that! They've got a right to do as they please! You may have the whole thing wrong—and I'm darned if I'm going to mess around with it."

"I'm not generally wrong about things like that, am I, Crunch?"

"You *could* be," he said doubtfully.

"Nevertheless—I want you to try to stop it. If Pinney must go, and the Jameses must, they can fish at Bimini. Troll the same water—and it isn't so swank. You don't have to dress for dinner every night. The Jameses may not even realize that. And if Janet has more than one evening dress, I'll eat the surplus! You surely realize how sensitive people feel in a spot of that sort. Women, especially."

Crunch assayed the girl's darkling eyes—and especially the locked angle of her jaw. He said rather hopelessly, "I can't go pushing into other people's business like that!" The words fell on flint and struck not even a spark. "How'd you find out?"

"Because," she made her voice chastising, "everybody at the Gulf

Stream Dock knows about it, and they're all laughing their silly heads off—just as you did!"

"Oh—well—"

A man on a diplomatic errand for his wife, one which involves duty to a detached idea, is a man in a vulnerable predicament. Crunch had refused point-blank to approach the Jameses. But he had announced a reluctant willingness to interview the skipper of the boat in question.

Late that afternoon, he went down to the Royal Hammock Dock. It was a tottering pier with loose planks; jury-rigged piles bolstered those which had been eaten nearly through by marine worms. The boats moored along it were ancient; derelicts with open cockpits, antique commercial fishermen, quondam rum-runners, dories with outboards, a dismasted sloop, and a houseboat that had actually sunk and was being used as a site from which to fish. Some of them were marked, "For charter—rates reasonable."

They'd have to do, Crunch thought. He sat down on a box and watched two kids who were catching snapper, to the annoyance of a middle-aged man beside them who was not catching anything. Cracker kids. They knew when and how to set the hook. The tourist didn't. Crunch decided to go over and show him—and then the *Aurora* hove in view.

She came not through Government Cut but through a Conch channel to the southward. She pushed slowly across the Bay, at what was probably full throttle. *Aurora*—goddess of the dawn—and standing joke of South Florida. She was short and stubby, basin-shaped. Old and needing paint. Outriggers sprouted from her like stems of a leafless fern. Five of them. Her small canopy was crammed with chairs. There were lines enough in her top-gear to make a cobweb. When she turned to run stern foremost into her slip, she showed a cockpit filled with chairs. There were two bunks below, and none on deck, because there was no space for them. Aboard her, at the moment, besides her skipper and his scrawny mate, were several passengers. Crunch counted. Six. Her single motor clanked, wheezed, ground in reverse, and Crunch rose to throw a stern line.

Her skipper waved at him delightedly and grabbed the controls again to keep from hitting the pier.

Cheerful little guy, Crunch thought. You wouldn't believe the *Aurora* was seaworthy enough for the Bay on a breezy day. But he'd seen her outside many a time, in a heavy easterly and a cold northwesterly, and a straight south semi-gale, bobbing in the big seas, dragging a slew of baits, loaded with people. An ugly little hulk—but a good boat for weather. And, of course, the number of passengers explained her existence. Pinney took as many as eight, fishing them in relays, if necessary. He accepted them in ones and twos and threes—strangers to each other; men who wanted desperately to have a crack at a sailfish or a white marlin or anything else in the blue water; men who couldn't afford thirty or thirty-five dollars for a day of trolling. Pinney charged them three dollars each. He made a meagre living out of it.

The mate opened the fish box in the stern. He began tossing out the catch—including two sails; he didn't look strong enough to heave them, but he was. People scrambled ashore, proud and excited, and women came down from cars to look breathlessly at the fish.

When his boat was secured, the skipper hurried toward Crunch. "Well, well! This is quite an honor for Royal Dock! Haven't seen you in an age! Say, Crunch! You heard the news?"

Determination began to wither in the master of the *Poseidon*. "News? What news?"

Lucius Pinney was laughing. Laughing with his blue eyes, his lips, his voice. "Tell you in a minute. Want to introduce a few of my passengers to you. Fellow named Grigg—sells wallpaper in Kansas City—and an accountant from Duluth—mighty swell chaps, all of them. Not rich, like your customers—but I sure do love to hitch a poor man to a big fish!" He raised his voice. "Say, men! Like to meet one of the most famous fishing guides in America?"

They crowded around Crunch, shook his hand, bashfully introduced their wives, thanked the captain profusely—and commenced to drift away with parcels of the fish they had caught. Crunch hoped his customers were as happy and excited when he brought them in as were those of Lucius Pinney. It would be fun to fish with Pinney. His enthusiasm never ebbed for a second.

The little man came back from wrapping fish. He tried to be modest. "The news, Crunch, is that I'm going across!" He said it as if he were talking about the inheritance of a million dollars.

"No!"

"Yes, sir! Yes, siree! Me an' the old *Aurora*. My Lord! For eleven years I been putting out of this stove-in dock with a deck-load of landlubbers, dragging baits in the Stream and getting my share of fish—maybe more." He chuckled at what was evidently a standard joke. "Yep. Maybe more— because the way I charter, I take so many people the baits behind my boat look like a school of herring. That gets up a raft of stuff. Yeah. Yep. I'm goin'. Eleven years—and I've dreamed all that time somebody would come along with money enough to say, 'Skipper. Get some clearance papers. We're goin' to wet a line in Bahamas waters!' And now—somebody said it and I still can't believe my luck! Imagine me over in that mako and marlin water! Me! Pinney!"

Crunch peered over the pale blue Bay and bit hard on both his lips.

He thought about Sari's demand, and he thought about the little guy at his side. Crunch knew the feeling that man was having. He turned back and held out his hand. "That's swell, Lucius. Dandy! When you going?"

"Next week—Wednesday."

"Bimini?"

There was scorn in the man's voice. "Hell, no! It seems that when I do it I do it up brown! My customers are going right to Cat Cay—and there they're going to stay."

"How long you be there?"

Lucius Pinney's eyes were evasive. "Oh—quite a while. It's a first-rate charter. Yeah. Yep. Quite a spell."

"I see." Crunch wanted to help, then. To help and to instruct and to find out things. "Well—I'll be there myself. Leaving tomorrow. Tonight, we're packing the *Poseidon* full of dress clothes and champagne, and generally making her a sissy-ship—"

Lucius interrupted. He was worried, and horribly embarrassed. "Say." His voice became a whisper. "Over there—I wouldn't want to look like a greenhorn! The—the guides—don't wear no tuxedoes at night, do they?"

"They do not! They have a special place to eat—a bar of their own—"

A sigh escaped the other man. "Swell—isn't it?"

Crunch's eye was traveling over the stern of the *Aurora*. "What kind of an outfit you going to fish?"

"Well—my customers—people named James—banker" Lucius flushed abruptly. "You know them, I think. They've been fishing with me for years, off and on. I should say—the chap works in a bank, hunh? Putting ont he dog, myself!Well—they were willing to try it with my two fourteen-ounce rods and twenty-four-thread line. Thought it would be sportier—"

"I've got a spare heavy rig, Lucius. Be glad to lend it to you—"

There was hurt pride—an infinitude of it—in the response. "Why Crunch, you'd oughta know me better'n that! When I take people across, I do it right! Comm'ere!" Secretively, jubilantly, he led Crunch through the jumble of chairs and gear on his boat and down into the cabin. Lying on one of the bunks was a thirty-nine-thread outfit, not a new one, but one that had been painted and polished till it shone. "I bought that," said Lucius, "just for the trip. It'll take the profit out of it for me—but I may wangle some more trips, with gear like that, hunh? And—the best part is—the Jameses don't know I've got it aboard! They still think they gotta fish my light stuff exclusively!"

"That's elegant, Lucius," Crunch said. He tested the reel. He jerked on the line. He cocked his head appreciatively. And, as soon as he could, he got away from the exuberant little man.

When he came in for dinner, Sari said, "Well? Did you persuade them to go to Bimini—or down in the keys—or some place where they won't get their feelings hurt?"

Crunch looked at his wife thoughtfully. "No, Sari. I didn't. They're going to Cat Cay."

"But—Crunch!!"

"This is a free country," Crunch answered. "I said—they're going."

The dark-haired girl sighed. "You kind of let me down, Crunchie."

To big game anglers, Cat Cay is Valhalla, Mecca, the Kohinoor and the Empire State Building. It lies on the eastern side of the funnel through which pours the hot, transparent bath of the Gulf Stream. It was once merely another key—a ragged reach of coral, breaking the blue water into foam, covered with a rug-like green jungle, and guarded by ostentatious birds. But the day came when men who had once exulted over a three pound trout taken on a rod and reel began to think three hundred pounds was no great shakes for hefty relatives of the same species of tackle. This new sport was dashing, daring—and expensive. And, for those who could afford it, there was need of a base suitable to the tastes of the elite.

Cat Cay became such a base. There the conventional clubhouse sprang up, the gaudy modern barroom, docks, beaches for swimming, fruit groves, winding trails paved with concrete and trespassed by tricycles in which guests could lounge while Negroes pedalled them through tunnels in the tropical trees. Tennis courts came to Cat Cay; a golf course was started, hole by hole, in the soft rock of the island; fine plate, cutlery, silverware, luxurious beds, paintings, archery butts, croquet mallets, the seedlings of rare flowers, tall mirrors, glittering plumbing, stemware with monograms—all that and much more—reached the island by boat. Then came the people, dressing for dinner each night, fishing every day the wind let them, eating steaks flown to their table through the air. The names of those people, signed in colors on the barroom wall, were such as might be expected: the names of fortunes and celebrities, of famous beauties and renowned athletes, of society and café society, of foreign notables, princes, dukes, duchesses, and nobody at all who wasn't somebody.

Crunch was there—on the other side of the island, where the guides lived and the boats docked—when the *Aurora* put into the harbor.

It was a little worse than he had expected. Quite a little worse. And he'd already had bad moments imagining it. The guides on their boats and those on the dock set up a cheer—a cheer of astonishment and mirth. The anglers and other guests in the area came down in their white flannels and their slack suits and their lavishly simple sports dresses, and they, too, stared at the miniature burlesque of what a fishing cruiser should be. The boatmen thought that Lucius had aimed at Bimini and missed—and they found that hypothesis a reason for hilarity. Many of the guests, judged by their expressions, thought that, in any case, the *Aurora* should be shooed away from the Cat Cay basin. But it came in and moored—amidst the nautical splendor of fifty and hundred thousand dollar yachts—of boats that made even the gleaming *Poseidon* look rather unimportant. For there was no chrome on the *Aurora*. Just brass and bronze, dulled by hard wear and salt water.

Lucius Pinney, ignoring the laughter, ran in close, asked where his moorings were, and stopped his incredible boat in the midst of the grandeur. He was blushing slightly, and his eyes kept avoiding other eyes, but his mouth was smiling. A mouth that said: Let 'em laugh. I suppose we do look funny. But we're having a better time than they are!

It was in a similar humor that the Jameses appeared from below, carrying their unprepossessing luggage. Jeff beamed at the people. Janet saw Crunch and waved. Crunch went down to the *Aurora* and took their bags. He walked with them between the people—and the way he walked quieted them a little.

Janet was pretty, and much less frail than she had been when her health had caused the Jameses to come south, with no prospects. She whispered to Crunch, "We made it! Imagine, Crunch! And we've saved up enough to stay here five whole days!"

Jeff, lean and wiry—he'd been stroke on his hundred and fifty pound crew at college—looked straight ahead. His eyebrows were sardonic and he didn't whisper, but his voice was low: "I knew, Crunch, that the *Aurora* would be a sort of skeleton at the feast. But people don't need to look at us as if we were lepers. It's all for fun—or am I wrong?"

"If anybody in the world *isn't* wrong," Crunch replied, "it's you two kids." Then he growled at a mate. "Gangway, lug!"

After Crunch had started the Jameses and their luggage across the key, he strolled toward his boat. Mr. Whetencoat, who had chartered him for this trip, touched his arm. "You mean to say, skipper, those people actually have *reservations?*"

Crunch looked at his customer coldly. "Yeah." Mr. Whetencoat was a noted polo player. He was trying big game fishing for the first time and was not yet sure that he liked it. Crunch was pretty sure that he didn't like Whetencoat.

"Must be some mistake, old man."

"No mistake. Those kids aren't rich—but they know more about fishing than you do about horses."

"Really!" said the poloist. He didn't say any more because of the expression in Crunch's eyes.

Linda Bonnelle came tripping down the dock, streaming dark hair and nickel-plated laughter. Crunch could never remember whether Linda was the Number 3 or the Number 4 glamour girl of the current season. She snatched his arm with both of hers. "Crunchie! How perfectly priceless! What a stunning gag! Who are those fascinating people! I'd give anything to have thought up a rib like that!"

Crunch detached the lady. "It isn't a rib, Linda."

She stood there, slowing understanding that. "If it isn't a rib, then it's rather nasty! I mean to say—"

Crunch's insides felt as if they were injured and full of salt. "Nasty? I wonder, Linda, if you ever heard the word 'pathetic'?"

Her eyes flashed. "Aren't you being rather impertinent, Captain?" She turned and yelled, "Oh, muzz! No gag! It's for real! Can you top that!"

The *Poseidon*, throbbing gently, trolled along the edge of the islands toward Bimini. Mr. Whetencoat got a strike, fought a big grouper, and brought it to boat. Crunch gaffed it. "Keep it?" he asked.

The lone passenger scowled. "Certainly. What do you mean—keep it?"

"We've got enough for the dining room for a day or two—"

"What's that got to do with it? I caught it, didn't I?"

They headed out toward bluer water. Crunch put over two marlin baits. They danced and slid on the waves, jerking the lines to the outriggers as if they were marionettes.

Much later, Desperate, the mate, leaned over and said to Crunch softly, "Hey. Commere."

Their passenger was dozing. Crunch hopped aloft.

Up ahead was a cluster of boats—boats from Cat Cay and boats from Bimini. Conspicuous in the flotilla was the *Aurora*; her many outriggers, for her usually many customers, made her the most noticeable of all. From the others came, at intervals, the sound of horns and whistles. Musical blasts and shrill, metallic sirenings and basso-foggy bleats.

"Very funny," said Des.

Crunch scowled. "I don't get it."

"They're kidding the *Aurora*. Every time they troll past—they salute her."

Crunch looked and listened a while. "Yeah," he finally said. "Very funny. So funny, that if the captains keep razzing poor old Pinney, somebody in these parts is maybe going to get hurt!"

There was a yell from below. Crunch spun around. He was just in time to see that something had snatched a bait, pulled the line out of the clothespin, hauled it tight, and wakened Mr. Whetencoat. A fish, blue and gigantic, split the sea. Mr. Whetencoat, in an agony of excitement, threw the reel on free-spool. Crunch yelled a warning. The reel, without a drag to check it, spun like an airplane propeller and backlashed. The line broke—whizzing back into the cockpit. The marlin leaped again, trailing leader wire, and was gone.

Then Mr. Whetencoat realized anger was in order. "Captain," he began, "should you or should you not have been at my side for that strike? Am I or am I not paying you some fifty dollars a day—"

One of those "am-I-or-am-I-notters," Crunch thought, and he took his scolding patiently.

He didn't see the Jameses that night. But the next night he did. They came over to the guide's side of the island for a visit with their old friend. Crunch welcomed them aboard and set out cigarettes and candy.

"How's it going?" he asked.

Janet answered. "It's wonderful! We had two blues on this afternoon. We saw a baby whale. We caught a white marlin on twenty-four-thread— seventy-seven pounds. It's just too swell to believe! And this place—is heavenly!"

Jeff was looking quizzically at his wife and rubbing his chin. "I could do without a couple of the people, though."

The girl nodded. "Yes. But the management's lovely about us being— not very well off, and having a funny boat. There are some snobs, always, in a place as expensive as this."

Crunch looked at the stars, feeling relieved. They were juicy stars, set in the special Bahamas brand of black plush sky. The youngsters could take a kidding and still like it. Game. Or maybe just crazy about fishing. Both, to be exact. He began to talk. "Snobs. Yeah. A lot of people want to be snobs. All of us—in a way. I've fished some very ultra people—that I liked to beat the devil. Many. I always kind of figured that a true snob was somebody who was snobbish only toward phoneys, impostors, hypo-crites, and so on. I mean, he'd get along with anybody who was sincere— you, or me—or the King of England. Only, a lot of snobs figure things out just the other way around. I heard 'em whistling at you the other day."

Janet chuckled. "Did you? You know what? Every time they whistled, Lucius picked up his lung-power horn and blew a salute right back at them. He did it till he was dizzy. And today—they didn't bother us."

Crunch didn't explain that he had spent a whole evening telling indi-vidual boatmen in vivid detail what would happen to them if they main-tained the razzberry of the *Aurora*. There was a tranquil pause. He won dered why he always thought of them as youngsters. The Jameses were the same age as he and Sari. You just did, that was all. Everybody thought of people like the Jameses as youngsters.

"We're fishing from now on," Janet presently said, "on lighter tackle. One of those blues this afternoon sounded—and ran—and sounded deeper—and took the whole thousand yards of thirty-nine-thread! It popped at the spindle. I was so sorry for Lucius I could have cried. It was so perfectly darling of him to buy that gear just for us—!"

"I'd be glad—" Crunch began.

Jeff checked him with a smile. "We said you would. No use. Lucius is as proud as a Turk. Anyway, if we do boat one on twenty-four-thread, it'll be that much more of a trick. We did it once—remember?"

"I'll say I remember!" Crunch ate a caramel, reflectively. They had only three days more—even if the weather held. And they were going to use twenty-four-thread. He wondered how many marlin had been boated, through the years off Cat Cay and Bimini, with that size of line. A couple of dozen, perhaps. It was true that on their first day of deep sea fishing the Jameses had been lucky; and there is a superstition among fishing men that some people are lucky—while others are not. But Crunch felt their chances with twenty-four-thread were mighty slim. Painfully slim. He wanted them to get a fish.

For a while longer, they talked. Then they meandered along the dock together, looking at the vast dark shapes of the prizes which had been brought in.

Crunch was up exceptionally early. He prodded Des awake and together they slipped the *Poseidon*'s moorings. They shattered a glassy stillness by starting their motor. And they headed out to sea. Their passenger wouldn't be down for at least three hours; he was a tardy riser. And even the Jameses wouldn't appear for an hour and a half. Crunch had an idea— an idea that was Quixotic—and typical of him. He ran the *Poseidon* far out into the Gulf Stream, cut down the motors, and cruised in random curves, far from shore. After a suitable interval, he headed back.

The dock, which had been deserted at the time of his departure, was now a scene of sunlight and busy expectancy. Crunch walked over to the *Aurora* with a hank of wet line on his arm. Lucius was whistling merrily as he prepared baits for the day's trolling. He winked at Crunch, said, "Fine day! Great to be here, isn't it?"—and saw the line. His jaw shot out.

Crunch dropped aboard. "This yours, Lucius?"

The blue-eyed man was sullen. "You know it isn't!"

"I'm doggoned if I know anything of the kind! How big a fish was the one that ripped off what you had?"

"Dunno. It didn't come out."

"Mmmm. Look. Ever hear of a guy hooking a fish—and losing it—and catching the same one later, with his own hook and leader in it?"

Lucius was red of face. "I've *heard* of it."

"Well—listen. Des and I thought there might be some schools of pil-chards hanging around farther out today. Got up early just to find out. Put a bait over—for the hell of it. And we hung one. A nice blue. No fight in him much, though. Hauled him in and darned if there wasn't another line dragging away from him. So I grabbed up the other line, too, and the next thing you know he gave a terrific surge—and broke off both. If this isn't your line, I'll wear it around my neck for the rest of my life."

Lucius' eyes, pale, reddish at the rims, moist—met those of Crunch squarely. Lucius, knew Crunch was lying; he knew why Crunch had wakened everybody by starting his motor at the crack of dawn. And Crunch knew Lucius didn't believe him. So Crunch just kept staring back, daring the smaller man to say anything. It was a long, quiet bat-tle—funny perhaps—but not to either contender. Finally Lucius reached out. "You like those kids, don't you? So do I." And nothing more was said about the line—then, or ever.

Crunch was very glad about that line.

Not that day, but the next.

He'd thought of the Jameses as lucky. He also thought that there ought to be some justice. And there was. He didn't see them hit their fish. He heard about it on the ship-to-shore phone.

Somebody had been using it to discuss the matter of flying a certain kind of wire over to Cat Cay. Crunch had listened, and was about to turn off the apparatus. Mr. Whetencoat was asleep again. The baits were rock-eting along. Crunch reached for the switch and then an excited voice cut in: "Hello, *Pandora*! *Go West* calling the *Pandora*! Say! . . . You any-where near us? . . . Yeah . . . The *Aurora*'s just hung something terrific. Can you imagine that! . . . Yeah—where I said I'd be—off the north end of the island about four miles. . . . They're right near. . . . It's a whop-per, all right!"

Crunch turned the *Poseidon* toward the spot indicated, and notched up the motors. In half an hour, he could see the fronds of the *Aurora*. He could also see a couple of other boats approaching the spot. Barker's new one, for example—the *Sea Dog*. Crunch thought acidly that Barker was the very man to rush up and interfere where another had hung a fish. Many skippers did that, on the thin hope of hooking a mate.

But Crunch wasn't expecting what he saw when the *Aurora*, her two frenetic passengers, and her crazed skipper became visible through the glasses. Their fish leaped. Mr. James rocked and cranked. It was a big one, all right, but not a record, by any means. It broke again. Crunch looked again. Then he handed the glasses to Des. "See if you see what I did."

Des grinned. "I saw—with my own good eyes. Broadbill."

Crunch whammed his hat on the canopy and stamped on it. "God bless those Jameses!" he said fervently. "And heaven help them to get it in!"

From below came the querulous voice of the awakened Whetencoat. "Look here, you two! You're not paying any attention to me, again! That cost us a fish the last time, you may recall. I'm paying you an exorbitant sum—!"

Crunch watched the battle. He also watched Barker troll the *Sea Dog* round and round the area. Finally he went over close to Barker's boat. Crunch was feeling a sort of super-glee—suspended and prayerful. He yelled at Barker, "Ain't that somethin'! How often does a broadbill take a trolled bait? Once every fifth blue moon! And say! Give 'em more room!"

Barker swore. Barker's two men passengers also looked unhappy. One of them bawled at Crunch, "Maybe you think it's funny, Captain! But we've been fishing here for nine days without a hit!"

Crunch nodded sympathetically at the men.

The swordfish stayed deep for a long time. An hour, perhaps. Mr. James worked like a Trojan. Crunch saw his wife wiping the sweat out of his eyes, getting a hat for him, and a drink of water, and a stick of gum. Then the fish broke and raced on the surface toward the place where the *Poseidon* and the *Sea Dog* were working. That, apparently, was too much for Barker. Full of envy, disappointment, and spite for Crunch, he swung his boat deliberately toward the line that connected Jeff James with his fish. Crunch saw it; his face turned white. He stabbed the *Poseidon* ahead at full throttle. She was fast. She intercepted Captain Barker so that he had the alternative of smashing into the *Poseidon* or sheering off. He sheered—spitting overboard in derision at Crunch.

It was then, or thereabouts, that Des voiced a problem. "Look, Crunch. You said you were praying they'd get that broadbill in. How are they going to get it in? I never saw a block and tackle on the *Aurora*. He hasn't any panel in the stern. He and that scrubby mate can't lift it. Of course, if they get a rope on its tail, they can inch it out in time. But this water's liable to have sharks in it—which you know as well as I do."

"Yeah," said Crunch. He began to watch the fight narrowly. Barker had given up the district and trolled away. Jeff James, who had once come aboard the *Poseidon* with hydrographic maps and theories about fish—and proved his theories—was laboring expertly. The broadbill, under the surges of a collegiate stroke, wasn't going to last much longer. In fact, it broke and rolled on its side—a sign of fatigue. Crunch edged closer to the *Aurora*.

Mr. Whetencoat spoke rancorously. "See here, Captain. If you have any intention of helping with that fish, I forbid it. After all, you're under my charter!"

Crunch looked down. "And you're my passenger. I'm the Captain."

"You do this—and I'll call this trip off, immediately we dock. You've no right—none whatever—to give away my fishing time!"

Crunch came in close to the *Aurora*, on the side away from the bucking fish. He lifted a megaphone. "Hey! Lucius! How you going to take him aboard?"

Lucius cupped his hands. "That's what we're wondering! Rope his tail, I guess, and lift him an inch at a time."

Des pointed to an inquisitive and ominous triangle of fin. He bellowed, "See that! You've got to yank him out fast—or he'll be chewed and ineligible!"

Lucius looked at the shark and his face sickened.

Crunch bellowed again. "When the swivel is in sight, I'll come up alongside, stern first. Have your mate grab it—and pass it to Des. Have Jeff slack off on the drag as we pull away. We'll take him aboard!"

The boating of the broadbill later became one of the high moments in the annals of Cat Cay. Des took out the *Poseidon*'s panel and the sea slopped into the cockpit. Mr. Whetencoat snarled. Lucius' mate yelled that the swivel was in sight. A moment later he had the leader, and the broadbill was thrashing astern. Des put a fender over and the boats touched. One of Crunch's outriggers snapped off one of the *Aurora*'s. Des reached five times for the leader before the mate could get it to him. The shark—not a fin, but visible as a huge shape—moved in. The broadbill was bleeding. Crunch left the controls for a few perilous seconds, yanked open the fish box, heaved out Mr. Whetencoat's big grouper, and fed it to the shark. That gave them a short respite from one hazard. Des was pulling in leader, gently, strongly. Crunch eased the *Poseidon* off a bit. Then he came astern with ropes, a block and fall, and the big flying gaff. The job was finished when Des fell upon the floundering giant with a billy.

Evening came. Then night. Crunch was sitting in the black beatitude, alone. Every once in a while, he smiled.

The Jameses—and several other people—came roistering down the dock in tricycles and on bicycles. Janet began introducing people to Crunch. "They've just given us the most marvelous party! We didn't realize what an event the taking of a broadbill would be! You've got to come up to the bar and have a drink, Crunch! You've got to!"

He had a beer. He listened to the music, and watched the impromptu dancing. By and by he wandered again into the darkness. Jeff came out and joined him. Jeff was disturbed. "I've just found out that what you did for us—made that fellow Whetencoat mighty sore."

Crunch's eyes shone. "Yeah. He canceled me."

"Good Lord! That's awful, man!"

The captain's head shook. "I've been sitting here smirking. One of the things that made me do it was Whetencoat. Ever since the first day he fished me, I've been wondering how to get rid of him. In Miami—waiting for me—there's another much nicer party that wants to come over here. All I have to do is radio them to hop a plane." He grinned at Jeff's sigh of relief. Then he went on, "I was worried as sin about you kids coming over here."

"Worried? Why?"

Crunch was uncomfortable. "Oh—the people here—and the *Aurora*—"

"The people?" Jeff sounded surprised. "Why—we know a lot of them. Janet was a debutante once. Didn't anybody ever tell you that? When she got sick we gave up New York—and everything—and sort of sneaked down to Florida. We haven't run into many of our old friends for several years. But they were delighted to see us. A few we didn't know were snooty, of course—at first—"

Crunch went back to the *Poseidon*. He thought about a debutante who would go to Florida and live on twenty-eight a week. That was their salary when Crunch first knew them. And he thought about the kind of a guy who would go with her, and do it for her. He also thought, that for just this once, Sari had been wrong.

Barker came along in the shadows.

"I been thinking," he said, "an' I think that when it takes two boats to catch a fish—it isn't legal."

Crunch budged only his eyebrows. "And I went to the authorities here and I asked—and they flagged Miami on it—and that broadbill is already registered in the Tournament."

Barker spit. "And you're a louse," he said. "And your old woman is a dirty rotten busybody and a party-snatcher."

That moved more than Crunch's eyebrows. He came up and stood in front of Barker. "You've been asking for this a long time," he said.

Barker, who had once boasted that he could kill Crunch because he'd been a professional wrestler, removed his jacket. It was a long fight. The people at the bar didn't know about it until Crunch came in, unconsciously massaging his knuckles. "There's a man lying on the dock," he said, "—sort of a man, that is—and he needs liniment, iodine, adhesive plaster and a stretcher." The crowd fell silent. Crunch caught sight of its most ecstatic member—Lucius Pinney. "It's Captain Barker," he explained. "Looks like he got bit by the *Aurora*'s broadbill."

THE AFFAIR OF THE ARDENT AMAZON

THE WINDS of March, unaware of the calendar, went on blowing until mid-April. That kept Miami's sportfishing fleet tied up; tourists wouldn't brave the windstacked seas, and local people could wait for better weather. By mid-April, the guides at the Gulf Stream Dock were restless from inaction. However, Crunch Adams, the *Poseidon*'s captain, was less impatient than most of his colleagues, though no less ready for a charter. His relative calm was due partly to temperament, but partly to the winds themselves. The fact that he and his mate, Des Smith, were stormbound had been put to use by Crunch's wife, Sari.

It was Sari's opinion that boatmen made good husbands. It was also her belief that womankind had a natural equity in all men who were attractive, courageous and able. Des Smith was such a man—but Des was a bachelor. So, during the windy weeks, Sari had paraded past Des a series of likely but unwed young ladies.

To her surprise, Des commenced to take an interest in a certain Eloise Derby. Sari was so pleased that Crunch regarded the stormy weather as only a partial calamity.

Nevertheless, his desire for business grew great. And when the wind dropped, he enthusiastically welcomed aboard a man who said he wanted to make a deal. He was a thin, small man, and citified; he wore a natty felt hat and two-tone shoes; he had a moustache like a hairpin—and office pallor.

"I have a client," the man said, holding out a card, "who wants to fish up some publicity for herself."

Crunch waved the man to a seat in a fighting chair and read the card: ALFRED RAINEY, ARTISTS' REPRESENTATIVE. The address was Broadway and New York City.

Crunch repeated inquiringly, "Fish up publicity?"

"Here's the pitch," the man said, his eye taking in the outriggers and tackle with some apprehension. "My client is Beulah Boyd." He paused for a second, received no sign of recognition, shrugged, and went on. "She's the strongest woman in the world. Natural athlete. Circus trained. Used to be a wrestler, but wrestles only for charity now. They billed her then as 'Beauty and Beef'—she's a looker. I'm grooming her for TV and movies. She can act."

"What does she want us to help her do?" Crunch asked without enthusiasm. "Wrestle a shark?"

Mr. Rainey's look of anxiety increased. "Nothing like that! She's strictly legit! Has a lot of records and firsts. She's got a short night-club spot here, next week. Five-day layover. I'm building more firsts for her. Kick a football farther than any living woman. Like that. In Peoria, a while back, she broke two plug-casting records for women. Never had a fish-pole in her hand before. I decided if she could nail a big fish of some sort, and we had a cameraman there to shoot the action, it would be another first for Beulah. Make good pix. Hit the papers. See?"

"Sure," Crunch said. "But sometimes big fish won't co-operate. Unless you'll settle for a shark."

"That'd be your problem. Beulah's got these five days to fish. I could afford to risk four hundred, for a real publicity fish."

"We couldn't guarantee it," Crunch answered.

"I'm gambling on you. Fishing's class! Beulah needs class build-up. I've got to get back to little old New York on biz, for a few days, see? Fishing'd keep Beulah out of—keep her occupied."

Crunch wondered what Beulah needed to be kept out of, but didn't ask. Four hundred dollars for five days was good money. "We'll do our best," he said.

Mr. Alfred Rainey pulled out a billfold. "Pay you in advance," he said. "Might as well. If she knows I've spent the money, she'll be sure to go fishing."

From the dock, he called down, "I'll hire Wally Bates to go along to get the pictures."

"Know him well," Crunch called back. "O.K."

Crunch was feeling extra bland on the morning following the deal. He had a good idea about how to get a fish that would be big, though not especially sportive. He had a tidy charter, signed and paid for. The weather was serene, and Des had gone up to the end of the dock to await their customer. Crunch expected that Beulah would be a fading Diana, a Mrs. Five-by-Five, like most lady wrestlers. He was stowing a case of colas when he heard his mate's call and hastened to the cockpit.

He saw Des, burdened with a motion-picture-camera tripod, a suitcase and a lunch basket. He saw Wally Bates, gnarled and grinning. The two men then separated, and Crunch saw Beulah.

She was a big girl in her late twenties, rather than the envisaged forties. She had wavy hair. Her eyes, large and incandescent, were fixed on Des approvingly. She wore a boy's checked-gingham shirt—and shorts. From the shorts there extended limbs which showed no muscular ropiness. She was, Crunch decided, one of the best-looking young ladies he had ever seen. That was all he had time to decide.

Beulah ran at the boat. She left the dock in a flying dive. Crunch, standing below in the stern cockpit, ducked—because she was sailing right over his head. She sailed across the cockpit and caught the footbrace of a fishing seat on the canopy deck, as if it were a trapeze bar. She jackknifed her legs, arched into the cabin space, swung back, skinned the cat and straightened her body, vertically and upside down. She let go with one hand, did a slow roll, chinned herself with her right arm, and dropped to the deck.

"You're Crunch," she said. "I'm Beulah. Shake!"

He shook hands. He felt that he was engaging a power-driven vise. However, Crunch was male, Crunch had once been a prizefighter and Crunch kept in condition.

In a minute, she laughed. "O.K.! I give up! I couldn't mash Desperate's hand, either."

Crunch looked at his fingers. They were still in place, but not many men could have given him as hard a struggle. "Make yourself at home," he said. "Hi, Wally!"

The cameraman came aboard familiarly, sat down and lighted a cigar.

Des leaned over his skipper and whispered, "Brother!" Crunch had a sudden feeling that perhaps this charter, like some others, would present special difficulties. "Let's go fishing," he said, and started the motors.

Des went forward to handle the lines. Wally stretched out on a day bed and smoked. Beulah began doing tricks on the ropes of the block and tackle that hung from a stubby mast and was used to haul big fish into the boat.

They left the Government Cut and headed south, hooked-up and not trolling; they had distance to cover. Some months before, Crunch had seen, on the reef below Fowey Light, three large jewfish. Jewfish are sea bass and considered, by sports anglers, somewhat turgid. But they can weigh as much as half a ton. And half a ton, or even a quarter of a ton of anything with fins, is generally able to provide the angler with excitement. Furthermore, jewfish are photogenic; they look like the mystic deity of all the basses, fresh-water or salt.

Crunch headed for the spot where he'd seen the monsters, knowing that such fish are usually residential; they have "homes" and stay around them. Beulah soon went forward and sat down beside Des. She had removed her informal shirt and now sun-bathed in a halter. This gave Crunch a further chance to marvel. Beneath her sun tan was no conspicuous show of sinew. She was not muscle-bound. True, she had broad and slightly thick shoulders. But Nature had shaped her in proportion.

The skipper could observe more. Miss Boyd was making an impression on Des Smith, a vast impression. They were talking. That is, Beulah was talking. Des was mostly listening, as usual. But he had stopped chewing gum. His eyes were slightly glazed. His yachting cap, which he wore as level as an officer in naval reserve, now hung jauntily over one ear. And these were the symptoms, in Des.

Crunch thought ruefully of his wife's campaign — and of Eloise Derby, of whom Sari intensely approved. He somehow felt that Sari would take a dim view of Beulah. He shook his head morosely. Old Des, he hoped, would be only momentarily bemused, or stunned. He set aside his worry; he had other things to consider.

He took a compass reading, changed course, and ran on a specific bearing with Fowey Light exactly astern. He watched the shore until a clump of distant Australian pines fell in line with a beacon. At that point, he cut the engines. "O.K.," he called.

Des brought Miss Boyd back to the cockpit, holding her arm. "We're going to drift a live bait," he explained.

"Meaning what?" she asked pleasantly.

Des looked over the side. Here the water was many-colored — dark blue over rock patches, light blue over the sand, and glacier-green inshore, where the reefs rose close to the surface. These colors, like the purple edge of the Gulf Stream, were sharply delineated; and so much sunshine poured upon the water that it seemed to glow and shimmer.

"Down there," Des said to the girl, "some mighty big jewfish live. We'll put a grunt or a yellowtail on your line and let it swim toward bottom. Maybe an ordinary grouper will take it or maybe a shark. But maybe one of the jewfish. If he does, you'll have something to take your picture with. If you boat him, that is."

She watched while he baited up and arranged the line in a clothespin tied to a stern cleat. "That'll hold the bait off bottom," he explained. "Then, when something hits it, the line'll snap free of the clothespin and you'll have a fish on. Practically automatic."

The *Poseidon* drifted. Wally Bates lay down on the day bed again, after arranging his cameras; he soon began to snore. Crunch went up to the top controls. On the edge of the reef, there was only a slow current. But occasionally he started one motor and ran back to the spot he had discovered. For an hour, nothing happened. Then a barracuda ripped off the live grunt and Des put on another bait.

A second hour passed.

From the mate's standpoint, it was not an empty interlude. For now, Des talked. Crunch thought he had never heard his mate say so much, in any previous month. Des even flirted, almost brazenly; and that was also without precedent.

Beulah Boyd talked too. In fact, she told Des a large part of the story of her life: "I had five brothers," she confided, "and we lived on a farm. They taught me to wrestle and even box, and to swim in the creek and dive. I got real husky. I loved rovin', besides, and when I was fifteen—I looked eighteen—I ran away with a carnival. Then the circus. I learned the trapeze and the high wire, a little. One day, the strong lady got sick. I'd been watching her. I knew I could do her tricks and then some, so I filled in—and got her job. Then vaudeville." Beulah sighed. "Now it's TV, even, sometimes! And Mr. Rainey thinks he can get me in pictures!"

"You'd be—magnificent," Des said.

Crunch was barely able to restrain sarcastic utterance. For he could now see that Beulah Boyd was definitely not a suitable young lady for his mate. Beulah "loved rovin'." A man fond of her would spend his life making sleeper jumps and flying from New York to Hollywood. A man married to Beulah would, Crunch bitterly perceived, merely hang around to hold her coat.

He had reached that point in his meditation when the jewfish hit. It astonished Crunch that they should have luck so soon; but that was only the beginning of amazement for him.

It was a big jewfish. After the first flurry of excitement—in which Des yelled, Wally Bates woke and started grinding film, and Beulah grabbed the rod—Crunch could see a dark, broad-backed blob, deep down. That was their fish—charging across an azure desert of sand toward a deep blue area of submarine coral.

"Stop him, if you can!" Crunch yelled.

The jewfish, a bottom-dwelling species, usually heads for the nearest rocks when hooked. He is doubtless merely in search of familiar seclusion of the coral arcades and caverns in which every jewfish enjoys hiding. But the effect is to cut lines, to foul them up, and to snarl steel leaders.

Miss Boyd, however, was using thirty-nine-thread line, a heavy rod and a large reel with which Des had somewhat familiarized her. When told to stop the fish if she could, Beulah screwed up the drag, tight. The rod took a croquet-wicket set. The reel grunted in pain. The line grew so taut that it gave forth a cello note. Miss Boyd's arms flexed slightly, and firmed. Des had leaped to the girl's side; but he was afraid to advise her to touch the drag. If she unscrewed it too far, the fish would surely reach the rocks. So, like Crunch, he stood there, open-mouthed, waiting to see which disaster would follow: a broken rod, broken line or ripped-out hook.

What happened was different.

Maybe that particular jewfish was lazy, or unfrightenable, or had bad judgment. At any rate, it stopped dead in the sea. Then it tried to go ahead and couldn't — Miss Boyd held it. Every time its mammoth tail beat, her arms shook a little. That was all. Neither skipper nor mate had ever seen precisely the same thing before. The great fish pulled with a force that must have been a hundred pounds. He didn't turn aside, try coming back, or sound, or relax; he just kept up the steady beating of his tail. And the girl merely held on. And the reel didn't turn.

Afterward, they disagreed about how long things had stayed at a dead-lock. Des said twenty minutes. Crunch said ten. Anyway, the fish eased around finally, and Miss Boyd began to wind in, horsing as she did so. Maybe the fish had a weak heart; possibly it was a fatalist. Whatever the cause, the leader suddenly shimmered in the sun. Des reached out and grabbed it, Crunch thudded into the cockpit, bent over the gunwale, and rammed home the flying gaff.

Des yanked out the stern transom. The block and tackle squeaked. Wally Bates, who had ground film throughout the fight, now photo-graphed the girl gazing at the huge brown fish when it slithered aboard.

"Go around five hundred," Crunch said. And he swiftly added, "There's the picture your manager wanted, for sure! We'll go right in, and get some shots of you and him on the dock rack. Then — if you want — you won't have to spend any more money. I mean, I'd be glad to give back the other four days' pay. After all — "

The girl was not panting. She might have been knitting rather than holding five hundred pounds of seagoing bass. She said disappointedly, "And that's all there is to this big-game fishing?"

"That's all," Crunch replied, not honestly, but in what he felt to be a good cause.

"Unless," Des added in a low, anxious tone, "you'd hung a broadbill on that bait, say. Like Charlie Apperson did last week off Fort Lauderdale."

"A broadbill?" the girl echoed with interest.

Crunch glared at his mate. "They go by this coast, deep, in April. But you'd have to fish for weeks to nail one."

Beulah eyed the dripping fish. "And they're — harder to pull in?"

"Much," Des said.

She smiled rapturously at him. "Well, let's try! After all, Alfie — Mr. Rainey — paid for five days. And I'm having a luscious time!" Her big eyes made it evident that her pleasure was related not to giant bass fishing, but to one Des Smith.

Under the circumstances, there was not much that Crunch could do. True, when he went back to the top controls, a kind of nervous indignation made him fumble a cigarette, and when he bent to retrieve it his yachting cap fell off. True, seeing his hat on the deck, he stamped on it. But that was all he could do, until he reached home.

Sari, in a crisp, green-checked dress she had made herself, ministered to her husband, on their back porch, with iced coffee. Then she listened. She decided that Crunch had sized up correctly a perilous situation; she recommended strategic action:

"We'll take Eloise and Des out for dinner and dancing tomorrow night. I've been afraid, for years, Des would pick a wrong girl. He's utterly helpless where women are concerned."

"With Beulah Boyd, he doesn't seem helpless."

"I mean, he is devoid of judgment. Doesn't know his own mind!"

Sari started to the telephone to communicate with Eloise Derby. Crunch sipped coffee, admiring the bloom on Sari's gardenias and watching his son mow grass under the fruit trees.

On the evening following the two couples enjoyed a steak dinner at a restaurant far out on Bird Road. Afterward, they journeyed to Miami Beach for a few rumbas with the Havaniers, at the Pelican Patio. Des, who liked to dance — in spite of his overwhelming shyness — took Eloise out on the floor. It furnished Sari her first good opportunity of the evening for private talk with her spouse. "What happened today?"

"We drifted live baits, deep, for broadbill. We hung a Warsaw grouper and lost it. We boated a small shark. Rest of the day, I ran a sort of cruise ship. Flat calm. Wally Bates slept most of the time. Our Des gave Beulah the sweet treatment."

Sari nodded and looked, with concern, at the dance floor, where Des was sweeping the lissom Miss Derby about in rumba figures. She was chattering feverishly. "I shouldn't have told Eloise about Beulah," Sari said. "It upset her, and she seems the type who can't keep quiet for a second when she's nervous."

"So I noticed," Crunch muttered. "During dinner nobody else could get a word in. And I think old Des noticed too. I am afraid his interest in Eloise has waned, in two different ways."

"Crunch! We can't let him do a thing like that! I've got to try to find somebody else — somebody completely dazzling — and arrange something tomorrow. Why, he might marry that person and go away with her, quit fishing — everything!"

"I never saw him quite so—" Crunch sighed. "Come on. Let's dance."

But before they could get out on the open-air dance floor, under the palm trees painted with colored light, Des and Eloise came back.

"He's got to leave!" Eloise wailed "Migraine headache!" Her eyes looked accusingly, almost angrily, at Sari.

"Mighty sorry," Des murmured rapidly. "I'll take a cab. You folks enjoy yourselves!" And he left before they could reply.

"I personally don't think he has a headache whatsoever!" Miss Derby said vehemently. "I think he's going to see that Beulah."

The following morning was also calm, clear and warm. However, the coolness between skipper and mate was of the degree of ice. Des seemed almost unaware of it. Solicitude for the passenger so occupied him that he also seemed nearly unconscious of the fact that they were trying to fish. They caught nothing.

They caught nothing on the fourth day. Wally Bates slept most of the time. Crunch merely wished he could emulate the cameraman, but the spectacle of his mate's behavior made it impossible for him to sleep much, even at night.

The fourth day had been like the third; but the fifth differed, though the weather remained beautiful. Des was anointing the lady's shoulders with sun-tan oil. He did it with such affectionate tenderness that Crunch was of a mind to jump overboard and try to swim in to Miami Beach.

"That line," said the girl suddenly, "just clicked out."

Crunch could not recall a time when a customer had heard the clothespin snap and Des had failed to hear. Beulah picked up the rod, got set, waited for the slack line to come tight, and struck—three times, hard. The reel responded by starting to turn like a rotor in a jet stream.

"You got one!" Des yelled. "That's no shark, no Warsaw!" He whirled and addressed the awakening Wally: "Put on a telephoto, man! You're going to see some jumps!"

Wally did so. The reel kept caterwauling. The camera pointed out toward sea. And soon, some three hundred yards away, the ocean split open. It tossed forth a biological dynamo, a blue-and-silver being, upward of ten feet in length, with a nose sword as wide as a man's hand and nearly a yard long. This beast seemed to ride on the air, leaving a brief trough in the water. It rolled on one side and then the other. It bent itself almost U-shape. It flexed straight and re-entered the sea, bill first, neat as a diver. It came right back out, as if bouncing, and tail-walked in a great arc that brought it closer to the boat.

When it vanished, Wally muttered, "Got it! And a silhouette of the girl's head! What a shot for the newsreels!"

Crunch said, "Fine." He said it flatly, unemotionally. Ordinarily the fish, the jump, the picture, would have filled him with delight. He looked at the girl. She was winding to get the belly out of the line—winding as hard and fast as any male angler Crunch had fished, with one or two exceptions. Her hair flew. Her eyes shone. She was loving the battle. And Wally, with a different lens, was moving in to take pictures of that mood. They, too, would be good shots.

Crunch looked at his mate and thought: *Des is praying.*

His eyes were closed. His face was pale. His fists were clenched. His lips were moving. If he was not actually praying that his inamorata would nail the broadbill, Crunch decided, Des was doing the biggest job of wishing in the history of hope.

Meantime the broadbill, having decided that nothing could be accomplished by leaping or by tailwalking or by greyhounding, was down in the sea—perhaps a hundred feet down—fighting wildly. The reel screamed and whinnied. Line slacked as the fish shot back toward the boat. Beulah's hands flashed as she cranked. Her shoulders shook as the great fish slammed its head back and forth.

Her body, in the fighting chair, was yanked and jostled in a way that suggested the fast-changing postures of a cowgirl on a busy bronco. But Beulah Boyd kept smiling with girlish ecstasy. Her breath went in and out smoothly.

By and by the swordfish sounded; line went out in lunges as it swam down toward the abyss. Agony shone on Desperate's face. Interest appeared on the skipper's. When it was perhaps a thousand feet down, the fish took to horizontal maneuvering and slanted plunges, throwing a great strain on the angler.

After perhaps twenty minutes, Beulah asked brightly, "How long can they do like this?"

"Hours," Crunch said.

"For heaven's sake," she replied. "They're really quite strong—in a way."

The broadbill bulldogged and busted about in the depths for an hour.

"Try," Des said, in a taut, metallic way, "lifting him a little. An inch or so at a time. If you can start him at all."

Lifting was nothing to Beulah. Daisy-fresh, she lifted. Presently the beleaguered broadbill gave a foot, then two, then six—and at last he made a rush for the surface. Beulah kept up with him. The fish came clear up and clear out, spun on the surface—throwing a great white wave—and decided on speedy surface runs. It made six. By then, Beulah was actually perspiring. It showed, Crunch thought, that the girl was human, more or less.

At the end of the second hour, however, the broadbill's runs slowed and shortened. It struggled with what looked like uncertainty, threshing about, rolling, shooting around in slow circles, its dorsal fin out like a flag. It quit trying to leap, and settled for mere thrusts at the sky with its bill—thrusts that brought it only head-and-eyes clear of the sea.

"I think it's giving out already," she said.

That did it. As if the great fish had heard, it half rolled on its side and lay almost dead. She pumped it toward the boat. It came, reluctant, sidewise, pushing a wall of water, but it came in. Des grabbed the leader. Crunch rammed the gaff. When the huge head slid into the cockpit, he lifted the marlin billy to make the kill. Then he put down the billy. The swordfish was no longer of this world. He looked at the girl. She was smiling, still, and just about as she'd been two hours before.

"That's fun," she said. "And it's only three o'clock. Let's get another if we can!"

Crunch looked at Des. The mate's eyes showed pride.

Crunch quietly put back the marlin billy in the proper hole in the little billy rack. He removed his hat. He held out his hand.

"Congratulations," he said to the lady. "That was great fishing; great! We haven't time for another."

She batted her eyelashes and turned. "Des," she said, "kiss me."

Des obliged.

And the *Poseidon* started in, to expose its prize to the cameras of what would be, for certain, an exuberant press. They had a huge fish—rare for Miami waters—and they had Beulah. *Cheesecake*, Crunch told himself, *in any language*. She was truly photogenic.

Sari was on the dock. She had seen the broadbill flag flying from the outrigger when the *Poseidon* came across Biscayne Bay. She had done her duty, phoning the newspapers immediately. She saw—though she did not need confirmation—the girl's happy expression, and Desperate's unconcealed joy, his virtual hysteria. She saw her husband's licked look. She shook her head sadly, thinking of all the very suitable girls Des had eschewed. But Sari was game. She was the first to call across the water, "Congratulations, Miss Boyd! That's a great fish!"

It was. It lay, roped, across the stern—tail and bill hanging far out and down. Every person on the pier was there to see.

The sun had set by the time the newspapermen and the press-association photographers had finished shooting the girl with the fish, the girl and the fish and the mate, and such other combinations as occurred to them. The dock was graveled with flash bulbs. Wally Bates had gone, long since, to speed the development of what he stated would be some of the best fishing shots ever made.

Des said to Beulah, and only to Beulah, "What about supper?"

She threw her arms around him. "I'd love it. I—"

Right then, it happened. A small but rather penetrating voice called out, "Cut!"

Beulah gasped and released Des. "Alfie!" she cried.

"I see you got one," the artists' representative said rather peevishly. "Oughta make good pix. I just flew in!" He came up—a pearl-gray hat on the back of his head, a hostile look in his eye. He set himself squarely in front of Des. "Sorry to crowd you out, fella, but I wanna greet my wife proper."

"Alfie!" the girl gurgled. "I've been so lonesome!"

They embraced—warmly, even hotly. Then Alfie pushed the girl away as if he, not she, had the horsepower.

"Appreciate what you boys did for my little girl!" He turned to Des. "Hope she didn't give you more trouble than you could handle, Mr. Smith. My baby is kind of flirtatious when her daddy's away."

"I never—" Beulah began indignantly.

"Don't lie to poppa," Alfred rebuked her. He winked at Crunch. "She always tries to raise a little devilment when I'm away. Think nothing of it! And now, dear, say good-by to the nice people! It's late and your daddy's hungry!"

Beulah said a happy, irresponsible farewell. She whispered something to her husband. Alfie turned. "This business about us being married," he said—"it's a professional secret, kind of. We've been hitched eight years."

Sari walked to the edge of the dock, through straggling people who stared at the great fish. She tried to find something—anything—to look at. Crunch glanced once at Des, covertly, and joined Sari, searching also for something distant to concentrate on. Des walked off, his hands in his pockets.

After a moment Sari said, "Maybe we better follow the poor guy. You can't tell. A blow like that. He might—"

"Anybody might," Crunch agreed somberly. "If it had been me, I'd have jumped off the dock and stayed under."

Near the fishing pier was a park. Not a big park; the random city kind that sustains a few trees, several benches. This one had palm trees and benches that faced the harbor, now rosy with reflected sunset. Des was there, alone, on a bench and his shoulders heaved.

"Poor guy!" Crunch whispered. "Poor guy." He had never seen Des cry before; hadn't believed it possible. "We better just sneak away," he went on in a whisper. "Not let him know we saw."

Sari nodded. Tears filled her eyes too—tears of sympathy. But as they started away, she turned. She stared, listened. "Are you sure he's crying?"

"Am I—? What!" Crunch also stared and slowly stole up behind Des, with the care of a stalking Indian. He leaned down. And he tiptoed back to his wife. "The son of a gun is laughing," he said dazedly. "Paralyzed with laughter. It's killing him! He must have known all the time she was married! Probably she said so. He was pulling my leg!"

"My leg," Sari replied softly. "He did it because of the girls I pestered him with. He wanted to scare us—so we'd let him alone, in the girl department."

"I'm going back," Crunch said with heat, "and knock his block off!"

He looked more closely at his wife. Sari's eyes had crinkled. Her lips had turned up. She tittered. She giggled. And Crunch snickered.

"The old houndfish!" Crunch suddenly exploded. Their laughter attracted pedestrians who stopped to share it. They hung on each other. Pretty soon, Des heard. He approached and tapped their shoulders.

"Something funny?" he asked innocently.

That did it. They had to move to a bench—all three of them. But even while mirth made her too weak to stand, Sari understood how greatly they had misjudged the *Poseidon*'s mate.

As usual, she thought, and she hugged Des.

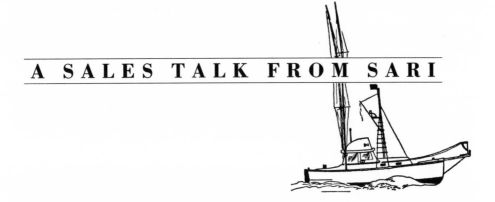

A SALES TALK FROM SARI

ON A sunny Saturday morning in February, at nine o'clock, the *Poseidon* shed her bow lines and took off for blue water. Crunch, at the top controls, waved admonishingly to Sari, who stood on the Gulf Stream Dock Sari acknowledged the gesture. Beside her, another girl waved. A very beautiful girl with long blonde hair that put to fetching use both the sparkling sunshine and the morning breeze. She waved rather dismally, however, and when the *Poseidon* had drawn far enough away from land so that the figure of the solitary passenger standing in the stern became identifiable merely as a man, she stamped her foot, sat down on a bench, and showed signs of tears—not the involuntary kind, but the kind that is the product of an emotion deliberately indulged.

Sari knew that the name of the girl was Susannah Ellis, that she was last year's Miss Dade County—which is the political boundary describing Miami, Miami Beach and a considerable chunk of Everglades, that she was a fashion model of considerable fame, and that she had "been seen" a good deal in the company of the eligible Mr. Howard Greene, now fading into a mere dot in the stern cockpit of the *Poseidon*. Sari kept up with the society pages and the gossip columns, in spite of the fact that she often found them altogether too interchangeable.

Sari's assignment was to "do something about" Susannah. Crunch had given it to her. "This dame," he had said, "is ruining one of my best customers. She keeps trying to stop him from fishing. Can you imagine that? You talk to her, Sari. You'll figure out some angle."

It is often hard to approach a girl on the verge of angry tears—especially for another woman. Sari walked past Susannah twice, hopefully, but the model showed no awareness of Sari's existence. Embarrassed, Sari sat down on the same bench and looked closely at Susannah. Observed thus, she was even more attractive: she had big, greenish-grey eyes and enough red in her long blond hair for stunning contrast. The mere existence of girls like Susannah, Sari reflected, made the business of being a man quite difficult; she wasn't just appealing—she was compelling. Sari worried a minute over Crunch, in the light of that reflection, and then, as all women like Sari do, she discarded the worry for a glow of pride. She touched her own dark curls lightly and attacked her subject with the most direct of all possible methods.

"What's the matter?"

Susannah turned and her grey-green eyes narrowed perceptibly. She was about to say, Sari knew, that it was none of her business. Instead, after an appraising moment, she replied, "You know Howie Greene?"

Sari nodded. "Quite well."

"I'm crazy about him," the girl said.

"He's a very nice person."

The model shook her head and laughed. "He is—week days. But on weekends—he just simply doesn't exist."

Sari considered that statement. It didn't make sense and then, abruptly, it made excellent sense. "Oh. You mean, he goes fishing."

"I *mean!*" Susannah said with emphasis. "On the *Poseidon*—or one of the other charterboats—or by car down in the keys—or in an outboard—or, maybe, even from his sea wall. Wherever there's water, he fishes. And, since Miami is practically Venice, he fishes all his free time!"

"I see."

"He's gone now. I got up early today just to ask him to take me to the opening of the Palm and Hibiscus Club tonight. What happened? Before I could get in a word edgewise, he and that Crunch Adams were talking a mile a minute about whether they'd troll strips or balaos, whatever that is—he told me that there were tarpon in the Cut these evenings and he was going to take a shot at them tonight. So what? So I'll go to the opening with some other boy—and while I'm dancing, he'll be out there on that old boat in a pair of fishy pants—trying to get a tarpon!"

"I take it," Sari said, "you don't like fishing?"

"I hate every part of it," the girl answered. "I get seasick. I get scared out on the Gulf Stream. I don't like the way fish smell. I don't like boats. I don't even like water—especially."

"I'm a fishing widow, too," Sari said.

The girl brightened. "Really?"

"Crunch—is my husband."

"Oh. That's different." Susannah was embarrassed, but not mollified. "It's his business—to fish."

Sari let the conversation die. Susannah was young and vehement. Rapacious, too, maybe. It was hard to tell. Young people, these days, were good at concealing what went on inside them. Frustration and disappointment are difficult for everybody to bear—and there's a good deal of both in every life. Sari thought a little while and presently she walked over to the dock locker which belonged to the *Poseidon*. She fumbled through her handbag for a key Crunch had given her and laboriously lifted the lid. For several minutes she bent into the big box. Presently she emerged with the articles she had sought: a hank of line, a small, cheap reel on a little steel casting rod, some coiled leader wire, and a cardboard box that rattled. She returned to the bench.

While she wound the line on the reel, Susannah watched with disapproval. "You probably like to fish," she finally said.

Sari nodded. "Moderately. Crunch thinks I'm crazy about it. I'd never let him know that I'm only—fairly crazy about it."

"With Howie," said Susannah, "it's not like that at all." Her pique, and Sari's presence as an audience, together with Sari's obviously confiding manner, had the effect of making her talkative. "Howie's a good lawyer and he works hard. I realize that. I approve of a man working hard. He earns quite a lot of money—but then—plenty of men with a lot of money have asked me—"

Sari looked at the gleaming tresses and the wide, passionate eyes. "Sure," she said.

"I like money." That was said frankly and it gave value to what she said next. "But I don't think I'd mind being poor—with Howie. Every darn time he looks at me, I get positively weak. Nobody ever did that to me before. I've got a crush on the guy you could wrap up a building in! Only—weekends—he goes fishing. Always. Says it's his way of life, and he won't change. He took me out—till he found I despise. it. But he'd rather go alone. He likes to sit by himself, and daydream, and when he gets a strike—he likes to have the whole boat to himself."

"Sounds selfish." *I like her*, Sari thought.

"It *is* selfish," the girl replied sharply. "We've had fights galore about it. I'm just trying to make up my mind to tell him it's all off. Only—if I do—it'll be mighty hard. He's nice."

"I always thought so," Sari said. She had finished winding the line. She gave the short little rod a flick and looked in the pasteboard box. It was full of plugs. She rose. "Well, I guess you two people will have to figure it out—yourselves. That's the rule about fights, isn't it?"

Susannah nodded moodily and stood up. "Where you going?"

"To get the bus."

"I'll take you—any place you like. I haven't a thing to do all day, thanks to Howie! I was positive I could persuade him to stay ashore. Positive. And then—seeing him—all excited and all set—I didn't even try."

"I know how it is." Sari paused and smiled. "If you want to, you can drop me off. In fact, I was going to ask you if you would. It's almost on your way. You see—I know where you live. From the papers—"

Susannah tossed her head, but not conceitedly. "I'd be glad to. I know about you—and Crunch—from the papers, too. I suppose it's kind of mean for me to be trying to spoil Crunch's business—but I am." They started to walk. "You're not going fishing yourself, are you?"

"Nope. I'm just going to see a—a person—who's as keen about it as your Howie. I promised to make the call—days ago."

Susannah drove her roadster into an unprepossessing street and followed it to the end of the pavement. Then, upon Sari's instructions, she parked the car. With Sari in the lead, they walked along two coral ruts, past small frame houses that needed paint. Some of the land around the houses was pine and palmetto waste; some of it had been turned into gardens—but most of the vegetable beds were very weedy. Presently Sari struck off through the weeds on a footpath.

"Snaky, isn't it?" Susannah asked dubiously.

Sari nodded. "I've seen a couple."

She went on—so Susannah followed, reflecting that she had as much nerve as Sari. They ducked under a fence and crossed a swampy patch of ground behind a particularly tatterdemalion bungalow. Then Sari raised her voice. "Hi! Sonny! It's me!"

The response was instant, enthusiastic, and rendered in a high treble. "Hello, Mrs. Adams!"

"It's a child!" Susannah exclaimed.

"Boy," Sari said. "Quite a boy, too."

They came upon him then. Sonny was sitting in an old deck chair beside a forgotten side-lead of one of the drainage canals. A big ficus tree grew on Sonny's side of the canal bank and its limbs had been chopped away to make a sun-dappled grotto for the boy. A plank formed a seat beside his deck chair. The dark, transparent water was at his feet. Also at his feet was an air rifle and an assortment of additional "equipment." In his hands was a bamboo pole. His eyes were a star-bright blue, his hair a cottony white on the verge of silver, his age about nine or ten, and his feet, propped in front of him, were in braces. Crutches leaned against one of the down-stabbed roots of the banyan.

He saw them and said exultantly, *"You brought the rod!"*

Sari smiled and nodded. "This is Miss Ellis."

Carefully, Sonny inserted his bamboo jack pole in a nailed wooden gadget which held it at the proper fishing angle. He held out his hand. His expression changed to awe when he concentrated on Susannah. "You're *beautiful!*"

Sari watched the girl. She flushed. She shook the hand. "Hello, Sonny. It's nice, if you think I'm beautiful."

"Anybody could see that," Sonny said. Then, manners having been observed, he took the little casting rod. "Boy! Boy-oh-boy!" He whipped it. "You know, Mrs. Adams, I didn't *really* think you could get hold of a casting rod for me when you said you would. Now—I can shoot a bait all the way across to Tasmania!"

Sari nodded.

Susannah said, "Tasmania?"

Proudly, Sonny indicated the canal before him—a deadend segment, about seventy five feet long. It communicated with a larger canal which was concealed by jungle. Sonny's area was half as broad as it was long. The banks had fallen in, making the shore irregular. Fast-growing tropical trees, creeper-choked, leaned over both sides. An old barge, abandoned at the upper end, emerged mossy and slippery from the deep tidal water, where it had sunk years before. Odd flowers bloomed on the weedy margins; insects buzzed in the shadows; butterflies flickered in the light: it was a jungle dell—lush, warm, weird, quiet, and as solitary as the last mile of time.

"Tasmania," Sonny explained, "is the island over yonder. The grass that sticks up. See that cove across the way? That's the Indian Ocean. I got everything named. There's Greenland—the white sand bar—and there's Africa—that's the whole opposite side, mostly. When the jacks come boiling and cutting through here—they usually chase mullet into the Indian Ocean first. Sometimes, though, the mullet run around the end of Greenland and the jacks are scared to go there—too shallow. Then, a bunch of old snooks live right near Tasmania. See that big root of the tipped-over tree? That's the Black Sea, in there. That's where the snooks live. I caught one, once. Three pounds and a quarter. On the pole I had before this one. It broke later—on a real big fish. A old jewfish, maybe. But I couldn't ever get a bait over to Tasmania—till now. Now I can. Now I can cast a bait there, as soon as I practice a little."

"You sure can," Sari said.

Sonny looked reverently at the rod, hefted it, and said, "You cast."

Sari thought of demurring—of asking him to be first. But she understood that he did not know how. So she took a plug from the pasteboard box, fixed it on a leader, which she showed him how to prepare, and deftly cast into the center of the Black Sea. There was a mighty boil and splash. For a split second a big, yellowish head showed. The fish hit the plug, knocked it into the air, and missed the hooks.

Sonny's eyes shimmered. "Snook! Didn't I tell you? Go on, Sari! Next time, he'll get it!"

She reeled in and shook her head. "Not me, Sonny. That's your snook. Next time—you'll be the one to hook him."

The boy said, "Gee!" and hesitated. "I'd rather kind of practice—by myself—till I get the hang of it—"

"Sure," Sari said. "You put on that little hookless plug and practice in the yard on the grass. When you're ready—try it here with a real one."

Sonny stared at his prize. "Boy! Am I lucky!"

Susannah said, "I'm afraid—I've got to be running along—"

His voice followed them through the trees, the weeds, the insects. "Thanks a million, Mrs. Adams! 'Bye, Miss Ellis! Come and see me!"

At the car, Susannah said, "I was afraid I was going to cry."

Sari nodded. "Yeah. Sonny got paralyzed a year ago. Doing fine—though. He gets back and forth to the house alone, now—with braces and crutches. He'll walk again. That canal-bank is his whole world. He goes out in the morning—and stays there all day, if it's nice. Takes his lunch. When it rains, he stays in. He fishes—and reads."

"All alone?"

"Often. Other kids come to keep him company, of course. And grown people. But his father's dead—and his mother works. He can reach the family next door by yelling—if he wants to. Never does, I understand." Sari was in the car. She slammed the door. "For nearly a year, now, he's been studying that mud hole—and every fish in it. I bet he knows things about the way of jack and snook and tarpon, too, maybe, that grown men would give a fortune to find out. Bob Breastedt of the *Dispatch* told us about him—a few weeks ago."

Susannah drove to the Adams' trim bungalow. She said nothing, all the way. Sari thanked her for the lift and added, quietly, "I thought, maybe, you'd like to see another—person—who's crazy about fishing."

Susannah bent forward over the wheel and her heavy, red-gold hair leaned forward, too. "I know. Awful game little kid. Thanks."

"I talked to her," Sari explained that night to Crunch. "She's pretty sore about the way Howie fishes weekends and leaves her in the lurch."

"It's a doggone crime," Crunch said indignantly, "for a dame to try to ruin anything a man is as batty about as Howie is about fishing. What'd she say?"

"We went over and visited Sonny Keller." Sari frowned. "What'd she *say*? Oh—she didn't say anything."

Crunch shrugged. "She better not! How's Sonny? Now, *there* is one fishing guy! You take him the casting outfit?"

Sari reported that she had.

A few evenings later, the cream and chrome sedan of Mr. Howard Greene drew to a stop in front of the Adams demesne. Young Bill Adams stopped chasing Noisy Groceries, the dog, long enough to shout, "Moooother! Company!"

Mr. Green grinned tentatively and came up on the Adams porch. "Just stopped by to make sure Saturday's charter is okay and tell you we're going to have another passenger."

Crunch had put down the evening paper. He looked surprised. "Thought you preferred to go alone?"

"I do." Mr. Greene lighted a cigarette. "Some friend of Susannah's. She insisted I take the palooka. Don't know him from Adam—but she made a terrific scene about it—"

Crunch shook his head sympathetically. "Well. We can fish two, easy enough."

"I suppose so. I was just driving past. Thought I'd tell you. We'll have to give up the idea of fishing with the deep rig Saturday. But Susannah is darned dictatorial—when she wants to be. Well—so long."

The Adamses said, "So long."

Mr. Greene turned on the walk. "Fellow named Arthur Keller," he said. "Know him? Susannah calls him Sonny."

Sari grabbed Crunch's arm and squeezed it, warningly. She said, after a gulp, "Guess we don't. Well. Good-night. Mr. Greene."

The cream and chrome sedan buzzed into the fragrant gloom. Crunch peered at Sari. "What kind of a job is this? Not that I—"

She shook her head. "I don't know, Crunch. I haven't seen Susannah since Saturday. It's her idea."

Mr. Greene waited impatiently in the stern of the *Poseidon* at nine o'clock on Saturday morning. From time to time he glanced at his wrist watch. He said, repeatedly, to Crunch: "Not only does she saddle me with some onion—probably some lug she's getting soft about instead of me—but the clown is late!" Finally he said, "There's her car!" A moment later, he was speechless. Down the dock came Susannah, followed by Desperate, who was carrying a medium-sized boy. The boy had his legs in braces and was looking, it seemed, at every separate object on the dock at once.

Mr. Greene breathed hard and said, "A kid!"

Crunch eyed him closely. He looked at his wrist watch again. He looked at the fighting chair. He shrugged. He put on a fairly convincing smile. By the time Sonny reached the stern of the boat, he was able to say without any show of irritation, "Well, well, *well*! So *this* is Sonny Keller?"

Sonny's eyes were on the bright verge of mist. "Boy! The *Poseidon*! Say, Mr. Greene, you must be about the most generous man on earth! I'm afraid I won't be much good, but I sure appreciate a chance to try. I'm a fair snook catcher."

Mr. Greene nodded. Susannah was standing near the boat. "You coming?"

She shook her head. "Heavens, no. But this child, Howie, is even nuttier about fishing than you are. I thought you two ought to get along."

Howie said, "Mmmm."

Sonny glanced at him and then, anxiously, at Crunch. The skipper winked. That consoled the child. The *Poseidon's* engines came to life.

When the girl on shore faded, Mr. Greene, standing behind the boy, pointed to Susannah and tapped his forehead. Crunch made no response. So Mr. Greene sat down. "Like to fish for snook, eh?"

The boy nodded gravely. "I love it. I hope I'm not in the way?"

"In the way? Mercy, No! Glad to have you along."

"I've never been out on the ocean before," Sonny said. "Maybe I'll get seasick."

"Well—if you do, we can bring you right in."

"I hope I won't. I sure would like to see one of those old sailamaroos in action!"

"Always a chance." Mr. Greene did not seem to be very good at keeping up a conversation with a boy. There was a pause.

Sonny again felt his superfluousness. "Course—if you think so, Mr. Greene, I wouldn't need to fish. I could just watch. I like that."

"Well—" Mr. Greene sounded agreeable.

Crunch said, "Nonsense! We'll put a belt around you and the fighting chair, both. Put a mop handle across the footrest and lash it fast. And that'll fix you up as fine and dandy as any man could be fixed. You got a nice pair of arms, there, from—" Crunch bit his tongue.

Howie Greene nodded. "Sure. We'll fix you up."

Sonny just breathed ecstatically—and watched the jetties go by. Presently he said, "You ever fish for snapper, Mr. Greene?"

"You bet I did. Smart fish."

"Yeah. They are. And the people that fish for 'em are dumb. Now—we got a lot of snapper—under the mangrove roots. That's along the coast of Siberia. I watch 'em all day. I watch what kind of minnows they chase and what kind of bugs they eat at what time of day. Ever see a snapper come out and grab a butterfly?"

"Can't say I ever did."

"Well—I did. Lemme tell you, if people knew what fish ate, when— and how—they liked to grab what they ate, they'd catch all they wanted. You come over sometime with a fly rod and I'll show you how to get those Siberian snappers. That is—if you fish a fly rod."

"I do. Siberia's a long way off, though."

"That," Sonny said, "is just the name of part of a canal bank."

"Oh?" replied Mr. Greene. The dialogue was beginning to make sense. "What about—how snappers feed?"

Sonny told him—told him the results of watching the fish life in one large pool—day after day, week after week—with intelligence and the intensity of a person who is able to do absolutely nothing else. Mr. Green listened with growing interest. And when Des announced they were ready to start fishing, Mr. Greene treated the boy with a certain deference—the sort one expert shows another. "You sit right where you are, Sonny. I'll take a side chair. You sure that snook'd go better for a plug with orange-yellow rings?"

"I'm not sure," the boy answered, taking a light rod from Des, "but I suspect they would. If I had some paint, I'd try."

"We'll try together," the man answered, "if you'll let me come over and cast around Tasmania and Siberia and the Black Sea, sometime."

"Any old time," Sonny replied. Then he said, "Des, this rod's so big I'm scared."

Des grinned. "You just hang on, Sonny. Just hang on."

Unfortunately, it was one of those days. One of those February days. The *Fantasia* hung a white marlin and lost it. Doc got an Allison on board and trolled through the fleet, displaying his red flag gloriously. There were sailfish to be seen tailing south—as well as turtles, gulls, pelicans, cormorants, several sharks, and jellyfish. It rendered Sonny ecstatic. But his host, toward the middle of the afternoon, climbed up to the top controls and said to Crunch, "Couldn't we go over the reef or something? I swear, I'd about give my soul to have that kid get a strike. Maybe, on the reef we'd pick up a barracuda. The little nipper's a born sport!"

Crunch nodded and put the helm over. The *Poseidon* slid from the Gulf Stream into the green water.

"That kid," Mr. Greene continued, "is bright. A young genius. Knows more about shallow water fish than most veterans. Likable, too. Tells me he lives alone—daytimes. Imagine that!"

Nothing showed over the reef. Crunch was getting discouraged himself. And Sonny, his line in an outrigger, was dozing. He had neglected, carefully, to tell them that he usually took an afternoon nap. Four o'clock passed and the sun dropped all too swiftly. Mr. Greene looked no longer like a handsome and self-possessed man of affairs; he looked like a man whom fate had harried.

Then, quite suddenly, Des murmured, "Sailfish." A big sail was running on the surface about a yard behind Mr. Greene's bait—which trolled straight back.

Sonny opened his eyes at the magic word, exclaimed, "Where?" and then bellowed, "I see it! I see it!"

Mr. Greene glanced up, disappointedly, at Crunch. He had wanted the boy to get the strike, if there was one. Suddenly, impulsively, he began reeling in. The saifish speeded up with the accelerating bait. But it did not speed up fast enough. Mr. Green reeled until his bait was about twenty feet behind the boat's stern. Then he whipped back his rod. Bait, hook and leader flew into the air. Des ducked down to protect the boy. Mr. Greene reached out like a fielder and caught the hook in his bare hand. Afterward he stood fixedly, staring at the water. The sailfish had disappeared. Only one bait skittered now behind the *Poseidon*: Sonny's balao.

For two or three seconds there was a rigid concentration of eyes. Would the cheated fish merely swim away? Or would it attack the other bait? Then, all at once, the sea furrowed and the sailfish came out—swindled and sore—charging Sonny's bait with its purple dorsal fin stretched taut. The balao was seized by both bills. Line floated from the outrigger. Des whispered, "Doggone," and added, sharply, "Get set, Sonny!"

Mr. Greene threw his rod on the floor and came to the boy's side. The line tightened. The youngster was hauled heavily against the belt and the mop-handle footrest. "I got him!" he yelled. "I got him *on!* I can feel him!" Then he shouted, "Lookee! There he is!"

And so, indeed, he was. It was one of those "fast babies," Des explained later, to all who would listen. The kind that tower straight up, zig-zagging like the rope behind a thrown harpoon, and turn, hitting the water, and bouncing. The kind that go crazy. The kind that start shooting back and forth in the air in one place, making hundred and eighty degree skid reverses barely under the surface, going faster than birds in a badminton game.

Sonny forgot to hold his rod up, forgot to try to reel, forgot to do anything but holler. A dozen boats heard the sound. Fully forty people in the region turned. All of them saw the ship, the child, and the silver and purple fish flashing and throwing a private surf. All of them grinned— and the skipper of the nearest boat yelled through a megaphone, "Ride him, cowboy!"

Mr. Greene tried, finally to give a little advice. But he was too excited. He said, in a frantic tone, "You tell him, Des! I can't!"

So Des knelt beside the boy, and began in his calmest tone, which presently penetrated the wild universe in which the boy was living: "Get your left hand a little higher . . . take a grip with your whole right on the reel handle . . . not just the fingers . . . keep the tip a wee shade higher . . . when he goes into the air like that, try to wind if you can . . . and when he rips off line like that, no use winding, because the reel spool just turns the other way . . . dandy! . . . fine! . . ."

Twenty minutes passed. The sail was sulking. Sonny's homemade coverall was soaked with perspiration. He looked tired. Once, when the pressure of the fish diminished, he let go of the reel handle and massaged his fingers on the arm of the fighting chair. Des asked anxiously, "You feel all right?"

"Swell."

"Take it easy, then."

"Yeah."

The sail stopped sulking and exploded three times in succession.

Up on top, with Crunch, Mr. Greene said in an anguished tone, "How is it going? I can't look!"

Crunch measured the situation. "All right. The kid's tired. He's kind of young for it, to start with—and—" He interrupted himself. "It's coming toward the boat."

"Toward the boat!" Mr. Greene swore with dismay and scrambled over the side to help, with his nervous system, even if he could not help in any other way. He hit the deck hard. "Gun her, Crunch," he yelled. "The darn fish is trying to go under the wheels!"

Crunch gunned her. They slid out of that predicament. Mr. Greene bent over the boy. "How you doing?"

"Okay! Kind of achy! Boy! Is *this* something!"

"Stay with it," Mr. Greene said prayerfully. "Stay with it, no matter what! A fisherman never gives down!"

"Yeah," Sonny said, and heaved dutifully.

The sail came close. Like most of those which concentrate their major pyrotechnics on the early stages of the fight, it was tired. It rolled on its side. Des waved the boy to wind. Furiously, fighting the rebellious fatigue of his muscles, Sonny wound. Des grabbed the leader wire. He brought the fish gingerly alongside. He made ready to reach for the bill with gloved hands. But the suspense was more than Mr. Greene could endure. He leaned over the *Poseidon*'s gunwale. Barehanded, he grabbed the bill. The sail surged, but Mr. Greene hung on. Hung on—and heaved. The great fish came crashing aboard and Mr. Greene fell upon it, wrapping his arms and legs around it. "Got him, glory be!" he bellowed, unaware of the fact that he had taken all the skin off one palm.

Sonny just sat there, looking at a fish as heavy as he was—and about a yard longer. He wore an expression that Mr. Greene plainly understood, as he hung onto the fish, spoiling his clothes and bruising his ankles in an effort to subdue the flailing caudal. Des got a billy and subdued the creature.

The lawyer rose, then. Solemnly, he shook the boy's hand. "A very nice piece of fishing," he said. "Magnificently done!"

As a matter of fact, it hadn't been at all expert—but that detail was forever lost to history. Sonny said, "Golly! Mother'll be pleased. And so am I!" Then he blinked and cleared his throat and blinked some more.

The *Poseidon* came around the turn from the Cut, blowing her horn and flying Sonny's shirt from an outrigger. The boy was in the fighting chair, waving. Mr. Greene was dancing a jig beside him. The crowd that meets the boats surged curiously to the *Poseidon*'s berth. Des dragged ashore the catch.

Susannah was there, too. She shook Sonny's hand when Des brought him ashore. Then she found a chance to speak to Howie Greene. "I'm awfully glad you got that poor little youngster a fish. He was so game— and so pathetic. And he seemed to be as crazy about fishing as you are."

Howie's expression was intense and searching. "Is that why you sent Sonny out with me? To give him a good time?"

"No," said the girl. "Not entirely."

Howie nodded. "So I thought. Look, Susannah. We're going to have a very serious talk—this evening. Meanwhile, I'm going to kiss you. Right here."

Crunch and Sari were invited to the Ellis-Greene wedding. They did not go because Crunch was in Bimini. But early one evening, a month or so afterward, when Crunch was checking the list of his charters, he complained about the number of blank weekends on the list. "That idea you had about the Greenes," he said, "was your worst fizzle to date! I suppose you figured that if she saw Sonny sitting all day fishing in the canal, she'd get to understand why her boy friend went fishing so much, and then she'd let him go. 'All men are just grown up kids.' Some sort of idea like that? Well—it backfired. Howie Greene's cancelled out nearly every weekend he had taken this spring."

"You'll get somebody else," Sari said.

"Oh—sure, sure. But you have to work hard for business—these days."

Sari considered, holding up a sunsuit which she was mending for Bill. "They wanted to get married," she said presently, "to have fun—each in his own way. Howie fishing, Susannah just playing around. Pretty selfish— of both of them. I thought that maybe—just *maybe*—Sonny would remind both of them that there are other reasons for getting married besides night clubs. Or even charterboats."

"You mean—you *deliberately* lost me a customer?"

"Yep," Sari said.

"Hunh!" Crunch shook his head. "That reminds me." He thrust his hand in the pocket of his khaki trousers. "Got a mess of old line for Sonny. Guess I'll stroll over with it."

"Go ahead," Sari said.

Crunch walked eight blocks through the fading sunlight. He took a cross-cut over a fence and through a region of pine and palmetto. He did not see the cream and chrome car parked at the end of the pavement. But he did see Sonny and the two Greenes in Sonny's back yard, practicing casting with hookless plugs. Sonny's mother was sitting quietly in the shadows of a vine-covered arbor. Mrs. Keller nodded proudly at her son. "See? He's standing without crutches, now. That sailfish—gave him a tremendous lot of self-confidence!"

"Gave other people a lot," Crunch said. It was all he said about the matter, ever, except for one further phrase. He walked home in the moonlight, whistling softly. When he was about halfway, he murmured aloud, "That Sari!"

Then he went on toward home, faster, whistling with vigor.

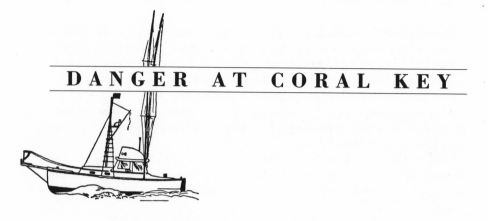

DANGER AT CORAL KEY

1

THE TENSION was almost tangible at Coral Key. When the sun rose on the following day, the Tuna Tournament would start. Fishing boats would line up at the harbor mouth, one angler to every craft; a starting gun would send them forth upon the great Gulf Stream; and the judge's yacht would follow at a statelier pace. There were to be thirty-eight entrants this year, which made the contest the biggest in Bahamas history. Meanwhile, with an afternoon and a long night to wait, the anglers and guides restlessly strode the dock and, from time to time, scrutinized a blue sky above a bluer sea. The wind was east and light: ideal weather. Even a stranger—even a stranger who knew nothing of the pursuit of horse mackerel—would have sensed the tautness of the men, and the women, too, who looked on quietly.

Among these people was just such a stranger, who readied himself like the others. A lean man, young, rather tall, whose broad back surged like an oarsman's as he nervously rehearsed for the contest. He was a man with reddish hair that curled with the sweat of effort. He halted, at last, and grinned up at his skipper. "How am I doing?"

"A hundred and ten!"

"The young man nodded and bent over the tackle again. His line was fast, not to a fish, but to the dock at which the boat, the *Poseidon*, was moored. He threw his weight against the harness on his back. Crunch Adams, the *Poseidon's* skipper, could feel his boat surge slightly with the practice lunges.

"You mean," the young man grunted as he shot forward, winding in a yard of slack and heaving again, "a fish can pull that hard?"

"And harder," Crunch grinned.

"Where does he get the purchase—in water?"

"A tuna," Crunch answered, "has to swim clear around the edge of the North Atlantic every year. Takes a lot of oomph. Gives him plenty of purchase."

"Boy!" said the young man. He seemed frightened for a moment. Then he set his jaw and threw himself into such an effort as a boxer might make when his last hope of victory depended upon risky violence. At last he gasped, "You mean it takes a workout like this to get a tuna?"

The skipper nodded. "A big one. In fast time."

The customer stood. His legs quivered under him. He looked, for an instant, up the path that wound from the festooned dock through the jungle toward Coral Key Inn. Then he looked at the guests—the people in shorts on the dock, the very successful business men and their wives and their daughters. He shook his head incredulously.

Crunch could read his thoughts. Coral Key, with its villas and homes, its inn and golf course, was among the world's half dozen most luxurious resorts. Only the rich could afford to vist there. Only the very, very rich could afford to own a house on the West Indian island. And one did not ordinarily think of the captains of industry, its tycoons and their sons, as men who kept in the physical condition required by such exercise.

"Guess I'll change," the young man said.

He waited for permission and leaped ashore when Crunch nodded. As he went up the dock, almost everybody looked at him. But no one addressed him by name though several men offered a polite, "How are you?" or a casual, "Nice day." The women, in shorts or slacks, in sports dresses—and a few in formal afternoon attire—particularly watched him pass and especially turned to follow him down the pier.

Amanda Barton, two hundred pounds of aggression and brains, stomped down the dock in the disk of rosy shade which her parasol shed. "Crunch!" she boomed in a froglike voice.

A delighted smile came on the skipper's face. "Hello, there, Mrs. Barton! Glad to see you! You're fishing this season?"

"Hell, no! If I followed my doctor's orders, I'd still be in bed in New York! And my blood pressure would be twice as high as it was!" She snorted. "But can you imagine me missing the Coral Key shindy?" She stepped out and down, onto the stern of the cruiser, which winced. "I'm a judge this time, you old fish thief!" She sat in the fighting chair after a long, fond look at the skipper. "Who are you guiding?"

"A lad from New York named Harvey Paul."

"I know some Pauls," Mrs. Barton reflected. "No Harvey."

"He doesn't belong to your crowd."

"Then how come he's here at Coral Key?"

The skipper offered a cigarette, which was refused; he lighted it himself. "I'll let you in on something, but it's private. This tournament—and being at the inn—is going to be rough for my passenger."

"Rough?" she frowned. "I dislike ringers, Crunch."

"He's not a ringer. Although he never went deep-sea fishing in his life." Crunch sat on the gunwale. His eyes, as blue as the Gulf Stream, squinted whimsically. "Here's the confession, Amanda. Des and I were set to fish Fred Maple this year. He canceled out three days ago. The State Department sent him on a hush-hush mission. He wanted to pay us—"

"But being the soul of honor—also blockheaded, since Freddie has millions—you two boys refused!"

Crunch nodded and chuckled. "Old Des and I were sitting around having the blues, over in Miami. We particularly wanted to be here. Remember the licking we took from Moon-eye Gletter last year?"

Mrs. Barton's wise face became sharp. "Is Moon-eye here? I haven't seen the entry list yet."

"Yeah. And we intend—"

"Crunch! I'm a judge now! I know all about Moon-eye Gletter and his tricks. I know—at least I suspect what he did to you the final day last year. But I'd hate to see you and Des disqualify yourselves because of grudge fighting."

Crunch stared over the silver-weathered planks of the pier. "We won't disqualify ourselves. But we mean to take Gletter. What he did last year—though we can never prove it—was to sneak aboard the *Poseidon* and shoot acid into every line we had. Deep down in—where we couldn't possibly notice. The lines didn't pop till after the tunas had made long runs. That was why we lost every single last-day fish, and lost the tournament."

"I figured it about that way."

"This time"—Crunch spoke with a nervousness she had never seen in him—"we intend to win. In fact, it's part of our contract."

Amanda Barton was startled. "You mean you made a deal with this—this Harvey Paul to win!"

Crunch nodded. "In a way. As I was saying, our charter was canceled. We were sitting around moping. This young guy came along. He told us he had a college pal named Millard Davis, who belonged to the Coral Key Club. Davis had invited him there to be a competing guest. So he only needed a boat. But he didn't have any ready cash."

"You and Des are fishing for free?"

Crunch grinned sheepishly. "Maybe yes and maybe no. There's a first prize, remember."

The prize was in keeping with the attitudes and fortunes of the Coral Key devotees—a fact whereof Amanda Barton was fully aware. Every year, to the lucky winner, a check for fifty thousand dollars was presented. There was no second and no third award. Even so, it was a token, a gesture; for nobody who lived or took a vacation at Coral Key needed money. Not even fifty thousand dollars. The prize was just a tradition, no more, no less.

Mrs. Barton thought for a minute and said, "You get paid if you win? Crunch! You know there's more luck than anything else in fishing."

The skipper nodded diffidently. "Sure. But we get paid double, if we happen to win. Nothing, if we don't. That's what Harvey Paul has: nothing. He did own a nice business. It went bust. Then all he had left was enough cash for a round-trip ticket to Miami and this invitation to enter the tournament and use his friend's villa. He heard about the big prize money. He figured if he could persuade some skipper to gamble with him, he could enter. If he won, he could start his business again."

Mrs. Barton was listening with incredulity. "You and Des always were the most quixotic fools on the Gulf Stream Dock! Your customer hasn't anything to lose. But you and Des will be out at least a thousand dollars, for expenses, when this is over! Not to mention—"

Crunch eyed her moodily and nodded. "More than anything, we hated to not be here. Besides, we liked the joe."

"What did Sari think of the deal?"

Crunch grinned, stopped grinning and sighed. "Sari is not even speaking to either of us. She didn't even come to the dock to see us off." His face displayed a pained recollection of his wife's anger. "Sari said that she thought I was showing the first signs of becoming senile."

"So do I!" Mrs. Barton snapped. She rose with surprising speed. "I'll look up your Mr. Paul at dinner, though. And if he's that nice, I'll introduce him around." She surged up on the dock. "Not merely senile," she said, to herself but conspicuously aloud. "Plain goofy. You boys really are slipping!"

Left alone, Crunch wondered for the hundredth time if she wasn't right. He and Des had been bitterly disappointed by the last-minute cancellation. But it certainly was not good business to gamble the cost of taking the *Poseidon* to the Bahamas against the insane chance that they might capture the grand, and only, prize.

There were other disadvantages, besides—too many to ponder. He sat down feebly and wondered where Des was.

Crunch's mate happened to be lying on a bed in a double room assigned to Crunch and himself, in the quarters for mates and skippers. Des appeared to be asleep; he was merely using the pose to hide his qualms. Now that they were actually engaged in a deal that would almost certainly cost them ten or twelve hundred dollars with almost no hope of return, Desperate felt unhappy. Ashamed. Uninterested in things.

Indeed, when Crunch at last came in to change for dinner, Des continued to feign sleep. He was not hungry when the dinner bell rang. And finally he did fall into the sort of slumber that is but a defense of the mind against unendurable anxiety. When he woke up it was dark. He switched on a light and looked at his wrist watch. The dinner period had passed. To his annoyance, he now felt severe pangs of hunger. That meant either going to the Snack Bar—which would be crowded with men in evening clothes and girls and women in dinner dresses, all feverishly excited about the coming morning—or it meant walking back across the key and rustling something from the *Poseidon's* galley.

Des took a shower, put on clean whites and started across the island. The path led through a grove of coconut palms and thence along an edge of the eighteen-hole golf course; afterward it traversed some hardwood and came out over a ragged escarpment pocketed with miniature beaches. There the sea played, silver in the moonlight. Des wore boat shoes which made no sound. Still, he would not have dreamed of eavesdropping if he hadn't heard his skipper's name, tossed by the breeze from the dark recesses of sand and lavalike coral.

"Of course I haven't got a dime! Crunch Adams is the whitest guy I ever met! He's betting on the trip!"

"Then he's mad!" said a girl's voice. "You never even fished bullheads!"

Des could make out the couple kneeling in sand, facing each other. The girl had blond hair and she had evidently used one of the new, diamond-dust powders, because the moon glittered in it.

Mr. Paul continued to defend himself, "If these decadent playboys at Coral Key can catch tunas, I can!"

Her answer was rueful, "Why does everybody like you assume, Harvey, that just because people are rich, they're not merely half-witted but decrepit besides? Am I?"

"I'm nuts about you," he responded irrelevantly.

"Well, I'm definitely not—about you! You shouldn't have followed me here! You know how dad hates you chasing me, anyway!"

"That prejudiced, Bronze Age big shot!"

"Don't you call my father names! He's all I've got in the world! And I'm all he has! I love dad! How could you ever expect me to care about you anyway, since you feel the way you do about him?"

Des scuffed a foot and approached. The girl tossed her gleaming locks and called, "Who's that?"

Harvey identified the intruder, "Hi, Des!" He waved a hand. "This is Miss Vanda Bradley. Des Smith."

The girl said, "You oaf! I've know Desperate Smith since I was knee-high! Dad and I often fish with Des and old Crunch. Hi! Did you hear us quarreling?"

"Quarreling?" Des murmured vacuously.

Vanda Bradley jumped up on the walk, brushing sand from her evening dress. "You're the most inept dissembler in the world, Des! I bet you heard the whole thing! So now you know Harvey followed me here."

"I did not," Harvey said flatly. "I came to get the money and start my promotion business again."

"You could have saved yourself all the toil and tears and had a better chance with a ticket on the Irish Sweepstakes!" She addressed Des in about the same acid tone, "Have you and Crunch lost your minds, by chance? Are you people serious?"

"Yes," Des said, "to both."

Harvey swayed toward the girl slightly, as if he were iron and she were magnetized. His ankles seemed to hold firm, however, and he resisted an impulse his motion made plain. But Des noted that Vanda also had swayed a little—not consciously. So the mate appreciated that Vanda's reproaches and denials were flimsy. *This*, he said to himself, *is going to be some trip.*

Vanda bade them good night. Her sandals clicked on the pavement. She went toward the inn, from which, on an abrupt veering of the night breeze, came the sounds of a dance orchestra. Harvey and the mate walked in the opposite direction, to the dock. It was deserted.

As soon as he came out through the trees, Des realized his frequent foreboding about the cruise had been utterly inadequate. There was something the matter with the pride of his life, the *Poseidon*. For an instant his shocked senses merely telegraphed trouble. But they identified the trouble quickly. The *Poseidon* was riding lower in the water than she should. That meant she was leaking. Des ran, followed by Harvey, who called, "What's wrong?"

Des didn't take time to answer. He leaped aboard, yanked up a hatch cover and disappeared. He found the sea cocks open. Reaching down through a foot of sluicing bilge, he closed them. Then, grimly, he went to the controls, pressed an engine-starter button, warmed a motor and engaged one of the pumps. Dirty water splashed into the harbor in the dim dock light. Harvey, meanwhile, stood in the stern cockpit, watching perplexedly.

"Gletter," Des began at last, "or his mate, Fiddler, must have come aboard after the coast was clear down here. Opened the sea cocks. She was settling."

"Who's Gletter?"

For an answer, Des leaped back onto the dock and strode toward its T-shaped far end. He walked out on one arm of the pier and stood astern of a rakish modern cruiser. The *Poseidon* lay midway between two dock lights, in deep shadow, but Gletter's boat was moored beneath a cone of feeble light. Des noted drops of water on the bottom of an upended dinghy, forward of her canopy. Someone had put the little craft overboard recently. Rowed to the *Poseidon's* night-hidden bow, doubtless; climbed aboard, opened the valves and rowed away. Des explained.

Harvey Paul listened with a furrow of anxiety on his forehead. "Why, Des? Why would this Gletter or his mate, Fiddler, do such a thing?"

"Because he's been doing things like that to Crunch and me for a long while," Des answered with quiet anger.

"What's he got against you?"

"Nothing." Des started back down the dock. "Nothing! Except, four or five times in the last ten years, we've licked him fair and square for trophies. And three or four of his pet customers have changed over to us. We didn't steal 'em. They quit him—tried different boats—and settled on the *Poseidon*. Gletter hates losing."

"I see." Young Mr. Paul meditated a moment. "That's going to make one more handicap for us."

"Yeah."

"I'll stay aboard tonight," Harvey offered.

Des shook his head. "You go up to the shindy. Find Crunch. Tell him about it, privately. I'll sleep aboard tonight. You tell old Crunch that too."

Harvey took a direct path toward the Coral Key Inn. As he passed near the stucco houses of the native help, he heard a band playing in the calypso-like rhythm of the Bahamas and he also heard the high, excited voices of men in a dice game. That appeared to be the reason the dock had been altogether deserted. He moved on into the jungle.

Up ahead, presently, the lights of the inn glowed through dense foliage. Harvey stepped from the wall of trees onto acres of clipped lawn. Before him was the island's main building, three stories high, pouring light across the lawn from every window.

The spectacle was glamorous, but it had a stifling effect on the young man. He stopped uncertainly. Who was he, to pit himself against such opulence? A small-town kid from the Middle West. One who had worked his way through two years of college, fought the last year of a war and finished school on the GI Bill. One who, after that, had started his own business in Manhattan on a shoestring, built it up until he'd had seven clients and a good income, and stupidly failed. He'd been having lunch at the University Association right after the disaster, when Millard Davis, 3rd, a classmate, had casually invited him to use his Coral Key cottage during the tournament. Harvey had been on the verge of explaining his destitute circumstances when Millard had mentioned the prize money: "But money or marbles, you'd have fun!"

In the dining room of a club in New York City, that money had seemed a possibly achievable goal. But now that he was actually entered in the tournament, the money seemed as far away as the moon. And Vanda Bradley—undoubtedly among the dancers—was as remote from Harvey as the outer planets. He sighed ruefully then, but spiritedly, and strode toward the glass doors.

There were pretty girls and middle-aged women in dinner dresses. The men were of every age too. But even those with gray hair looked muscular. Most were sun-tanned. In the big room there was no visible evidence of self-indulgence and decay. Dancers and spectators would have pleased a physical-culture fiend, Harvey thought. He saw Vanda dance past in the arms of Crunch Adams.

Then, to his surprise, somebody spoke his name and gripped his arm so powerfully that he expected, as he turned, to confront a man. But it was a woman, a hefty, handsome woman with abundant white hair who wore a dress of rose.

"My name," she said, "is Amanda Barton. And you're Harvey Paul. Crunch told me. I promised him, young man, that I'd introduce you around here." Her eyes searched the dance floor and she said idly, "I wonder if I'm too old and too spavined to learn the samba, myself? There's Crunch! Picked the prettiest female on the island, didn't he? What a figure that girl has! Brains, too! Let's start in the bar, Mr. Paul. You'll meet some of the oldest families in America, some of the nicest people—and a few of the biggest bores! Crunch tells me you never fished before. I admire your gall! By the Lord Harry, I do!"

She winked at him. He laughed. He liked her. Everybody did, save for a few rival hostesses in Bar Harbor and similar places. He found himself in the Coral Reef Bar, holding a planter's punch as he and Amanda moved from table to table.

Harvey Paul was handsome. He was courteous. His way, upon being introduced, seemed shy, but he was not shy. And he had a quiet quick-wittedness which caused him to find, almost invariably, amusing words to say to everybody. Coral Key tentatively adopted Harvey, half because of what he appeared to be and half because of his sponsorship by Amanda.

He danced with several girls and women. He tried three times to dance with Vanda Bradley, but each time he was met by a faint shake of her silver-gold head and a negative sparkle of the glittery stuff she had powdered into her hair. He forgot to tell Crunch about the near-disaster to the *Poseidon* until, at midnight, a big gong sounded and the orchestra played "Good Night, Ladies." The anglers had to be in bed. Belatedly, apologetically, Harvey hunted up his captain.

Crunch listened to the story and nodded with the same grimness Des had shown. "I was dumb not to have made sure there'd be a dock watch-man. Get some sleep." They shook hands. Crunch cuffed Harvey with approval. "You've made quite a hit down here so far, boy! People keep asking me what you do. I tell 'em, nothing." Crunch's eyes were amused.

Harvey blushed a little. "I wouldn't want people to think I was just a playboy, like some I met this evening."

"Why not? If you told 'em you were broke, a few would cut you, and the rest would try to lend you money."

The crowd was already thinning. Harvey looked at those who remained and shrugged. "Tell 'em anything you please, captain. After all, if we win, we'll be rich, for me. And if we don't, it won't matter what they think!"

The Coral Key cottage lent to Harvey by his casual classmate was one of the smallest of the private houses. A sea-facing villa, it contained a two-story living room about fifty feet long, and two lavish bedroom suites. As he unlocked the modernistic front door, Harvey reflected that the small palace had doubtless cost more than the prize money he no longer had any real hope of winning. And he remembered that his classmate, when offering it, had simply said, "I've got a little shanty on Coral Key you could use, if you can get off for a couple of weeks this spring."

Harvey switched on the lights of the "shanty." He hurried through the splendor of its main chamber and entered the downstairs bedroom suite. He hung up his dinner clothes carefully, so their creases would be pre-served; he had very little cash to waste on tips for valets. He turned out all the lights and dropped with a sigh into a voluptuous bed. Outdoors, easy surf from the moon-spattered sea gurgled though jagged oölite where little fish swam in tidal pools, crabs scuttled and a thousand other forms of obscure life went about their weird nocturnal doings.

The thud and gush of sea that lulled the tropical landscape seemed to bring ashore, like driftwood, his various anxieties. They circled in his mind for a little while. He'd gone broke being headstrong, and because he had been determined to work for himself. He was in love with an unattainable girl. The girl's father detested him. He had invaded a private paradise inhabited by nice people, who, if they knew, would be outraged by his conduct. He'd undertaken a gamble for a fishing prize without fishing experience. Finally, the skipper and mate who were so generously helping him had their own reasons for the gamble—reasons which in-volved an apparently dangerous feud. . . .

His alarm clock summoned him back to a turquoise morning spangled with orange over the Bahamas Banks. He showered and dressed. In the dining room of the inn, the people who had been amiable the night be-fore were preoccupied. Men in shorts, sports shirts and long-visored "bill-hats" ate hurriedly, without much talk; they were, this day, deadly rivals.

On the pier, the skippers and mates also were quiet—which was not their wont. Even engines, started tentatively, seemed to run without their customary clangor.

Crunch merely asked, "Sleep well?" and Harvey realized that the difference between a good sleep and a bad one was vitally important.

The boats cast off and lined up, one by one. The *Poseidon* took her place. Looking along the line, Harvey could see the anglers, fiddling with the winch-sized reels, pulling out line against heavy drags, feeling hook points. These men—young, middle-aged, two or three with white hair—seemed to be built like stokers, wrestlers, football players. Harvey's own wiry body, city-pale, was foreign here. The judges' yacht, the *Dorado*, steamed importantly to the harbor mouth. Crunch called a few questions to a colored youngster who, Harvey suddenly perceived, had taken a perch on a cross-piece on the mast. A cannon boomed. Every pair of engines in the fleet roared at maximum speed.

Harvey glimpsed the sandspit on the southern side of the harbor. He saw the *Dorado* drop astern. He had a view of the coral reef opposite the sandspit—a white beach with a topknot of cocoanut palms. Then the water turned emerald, pale blue and, presently, the translucent indigo-cobalt that marks the Gulf Stream. A ground swell, tired after a long run from some remote and stormy surface, smacked like drum beats against the racing *Poseidon*.

Minutes passed—five and ten and twenty. The sun hove up, hot and bright. Sitting in the fighting chair, riding the ground swell like a man out on a trotting elephant, Harvey realized that Des had been beaver-busy. Two heavy rods had been set in the sockets. Coiled cable leaders lay on the stern gunwale, each rigged with two huge hooks, both pairs of hooks concealed in bunches of white feathers almost a foot long. Now Des slammed one rod into the gimbal on the edge of the chair in which Harvey sat. He made fast a safety line from the rod to the base of the chair. Again Harvey could guess the strength of a tuna.

Des snapped a leader onto the line and smiled vaguely. "All set! We'll offer a white feather, to start with."

The fleet was spreading out, each boat pursuing a course chosen by its skipper; all searching for the far, dark shadow of northing tuna schools.

From up on the canopy, Crunch's voice came clearly, "Moon-eye's fast on one! Lucky guy!"

The harness on his back, the straps at his side, the huge reel above his knees and the rod in front of him were encumbrances. Nevertheless, Harvey managed to crane around. He saw, perhaps a quarter of a mile across the very blue sea, a boat lying dead in the water. He also saw, in its stern, the figure of a man surging up and down with formidable activity. He knew the man would be Mr. Bradley—Vanda's father, and fifty if he was a day. A wave of fear attacked Harvey.

Des said, "Feel O.K.?"

"Tops," Harvey lied.

Around them, now, the sea was a Prussian-blue desert, with, here and there at different distances, the shape of a fishing boat or a mere dot across the water that served to show a boat's position.

"Off the starboard bow!" Crunch called in a peculiar tone. "About thirty degrees—twelve hundred yards!"

Des looked intently, leaning out over the water. "Yeah," he murmured.

Then the native boy, who should have seen first, yelled, "Tuna!"

Crunch and Des laughed. The youngster lacked their experience in sea vision; even the advantage of his high perch did not make up for the difference.

Harvey asked worriedly, "What do I do?"

Des tossed the feather into the sea. He made sure the younger man had his rod well seated and held at the proper angle.

"Hang on," he then counseled succinctly.

He hung on. His heart began to pound. He hadn't felt any of that precise sensation since the war. The *Poseidon* hurried ahead, slowed, hurried again, cut in an arc and turned back. Then he saw the tunas, and the sight shocked him nearly as much as enemy planes once had.

The tuna is a bluish fish, a steely-blue fish. Owing to refraction, it usually appears beneath the surface of clear sun-spangled water as chocolate brown. It is a teardrop-shaped fish; the forward third is enormous and tapers perfectly in the hinder two thirds to a very narrow, metal-strong band of sinew that flares in the caudal fin, or tail. This is dark blue; it drives the tuna annually around the food-rich perimeter of the North Atlantic. The fish then passing Coral Key would next pass Cat Cay, Bimini and Walker Key; thereafter they would head for Hatteras. In the summer they would appear off Montauk Point and anglers there would go after them. Massachusetts and Nova Scotia would be followed by the long, cold trek to England. After that, Breton fishermen off France would find their sardine nets ripped up by these unwanted "horse mackerel." When spring came again, they would head—millions upon millions of them—for South America, the Caribbean and so back to the waters of Coral Key, in an interminable itinerary.*

Individuals in these nomadic schools may weigh two hundred pounds apiece up to more than a thousand pounds. Those in the school Harvey now saw ran from four hundred to six hundred pounds. They were directly astern of the *Poseidon,* which had been maneuvered to get them there. They swam three or four feet below the surface. There were about twenty of them and they appeared to be following a lead fish slightly larger than the rest.

In front of the school, about twenty-five feet, Harvey saw another object—a smallish white dot that ducked and bobbed in the sea. He realized with shock it was the feather—his bait—and that it was attached by line, reel and rod to him. He found himself half wishing the tuna would not stike. But the *Poseidon* slowed remorselessly; remorselessly, the feather lure drew closer to the lead fish. When it had dropped back to within five feet of the sea-plowing fish, the tuna speeded up. For perhaps ten seconds he swam steadily and in plain view behind the white dot. A dark hole opened in the fish and the white dot vanished in the hole, which snapped silently shut. Harvey felt nothing after that for an instant. Then he felt as if his arms were being pulled out by the roots.

His hands, furthermore, were slippery with sweat—the drama of the past few moments had left him weak. The heavy rod bent toward the water, and he tried to hold it back. The great reel began to turn and he was engulfed in panic. There is a kind of "fever" for every fish—a nervous condition akin to buck fever, but different for marlin and tuna and broadbills and mako sharks. He had tuna fever. He hung on to the rod, but he groaned as, to his dismay, it slipped from his wet fingers.

The harness picked it up. A strain so great he could not hold it in his hands became, in a split second, a strain his back could endure. The padded-metal harness slammed against his spine and ribs. That thrust was conveyed to his legs and by them to the footrest. He straightened his legs instinctively, and the weight of the fish was then taken up by his skeleton.

After that, he sat shakily while Des murmured, "He's hooked; just stay as you are."

Harvey forthwith experienced the initial run of a hooked tuna of above-average size. Such a fish can turn a reel set at a hundred pounds of drag. Such a fish can run for a thousand yards—which is more than half a mile. And he had hooked just such a fish. It ran its half mile in less than a minute of reel-heating time.

"Wind!" Des yelled. "Crank in!"

The line had slackened. Harvey wound in line for a minute, two, five. He looked up, gasping.

"Wind!" Des urgently repeated. "He's swimming back!"

Harvey heard his own panting. He felt the blood stuttering in his ears. He believed he was going to expire from air hunger; and abruptly, like a distance runner, he began to feel the relief of second wind. But his arms ached. When he thought he'd have to rest, he felt the line come tight again. He also felt the surge of the great fish—the shake of its heavy head, the rhythmic beat of its tail. That sensation, somehow, gave him the grit to wind again—after the fish, stung once more by the hook, made a second, shorter run.

Harvey's fish soon sounded—boring down into the abyssal waters, five or ten yards at a time, so that the line descended vertically from the rod, and the weight of the downward drive hunched his shoulders and cramped his chest. As the tuna plunged into water where there was no light, no temperature change, only eternal blackness and fantastic pressure, it spiraled. Finally—perhaps when the fish reached bottom—its great dive ended. No longer did the reel grind and stop, grind and stop. No longer did the rod tip buck and bend.

"Start him up," Des said.

"How?"

"Put your back in it slow and steady. Raise the tip of the rod by main force a couple of feet. Then swing forward fast and reel in the slack line."

He tried it. "I only got a few inches!"

"Right. Precious inches too!"

"But, man, he's down there a thousand feet!"

"Then," Des grinned, "you've got to give a few thousand heaves!"

Harvey set his teeth. He thought of the times when he had found a hundred squats or bending exercises in the university gymnasium a hardship. He went doggedly after the unimaginable figure of thousands of back bends, leg thrusts. After a while, he found that by sliding a little in the chair, the rod worked more easily. He was learning to "fish with his legs"—the only way by which the average man can fight tunas. When he had brought his quarry some six hundred feet up from the depths, it came the rest of the way in a rush. "He's up!" Harvey gasped. "Now, what?"

Des looked at the sea, the line, the rod, the angler. "Now," he said quietly, "he's going down again."

And so the fish did, against the full strength of a drag set close to the breaking strain of the line. This time, as the fish corkscrewed its way, head down, into the deeps, Des gave Harvey a cola to drink and a cigarette. As he sweatingly pumped the tuna back to the surface, they poured buckets of water over Harvey. At the surface the tuna made a half dozen short runs. Then it tried to sound again. But its stupendous energy diminished.

In a dazed dream, Harvey heard Crunch say, "O.K., Des! Get set! I'll be down and we'll take him now!"

Harvey was urged to work faster. The transom was lifted from the stern. Presently Harvey saw through sweat-stained eyes a shape, dark and awesome, that lunged in the water not fifty yards from the boat—and as he heaved on the rod, the shape came closer. Des rammed home the flying gaff. A block and tackle tautened, squealed. And then an incredibly huge head with a gaping mouth was lifted up onto the stern roller and pulled forward. The tuna came aboard so nearly dead it merely flicked its tail and quivered its fins.

Harvey felt pain in every sinew. He breathed like a marathon runner. But his eyes gloated. He couldn't believe a man could catch anything that big.

"Nice one," Crunch nodded. "Around five hundred." And he said, "Let's go!"

The *Poseidon* shot forward—shot forward, Harvey realized with a feeling of horror—in quest of another tuna. He didn't believe he could handle another that day. Maybe not that week. And Des said, as if he had read Harvey's thoughts, "Pretty good time, too—under an hour. We should nail the next one faster, though. Some of these lads bring 'em aboard in about twenty minutes, occasionally."

The angler nodded. He unclinched fingers that felt permanently curled up. He rubbed an especially tender spot in his right forearm. He stared out over the vast expanse of morning-hot, calm sea and noted here and there the dots that were distant cruisers. It seemed to him that several were standing still—which meant they were fighting fish.

The *Poseidon* began racing and, in a moment, maneuvering. Harvey thought, almost prayed, *No. Not yet. Please, not yet.* And then he was in the chair again, holding the rod; a big tuna had turned from a second school to follow his bait.

They lost that tuna, twenty minutes later, to a mako shark. The shark cut in when the tuna was ending a long surface run and Harvey was braced and fighting. The boy on the mast saw the fin and yelled. Crunch snatched the heavy shark gun and fired, but not with any hope—tuna and the shark were both far from the *Poseidon*. The tip of the heavy rod yanked and wobbled for a few moments and then went dead. Out in the sea, red showed on the surface. Crunch approached the spot as Harvey wound in line. The tuna had been killed by two bites, each of which was a good eighteen inches across, and nearly as deep—each of which had taken about a hundred pounds of meat. "Mouth like a coal scuttle," Crunch said of the mako. They watched the carcass settle in the sea and journeyed on.

Harvey had respite then. It was more than an hour later when they hung their third fish. They caught it. This one was smaller than the first two, but it seemed to Harvey that it had fought even harder. It was not until evening that he learned such was frequently the case—the bigger tunas are often more sluggish; a two-hundred-pounder will sometimes put up more battle than one three times as large.

They had lunch while they kept "prowling," as Crunch called it, at full cruising speed. Toward three o'clock, Harvey hooked another. "This one," Des murmured, "is really a beaut."

"I wish," Harvey replied hoarsely, "that it was a trout! Or a goldfish! Anything but a beaut!"

The mate looked at him. Harvey was pretty tired—but not dangerously tired, Des thought. His shoulders were bare and sunburned. His hair was plastered on his head by salt water and perspiration. He breathed through an open mouth. But the arteries at his temples pulsed steadily, slowly, evenly.

The fisherman himself felt otherwise; to him, the world was a blue blur in which, like a galley slave in an everlasting sea battle, all he could do was bend his back one more time and thrust one more time with his legs and keep it up a hundred times, and a thousand, and ten thousand, while an arm numb with ache and fatigue cranked around and around forever. His fish fought on through the afternoon until the other boats began to start back toward the harbor. Only those with hooked fish, presently, were permitted to remain out. And the *Dorado* steamed slowly by.

From her decks, natty passengers and judges looked down at the working man and the waiting crew.

Amanda Barton bellowed, "How long you been on it?"

"Two hours and forty minutes."

"O.K.! How many you got?"

"Two aboard and this one coming in. Hooked five!"

"Good! May put you even with the top boats!"

Glancing up from his labors, Harvey saw Vanda among those who lined the rail of the luxurious yacht. The wind had blown her hair all day; it was tangled, beautifully tangled. Her eyes seemed to fix upon him with what he hoped was pleasure. So he bent his back even harder. It was, he thought, the best plan. For the past half hour he had realized that his last iota of strength was ebbing. He was by now reasonably sure that it was only a matter of minutes until he fell from the fighting chair, out cold. So he gathered up the last store of his energy and bade his wretched muscles make a final drive.

The result was dramatic. The tuna had been tugging near the surface, in a direction opposite to that of the boat. It had grown fairly accustomed to the pressure Harvey had put on it. Now, as that stress increased, the fish made a nervous forward rush. The drag held. The fish tilted up toward the surface, broke water, emerged for half its length, and fell over. People yelled on the yacht. Harvey tried it again. Again, the fish half hove up from the sea.

"It's jumping!" somebody on the *Dorado* yelled.

The tuna was not precisely jumping. It was not even trying to jump. But the new circumstance seemed to bewilder and tire the tuna, for, after four or five thrusts and a few disheartened surface rolls, it allowed itself to be brought near the boat.

That was when Vanda yelled with all her might, "There's a shark! Underneath! Deep down!"

Des seized the leader. Crunch rammed home the gaff. Harvey grabbed a boat hook and rushed to the stern. There, under the great blue back and white belly of the incoming fish, he saw a torpedo shape. The shark had probably been feeding on other hooked tuna that day or it would have made a faster attack. But when it did move in toward the tuna's flank, Harvey speared down hard with the boat hook. He felt a contact. The shark whirled, knocked the boat hook out of his hands and flashed into the somber, afternoon-lit depths. The tuna came in and the yacht's company cheered.

Crunch waved. Des headed for shore. Harvey lay down on the deck of the cockpit among his fish, as near to fainting as he'd ever been. It seemed only a few minutes to land. Actually, the trip, at reduced speed, took nearly an hour; the *Dorado* beat the *Poseidon* by a wide margin. And with the *Dorado* went the tale of "young Mr. Paul's leaping tuna." And with the tale, a considerable interest developed among other anglers. Most of them knew, of course, why the big fish had seemed to leap—a thing tuna rarely do.

But the fact that the young, unknown contestant had been fresh enough at the end of a very hard day's fishing to yank his fifth tuna hooked, and his third caught, halfway out of water, discouraged some anglers and impressed all of them.

Ike Bratten, of Bratten Shoes, standing beside the steelyard as his own fish were weighed, shook his big head dolefully. "If that's the sort of manpower we're up against, I'm fishing for fun, from here on in!" Others nodded.

Neville Bigman asked, "Who is this hot shot?"

Amanda Barton told his name and added some of his virtues.

"I know all that," Neville said impatiently. "Saw him at the dance last night. Sure, he's charming. But what's his business? Where's his home?"

"Lives in Manhattan," Amanda answered, wondering if Harvey would have the rent money to keep an apartment anywhere, when this contest ended. "Right now he's looking for a new business. He had one—promotion." She didn't say that it had folded up. By saying nothing, in fact, she implied to such people as these that he had tired of his business and sold it or maybe even given it away. It would have been very difficult for the Coral Key regulars to realize that all Harvey Paul had in the world was one hundred and three dollars and eighteen cents in his shorts pockets.

Neville Bigman flexed his tired muscles. "If he is as good in business as fishing, he's the next Morgan!"

Vanda had listened to that discussion with pleasure. Not so, her father. He jauntily supervised the weighing of his three fish—he and two other entrants had brought in three that day. But afterward he said, "Why don't you tell 'em, daughter, that young Paul's a fourflusher and a cadger?"

"Because he's not!" said the blonde argumentatively.

Pontius Bradley stared at his daughter, but thought about her mother. Laura Bradley, before her untimely death, had been something of a problem when crossed on delicate matters. And Vanda had not only inherited her mother's capacity for emotional combat but added to it an education which included a master's degree. Glumly, he evaded argument and watched as the *Poseidon* rounded the point.

On board, Crunch knelt over his passenger. "Better rise and shine, pal! There's a committee on the dock!"

Harvey peered over the gunwale. "Man! I don't think I can stand! I may have to be hospitalized!"

Crunch grinned sympathetically. "It gets worse for a few days. Then, better. I see Vanda on the dock."

"Where?" Harvey rose, forgetful of the awesome condition of his muscles. He saw the girl and waved.

The weighing began as soon as they docked. Harvey's third fish, the one alleged to have jumped, brought him a higher poundage than all but one of the day's four "triple-headers." That contestant, however, had fished with heavier line than the *Poseidon* had used, so that, in net points—which were all that counted—Harvey led for the day. When this fact was announced there was a good deal of applause and some backslapping. Harvey was invited up to the bar for a quick one before the dinner change, by half the inhabitants of the Key. He accepted; Vanda had done so.

But Mr. Pontius Bradley, seeing his name and his boat in third place, disgustedly withdrew from the group. He found Moon-Eye Gletter staring sourly at the scoreboard.

"If there's one thing I'm determined to do," said Mr. Bradley, "it's to wipe that twirp off the board! I think if he won I'd have a stroke!"

"Wouldn't mind seeing Crunch larruped, myself!"

"Then," Bradley grunted, "you've got to find me more and bigger tuna."

Gletter had a permanent vertical scowl over large, too-shiny eyes. "Or something," he muttered.

The magnate looked at the skipper, pondering his reputation. "Keep it clean, Gletter!" Mr. Bradley said. "We want to win, but win fair."

"Oh, sure." Gletter's eyes gleamed white and evil.

Mr. Bradley thought some more. "Remember that. No tricks, nothing illegal. I'll give you some incentive! Two-grand bonus if you bring me in ahead of Paul."

"For an extra two grand," Gletter smiled, "I'd dive in and heave your tunas aboard barehanded!"

After dinner Harvey went to his borrowed residence. The dance band played alluringly, but he couldn't dance that night. He'd hardly been able to eat. He'd been stunned, in fact, to observe that some of the men who had fished all day—who had hooked and fought, boated or lost two or three tunas apiece—were apparently eager to dance mambos and tangos. He undressed shakily and threw himself on the bed. Pain ran through him. His legs simmered. He was sure they would be immobile by morning. There was a knock on the door.

"Come in!" Harvey yelled.

It was Des, carrying a valise. "Give you a rub-down," the mate announced cheerily.

Gratefully, Harvey submitted. Des, it proved, had a keen knowledge of exactly what muscles were most distressed by big-game fishing. But as he worked he worried. "You sure got yourself stiffened up, boy!"

Harvey groaned. "I've been lying here thinking how crazy I was to tangle in a half dozen rackets that are all out of my class."

"You're not quitting on us?"

"Not quitting, no. That is," Harvey grinned painfully, "if I'm able to walk to the boat in the morning."

"That's the spirit! When I get through, you take a long hot shower, and then get some sleep. In the early morning, another shower, another rub-down, and you'll feel better. After a day or two more, all this soreness will go away—" His voice trailed off.

Harvey lifted his head.

Des was staring out the window. The siren on the power plant had sounded.

"What is it?" Harvey asked.

"That's the club alarm! Means fire! And it kind of looks bright in the sky, over by the docks!" Des went to the window, watched briefly and reported, "Everybody's running out of the inn! I better go see what's wrong, myself!" He turned and found Harvey in his slacks, already buttoning a shirt and shoving his feet into moccasins.

They went out together. The glare in the direction of the docks suddenly grew very bright. Des started to run. "*Poseidon's* down there!" he yelled.

His teeth clenched, Harvey followed.

2

IN ANY fire on or near powerboats there is a special danger of explosion—
of a mushy, blinding burst of gasoline. The men running through the key
jungle were fully aware of that. The light they'd seen in the sky had the
brightness of gasoline already ablaze. When Harvey Paul and Des Smith
charged out through the last fringe of mangrove they saw a picture in two
vivid colors—the color of flame and the gray of people and landscape
silhouetted by flame.

The fire seemed to be on the water, near the dock at about the position of the *Poseidon*. It was a bright, hot fire that bellied with the
night breeze beneath a canopy of smoke. Against it were outlined the
shapes of cruisers and their geometrical rigging and, against that complex
pattern, they saw the figures of men standing still on the dock or
approaching the flames cautiously, their hands held before their eyes
to fend off heat. It seemed, at first, that the fire came from the surface
of the water. But as Harvey and Des ran onto the pier they could
see what caused the conflagration and they could imagine what had
happened.

A half dozen outboard motorboats were kept by members of the Coral
Key Association for bonefishing, other inshore fishing and for fast trips on
calm days to Cat Cay and Bimini. These craft were moored to floats at
some distance from the shore. One of them had apparently caught fire
and, when its line burned through, had drifted on the outgoing tide
around the harbor rim to come to rest against the bow of the cruiser
Matilda, next to the *Poseidon*.

There were men on board both the larger boats. Harvey recognized
Crunch Adams among them and he made out Gletter on the *Matilda*.
These, with others, were trying to shoot fire extinguishers into the furiously burning small boat. They used hatch covers to protect themselves
from the heat as they moved on the decks of the two immediately en-
dangered boats. But they seemed unable to make much progress in putting out the fire; they couldn't get close enough, and the extinguishers
had little effect.

Both Des and Harvey leaped into the *Poseidon's* stern cockpit. Des
rushed forward where Crunch was crawling behind a hatch cover, passed
a fresh extinguisher to his skipper and dodged back behind the cabin.

"We're getting nowhere!" Crunch shouted. "And there's four or five
more cans of gas on board! Some fool—"

Beside Harvey, a man in dinner clothes said frenetically, "That's me! I
took my boat up to Bimini today, and bought the gas! I was going to store
it in the morning!"

"Those guys," said someone else, "better get off the decks, then! Because if one of those five-gallon cans goes—"

"If one goes, everything here will go!"

A hand-propelled truck came trundling down the dock; the natives who pushed it prepared to operate its hand pump. Someone profanely ordered them to stop. "Water," the raging voice commanded, "mustn't be used! Only spread the blaze!"

The harpoon pulpit of the *Matilda,* under which the outboard boat was burning, itself began to blaze. Crunch jumped back into the cockpit, behind the men who had been out with him near the fire.

"Get all the boats out!" he yelled. "Start the nearest ones first!"

Harvey had been standing there, by then, for a few minutes. They had seemed long minutes and his presence had been useless. But perhaps because he had not been engaged in any activity or even engaged in trying to find an act to perform, he had been able to size up the situation with detachment. Perhaps, too, there was something special to be said about Harvey Paul. He was a young man of unusual imaginativeness. Besides, he had been heaving on tuna all that day.

For another second or two, he watched the scene, as mates, skippers, owners, men and women from the inn leaped into the cruisers and fishing boats to start their engines.

"Couldn't we—" said Harvey to Crunch, in a voice that was actually a shout, and yet seemed quiet in comparison with the din. "Couldn't we rig an anchor on a wire line or something, and throw it aboard the dinghy, and let out line and tow the thing?"

Crunch turned. His face was smoke-streaked, reddened by the heat, glittering with sweat. He stared at Harvey for an instant as if wondering who he was and what he'd said. Then he leaped down the *Poseidon's* ladder and came back with the spare dinghy anchor.

"Des!" he bellowed. "Break out a roll of leader cable! Make fast this anchor! Make the cable fast to a heavy rig! Everybody else ashore!"

Things happened with incredible speed. Yet, to Harvey, it seemed they moved with nightmare slowness. Men on the *Poseidon* leaped back on the dock, some in mere response to Crunch's order and some because they apparently feared the order meant imminent new peril. Crunch started the *Poseidon's* engines and cast off her stern lines. Des made fast the anchor and the leader. Then he ran through the ship and forward, up through the hatch, where the fire was hottest. He reached out in the heat and cut the bow lines.

The *Poseidon* was moving before he was able to get back, blind and choking, to the cockpit. Crunch had to steer; Des couldn't see for a moment. So it was Harvey who picked up the light anchor and planted himself at the gunwale.

"Make sure," Crunch called, "the cable will run free! Duck below the gunwale! When we get alongside, pitch it in! Then duck and pay out line! Then take the rod, and we'll scrambola!"

It was a matter of seconds only until Crunch yelled, "Now!"

Harvey rose from his crouch into the glare and heat. The small boat's hull was alongside and the night breeze kept clear the actual flame. He threw the anchor and ducked again. He felt the *Poseidon* lunge ahead. He watched loops of cable slide over the stern.

"Get on the rod!" Harvey rose again and jumped into the fighting chair. He straddled the rod. The line came tight, the anchor held in the burning outboard and the reel turned under the pressure as the small craft swung about and pulled away from the *Matilda*. But the fire on board her roared with increased intensity so that, even at the widening distance, the heat was all but intolerable.

"Anchor must have busted open another gas can," Crunch said, from the wheel. "Probably about melted through, anyhow. . . . Des! Can you wet down the side? We're smoking!"

Des was still coughing, but he nodded, wiped his eyes and dropped overboard a pail on a rope. He began to slosh the *Poseidon's* side and then her forward deck. Harvey, following instructions, payed out line until Crunch felt they had their dangerous tow a safe distance astern. Then he ordered the drag set up and he increased speed. The heat and fire and smoke from the small boat bent away from them. The *Poseidon* made a big half circle in the harbor, keeping clear of everything moored there. Light from the fire gave plenty of visibility. At last Crunch straightened the course and the motors turned still faster. Thus they went through the harbor mouth, the long steel cable and the anchor holding in spite of the heat, and the heavy tuna line giving only occasionally on the reel as it served for a tow rope. Only Harvey, who was taking the pull of the boat on his tired arms and without benefit of harness, was unable, in that stretch of minutes, to breathe with relief.

When Crunch presently appreciated that circumstance, he left the wheel long enough to snap the rod into snaffles on short lines, so that it stood by itself. Harvey's part of the ordeal ended.

"Just keep the reel drag now, pal, so she drops back a bit all the time, but so we keep pulling her to sea!"

Harvey stood, panting and sweating, in the dark as he carefully managed the set of the drag.

Des came along soon and helped. "Sorry about not being able to give a hand!"

"You bore a hand!" Crunch said. "I was scared, when you went up through the forward hatch, you'd get killed!"

Abruptly, the line slacked. They did not know, immediately, whether the cable had burned through or the anchor had pulled loose or the line behind the cable had parted.

"Far enough out," Crunch said. He raced the *Poseidon* away from the fiery derelict, and then turned in toward shore, circling.

The boat exploded a minute or two later. Arms of flame seethed up. A soft "whoom!" came across the night. Pieces of burning wood and what appeared to be gouts of flaming gasoline rose high, spread and fell. The sea hissed. Its surface was briefly illuminated by pools of burning gasoline and flaming embers; this eddying conflagration became red-eyed embers that sizzled out and left, presently, deep darkness and a smoky smell.

The *Poseidon* headed for the harbor. Every vessel had returned to its moorings; every one was alight; and most of the people on the key either stood on the pier or sat on board their boats. Somebody blew a horn to greet the incoming cruiser, and most ships took it up, making a vast fanfare as the *Poseidon* was berthed.

Among those who pressed forward to greet her crew was the president of the Coral Key Association, Gustav Inwood, who was also the president of one of the largest insurance companies in the world.

He helped ashore three weary men, three men whose faces were fire-reddened and dirt-streaked, whose hair was singed. "Nice work, Crunch!" he said, above the still-clamorous horns, whistles and ship sirens.

Crunch jerked his thumb at Harvey. "Thank Mr. Paul. It was his idea."

Gustav Inwood did so, and added something about adjourning to the Coral Reef Bar, where drinks for the whole island would be on the house. "You boys probably saved several boats," he went on, to Harvey. "You may have saved the whole flotilla! And it's possible, if the fire had spread and gas tanks had started exploding, you saved some lives. It was a pretty heady scheme!"

The chief hero of the occasion mumbled something. Gustav Inwood gave him a sharper look and turned to Crunch. "Your passenger's about shot, captain. Is he all right? He didn't get hurt?"

"Just bushed," Harvey murmured.

Des grabbed his arm. Crunch explained, "He fished all day, and he's new to it."

"In the lead, isn't he?" Inwood asked.

"Yeah." Crunch sighed. "He needs some rest, not a big celebration at the bar. You see, just now he handled the rod we had that outboard fast to—without a harness. I imagine it took about all he had left in him."

"I do need rest," Harvey agreed apologetically. "Got to hit the deck at dawn and fish some more."

"Get the luggage wagon and carry this lad home," Mr. Inwood ordered. . . . "Des, you go along and see that he makes it to bed. I'll have the island doctor stop by and check him over."

The truck hummed up a paved path and into the jungle. Mr. Inwood looked at the crowd of people straggling back on various paths and then at Crunch. "You know," he said, "that guy isn't in any shape to go back in the tournament in the morning."

"Yeah. I know."

"Needs a day off."

"He does." Crunch hesitated. "But he's a mighty determined lad. Determined to win!"

"Any special reason? Or just competitive by nature?"

"Needs the prize money." Crunch said it hesitantly.

Mr. Inwood walked along in thought, beside Crunch. The jungle closed around them. "Why?" he asked finally.

Crunch told Harvey's story for the second time.

"Got enough brass for a brass factory," Mr. Inwood said as Crunch concluded. He chuckled softly. "Still, it's mighty high-quality brass! Deserves a break. I think I'll call a special meeting of the rules committee. After all, the *Matilda's* burned badly enough to keep her in tomorrow. Not anybody's fault. The tuna will run, off and on, for a month. You could claim the *Poseidon* needed a little overhaul."

"It wouldn't be far from the truth, either!"

"So we could suspend the tournament for a day. That would give the *Matilda* time to make repairs. And your man could rest up."

Ahead of them the inn appeared, like an ocean liner with every deck a layer of light. "I wonder how that outboard caught fire, and how it broke loose?" Mr. Inwood mused.

"So do I." Crunch spoke bitterly.

The president of the association was startled. "You don't believe anybody did it on purpose, do you?"

"I could never prove it. After all, the evidence, if any, was towed to sea."

"But who? What for? Why? Cutting loose a burning small boat!"

"There are some pretty hot feuds involved in these tournaments," Crunch answered. "And some skippers will do darn near anything to win or to beat somebody they hate. The tide was running hard. You could row out by that outboard and drop a few chips and see where they floated. Then, if the direction suited you, you could set fire to the outboard and let everything else happen—just as it did."

"Nothing much of that sort ever occurred on Coral Key. We've had trouble, sure. Fist fights. A couple of dozen dirty tricks played. But a thing like that would endanger a lot of high-priced fishing boats! And it could have been an accident."

"Some people, though, are really despised around here."

"Who, for instance?"

"For instance, Des and me."

"Nonsense!" Mr. Inwood answered. "Come on up and join the party!"

"If you don't mind, I think I'll turn in. I'm not exactly dressed for a party any longer. And I'm about three quarters tired myself. It was quite a day!"

Harvey woke in bright daylight. He moved an arm. It hurt. He sat up. It took time. He put his feet on the floor—and grimaced.

He staggered to the bathroom. He took a long hot shower, after removing the light dressing the doctor had put on his slightly burned face the night before. He shaved with immense difficulty. There was a knock on his door.

"Come in!" he yelled, tying his dressing gown.

It was a waiter with a large tray balanced on his head. "Mr. Inwood had a boy waiting to hear you waken up, sir. He had your breakfast thereafter sent over by me. I'm Victor."

Harvey grinned. That, also, hurt. "Thanks, Victor."

"I'll just spread it out here on the table. Overlooks the sea. Pictorial vista."

Harvey blinked. He was not accustomed to the eloquent vocabularies of British-educated colored people. His breakfast was spread. He sat down and found himself fantastically hungry. When he had eaten, and when he had finished his third cup of coffee, he found that his body was again a bearable place in which to live. He started to whistle. There came another knock on his door.

"Come in!" he called cheerfully. He wondered what Mr. Inwood would send this time.

The door swung in and Vanda stood there. She was not in an evening dress, but a play suit. She did not have diamond dust in her hair, but sunlight fell upon it, and the effect was as dazzling.

"Are you alive?" she asked.

He realized that the light of tropical morning was so bright she was unable to see into the cottage. "Three paces forward, step down, turn right and bend forward."

Vanda came in, her eyes growing accustomed to the change of light instantly, but she pretended to be following his directions in complete blindness. In fact, when she bent forward, she shut her eyes. She kept them shut while he kissed her, which he did for some time. He would have done it for longer, but she straightened.

"Darling," she said, "you're sensational! Everybody on the island is talking about you! Either how handsome you are, or how gallant, or how strong, or how fast your brain works in a crisis. I hurried over when I found you'd had breakfast, in order to get ahead of practically all the rest of the females on Coral Key!"

"I am fairly terrific," he agreed smugly.

"But completely terrific! Including your ego!"

"As a matter of fact," he answered, "and on careful second thought, I am terrific only sitting down. I can hardly stand. My back is unable to bend except about an inch a minute. My legs scarcely work at all. If you came over here to woo me, you will have to sit on my lap."

"I didn't come over here to woo you, exactly," she answered, taking a chair at the table and biting into the one, half piece of toast he had left uneaten. "Though you are attractive—even more so, when your eyebrows aren't burned off! I came to warn you."

"Can anything else possibly happen to me?"

Vanda laughed. "You think yesterday was rigorous? Wait and see! I came to warn you against daddy."

"What has he decided to do? Shoot me on sight?"

"You're going to go on trying to win the tournament, aren't you?"

He nodded. "I lead, as of now."

"And five days to fish! Dad is the only person here, apparently, who takes a dim view of you. He is simply furious at the fact that you've got everybody cheering."

"Pure accident."

"And he's going to lick you if it's the last thing he does on earth! He's been a deep-sea angler all his life. He's as strong as a bull. He never gets tired. Once, off Nova Scotia, he fought a broadbill swordfish for twenty-seven hours without stopping! Catching tunas—especially when they're running the way they were yesterday—is much more a matter of strength and endurance than anything else. In the shape you're in, even tomorrow, you won't have a prayer!" She saw that her words were having no effect on him. "Do you know what dad is doing now? Playing golf! Thirty-six holes! And before that he spent four hours on a rowing machine this morning!"

"Exhausting himself," Harvey murmured. "Great!"

So Vanda kissed him again. There was nothing else to do.

Vanda was not, usually, either foolish or flirtatious. When she had first met him, in New York, at a deb party, she had thought he was attractive. She had also thought him a rather lighthearted, lightweight person—a young promoter of trivial business enterprises—a war hero, to be sure, but someone just like thousands of other bright young men in the business world.

The early persistence of his attentions had, at first, amused her. His ardor, however, had soon become vaguely upsetting and annoying until, one evening on the terrace of a hotel ballroom, with music playing and people dancing behind them, that upsetting and annoying quality had suddenly seemed to be the most exhilarating and desirable human quality on earth. Vanda was a sensible young woman who would someday inherit and manage a fortune, and who, meanwhile, had a good job as a chemistry expert in a cosmetic concern. Consequently, she had reacted by becoming slightly afraid of Mr. Paul. Nobody, in her opinion, should be allowed to do such things to a girl's emotions, against her will.

She had eventually discussed the matter with her father, since their relationship was one of the utmost candor. Mr. Bradley had quietly, and without Vanda's knowledge, arranged to have Mr. Paul investigated. The inquiry had taken place at the moment of the collapse of Harvey's business. It was the one black mark the very shrewd inquirers could find, but it sufficed. "The man," Vanda's father told her, "is clearly a cheap fortune hunter." Mr. Bradley was a widower and Vanda was his only child. He did not know that he looked upon her with a jealous possessiveness so fierce that, as long as he could prevent it, no man, prince, millionaire or genius, would take Vanda from his side.

It was a faint inkling of those facts, however, which had prompted Vanda's morning call. And it was a distinct sense of the spirit in Mr. Paul which caused her to kiss him a second time. She felt annoyed at her father for taking such an extraordinary dislike to Harvey. She felt frightened for him because she believed her father could easily ruin Harvey's tournament ambitions even if—as now seemed at least possible—the other competitors decided to let Harvey win. She did not yet realize how sharply her loyalties were divided. And she did not in any way appreciate with what inner fury two men might struggle over her—as if she were not a person, but a prize. Neither did Harvey.

"Go warn your father," Harvey said, as Vanda stood in the open doorway. "Use a little psychology. For instance, chase him out on the golf course and tell him he might strain his heart. Have the doctor recommend some pills for him this evening. I mean, if you're interested in seeing me beat the old grampus!"

"I didn't say that, did I?"

He smirked at her. "No. But the lipstick I still have on my lips definitely means that's what you feel!"

She walked away, troubled.

Harvey's next visitor was Des, who came with his massage kit.

After the massage, to his horror, Harvey was made to walk down onto the dock, clear across the island. And then he was strapped into the fighting chair and set to pumping the heavy rod and reel again. The first few minutes were almost impossible. The next fifteen were better. The next half hour seemed to relieve his sinews of a vast burden of grief. People, moreover, kept coming up on the dock to congratulate him on his idea of the night before and to thank Crunch and Des for saving their boats. These amiable moments gave Harvey welcome rests between his efforts.

To his surprise, he ate a big lunch. To his astonishment, he attacked the tuna rig with violence in the late afternoon and "fought" the dock for two hours. Mr. Bradley came in on Gletter's boat toward sundown, with two tuna he'd caught merely for practice, and observed Harvey at work.

The sight surprised him, and he walked over. "How do you feel, Paul?"

Harvey stopped and wiped his eyes with a towel. "Dandy!" He didn't, quite. But Vanda's father would never know that.

"Must say, I admire your nerve!"

Harvey took a long, upward look at Mr. Bradley. There was, he thought, nothing visibly wrong with the man. He had been put together like a fullback and he hadn't gained a pound since he'd been one. He had straight, rather hard blue eyes and a square, but not hard face. He would, Harvey thought, be a pretty swell guy, if he liked you. But, Harvey recalled, Mr. Bradley did not like him, any.

So he answered, rather quickly, "I admire your nerve too!"

Mr. Bradley didn't get it. He had, once again, what was for him a fairly frequent sensation: that modern young people talked in a language wholly different from his own. "My nerve?" he repeated, puzzled.

It was the opening Harvey had hoped for. He began to rock back and forth in the fighting chair, bending the heavy rod and making line zip from the reel each time. "Sure. Man of your age. Overdoing! And just for fun! Taking a chance on a heart attack—on a stroke—simply to snag a few outsize mackerel!"

"Heart attack! Stroke!" Mr. Bradley looked as if he might have both, then and there. "Young man, my heart and arteries are in perfect condition!"

"For your age"—Harvey whipped the big rod—"no doubt! Still. Never tell about those things. Look at Alonso, the wrestler. Doctors said his condition was perfect too. Took on that French wonder and, zowie!" Harvey cranked swiftly. "Curtains."

Mr. Bradley grunted and stalked up the dock.

"Who was Alonso?" Crunch asked behind Harvey's back. "I used to be a fighter, and I follow wrestling. Never heard of him."

Harvey heaved. "Neither did I."

Crunch whistled softly to keep from laughing. He had a notion that his young angler would be able to fish on the next day, and for as many days as necessary thereafter.

Crunch was right. On the following day, Harvey fought five tunas and boated two. Mr. Bradley brought in three, but his were smaller. He took second place by a small margin over Harvey's third place. First was held, that evening—and that evening only—by Neville Bigman, with a remarkable catch of five tunas in one day, a record for Coral Key. The next day, however, Mr. Bigman retired from the tournament, so exhausted that he contented himself with four games of shuffleboard in the late afternoon.

On the third day, toward quitting time, Crunch ran the *Poseidon* close to Gletter's boat and saw, through glasses, three tunas unmistakably lying under tarpaulins. The *Poseidon* had three, and Crunch called down the fact.

"Harvey," he said, "we've got about a quarter of an hour left. If we hook one and get it—and they don't—I think we'll lead again."

They hooked one. A boat with a fish on at quitting time was allowed to fight it out; the fish, if caught, would qualify.

The trouble was that the tuna hung by Harvey was a giant, and Harvey had already put in a day of Homeric struggle. The sun set and the sky turned orange, vermilion, purple, bronze and then gray. Night fell. The other boats had gone in. The *Poseidon* stayed out—a dot of light from shore.

"Take it easy," Des would say, once in a while. "Keep your back straight, the way I showed you. Don't bend your knees. Let him swim against your bones, not your muscles. We maybe can lead him in where he can't sound so deep."

Whether they led the huge fish shoreward or whether it merely decided to conduct its fight in shallower water was a matter upon which experts might have debated. The fact was that, by heading toward shore and by exerting a steady but not extremely heavy pressure, they did move in—over ascending terraces scoured by the Gulf Stream—so that a time arrived when they were battling the monster over sandy bottom, not five hundred yards from the surf breaking along Coral Key.

"Now," Crunch finally said, "is the moment to give it the works!"

Harvey screwed up the drag and put his back in every surge against the fish. He was tired, but not as he had been, because he had learned to use long intervals of even pulling for recuperation. Crunch directed the *Poseidon's* searchlight out astern. By and by he reported, "Can't be more than sixty feet deep right here. Your fish is about halfway down. He's the biggest one, possibly, ever hooked by anybody on this boat."

Harvey fought the harder. Fifteen minutes passed, half an hour, forty-five minutes. And the monster fish appeared to give up. He quit rushing away whenever Harvey heaved him within a hundred yards of the stern. He crossed his self-chosen perimeter of flight. He came inside the fifty-yard perimeter. The twenty-five. Then Harvey began to get double line on his reel—which meant it was safe to double his efforts on the great fish. He thought he lacked the reserve for that agonizing spurt. Then he thought of Pontius Bradley, and found the reserve. The tuna came in even closer, and lay spent on its side, showing white belly, hardly fighting.

"Take it, Des," Crunch said quietly.

What happened then was such a disaster as can befall even the best of fishing guides. Des set the flying gaff on the gunwale. He seized the leader in gloved hands. Harvey lowered his rod tip and panted, not able to think, not able even to watch. The giant fish flurried as it was brought still closer by the mate. In the flurry, Des himself was violently tossed about. He hit the gaff. Somehow, he had set it on the outside of the gunwale cleat, rather than the inside, which was his habit. The gaff rolled overboard.

Des instantly yelled the news to his skipper. "Rig the spare, Crunch!"

Time passed, while Des held the surging, flailing fish in the down-slanted light of the spot. The captain called, "Not in the locker! Where'd you leave it?"

Des felt a cold sickness. "Ashore!" he answered. "Took it to grind the point! Left it! You'll have to haul in the one we're trailing!"

Crunch might have done that, save for the fact that the flying gaff was heavy enough to sink the wooden shaft inserted in it. On bottom, the gaff caught a coral outcrop in the sandy shallows. Line had payed out until it reached the block and tackle, which pulled taut and held. The momentum of the *Poseidon* was not used up and her tonnage strained on the light rope of the gaff. The *Poseidon* dragged a bit and veered a little, but something had to give. It was the rope, which snapped. The *Poseidon* ran slowly ahead again and the tuna thrashed alongside.

That was the moment when Des noticed how the tuna was hooked. It was hooked in the upper jaw, not deeply. Harvey's recent, tremendous efforts had eroded the bony area into a hole of such a size that any slackening of the line would cause the hook to drop out automatically. Des began to let the leader slide through his fingers, easing the fish back astern.

"Hold it!" Crunch yelled. "We can get a tail rope on it!"

"Not on this fish, you can't!" Des yelled back. "Hook's about to drop out! Bring it in position to tail-rope, and it would flop enough to shake the hook!" Des turned in the gloom. "Harvey, put the drag on medium. Get set to fish some more. And remember, if you give him six inches of slack, even, he's gone! We'll figure something."

Harvey wondered, crazily, what they'd think if he merely refused to try to fish any longer. He even wondered what they'd think if he started to cry—that was the way he felt. He tried to nerve himself to continue the now almost impossible contest by thinking of Mr. Bradley. It didn't suffice. But he thought of Vanda—and that did. Once again he felt the great fish drag against the rod and felt the tired, heavy beat of its tail. With the utmost caution, he began to play the tuna again—giving a little line now, taking line when he could. He heard Crunch calling on the radiophone, but he couldn't imagine why until he heard Crunch's words:

"This is the *Poseidon* . . . Charlie there? . . . Listen, Charlie! We've hooked a big one, inside the legal hours. Lost our flying gaff. Can't tail-rope the fish because the hook's holding in nothing but a big, bony hole. It would straighten any gaff we have left aboard. Could somebody run out with a flying gaff and find out if it would be legal in the tournament to use a borrowed one? . . . Yah, I think it would be too. . . . Offshore, not far, north of the point. . . . Roger, then! Romeo, boy!"

Mr. Bradley, sitting quietly in the stern of Gletter's boat, smoking an after-dinner cigar, heard all that came over the ship-to-shore phone.

So did Gletter, who chortled, "Is that a jam! They'll never take a tuna hooked that way—with just ropes!"

Pontius Bradley had been thinking, guiltily perhaps, about his duel with the vastly handicapped young man, about his daughter's excessive interest in the young man, and about his own possibly excessive objection to the whole business. He looked up and down the murkily lighted rows of moored charter boats, yachts and cruisers. None seemed to be manned. He thought, rather to his own surprise, of how he himself might feel under the same circumstances as those which now afflicted Harvey Paul.

He grinned faintly and sighed a little. "Moon-eye," he said, "get up steam and scram out and lend the *Poseidon* a gaff."

The ever-scowling skipper gulped. "Are you insane?"

"Nobody else here to do it, yet. Somebody will come along soon. Might as well be us."

"You promised me two grand to lick Crunch Adams!"

Mr. Bradley flushed a little. "Sure! Lick him fair and square, I said. But letting the kid lose because his crew fumbled isn't my idea of poker. Take him the gaff. Maybe they'll still miss the fish. Maybe, if they boat it, we'll do better tomorrow or next day."

The captain didn't move. "I refuse to be that screwy, Mr. Bradley! This is the best chance you'll get to win!"

Something—something that had made Pontius Bradley not merely an All-American fullback years ago but a corporation president afterward, now took hold of his voice. "Get going, Gletter."

The captain muttered an acid "Yes, sir."

In the night, off Coral Key, it was ticklish work passing the gaff. Crunch took it from the *Poseidon's* still-scorched harpoon pulpit.

After backing away to get clear, Gletter made an effort to come around in such a fashion as to sever the linen line that led from the laboring silhouette of Harvey Paul out to the sea, where the spotlight's cone held on it. Mr. Bradley took the controls by main force then, and adverted the deliberate act. He didn't say anything. But the way he looked at Gletter made that man turn his face toward the dark and keep it held that way.

On the *Poseidon*, Des said, "One more time, Harv!"

And the young man, astounded by the identity of those who had so swiftly brought the gaff, bent one more time. He had managed to prevent the tuna from getting any slack and he managed it, all the way in.

"You take it," Des finally called to Crunch.

But that, as Crunch knew, would be the worst possible psychology for his mate. He grinned and shook his head. "Gaff him, Des!"

So Des did. The tuna hardly reacted when the heavy iron went home; it was very nearly dead. Crunch lifted out the transom. The blocks creaked and the fish, gun-metal in the murk, hove up on the stern roller and plunged slitheringly into the cockpit. Harvey Paul passed out cold.

He had come to, however, when the *Poseidon* berthed—berthed, almost as on the night of the fire, in the presence of a large welcoming company. Vanda was the first to greet him, and she did it by throwing her arms around him. Harvey laughed, kissed her and hurried down the pier to thank Mr. Bradley.

But the tycoon's moment of good will appeared to have ended. "Somebody would have taken you out a gaff in a few minutes," he said surlily. "So we did. What the hell! You could have lost it, anyhow. And I'll take a bigger one tomorrow."

It was quite a boast. The tuna weighed six hundred and eighty-one pounds—the biggest ever brought in during a Coral Key tournament.

After a congratulatory dinner tendered by the island's people to Harvey alone—since he, alone, hadn't eaten—he managed to get Vanda to himself. They walked back down the path to the place where they'd had their quarrel on the evening of her arrival. They sat in the sand in the moonlight, in the night breeze.

"Father," she said rather sadly, "is going to have to go some to beat you now."

"He still aims to try!"

"Dad's impossible!" she shrugged. Then she said idly, "What are you going to do with the money?"

"Start my business again, if I win it. Why?"

"That's what you said," she answered rather disappointedly. "And that's what I've told people. They've been asking, since the big fish put you so far in front."

"What do other people do with it?" he asked sarcastically. "Buy fifty thousand dollars' worth of ice cream for the natives?"

"You see," Vanda went on, giving him the early onset of the most severe shock of his life, "none of the other winners has kept the money, so far. I mean, there's a tradition. Didn't you know?"

"Tradition? When he lent me his cottage here, Millard Davis didn't mention any tradition! He just mentioned fifty thousand golden bucks!"

"I thought you didn't know." Vanda looked sadly at the sad-sounding sea. "Nobody in other tournaments needed fifty thousand dollars! It makes a difference."

"I'll say." He shook her lightly. "Tell me this—tradition!"

"The winners always spend the money on something for Coral Key. The first tournament winner put in a nine-hole golf course. The next one made it eighteen holes. The year later, I think it was, the winner put in the big swimming pool. Then the tennis courts and stuff there. And so on. Nobody ever simply kept the prize. That's sort of—the spirit in which it was put up."

Harvey was silent. His New York friend had failed to mention that little detail, because his friend hadn't needed fifty thousand dollars, either. Now, Harvey knew, even if he did win, he'd be expected to landscape the crews' quarters or something of that sort. He thought of the appalling effort he had made. He looked at Vanda. He opened his mouth. But he found nothing to use it for, except to draw a deep, shaky breath.

Amanda Barton came aboard the *Poseidon* on Sunday evening. The cruiser flinched under her weight, as usual, and her voice boomed like a bullfrog's, "Hi, there! Crunch!" As usual, she was disobeying the orders of the doctor, who had forbidden her to risk her heart, heft and blood pressure at the Coral Key Tuna Tournament; she was eating intermittently from a large sack of saltwater taffy.

The *Poseidon's* skipper raised his head above the deck and vaulted clear, bringing along a muff-sized piece of waste on which he wiped his hands. His face was haggard but benevolent. "Hello, Mrs. Barton! How are you?"

"Fit as a fiddle," she answered. "Make it a cello," she amended. "Have some taffy." She held out the sack.

Crunch started to reach and saw engine grease on his hands. "Toss me a couple."

She did. She sat down on a daybed under the canopy; Crunch joined her. From the island came the sound of church bells, followed by the melodious drift of a native hymn. As a rule, the tournament lasted from a Monday through a Saturday. This year, owing to the fact that Tuesday had been skipped, the final day was to be Monday and the intervening Sunday also had been declared a holiday. The eyes of the New York dowager traveled ashore, where the steeple of the native church showed above the green embroidery of jungle; they moved on out to sea, where the red ball of the sun was setting over the Gulf Stream; they came back to the dock and fastened on a board where the contestants' scores were listed.

Of the original thirty-eight entrants, twenty-one remained. But of these, only two had scores large enough to be significantly affected by another day's fishing. Their names and current scores were chalked in a big circle:

> Leader: Harvey Paul . . . . 6157 points
> Second: Pontius Bradley . . . . 5882 points

Amanda Barton unloosened a sable stole—the evening breeze was cool for springtime—and lifted a lorgnette that hung around her neck on a platinum chain. She stared at the board as if the lorgnette might some-how change the scores. Crunch chewed candy thoughtfully and watched, without comment.

"Close," she sighed at last. "Too close for comfort!"

He nodded, but made no other response.

"You and Des have half killed yourselves," she went on.

A brief grin cracked his face. "What about Harvey Paul?"

"The young man has determination, I must say! And about everybody on the key is rooting for him. Never seen it so anxious around here—not even the year when the Vanderbilt girl led till the last day." Her fingers firmed involuntarily on the lorgnette—firmed with the grip of an old-time angler and threatened a valuable piece of jewelry. "What are his chances, Crunch?"

"You know as well as I do. The difference of one fish, tomorrow, ought to determine the winner."

"I know that, sure! Caught more tunas myself than this tournament has sent to the cannery! I mean, how's his health? He looked below par at dinner tonight."

"Physically, I think he's still O.K. Though he's taken about as much punishment as a mauled lion tamer."

"Mentally, then? Psychologically?"

Crunch considered. "That would be in Vanda Bradley's department."

Amanda made a sound which, in a man, would have been called a growl. "Ye gods! That girl! Can't make up her mind whether to root for the boy she loves or her father! You hear about boys tied to their mothers' apron strings. There ought to be a slogan for girls: 'Tied to their dads' suspenders,' maybe! More taffy?"

Crunch held out his hand. She tossed a few wrapped pieces into the broad, hard palm and went on, "I never saw anything like it in my life! Those two grown men actually fishing for that girl! The whole island's agog over it. And one, her father!"

"That's the reason. Mr. Bradley doesn't think Harvey's the right guy for his daughter."

"Do you?" She asked it sharply and waited alertly for the reply.

Crunch didn't hurry it. He juggled the pieces of candy, looked at the fading vermilion in the west, and pondered. "Yeah. He's O.K."

"That's what I came down to find out! Why didn't you say so half an hour ago?"

"Why didn't you ask me?"

Amanda chortled. "When I come any place this far away on foot, it's for a purpose. You're supposed to know why, Crunch—intuitively. There's just one other item."

His eyebrows wrinkled up at her inquiringly; his eyes smiled and he gnawed on a fresh piece of taffy.

"How come," she asked, "you and Des didn't tell Harvey Paul it was a custom here to turn back the prize money? Whoever had the luck to win it?"

The skipper's face fell. "Matter of fact, I assumed he knew. After all, he'd been invited down here by an owner member."

"And you figured you'd just let him break the tradition, eh?"

"I figured," Crunch answered slowly, and his face was a study, "that he hadn't a chance to win. But he was a nice kid. I guessed he had other motives than tuna—such as a girl. He wanted to get over here for the tournament in a desperate way."

"And so did you and Des!" She shook her head. "All charter-boatmen are crazed!"

"It's bad for our reputation to miss the Coral Key contest."

"And it's bad for your dispositions not to be out there trying to beat Gletter? Is that it, by chance?"

Crunch grinned. "Des and I never like to see Gletter fishing without top competition!" He walked to the stern as Amanda rose, and gave her an arm up onto the dock. "Why this FBI inquiry?"

"Reasons," she replied. "Reasons." She started away and turned back. "You and Des know, beyond doubt or question, I hope, that you absolutely have to win tomorrow?"

"We do, sure! But do the tuna?"

"They better!" she said menacingly, and strode toward shore.

Harvey Paul lay in a hammock outside his borrowed villa. The rather cool tropical night produced sea rhythms, bird calls and the scent of various flowers. With his hand against the bole of a gumbo limbo, he swung the hammock from time to time; it was, compared to chairs and beds, a comfortable resting place for Harvey. Even a week of fishing had not brought him up to that peak of condition boasted by Pontius Bradley. The harness had gouged a raw place in Harvey's back; his right calf inclined to cramps; both his shoulders ached; and there were line burns on the insides of his arms. He heard footsteps and sat up.

"I've been looking everywhere for you," Vanda said, as she spotted his silhouette. "I've got a wonderful idea!"

He put his feet down and she sat in the hammock beside him. The maneuver pressed them close together, but neither appeared to mind.

"What's the idea?" he asked. "I've been lying here without any idea at all. Except, every day, I wish I was a tuna instead of a person. The tunas either get away and live or perish relatively quickly."

"Poor boy!" She said it affectionately. "Then maybe you'll like my idea all the better."

"I hope so. The one about becoming a tuna isn't specially appealing."

Vanda laughed, a little uneasily. "You know dad's absolutely determined to beat you, even though you do lead by a few points?"

"The only thing I know better is, I'm determined to beat your beloved pappy. If my arms will stay in their sockets."

"Why not lose—deliberately?"

"What?"

"That's my idea! Lose. Let dad win. Then—perhaps—most likely—he won't be so darned angry and prejudiced about you."

He fell sideways in the hammock. "Wonderful! After last week's effort, I just quit! I work away ten years of life! I work so hard I bet I could row a trireme across the Mediterranean singlehanded right now! I'm a day from the end. So you have the wonderful idea that I quit."

"I thought you loved me!"

He sat up again. He embraced the girl. "Vanda, I do. I always have, since the day you drifted into my life in that little two-hundred-dollar dinner frock, woe is me! But your father fails to reciprocate my great passion."

"That's what I'm trying to tell you! If he won this contest—since it's got up to dreadfully high points for any year—he'd feel—"

Harvey took her hand. "He'd gloat. Or he'd say I quit, and claim I was a quitter, along with everything else. With a human being, it might be a good scheme. With your pappy, no scheme is any good."

"Vanda!" the voice of the man under discussion boomed over the lawns.

She lifted a cupped hand. "Here I am! Talking to Harvey!"

There was a short wait, followed by the sound of Pontius Bradley's athletic tread on the coral walk. "Ah, Paul! Good evening. I want my daughter for a bridge game."

"But I don't want to play bridge now, dad. I wasn't asked."

They could see him stiffen in the gloom and his voice had a certain rigidity when he replied, "I'm sorry, dear. I've promised you'd make a fourth—just now—with Amanda Barton and Ike Bratten."

"You can pick up a fourth easy enough," the girl answered. "Half the people on the key play better than I do."

"That's nonsense, Vanda. And, unfortunately, I agreed you'd play."

Sitting up again, listening, Harvey realized that the week's formidable competition had taken a toll on the nervous system of Vanda's father. The man's tone showed great stress. The knowledge pleased Harvey. His own system, nervous or any other, was below par. He looked, now, at Vanda and felt the tension in her body, felt her hands twist the fabric of the hammock as she tried to decide whether to jump out and accompany her father or to stay where she was.

"Look, dad," she finally said, and her voice was both sweet and slightly stinging, "sometimes you forget I'm twenty-four years old."

"I don't forget, Vanda. What you forget is that there are some occasions when you must defer to my judgment."

The hammock stopped moving at all, stopped every sign of slight agitation, as if the girl had frozen. "Dad," she said, "beat it!"

Mr. Bradley made a strange sound. He took two lunging steps forward and grabbed his daughter's arm. He yanked her bodily from the hammock. He started away.

Murmuring with surprise and rage, she followed. There was nothing else she could do, except to let herself be dragged like a child in a tantrum. And she, at least, was not in a tantrum.

Harvey then came out of the hammock like an arrow, and in ten racing steps set himself in front of the man and the forced girl. "Let her go!"

The three words held more fury than the rage shown by Mr. Bradley. They cut the night like steel. They frightened; they were intended to. The older man stopped, muttered and loosened his grip.

For a moment, nobody spoke. Then Vanda said, almost wonderingly, "Who do you think you are? Who does either of you think you are? I belong to myself, dad! I'm a grown woman!"

Mr. Bradley ignored the words. "I think," he said to Harvey in a near-crazed tone, "I'll take you apart, right here and now!"

"It would be better if you pulled yourself together!" In what seemed utter contempt, Harvey turned his back on the enraged father. "I'm sorry this had to happen, Vanda."

"So am I." She had stepped away from both men. She looked for a moment at her father. "I'm not playing bridge. You'll have to find another fourth." She wheeled to Harvey. "That bright idea I had just now—forget it."

Harvey said, "I never paid it any attention, Vanda."

The girl ran away swiftly, cutting across the lawn. Both men knew why she ran: she was going to weep.

"She's gone," her father said oddly.

In the light that swept the path from the inn, Harvey now could faintly make out the contorted expression of the other man.

"She'll be all right," he said almost softly. "Lot of strain around here."

"You have my apology."

"Thanks," Harvey nodded. "You have mine—if I did anything wrong. If I've ever done anything wrong!"

The older man measured the younger for a long moment and shook his head. "No. No, you haven't. Nothing personal about all this, Paul. Matter of fact, I find you a rather likable guy. It's just that—Vanda is my whole responsibility on this earth. I wouldn't want her to make a mistake. Ruin her life. It would ruin mine too."

Only the slightest sound of sarcasm was audible in Harvey's reply. "Of course, I never had an only daughter. But, on the other hand, I never thought of myself as bound to ruin the life of a girl I love!"

"See you," Mr. Bradley answered, "tomorrow."

The words contained both challenge and threat. They had a heroic, yet almost childish ring—a quality of, "Meet you at dawn—pistols for two—coffee for one."

Harvey snorted to himself on the way back to the hammock. As he lay down again he could smell—or imagined he could smell—the perfume Vanda had been wearing. It distressed him almost beyond endurance to think that, when the girl got over her embarrassment, she would probably become more attached to her father than ever, simply because of his dependence on her and this open confession of it. That was the way such things worked, he meditated, with considerable insight for his years. Nevertheless, it was better that way. If he could not separate any girl he loved from such childish feelings, he would not want that girl for a wife.

At the dock, at daybreak, there was such tautness as precedes a storm. Smiles were too bland—to hide discomfiture. Preparations were hurried and overdeft. Voices stayed low, as if in fear of an accidental timbre that might be caught by others and truly interpreted.

There was a definite sense of relief among the daybreak spectators when the cannon boomed and the boats surged forward into the final day's competition. But that sensation was followed gradually by another, which dried up the rush of sudden chatter: all day would be spent in waiting. It would be a long day for everybody.

Crunch, at the canopy controls, looked down grimly at Des. They didn't exchange their customary smile or wink. At first, their lead in the contest had been regarded by the two boatmen as a mere fluke. But soon the problem of holding the lead had become all-absorbing. Whoever won, whatever happened, both guides would be almost as tired as their tyro angler, when night fell and the tournament ended.

Crunch steered the *Poseidon* almost roughly out across the shallow stretch of pale blue water to the indigo rim of the continent-grinding Gulf Stream. Down below, Des was using glasses to add another pair of eyes to the constant search for northing tuna schools. Only Harvey seemed relaxed in the fighting chair behind the big rod—and that seeming was illusory, for when Des coughed absently, Harvey sprang to a ready position.

For an hour, the *Poseidon* raced hither and thither in swift seeking. Terns paddled themselves against a listless sky. The sea rose and fell almost imperceptibly. Little breezes moved on fringes of blue, out from the land—and were dissipated. The sun burned with ferocity.

"Tuna!" the boy in the crow's-nest called.

But it was a school of porpoise.

After another hour it became evident that, over Sunday, the phenomenal run had slacked off. There were boats on the entire blue perimeter, but every one was moving—moving fast, steadily, irregularly, like the *Poseidon*.

"Tuna!" the boy called again.

The *Poseidon* jumped.

For Harvey, it was a repetition of an act he performed all day, and performed in imagination during the moments before he fell asleep, and repeated even in dreams. The course changed two or three times. The white feather went over. The fish were big, dark blobs astern, then chocolate monsters that shouldered toward the flicking bait, and finally one brute that surged upon it with open jaws. But the tuna that approached from this school stopped before striking. It followed the feather for a hundred yards and turned away, rejoining its mates.

"Why was that?" Harvey asked disappointedly.

Des gave him a feeble, thin smile. "Be more sensible to ask why it was they hit feathers so hard all last week. Tuna are loopy. Sometimes they'll take one bait for days; then refuse it, but hit something else.

Sometimes, though, they won't hit a golden hook."

Crunch tapped the canopy with his foot and Des wheeled. "Try a feather with a strip," the skipper ordered. "And drag a whole mackerel on an outrigger. Put a red-and-yellow feather with another strip on the other high line. I have a hunch that anybody who makes them hit today will have to work for it."

So, as time passed, they charged back and forth on the paint-blue sea with two different sorts of bait leaping and crashing astern as the outriggers yanked the lines from the water. Two heavy rods slanted from the gunwale rests. Harvey still straddled a third, and its still-different bait was waiting in a bucket of cold water to be thrown overboard if tuna appeared. Thus they gave themselves three chances instead of one for a hit.

But they ate lunch anxiously, almost silently, without sighting another school. "If nobody gets anything," Des finally said, "we win."

It was a thought in the minds of all. But that thought was paired with another. On a day when fish were so scarce and those present so unwilling to hit, a single catch by either of the two lead boats would throw victory that way. Two o'clock. Three o'clock. They passed Gletter's cruiser and eyes strained from canopy to cockpit. Nobody waved or hailed. There were no fish in view. Nobody had taken one on Gletter's boat either.

"Tuna!" the boy yelled with unusual loudness.

It was a quarter to four. The school showed astern and two fish lunged forward. One seemed to sniff the stern bait and reject it. But the starboard outrigger went down. Des snatched the rod from the center chair. Harvey leaped for the gunwale and grabbed the rod there. He slammed it into the gimbal and straddled it just in time to feel the revved-up start of a first run.

"Hooked," he said softly.

Des buckled the harness around him. The angler snapped the snaffles. The back of the fighting chair was whipped out. Harvey, after what seemed too long a wait, was free to strike with his back, putting a heavy lunge behind the arm yanks with which he'd already tried to drive in the hook.

The added effort hadn't been necessary. For the tuna—a fair one—after yanking out the outrigger line, had gulped in the cut strip of fish and the feather. It was hooked very deep, and from the first it bled badly. The angler put into the fight the nervous energy stored up by the long day's waiting. He knew the strength of his tackle now, and how his quarry would behave. From the onslaught of the battle, he screwed up his drag to the tightest possible point, and he gave himself not a moment of rest. Every second of the flying minutes was spent either in standing hard while the fish ran or in a furious assault of back and shoulders.

When the medium-sized fish was gaffed and slid aboard, Crunch called, "Nineteen minutes, Harv! That's some time!"

The younger man laughed shortly and spoke like a veteran, "He was belly-hooked! Quit quick! Let's get another!"

"Let's get another." It was easily said. It couldn't be done.

The sun went lower and lower. Half hours, quarter hours became vital. They could see most of the other boats turning toward Coral Key; quitting early because of the bad fishing that day. The farthest-out boat was the *Poseidon,* and soon the next farthest was Gletter's. Crunch dropped down on deck and bent over the *Poseidon's* chronometer.

"Twenty-one minutes to go," he said. "Let's take a turn over Gletter's way. When we get there, it'll be pretty close to finish time and we can see if they have a fish. Or two fish.

Gletter's boat—trim, jaunty, with slanted outriggers and a blue-and-orange paint job—drew near. The men on the *Poseidon* could tell by the very sag of the skipper, mate and angler that they had boated nothing. And the time left was seven minutes. Crunch presently lifted a megaphone to make some jeering comment, and put it down with the thought that he'd wait till the last second had run out.

He was glad of the decision. Suddenly the people on board the other boat were electrified. The boy on the mast yelled thinly. Gletter rushed to the after end of the canopy and yelled something. Mr. Bradley sprang to life in the fighting chair. And, as he did, his big rod took a set and his big shoulders reared back to strike three mighty times. They were near enough to see a boil astern as the hooked tuna took off—near enough to see, even, that it headed diagonally away, toward the *Poseidon.*

Crunch shoved the throttles to full speed and cut the *Poseidon* around to get clear. Des called, as the boat turned, "Look, Crunch! See him!"

They could see. The great hooked tuna was tearing toward the *Poseidon* hardly a foot under the surface. It came at perhaps twenty knots, and behind it was the rigid, white line that led to Mr. Bradley's rod and his screaming reel. Under that, a shadow.

"Something's after it!" Harvey shouted.

"Mako!" yelled Crunch, from the canopy, where he could see better.

Des turned expressionlessly to Harvey. "There goes his tuna—and here comes our prize!"

Harvey was never able, afterward, to explain exactly why he did what he then did. He said it was in impulse—which was true. He said tuna fishing had made him hate sharks. He said Mr. Bradley had once been sporting enough to bring them a gaff for their record-breaking tuna.

Perhaps he did it because he felt sorry for the man in the fighting chair. In any event, he did it.

As the tuna flashed monstrously across the *Poseidon's* stern, Harvey hurled into the water, behind it, the feather and the strip of mackerel with which his line was then baited. It fell not ten feet from the running tuna's tail and perhaps thirty feet ahead of the chasing shark. The mako, diverted for an instant, seized the easy prey almost without deviating from its pursuit. Feather and fish slab were engulfed in its tooth-horrible jaws, and it plunged on after the tuna. But too late. Harvey's line came tight like a lariat thrown from a plane. He was banged into the chair. Line raced out. He struck and struck and struck.

Up on the canopy, Crunch stared with complete astonishment. Then, for an instant, his face was sick. Immediately after that, he grinned.

"By golly!" he breathed and he shook his head. "By golly!"

He had time to reflect no more. The mako, shooting off at a tangent, demanded instant work at the controls. And a moment later it leaped. It leaped three times, clean out, spinning, and back, splashing so that all those on Gletter's boat saw what it was and, having seen what Harvey had done, understood why. In Desperate's eyes, too, there was now a certain mixture of admiration, wonder and despair.

"I hung it!" They were Harvey's first words as he wound line.

"Brother," said Des, "you really did!"

The tuna—and Gletter's boat—went south; the mako, with the *Poseidon*, flashed and greyhounded toward the north; so the boats separated. Harvey, who had never fought a leaping fish, bent himself to the dilemma. The sun went clear down as he battled and the sky became orange and went out slowly. Night fell long before they hove in the huge shark.

There was, on the Coral Key dock, utter silence as the *Poseidon* came in. Few of the anglers and not many of the women had had dinner. They were waiting. Pontius Bradley had boated his tuna, and it weighed five hundred and sixty-two pounds. That gave him a big lead in points. But the waiting throng knew there was a tuna on board the *Poseidon*—as well, perhaps, as a mako—which wouldn't count.

Utter silence, save for the creak of gear, when the tuna was lifted from the *Poseidon's* stern and hung on the scales. There was a deathly stillness afterward while the judges computed.

Finally one spoke. "Mr. Paul?"

Harvey felt his heart dive inside him. He stepped away from the dock rail. "Right here, Mr. Inwood."

"You put up a noble—an unprecedented fight. We all congratulate you. Unfortunately, owing to the size of Pontius' fish, he leads by twelve points. A matter of a very narrow margin, in pounds."

There was still that strange silence. Water could be heard falling drop by drop from the last tuna's tail through a crack in the dock to the smooth sea. Harvey looked among the faces for one—Vanda's. He saw her suddenly duck her head and turn away as sobs shook her. But he couldn't tell whether they were sobs of relief or disappointment. He had a glimpse of Crunch's face, furrowed and fixed, like an iron face. He found Mr. Bradley and walked toward him, thinking of an old popular song about, "this is how the story ends."

He held out his hand. "Congratulations, Mr. Bradley. Nice work."

Only then was there a little applause and scattered talk. No cheering. People started strolling dissatisfiedly toward the inn and belated dinners. Even Mr. Bradley didn't seem especially happy. His hand was shaken half a hundred times, but his responses to congratulations sounded automatic. He finally started toward shore, passing Crunch on the way.

"It hardly seems fair," he murmured.

Crunch managed a smile. "It's fair. That's fishing. Our boy took the shark off your tuna. But you brought him the gaff. We're even."

The older man's eyes were bright with gratitude. He overtook his daughter, who was crying no longer. Arm in arm, they walked away.

"Let's go eat," Des said.

"You go," Crunch answered. "I'll sit here a bit."

The mate thought of insisting and realized Crunch did not merely want but had to be alone. Des understood and walked slowly toward the crew dining hall alone. Harvey had vanished minutes before.

Now Crunch, by himself, could give vent to emotion. But he seemed void of all feeling. He lay down on a daybed under the canopy. The duel was over. Harvey had lost. The *Poseidon* had lost. His wife, Sari, could say what she pleased—even that he was getting senile—and it would be true. He'd been a fool to take the risk, and a worse fool still because he gambled for a prize it wasn't quite cricket to accept. He wondered how often in his life he would fall prey to an impulse, to a quixotic impulse. And he thought of Harvey, tossing the bait to the mako—and by and by Crunch's hurt began the process of healing. He grinned in the dark and smoked.

Some cruise. One for the books, even if he was paying the freight. And Sari wouldn't mind too much. She'd be disappointed, but she'd understand; she was a fishing woman in the sense he thought of himself as a fishing man. He lay quietly, not content, but not wholly depressed. By and by, the dock quieted down as boats were hosed, gear was stowed and hungry mates and skippers left. By and by, also, because he had not slept at all on the night before, Crunch dozed.

Up in the shadows beside Millard Davis' villa, Harvey rocked himself in the hammock. He wasn't hungry. He wasn't anything. It was all over. He'd almost beaten the best tuna anglers in Coral Key and he had caught a walloping mako, besides. Maybe he wasn't too spavined now to swallow his various defeats—Vanda included—and go back to Manhattan and earn a living.

On the pier, time passed and Crunch slept. Now and again sounds of dance music came from the inn and sounds of revelry came from the crews' quarters as the end of the tournament was celebrated. In due course, a rowboat put out quietly from shore. It contained four men and they moved cautiously along the bows of the moored vessels, peering. When they were sure no one remained on the poorly lighted dock, they vaulted up. Their feet were bare, so they didn't make any sound. They carried knives—the long, thin-bladed kind boatmen use, the very sharp kind.

The cannery boat had not yet come for the day's catch—so it wouldn't arrive till early morning. A slim catch—only seven fish for all twenty-one boats. The men moved along the pier till they came to the winning fish— Mr. Bradley's fish. They talked in low tones.

"How'd you do it, with Bradley there all the time?" a lean, unshaven man asked.

Gletter chuckled. "On the way in, after getting the fish, he took a nap. Bushed, Bradley was. This tournament half killed him." Gletter knelt. "Two of you, hold the mouth open."

Two men squatted in the murk and opened the tuna's jaws. Gletter thrust in his knife, arm-deep, and hacked. "Got up weights from my ballast. Sewed 'em in good with bonefish-bait string and a needle. Wouldn't do," he grunted as he worked, "for a lot of iron to fall out of the fish while they weighed it!" He reached deeper and extracted from the tuna a rusty, heavy sash weight. One of his helpers started to throw it overboard.

"Hey!" Gletter called, *sotto voce*, "Wash it! We'll put it back aboard. Don't want anybody to spot a lot of sash weights on the bottom, come morning!"

Crunch woke then. He heard a murmur of voices. He stretched and almost yawned loudly. He repressed the yawn because he realized, quite suddenly, that the murmur he'd heard had been furtive. He slipped out of his shoes and moved astern, keeping low. He brought his head above the level of the dock in time to see Gletter pull a sash weight from the tuna's mouth. "That's six—the lot! Wash it! And wash down the mess here. We'll stow the ballast and scram." Gletter laughed nastily. "We couldn't burn Crunch out, but we sank him anyhow!"

Crunch did not stop to think at all. He might have realized that an examination of the tuna by daylight would reveal the string stitching, the iron rust—the fraud by which Gletter had brought Mr. Bradley the first prize. But all he realized was the overt fact. He might also have observed the men's knives. He didn't. He was on the dock and down the dock like a panther, standing over the kneeling men—Gletter and his mean mate, Fiddler, and two other lads from the boats, lads Crunch knew and had mistrusted always.

"Just leave those weights right on the dock," Crunch said.

They looked up then; hissed as they drew in breaths and tensed muscles and made ready to jump him. Fiddler was nearest, and Crunch hit him so hard he went overboard under the rail, falling with a splash between two cruisers. Bimbo Melby rushed him with the knife glinting, but Crunch was twice as fast as his opponent. He had the wrist and the knife, and it flicked way out into the harbor. Gletter came in, smashing Crunch with his fist. Crunch threw Melby over the rail and caught Gletter with a right, a little high on the chin, but Gletter staggered. It was the fourth man who did the damage. He had the sense not to knife Crunch, but, instead, he picked up a sash weight and swung it from behind at the unguarded head. Crunch was moving so fast then that the weight missed his head, but it came down on his shoulder with full force.

Pain flared in him and through him, and his right arm collapsed at his side. He tried to bring it up, but it merely flopped against his body. He saw Gletter move toward him again, turned and ducked the second blow of the sash weight. After he ducked, he had his left waiting for the man who swung it, and the man took it on the cheek. He fell back, bleeding.

"Easy!" Gletter warned sharply. "We got to do something about this guy!"

Gletter circled away from Crunch. He had his knife out then. The man with the sash weight couldn't lift it for a moment, then he could—and he, also, closed a little.

Crunch saw Fiddler scrambling back, dripping, a few rods down the dock. Then Melby. He had only one arm he could use and there would be four of them again—and this time they were going to "do something." There was only one thing they could do to save themselves—put the knives in Crunch and the sash weights on his legs and row him outside and leave him in deep water for the Gulf Stream. It was likely that Gletter had that in mind. For the first time in his life, Crunch was panicky.

The sick presentiment of disaster overcame him. He looked wildly for a way in which to run. He could dive overboard. But he had one arm— and they had a rowboat. He'd die faster in the water. He could yell. Who would hear, on the celebrating island? He could promise to shut up about the cheating, and perhaps they'd accept his word as a better risk than murder. And—*The hell with it,* he thought.

He put up his good arm and backed against the rail as if it were the rope of a ring. He cursed them. But they came cautiously, because the *Poseidon's* skipper still did have that one arm.

Feet pounded on the end of the pier. A big man rushed toward them.

"Beat it," Gletter muttered.

"What goes on here?" Mr. Bradley called. "I thought those guys were after you. Thought they had knives! Man! Your shoulder's bleeding!" He came up.

Crunch rubbed his shoulder. "Sort of stunned—locally, I think. Maybe a broken bone. Probably just hit a nerve. You got here at a real useful time, Mr. Bradley!"

"Who is it? Where'd they go?" Mr. Bradley peered across the dark harbor. He heard fast-dipping oars.

Crunch kept rubbing. "Gletter and Fiddler and a couple of boys. I caught 'em taking out sash weights they'd sewed in the belly of your tuna."

"What?"

Crunch was calming down, recovering from his moments of stupefying fear. "Yeah. Take a look. I caught 'em at it—and they didn't like being caught."

Mr. Bradley shook his head and examined the tuna carefully enough to assure himself that what Crunch said was true. "I'll help you ashore, and get you the doctor."

"Thanks. My fingers are beginning to work now. Guess it's O.K. Paralyzed my arm awhile, that's all."

"I had dinner," the older man said, still a little incoherently, "but I couldn't eat. I saw that boy deliberately hang that shark when it would certainly have ruined my chances. That's sportsmanship! I came down because I don't want this prize—don't want victory that way. I believe in fair-and-square fighting—love it—but—"

Crunch pointed with his good arm at the tuna. "You didn't win."

There was a stillness—a vast stillness. Then Mr. Bradley said, "If you feel equal to it, let's go up and tell them."

"Right. We'll have to post a guard over the evidence, though. A fairly heavy guard."

Crunch massaged his limp arm, and slapped it as it began to tingle with sensitivity again.

When Ike Bratten came over from the inn, Harvey was still moodily swinging himself in the hammock. Mr. Bratten called out his name and took a chair. He lighted a pipe, and Harvey, who did not know the purpose of the call, saw the square, blue-eyed countenance in the match light. Mr. Bratten looked like a cop—a good-natured cop on a peaceful beat. He talked, however, with a Harvard accent. He was the sort of man, furthermore, to whom people paid attention. And, incidentally, millions of people wore Bratten shoes.

"You aren't busy?" he asked, puffing on the pipe. "Mind if we chat awhile?"

"Busy?" Harvey chuckled. "No busier than I look. Sure. Enjoy a chat. About anything special?"

"Let's talk about your business, Paul."

Harvey chuckled again. "Haven't one. Failed."

"I know. You put all your dough on that electronics cooking gadget. It's ten years ahead of itself, boy. That's why you couldn't sell it. But you did successfully sell that citrus candy, and a line of cosmetics, and bathing suits."

"How do you know that?" Harvey sat up in the hammock.

"Funny thing," Ike Bratten said obliquely. "I'm supposed, in business, to be a first-rate judge of men. I believe I am. But I've been on the island all week, and every man and woman except Bradley has been singing your praises. Yet it never occurred to me that Bratten Shoes—which badly needs a new top man in its promotion department—would miss the best, if I missed you. Not till Amanda Barton put a bug in my ear last night! I didn't fish today—spent the whole day on the radio-phone. Know a lot about you now, Paul."

"You mean you're offering me a job?"

"Right."

Harvey dropped back in the hammock and looked at the stars for a moment. "Always figured I'd work for myself."

Ike Bratten drew his pipe till it made a red eye in the dark. "I found that out—among many things. I'd like you to work for me. Give you a five-year contract. At the end, you can take my firm as a client and strike out alone again, if we both agree. Or you can renew, if we agree. The last man I had in promotion was a dunce. You seem to have more fresh ideas than a skyrocket leaves sparks. I paid the dunce fifty a year. I'll start you there."

"Fifty. You mean fifty grand?" It was a figure which had long haunted Harvey's mind. A special figure. And now, as he uttered it, his voice broke, for the first time since he'd been eighteen.

Mr. Bratten smiled to himself. "You were making thirty when your own firm folded."

"And plowing it back. Sure."

"And you plowed all your capital back in a wrong furrow. If you hadn't, you'd be making fifty in a year or two. I buy brains, son. I pay well for them. Let me know in the morning, hunh? And congratulations, incidentally, on the fishing. If I ever saw a moral victory, that was it! I think the battle you gave Pontius is what decided me on you!"

He strolled away.

Harvey lay down again, because he couldn't sit up. The stars were moving in odd ways. He had no thoughts at all, and then he said a thought aloud, "Why, I can pay old Crunch and Des, after all!"

He had, in a sense, accepted the offer. But he lay a while longer in a rapturous stupor. Only gradually did he become aware of a rising din in the direction of the inn. People there were yelling. He got up and looked around the hibiscus. People were out jigging around on the lawn as if they'd gone utterly nuts.

Harvey walked toward the inn with the feeling that perhaps they had gone crazy—everybody, including Mr. Bratten. Then he was seen and the crowd cascaded toward him, yelling, "Here he is!" He was sure they had lost their minds when the men who reached him first summarily hoisted him on their shoulders and started a snake dance. Everyone got into the hysterical parade, and Harvey, twisting to try to get back to earth, felt his own senses rocking. It was Amanda Barton who had the alertness, upon seeing his expression as he was carried into the ballroom, to bellow in her magnificent voice, "You won, Harvey! Gletter cheated!"

The party that followed was remembered in Coral Key annals as the one nobody could ever hope to top. The band played all night long, the Coral Reef bar stayed open and one event followed another swiftly.

The first was the formal award. It took the drummer two minutes to quiet the throng. In giving the cup, and the check, Gus Inwood wound up a graceful speech with the words, "I would like to add, we've never had a winner we were prouder of!"

The rafters shook. They shook again when Harvey ended his words of acceptance by saying, "And now, because of complaints, failures, and particularly because of the dangerous darkness on the docks, in keeping with a great local tradition, I'd like to turn over the prize money for a new Coral Key lighting plant."

The statement left many people—who knew all about Harvey from Amanda—in a state of speechlessness, but it prevented no one from applauding, whistling, stamping and creating general pandemonium.

These circumstances, however, were less dramatic than the entrance of Vanda and her father, arm in arm and smiling. Harvey had missed them instantly. Like the others, he had assumed they would stay in their villa that night, somber, defeated, consoling each other. But the smiles they wore, Vanda's splendor in a new evening dress and Pontius Bradley's look as he stepped up on the bandstand changed all such opinion. They had entered the ballroom just as Harvey astonished his audience by contributing a new lighting plant.

Mr. Bradley extended his arms and silence returned in the huge, beautiful room. "Most of you," he said, "are old friends. Many of you are lifelong friends. So all—or nearly all of you—realize there was more behind my zeal in this tournament than a cash prize." He hesitated and glanced at Vanda for encouragement. People stirred uncomfortably, hoping Pontius Bradley wouldn't go overboard in some sort of misplaced emotion. "The young man," Bradley continued, "who just so gallantly turned over the prize for a power plant, has also pursued my daughter for more than a year, against my orders, my will and my whole determination."

He took a great breath and expelled it. "I hated to lose Vanda. It has only just occurred to me that, by losing her, I might regain her—and a son to boot! A son," he hurried on, as a tendency to shout became evident, "who is the only living man who ever licked me at my own game! A son who went broke just now to maintain not his but our tradition! A sportsman, furthermore, who not only won a great victory, as he thought, for me, but who did something I've longed to do all my life! He caught a mako! I'm proud to tell you that he has caught my daughter too!"

That did it.

Crunch and Des, coming in then, were seized upon by Amanda, who bellowed, "Boost me up, boys! I want to swing from the chandelier!" She roared with laughter, grabbed them both, kissed them—and only then saw Crunch's face. "Skipper!" she roared. "That shiner looks like the entrance to a coal mine!"

"Best black eye I ever got in my life," Crunch chuckled. "Come on to the bar. We'll buy you a drink."

"The drinks," she answered, starting with alacrity, "are on me, all night long!"

Later on Harvey managed to get Vanda out of the ballroom into a thicket of night-blooming jasmine. "I've got to tell you," he said earnestly, "that maybe I didn't cheat in the tournament, but I'm more or less cheating now."

"I love it!"

He brushed aside that comment. "I mean it. You and your dad think I'm penniless. I'm not. I've got a job. Fifty thousand a year!"

Vanda stepped back a little. Her voice was startled. "In that case, we better find dad. He was planning to hire you tomorrow."

"Hire a relative!" Harvey responded in extravagant horror. "Only congressmen and movie producers do that!"

People yelled their names. She shushed Harvey by kissing him. The searchers hurried on, calling, and the scent of jasmine floated around them like currents in a perfumed sea.

Outside the nest of blossoms where they hid for a few minutes longer, Crunch, Des and Amanda walked by, also looking for them. Crunch pointed toward the waving tops of the night-blooming shrubs. Then he pointed away, and the three walked on together, smiling conspiratorily. At that moment the skipper felt a small, ecstatic tear form in his eye, and he brushed it away with the thought that Sari sure was right. He was getting to be a senile, sentimental old seadog.

Only, he thought to himself—and his happy grin returned—Moon-eye Gletter wouldn't buy that bill of goods. Not by a long shot!

Editor's Note to page 270: We now know more about the northern Atlantic bluefin tuna *(Thunnus thynnus)* than was known when Phil Wylie wrote these stories. These giant fish evolved during the last glacial epoch; they are part of the post-Pleistocene "megafauna," along with mammoths and sabertooth tigers. Each year the adults follow the Gulf Stream north and then east across the North Atlantic, feeding all the way. They then migrate back, south and west from the coast of Europe to spawn in the warm waters of the Caribbean and the Gulf of Mexico.

Spawned-out and hungry, the giant fishes, some of them fifteen years old or more, then begin the circuit again. Probably there were never "millions and millions" of them, but a few hundred thousand or less. In the 1940s the Bahamas sports fishery, including the famous Cat Cay Tuna Tournament on which this story was based, took a few hundred a year; similar numbers were caught off New Jersey and Long Island, also on rod and reel.

Today, although the northern bluefin makes up less than 2% of the world-wide commerical catch of tuna, long-lining and other commerical fishing techniques have virtually eradicated these exotic giants. The Cat Cay Tournament is no more, and the hooking of even a single adult bluefin is front-page news in the Miami papers. K.P.

COMPANY FOR
CHRISTMAS DINNER

JUST AS they were about to go to bed, the phone rang. Crunch answered.
When the caller identified himself, the fishing skipper's response was gay.
Afterward, as his wife listened, his tone lost a little of its cheer. Once, he
said, "I'd figured staying ashore tomorrow. Things to do. Next day's
Christmas. But if you say so—" Presently he hung up.

"Crunch!" Sari didn't need to say more.

His deep blue eyes were evasive. "I know. But it's seventy-five bucks.
And it was J. H. Porter."

"And you haven't brought a tree, yet. Or shopped. And I have Christmas dinner to get set for."

"And J. H. will turn into a good customer if I treat him well. Besides,
he doesn't know a soul in Miami and I guess he feels lonely, this time of
year."

"Lonely? J. H. Porter? Crunch, will you never learn that all people
don't suffer from sentiment the way you do? He's a president of a steel
company, isn't he?"

"He's retired."

"And just about as selfish as they come! He's bored, so you have to
fish, the day before Christmas. No time for the family." She looked at
their son, Bill, who had been permitted to stay up late to make ornaments for the tree.

The skipper's brow was more deeply creased than on days when no fish
struck and he scowled in the anxious search for a fin or a splash that might
produce action. "If you say so," he answered, "I'll call his hotel and cancel."

Her mood of disappointment was exchanged for her more customary
attitude of practicality. "Seventy-five dollars," she murmured.

"You could buy a tree, instead. Have the store send it."

She nodded and turned to the bright-eyed, oversized boy. "Bill.
Bedtime."

He grinned at his parents and rose with a mixture of obedient alacrity and natural reluctance. The living-room floor was a sea of popcorn, colored paper, paste and paints. Crunch whacked him amiably; Bill feinted, punched, missed and said good night.

Before they slept, Sari asked, "You want anybody for Christmas dinner, skipper?"

His negative was blurred. "Not especially. Like who?"

"Oh, I'd thought of Alma Pullen and her kids, maybe."

"They were here last year. Nearly wrecked the joint. Let's just have ourselves, and old Des, for a change."

"Okay."

He rose in the dark, beating the alarm clock by his usual five minutes. He shut it off, made his own breakfast, started the car and drove to the Gulf Stream Dock with Des, his mate. They, like the others, busied themselves about the boats; by and by, the east shone where the sun would rise and the dock lights went out.

J. H. Porter came from a limousine, strutting as only small men can. "Got a hunch, captain," he said, repeating a part of his telephone conversation. "Feel lucky."

"Come aboard! Going to be a fine day."

The steelmaker stepped briskly into the cockpit. His hair was white and his eyebrows were white; but his eyes were clear and sharp. They had the quality of the metal he had manufactured all his life.

From the limousine came the chaffeur, bearing a large hamper of lunch. "Never overlook a hunch!" said Mr. Porter, beating Des, the mate, to the stern and taking the basket. "Been a business rule! What's the day before Christmas but another day? And who wants to sit around a hotel lobby among a lot of dodos, listening to carols on a radio? Phooie!" He thought that over. "Triple phooie!"

Crunch grinned. "Then let's go fishing!"

The captain wasn't surprised, an hour or so later, when the white marlin showed. Guides had been "raising" a lot of them in the early morning, on the edge of the Gulf Stream, in front of the grandiose sky line of Miami Beach. He was surprised, however, at the energy, the near-violence, with which his customer attacked and fought the fish. A big one—and they boated it in less than an hour.

"Maybe," Crunch had a chance to murmur to Des, "he'll call it a day now, and we can catch up with Christmas."

"Hope so."

But the steelmaker, after staring with joy at his catch and boasting about his hunch, once again showed the metal of which his spirit seemed to be composed. "Most fun I've had since I left the plant!

Now, let's bait up and see if we can get another!"

So the *Poseidon* trolled its solitary angler through the sunny afternoon and until she and the other fishing boats headed toward the Government Cut at the conventional hour.

At noon, Sari had phoned to Gulf Stream Dock. The possibility of a short day's fishing was on her mind, also. She was told that the *Dixie Star* had reported, on her ship-to-shore phone, a marlin flag flying from the *Poseidon's* outriggers and that, since the *Poseidon* hadn't come in, she'd probably be out until dark.

Sari was enthusiastic about the marlin flag. But she hung up and sighed. A marlin meant photographs at the dock and perhaps a drink with Mr. Porter. It meant, to a skipper's wife, a husband late for dinner and, of course, everything undone for Christmas.

She took off her apron. In the living room her son, Bill, again sat on the floor patiently pasting links of colored paper to form a chain. Beside him were strings of popcorn, dyed and threaded.

"Bill," she said, "go get a hatchet. Crunch will be late, so we'll chop our own tree."

The boy glanced up disappointedly. "Gee!"

"He's got a marlin."

"Gee!" Bill rose quickly and with no further protest, brought a hatchet.

Mother and son walked down the street to a real-estate development that had faltered in the memorable twenties.

Two kinds of trees grew in that no man's land: Australian pines, which are not pines, but look as if they were, and the Caribbean long leaf. Sari and the boy searched in a stand of the latter until they found one of the right height, with suitable foliage. Before he began to chop, Bill said, "Golly. I thought we'd get a store tree this year. These have branches like old sticks. And they don't smell the same."

Sari understood his feeling, even shared it. But she said, "You know how much a store tree that big would cost? Ten dollars."

Bill whistled and assaulted the Caribbean pine. Together, a little self-consciously, they dragged it back down the lane, across the bridge and into the carport, where Bill sawed the butt squarely and affixed a stand he had already fashioned from two-by-fours. In the Adams living room it towered almost to the ceiling. Sari brought cardboard boxes that contained ornaments bought in past years. Some were battered and tarnished; all were dusty; but Bill greeted each with remembered delight. Together they began to decorate the tree.

They were arranging the paper chains when a knock came at the door. Outside stood an angular young woman in a faded cotton dress; behind her, peering earnestly, were three young children. The woman was smiling.

"We saw you testing tree lights, Sari. Can the kids come in and look?"

"Hello, Alma! Sure! Hello, Kirk, Betty, Ellis."

Bill Adams glared at the worried children for an instant, looked at his mother and then approached Kirk, the oldest boy. "Come on," Bill said, "and help me."

"Let me!" The little girl rushed to the tree.

Alma sat down tiredly in a big chair. Sari went to a closet, unlocked it, and took out a box of candy intended for the next day. Alma's children each accepted a piece politely. Sari caught herself almost wishing they hadn't come—there was too much to do, as it was. But instantly she was ashamed. Alma's Jeff, the father of the children, had been killed two years before in a car accident. He'd been a skipper, so the Boatmen's League had helped the family. Still—

"How's the job?" Sari asked, passing a second round of candy and smiling at the children.

It was the worst possible question. Alma's gray eyes ceased even to see the tree. "I lost it, ten days ago. Ellis had a croupy cold and Betty came down with it and I kept being late, and—out I went."

Sari hung a loop of colored popcorn. "That's—awful!" She knew what she was going to do and hoped Crunch wouldn't mind too much.

The children ate their chocolate creams. The younger two were ordered to be watchers by the eldest. "You might break one," Kirk told them. "And they're very valuable ornaments."

"I'll get something else," Alma said steadily. "I've got leads. After Christmas is over." She spoke with sadness. To her, this particular Christmas was unrelieved ordeal.

"What are you and the kids doing, tomorrow?"

Kirk answered proudly, "We got a whole half a ham!"

"Why," Sari asked softly, "don't you have dinner with us? The ham will keep. And there were just going to be the four of us—and turkey."

"Could we, mother?" Betty ran up with the question. "Then we could see the tree all day! And there'd be more candy!"

Alma shook her head.

Sari looked at the children. Eight and six and five. Boy, girl, boy. With a whole half a ham and no tree and no candy. She glanced at her own twelve-year-old. And he was looking at the other children too.

"You better come over," Bill said. He reached out and patted the little girl. "You can have a box of candy."

Crunch Adams' wife smiled gently. "It would be fun. And you could help me with the dinner."

Alma wasn't pretty. She wasn't trained to do anything remunerative. The job she'd lost was not a good one—clerical work in a laundry. Sari wondered how it felt to be a gifted cook and never to have anything but the plainest, simplest food to prepare. Never even enough butter. "Maybe," she said, "you could even make us a plum pudding."

Four pairs of eyes considered the suggestion enthusiastically.

The *Poseidon* docked in *twilight* and pictures of the white marlin were taken by flash bulb before the taxidermist's truck carried it away. Des began to hose down the boat and Crunch accepted payment for the day's charter from Mr. Porter. The old man didn't leave. Another limousine waited for him in the parking yard—a limousine sent by his hotel; its chauffeur paced with Christmas Eve impatience.

Finally Mr. Porter said, "Hate to go home. Had a wonderful day. Hate it, I guess, because it's not home."

"Nice hotel, though."

"Yeah." J. H. brushed luxury away. "Family's scattered, this year." He shrugged. "My Evelyn's in London; married a guy in the State Department. Junior and his family are moving out West where we've built a new mill. Young Harry's in Vermont. Leaves me kind of at loose ends. Always used to get the gang together."

"That's tough."

"I don't like it," the steelmaker said. His tone became, for him, uneasy. "Why don't you let me take your wife and kid and Des, here, out for dinner tomorrow?"

Crunch was surprised and faintly embarrassed. There was some sentiment, or at least a great loneliness, in the old bird. "That's mighty nice of you. But Sari, my wife, is all set." Crunch had an idea, rejected it and found that it returned of its own accord. "If you don't mind a simple dinner, and one noisy kid, aged twelve, and if you're willing to take your turkey with trimmings in a boatman's bungalow—"

The old man's eyes flickered. "That's what I was hoping you'd say! What time?"

Crunch grinned. "Oh, around one-thirty." He wrote the address.

His grin lasted all the way home. The surprise of his mate increased it. And the sight of the homemade Christmas tree brought it into full bloom, a warm and glowing Yuletide smile. Sari called congratulations on the marlin from the kitchen and Crunch called back the weight of the fish. His wife came into the living room with a saucepan in her hands which she kept stirring as she looked at Crunch. She was feeling proud.

"It's beautiful!" the skipper said of the tree. "And if it won't do for old J. H., we'll toss him out."

Sari stared. "Old J. H.?"

"Mr. Porter," Crunch answered mildly. "Coming to dinner tomorrow."

Sari nearly dropped the saucepan. "Crunch! You couldn't!"

"Come Christmas Eve," he answered, "even those steel magnates get lonesome. He asked himself, just about."

The handsome girl with the now-alarmed expression swallowed twice. "Alma Pullen and her three kids are coming, too, Crunch! They only had a little food in their house and she's lost her job."

The captain dropped into the easy chair where he usually sat after dinner reading the paper. He looked at his wife, his mate, his son and their Christmas tree. His grin ebbed while he wondered how the tycoon would react to Alma's plainness, her poverty, and three additional kids. But his eyes met his wife's softly. "Between the two, Sari, who needs a dinner more. J. H. — or them?"

She kissed him in a certain way and the hot saucepan touched the back of his hand. He jumped and they both laughed.

"Suppose," said Sari, and again it was just before they went to sleep, "he brings some present for Bill and then has nothing for the other kids? What's he like, Crunch?"

The skipper answered sleepily, "I thought he was a pretty cold and rugged guy, till he asked about Christmas dinner. Now, I don't know. It's after midnight, gal. Merry Christmas and go to sleep!"

Mr. Porter arrived, by limousine, a little early. All he brought was a big bunch of red roses for Mrs. Adams. He looked over the neat bungalow with approval as he came up the walk. He stared at Sari with frank astonishment as he handed over the roses. He shook young Bill's hand solemnly.

And Bill, with the candor of the young, began to talk immediately. "How do you like our tree, Mr. Porter? Mother and I chopped it down. And look at the holly in the window. It's Florida holly. I gathered it myself, this morning."

"Holly," said Mr. Porter with a smile, "is my middle name."

"That's just what dad said."

Sari laughed embarrassedly. "Bill!"

The Pullen family swarmed up the sidewalk at that moment. There were gifts under the tree for the three children, gifts hastily assembled and wrapped by Sari. The two women went to the kitchen. Young Bill supervised the giving. Mr. Porter took Crunch's chair and watched. Des, being what his skipper called a "squarehead" in moments of exasperation, prepared the eggnog according to an old Scandinavian recipe. The men toasted one another; the two women had a taste and Sari said, "We're ready."

During the meal, as he watched the three appealing Pullen children eat their way through shrimp cocktail, turkey, dressing, mashed potatoes, gravy, vegetables and plum pudding, Mr. Porter pieced out by gentle interrogation the status of these guests.

Only when he had the story of the father's death and the mother's destitution did he comment: "Life's mighty hard, sometimes, Mrs. Pullen. I was left, myself, an orphan at eleven, with two younger sisters." He thought silently about it for a while and then, with a shrug, returned to the Christmas mood.

The Adamses had expected that the retired steelmaker would leave after the properly polite interval. But he showed no sign of doing so. He accepted a glass of apricot brandy that a friend of Sari's had made, seated himself in the living room again, found some carols on the radio, and talked amiably if rather tritely about the oddness of Christmas in a place where there was no snow, where the temperature was seventy-eight, where flowers bloomed and kids went swimming after their turkey.

That talk, coupled with the fact that the children were growing restless, gave Crunch an idea. "How," he asked the Pullen children, "would you like to do some fishing?"

There was no doubt that they would like it.

"You mate for 'em," Crunch said to his son. "Break out the casting rods and swipe a few shrimp from Sari and try the bridge."

It was a happy idea. Shortly afterward, the fishing expedition, four kids strong and conducted by the already-expert Bill Adams, left the bungalow. The grownups then listened to J. H., who told them, as the afternoon progressed, how a boy born on the wrong side of the tracks and orphaned early in life could and did make a living, get an education at night school and become, at last, the board chairman of a big corporation.

"Board chairman," he said, "and then retired board chairman, an old museum piece hanging around hotels. That's why, Mrs. Adams, Mrs. Pullen, and you two boys, I appreciate—"

He never got it said. Betty, feet racing, curls flying, burst through the front screen door. "Captain Adams! Bill says to come quick!"

Crunch blanched. "Is something the matter?"

The little girl nodded furiously. "It's Kirk! He's got a great big fish and he and Bill had to climb down the rocks—"

Crunch ran. Behind him came Des. Sari and Alma and J. H. brought up the rear.

Half a dozen Christmas anglers had wound up their lines to watch. A few cars had parked beyond the bridge; their occupants were now shouting advice from its rail. Down below, on a narrow bank where the eroded coral walls of the canal met the salt water, stood Kirk Pullen with Bill at his side. Ellis was stashed in an overhanging tree, apparently for safety, although the perch seemed somewhat precarious.

Kirk's casting rod was bent formidably. Now and again his reel sizzled as his fish made a hard run. When that happened, he kept changing hands and sucking his spool-burned thumbs. Between runs, he would back line.

Young Bill coached him as ardently, as effectively as Crunch or Des ever coached a tyro at sea: "Keep the tip a little higher, Kirk! Good! Don't thumb the old reel quite so hard! Might break the line! If your thumbs get too darned hot, squat down and ram the rod under water."

"Reel and all?" Kirk asked feverishly.

"Yep. Cool your hands off. Won't hurt the reel. There he goes! Try it!"

Kirk squatted and submerged the whirling reel. Its handles churned the water like an egg beater. But a look of relief came on the young angler's face as he discovered how the trick prevented his thumb from further burning.

On the bridge, Crunch took in the scene and winked at Sari.

"You go down and help," she said.

Crunch shook his head. "Couldn't do a darn thing Bill and Kirk aren't already doing. It's their show."

"What is it?"

Crunch turned to his dinner guest. Mr. Porter was standing with both hands on the railing. Their knuckles were white. His jaw was set and his eyes were brilliant with excitement.

The skipper eyed the rod, the sizzling sweeps of the line. "Jack, I guess," Crunch answered. "Nice one, for that tackle."

J. H. cupped his hands. "Stay with it, son!" he boomed.

Kirk glanced up, grinned faintly, and called back in a worried soprano, "I am."

The jack, if jack it was, decided to run up the canal. Yard by precious yard, it ripped out line against the boy's best effort to hold it. Bill showed him how to thumb the flange of the reel spool when the line on the spindle dwindled to a frictionless remnant. But the jack lunged on.

Silence dominated the bridge, silence that made the conversation of the angler and his "guide" clearly audible.

"She'll pop soon," Kirk murmured frantically.

Bill stared at the rocky shore. "Wade."

The boy's eyes dropped. "It's my good suit."

From the bridge came Alma's voice. "Wade, Kirk, if you want to!"

So Kirk and his escort strode into the canal. Knee deep. Hip deep. They toiled along, splashing and stumbling, behind the jack.

J. H. was whacking the rail now. "Get it! Get it, boy!" His eyes met the eyes of Crunch. "Man! Imagine that, at Kirk's age! I'd rather see that boy land that jack than catch ten marlin like the one we took yesterday!"

The skipper kept looking, and realized that J. H. meant exactly that.

But a jack is a fast fish, a strong fish, and bait-casting tackle is tricky. For another ten minutes the two boys pursued and fought their fish. Then, somewhere in the murky depths of the canal, the jack found a snag, cut across it or went around it, and parted the line.

For a moment, Kirk stood still, saying nothing. Then he looked at the stunned and disappointed spectators. He might have cried; his face showed that. But his gaze came to rest on Alma and because of her expression his small shoulders straightened and stiffened.

"Mother!" he called. "I nearly got it! Next time, I will! Wasn't it fun!"

Crunch heard the magnate utter words appropriate to some august bungle in a steel mill, words most inappropriate to a peaceful, sunny afternoon on a pretty bridge. The last of these were ". . . what spunk!"

It was Sari who collected the exceedingly wet boys and hurried them toward home. Crunch and Des followed with the younger children and the tackle. Alma Pullen and the steelmaker came last. They took a long time to make the short trip and when they re-entered the house Crunch noticed that J. H. looked embarrassed and Alma seemed flabbergasted.

"You don't happen," said Mr. Porter, "to know a good real-estate man, do you, Crunch?"

"Sure. Three or four."

"H'm'm'm'm." The elderly man sat down. He looked at the little girl and her brother playing under the tree. He looked at Alma. He lit a cigar and looked at that. "I've decided," he said finally, "to make Miami my base. Too old to be a rolling stone. Have to get back to Pittsburgh after New Year's and clear up a few things, so I thought you might start somebody house-hunting for me. Need a pretty good-sized place. Three—four bedrooms. On the water, a canal would do. If there were fish in it!"

Sari returned in time to hear. She glanced at Alma, who nodded dazedly. Then Sari glanced toward her husband with a worried expression.

These uneasy exchanges irritated Mr. Porter. "All right!" he abruptly exclaimed. "It's Christmas Day. And I'm a sentimental old ass! Possibly you think a dram of apricot brandy went to my head. See here! I'm old enough to be the father of everybody in this room! I've run a corporation I built myself that hired twelve thousand people! Every dollar I've got is my own and I've got several! If I want to buy a house, is there anything wrong with that?"

"Nothing," Crunch admitted.

"Alma's a fine housekeeper, isn't she? A superb cook, isn't she? A wizard with a needle, isn't she? Look at the kids' clothes! Darns you damned near need a magnifying glass to see! Now look at my socks!" With two petulant kicks, he removed both shoes. His bare heels were revealed. Morosely, he stared at them. "I own over two million dollars' worth of Government bonds and not one single perfect pair of socks! Furthermore, I'm the type of codger who lives forever. The doctors have promised me I'll break eighty, but the way I've been living, I haven't been very interested in that. The marlin helped." He looked at Crunch. "Understand?"

"Yeah," the skipper answered.

"You, Sari?"

She nodded.

"But the jack helped even more." He stared at Kirk, who had appeared in an old pair of Bill Adams' shorts that exuded the aroma of moth balls. "I raised one family and they did okay. Is there any law to prevent me from hiring a housekeeper and helping to raise hers? A lot of dodos in my category attach themselves to chorus girls. Phooie! Alma's a grown woman with a prefabricated family. That, my friends, is my idea of life! Kids! I'm a self-made man, why shouldn't I wind up my years as a self-made grandpa?"

Sari looked at Alma and then the children and sat down quickly, turning her head away.

J. H. strode up to her in his ragged socks. "You're the type, Mrs. Adams, who'll blame yourself for 'saddling' me with these children, if you're not careful!" He shook his cigar at her so hard that ashes fell on the carpet. "Don't! Think of it this way: I've been giving presents to my family for a generation. Now, for a present, I've got a family! And one more thing. Stop crying this instant!"

Sari raised her head. The eyes of a very tough little man met those of a very exceptional and exceptionally attractive woman. Both of them began to laugh.

Crunch had reflected on the matter of luck, which is a subject familiar to fishing skippers. Some men can catch a hundred-pound marlin and it doesn't matter much; but a kid may lose a ten-pound jack and his sportsmanship will change his entire life and the lives of his brother, his sister and his mother. Crunch was still thinking about that when the steelmaker whirled on him.

"As for you, captain, get that sappy smirk off your face and break out that cordial again! We've got to toast my new folks! We've got to find a real-estate man with good judgment! We've got work to do! Lots of it!" He scooped up little Betty and sat her on his knee. "How you going to like having a grandpa roaring around, from now on?"

"Roar right back," Betty said. And she did.

J. H. was still laughing when Crunch came from the kitchen with the homemade cordial and five tiny glasses. He winked at Sari and Sari winked back, a little damply. When she had a chance she whispered to Crunch, "The *Poseidon* will never make a better day's haul in this world, skipper."

SMUGGLER'S COVE

AT THE last minute, Crunch decided they should be alone for the introductions, so he snapped his fingers as if he'd forgotten something and stepped from the Gulf Stream Dock to the stern of his fishing cruiser. From there he went up topside. The palms of his hands, he noticed, were damp; he was nervous because he liked the young couple so much.

Larry Wood had given him a worried but understanding smile as Crunch deserted. Now, Larry peered up the dock and looked again at his wrist watch; then he saw his guests, a beautiful girl and a man.

He made a step toward the girl spontaneously—as anybody engaged for less than a month would do. But he didn't take a second step; instead, he let them approach in order to study his girl's father. Then Virginia saw him, left her father, ran up and kissed her fiancé. That was like her. She looked haughty—or at least, reserved; she was actually the opposite: outgiving and impulsive.

"Dad!" Virginia called. "Come on! Here he is!"

Crunch didn't watch the kiss; he watched the father.

The admiral had been staring at the boats. Now he examined Larry. And since Crunch knew the importance of first impressions he exerted his faculties, but he couldn't tell what the admiral's first impression was.

Larry said, "I'm mighty happy to meet you, sir."

The admiral was smiling, a good thing. *All admirals,* Crunch thought, *look like admirals. Tall or short, blue-eyed or brown, fat or thin—they all look like admirals.* This one was tall, gray-eyed, and dressed in civvies, mostly. Blue slacks, but navy blue. Gray shirt, a Navy shirt. No tie. Yachting cap, worn rakishly. But he had the gold-braid bearing. The admiral had a deep tan too. Crunch reflected that you undoubtedly got one in the Philippines as easily as in Miami at that season.

The admiral said, "So you're the cause of all those ten-page letters!"

Larry flushed. He also grinned. He looked at Virginia and asked, "How

320

did you find anything about me worth ten pages?"

The admiral snorted. "About you! What she filled those scented sheets with was a play-by-play discussion of her own emotions! It's a wonder she graduated, under the circumstances!"

Larry turned, now chuckling. He waved his arm. "That's Crunch Adams, our captain, up there."

The admiral wheeled and half saluted. "Skipper!"

Crunch nodded amiably but casually. Somebody, he felt, ought not to be overwhelmed. He and his mate had fished many an admiral in their time. Not one, perhaps, who had flown all the way from Manila to check on his daughter's choice. But admirals, all the same.

Des, the mate, came along with the big basket of lunch which Larry had ordered from a nearby restaurant. It was to be a four-day trip—but meals beginning with dinner would either be served on shore or put up in boxes at Ed's Yacht Motel on Upper Matecumbe Key, where the *Poseidon* would be berthed before nightfall.

Larry introduced the mate to the admiral, and Des gave the man his usual slow stare. All he said was, "Hi!" A decade and a half of mating hadn't lessened Des Smith's self-consciousness about meeting new people; and the more important they were, the more self-conscious he became.

There was a brief pause after the introduction. Virginia said, "Dad, don't you think the *Poseidon* is perfectly ducky!"

"Fairly shipshape," the admiral nodded.

Des instantly noticed the "fairly." *Probably,* he thought, *the ice pick is rusty. Or, maybe there's a fly-speck on the compass.* He went below with the lunch. The cruiser's engines roared as Crunch pushed the starter buttons.

Soon, with her outriggers spread like a giant **V** and the baits skittering over a sea like luminous blue ink, with the admiral and his daughter relaxed but alert in two of her fishing chairs, the *Poseidon* trolled past the pines south of Miami Beach, headed for the keys. Larry, as befitted a host, climbed up on the canopy to talk over the trip with his skipper; or, at any rate, to talk.

"He doesn't think much of me!" the young man said.

Crunch glanced down at the admiral. "Give him time, boy."

"Sure! Four days! Time enough for him to get Virginia off me! He's all the things outside that Navy officers always are. Courteous and tactful and friendly. A good joe. Inside, this one's as cold as a fluke's liver."

Crunch laughed. "Doggone it, Larry, if you start quitting at this point, you sure will lose! After all, you want to marry Virginia, not her old man."

"She's crazy about him, Crunch! To marry her, I gotta be." He shrugged. "And he has to like me! That's the size of it. Right away, he asked me what I was going to do after I was 'over this football-coaching phase at Miami.' I told him I hadn't any larger plans. I explained that a good coach gets well paid. I even humiliated myself by pointing out that my folks left me a few pieces of property that'll keep Virginia in short mink, if not long ermine. And Virginia tried a spiel about coaching being leadership—and influencing hundreds of boys. No dice.''

The corner of Crunch's eye had been devoted to the area behind the baits, as usual. An optical change in that area now attracted the whole of both eyes. For an instant he thought he had been deceived. Then, deep and a little darker than the blue water, it came again: the long shadow.

"On the right outrigger!" he called. "Watch it!"

The right outrigger—as the anglers sat—was the admiral's. He did not watch, however. Instead, he turned with a pained expression and yelled back, "Good Lord, man! The port outrigger!"

"He knows that!" Virginia said excitedly. "He only says 'right' and 'left' because most of his customers aren't as salty as—Dad! It's a sail!"

The admiral said, "Hunh!" He turned to look.

The sail was, by then, on the surface. It opened its dorsal with the slow dignity of a dowager opening a fan—a purple fan with black polka dots. It aimed its bill with the sadistic deliberation of a duelist who has disarmed his opponent. It charged. The clothespin, which held the line daintily at the tip of the outrigger, clicked faintly—a sound that always thrilled Crunch. Slack line drifted down to the smooth sea, lay in a zigzag for a moment, then straightened and submerged.

"Strike it!" Des appeared behind the admiral.

He struck. The sailfish ran. The reel yelled. So did the girl: "Dad! You've hooked it!"

"So I have," the admiral replied. It sounded like, *Naturally. What did you expect?*

He was no angler. And he did not enjoy being coached by the mate— although he followed directions and in due course, brought the sailfish to boat. Des expertly took the leader wire and, after a splashing struggle, he grabbed the bill of the fish. "Want to keep him? Or turn him loose?"

"Let him go," the admiral answered. "Inedible, I understand."

So they released the sailfish. Des broke out a flag which would signify to all who saw that the catch had been made. But before he could attach the white triangle to the outrigger halyard, a barracuda spoiled Virginia's bait. Des set aside the flag and prepared to change the de-tailed balao.

"I'll put it on and pull it up," Larry offered.

Again, the admiral bristled. "Run it up! Hoist it! Bend it on! Ye gods!"

Larry bit his lip. Virginia said, "Oh, daddy, don't be such a stickler! Fishing's for fun! It's informal!"

The admiral stood up and looked at his daughter severely. "Would he like it, if I talked about football that way? If I called them 'forward pitches'? If I said a line buck was a 'line butt'? Or talked about making a 'thump-down'?"

Larry chortled. "By golly! No, I wouldn't!"

"Exactly," the admiral said, and went below. When he came up in the cockpit again, his face was formidable. "There's a box under the forward bunk labeled dynamite."

"Is there?" Des said. "I didn't see any label."

"On the end! I thought I smelled dynamite, so I moved it to see."

"Maybe it is dynamite, then," said Des.

"What!"

"Friend of ours asked if we'd deliver a box to a mutual pal in the keys. He put it aboard. I didn't look. The guy in the keys has a new house. He's planting fruit trees. So maybe the box is dynamite."

"Look!" the admiral commanded.

Des went below, returned, and nodded.

"Captain," the admiral then shouted, "do you realize you're carrying a box of dynamite? Against all regulations?"

Crunch remembered the request to deliver a box and murmured an internal *oh-oh!* "Guess it'll be all right, admiral. Stuff's no doubt low percentage. Doesn't blow up without good cause. I wouldn't have taken it if they'd told me—which is why they didn't. I'd toss it—jettison it," he amended, "if it were rough."

"Not a question of danger," the admiral replied. "Regulations."

"The guy built his own house. Kind of hate to make him pay for an extra case. Kind of hate to pay myself. But I'll chuck it overboard if you're at all afraid—"

It was a bad word to use. The admiral's long, impressive face took on the hardness of granite. "I have something of a reputation, skipper, for not being afraid! Question purely of regulations."

"You mind, Virginia?"

The girl glanced up at Crunch. She had been gazing at the sea until then, gazing with embarrassment. "If you think it's all right, I don't mind in the least."

"Larry?"

The unhappy assistant coach shook his head. "Must be Hughie Nor-thrup's new house, hunh? Heck, no! Glad to do him a favor." He turned to the admiral. "Veteran. He built his place—with one good leg—only. Bought a remote little key."

"The sentiment's fine! Carrying explosives on a fish boat is something else. However—" He sat down in his fishing chair.

After that, the admiral quit criticizing and quit correcting unnautical terminology—which was worse than his heckling, Crunch felt. For it meant that he regarded all of them as beyond the pale, lubbers and fools, not seamen, operators of a—fishing boat.

Crunch realized that he should have chucked the dynamite overboard immediately, and ordinarily he would have done so. But he, not the admiral, was the *Poseidon's* skipper. Keeping the explosives on board gave Crunch a certain human satisfaction, a sense that not all prestige and command had been filched by the gold braid.

In the evening, Virginia strolled down the dock to the place where the cruiser was moored. It wasn't quite dark. Crunch, in the stern with his silent mate, saw her coming, the rising wind blowing her long, dark hair sideways and whipping her skirts.

"Hi," she called. "Can I come aboard?"

Crunch and Des had risen. Des held out a hand and she jumped down lightly to the deck.

"Going to blow," she said. "But it's nice and warm. I sure love hot weather! That's really why I picked Miami University. That, and the glamour."

She sat. All three watched the evening darken, without saying a word; it was permissible, even customary, amongst old fishing friends. Besides, Virginia had come to tell them something, so they waited for her to begin. Finally, she did. "Dad and Larry are up in the bar buying each other a couple of highballs and fighting the war." She paused. "I never saw dad act badly before, in my whole life!"

Crunch said quietly, "Give him time."

Virginia nodded. "Of course. But it frightens me, just the same. He's always been so right about things, Crunch. He gave me the devil tonight. Said I'd just drifted into an infatuation with a second-rater because I was lonely and out of my natural environment. He admitted Larry was well bred and well educated and all that. 'A very pretty boy too,' he said. I was furious!"

Crunch sighed. He didn't mean to, but the sigh escaped him.

It had a curious effect on Virginia. "Is that all you have to say? I expected you'd be as angry as I was! After all, you and Des know Larry darned well! You know how he's battled and struggled to help the university—in lots of ways besides football! You know he's a perfectly swell person! Why don't you say what you think? Why don't you agree that my dad's being perfectly loathsome?"

"Because," Crunch answered, "according to his beliefs, I don't think he is. And because it seems you may have to decide, Virginia, whether you

care enough about Larry to do something that's going to make your dad
sore at you for a long, long time. Maybe forever."

"Why couldn't they just have liked each other on first sight? I know—I
know for sure—Larry thinks dad is a jerk! All brass. And that makes me
mad at Larry! Why does it have to be like that?"

It was a question Crunch could not answer, a question no one could
answer.

"I guess I better go back," the girl said, "and make sure they are still
just fighting the war, not each other."

When she had gone, Crunch said, "Rugged."

Des hadn't said anything at all. And now he merely made a sound in
his throat which meant he was sorry for the girl and her fiancé and sorry
that a hopeful trip had soured. The sound may also have meant that his
opinion of admirals had dropped many notches.

They were still sitting there, when they had another visitor. A man,
this time, whose narrow, sun tanned face showed momentarily in the
glow from a light on the dock. Darkness engulfed him after he passed
the light.

"Captain Adams?"

"Right here."

"Oh. Didn't see you. My name's Cutter. Wanted to talk to you a
minute."

The skipper reached out and the cockpit was bathed in light. The man
jumped down—a shrewd-looking man whose eyes took in the boat and
the boatmen swiftly.

"I'm Adams. This is my mate, Des Smith."

The stranger, Cutter, immediately offered his hand. He smiled slightly.
"Ed Fairrier said you boys were reliable, had fished these waters for
years. Where you planning to fish this trip?"

"Outside, some. Bonefish, inside, maybe. If the wind stays up—and the
eight-o'clock weather report says it will—it may be too muddy for either.
In that case we'll probably shoot across toward Cape Sable and do some
fishing around there. Rivers and bays behind the islands. Got an errand
to do up that way, anyhow."

Mr. Cutter produced what looked like a wallet. But it was actually a
badge issued by the Treasury Department. The mate looked at it and the
skipper looked, and Mr. Cutter said, "I've told about a dozen guides who
get up toward the cape and around the gulf-side keys what I'm going
to tell you. All of them men who can be trusted to keep their mouths
shut. We think"—he glanced at the leather-covered identification before
pocketing it—"a load of contraband, a very high-priced load, is coming
through here soon. We missed it in some other ports. And this part of

Florida"—he grinned faintly—"has been used for smuggling, before."

His grin was reflected, twice. "Some," Crunch said dryly.

"I don't know what I want, really. It isn't bulky contraband. A small boat could handle it all. There aren't agents enough to watch this salt-water maze down here. Even a tenth of it. What I mean is, I'd like a report of anything suspicious. Fast running at night. I'll give you a phone number, and I'll give you a simple set of code words to use on your ship-to-shore if you see anything or anybody needing close study. You just call the number and you say you saw 'Joe's party' and you use the code to tell us where, and then you go about your business. In fact, if you by any chance found the people we're hoping to locate, you'd be out of luck if you did do anything but go about your business."

Crunch nodded. "Okay."

Cutter said, "I mean it! Don't fraternize, if you happen to see anybody suspicious. Don't try to learn more. Don't tag any boats. It's something we've been on for years." For an instant Mr. Cutter's eyes opened wide and round. "On it for years," he repeated, "and lost men in the Middle East, and Cuba—and gotten nobody. Yet."

"I see."

Mr. Cutter rose then. "Unlikely you'll spot a thing. Totally unlikely. But I figured it wouldn't hurt to add the eyes of a few reliable boatmen to the effort. Just phone us. That's all."

He handed Crunch a carbon copy of a typewritten list. He showed how phrases referring to fishes meant landmarks on the chart, directions of the compass and distances, so that any place in a vast watery wilderness could be pin-pointed by a few sentences of fisherman's palaver. He thanked them and shook hands and went away.

"Jewels," Des said when his footsteps died.

Crunch shook his head. "Middle East. Sounds more like dope."

Des unwrapped a stick of gum. He chewed it up slowly. "Yeah." A few minutes passed. "Lousy thing—dope."

Crunch yawned agreement. He closed the code in the logbook. "Hit the sack?"

"Check."

Before they fell asleep, the mate made one more contribution. "I wouldn't mind seeing that admiral sit down on a gang hook. Not a big gang hook—just big enough. Swivel-chair sailor!"

"Me, either," the skipper replied. "Still, maybe he's right. Maybe Virginia would be happier with rank. How can you be sure?"

"Glorious morning," the admiral said.

"Windy." Crunch took another bite of his flapjacks. There was no one else in the dining room; the admiral, evidently, was an early riser.

"I really like a boisterous day at sea," he said as he sat down.

"I'm afraid," Crunch answered, "we won't get outside."

The handsome man's brows raised slightly. "Engine trouble?"

Crunch shook his head. "Too rough to fish comfortably."

"No!" The admiral thought that over. "Funny! I've always had the impression fishermen never considered the weather. Rain, sleet, snow—like postmen. Before the war, I've seen flimsy Jap fishing craft out in a near typhoon!"

Crunch felt a flush come to his cheeks. Now he ate pancakes for a moment to recover his poise. He summoned a grin.

"Admiral, when it was a question of saving lives, we've had the *Poseidon* outside not in a near typhoon, but a real one. Hurricane. But I'm what you might call a conservative man. Don't like to fish people when the seas could break a plank. When fishing is just hard work and no fun; when you can neither rest nor relax a second."

A waitress appeared and the admiral ordered a solid breakfast. "What do we do, then? Stay ashore?"

Crunch began to outline other possibilities.

Presently the door opened and Larry came in—the full six feet, one hundred and seventy-five pounds of pleasant nature, common sense, blue eyes and curly blond hair.

"Good gad, man!" cried the admiral.

Crunch couldn't quite keep his lips from twitching, although he knew the poor auspices of the day had suddenly grown poorer. Larry was wearing a bright yellow shirt—and that was the rule in the keys. But he also sported a pair of Kelly-green trousers tied with an orange cord that hung down on one side. They were the loudest pants Crunch had ever seen— and he remembered Virginia. One day, while they had been fishing, she had argued at length that it was absurd for men to wear mousy colors. This, evidently, was the result.

Larry had heard the outraged exclamation. He chuckled. "Wow you, admiral?"

"Certainly you don't intend to go fishing in that getup?"

Larry seated himself with gusto. Crunch could see that, beneath the apparent high spirits, uncertainty struggled with irritation. "Why not? Cool and comfortable. Latest thing, they said at the store."

The sea hero closed his eyes and shook his head sharply. And Virginia arrived. She looked, whooped, ran across the room and embraced Larry.

"Darling, you did it! You look gorgeous! You look like a big daffodil!"

"He looks," said the admiral coldly, "like the press agent for a third-rate bull fighter."

Crunch didn't blame Larry for heaving the harpoon at the shark. Ordinarily, Crunch wouldn't have bothered with such quarry. But there were factors. One was the admiral: sailfishing had not seemed to afford him much of a thrill, and bottom-fishing in the lee of a key had pleased him even less. Another factor was weather.

Warm and steady, at twenty-five miles an hour, the wind came from the southeast. It turned the usually glass-clear water to a milky blue. It drove the bonefish and the permit off the flats into the channels. It picked up the suspended and chalky marl of the bottom so that other fish fled to places where their gills were less distressed and breathing was easier. It set up waves that tore loose eel grass and lined it in rows that spoiled the surface for casting. Good weather, as weather. But for fishing, poor.

So the *Poseidon* was on the way north and west toward the aquatic labyrinths of the tip of Florida where there was shelter, better water, and a chance for strikes. She was going fast when Virginia saw the shark's dorsal; Crunch saw it too: a blacktip, not big; six-seven feet. He steered toward it so they could see it better. And Larry, a man who felt himself well to the rear of a very large doghouse, picked up the harpoon.

Maybe, Crunch thought, harpooning a shark would help. Help alter the admiral's look of grim distaste and his daughter's expression of nerves frayed by loyalties divided. Crunch cut the engines and swung the cruiser in such a way that Larry, by then poised in the harpoon pulpit, would have an easy throw. Larry took aim.

Virginia, a little excited, cried, "Don't miss!"

The admiral, intent on the quest, also felt called upon to give a command. "Fire away, boy!"

His voice was enormous; it came thundering across the wind just as Larry began the downthrust. Into that sweep, the assistant coach put the pent-up fury of a frustrated twenty-four hours. But the command jarred him. The harpoon glittered in the air, drove into the water—and hit bottom, hard. It stuck there, almost vertically. The *Poseidon* heaved on a wave. And Larry fell overboard.

He was quick. As he lost his balance he leaped. He grabbed the imbedded shaft like a pole vaulter. His weight drove it deeper in the marl and, for a second or two, it seemed that it might support him. But slowly it canted and let its burden feet first into the sea—near the spot where the shark had been.

A little shark and it had not been hurt; at most, scraped by the harpoon shaft. And yet, Crunch saw, from the top controls, it whipped around under water and raced toward the splash made by Larry.

Once in a while—once in a very great while—even the little sharks—even the three and four footers—get mad. And even they have shark teeth.

The water wasn't deep. Enough to float the *Poseidon*. Enough to reach the shoulders of the man standing in it. He was trying to free the harpoon. He ducked under for a better grip. Crunch saw the shark's dorsal emerge and slice toward Larry.

He yelled, "Des! Get the shark gun!"

There was a thump as the mate took the ladder in a jump.

Larry was still under water, heaving on the pole. It came free suddenly, tipped over and floated. Then there was commotion. The shark's head broke water, threshing violently. Larry broke water. He had hold of the shark's tail! He hung on grimly for a wild instant and then let go. With his fist, he gave the shark a mighty blow. It streaked away. Crunch backed the boat and came in closer to pick up his passenger and the harpoon. In the short space of time that bizarre action had consumed, the skipper had sweat himself almost as wet as Larry.

Des yanked the coach on board.

Larry was grinning, hardly panting. "You know," he said, "that darned blacktip turned on me! I think he was making a pass! I grabbed his tail as he went by. Couldn't hang on, though. Strong devils!"

"Of all the foolhardy, asinine—" The admiral broke off. He stared. "Man. Your pants are running!"

Larry looked down, past sodden shirt, at his soaked trousers. Kelly-green rivulets were spreading Kelly-green puddles on the deck and Larry's white canvas shoes were already dyed green. He took them off. The socks underneath, and the feet beneath them, were also green. The unmistakable assumption was that all the lower half of Mr. Lawrence Wood was the color of St. Patrick's Day.

Usually Crunch had a few terse if not harsh things to say to customers who took idiotic chances on the spur of an excited moment. In this case, however, he refrained. The admiral had commenced to roar with laughter. His daughter gazed at her jade-oozing fiancé—a mixture of panic and risibility in her handsome eyes. It was, the skipper thought, punishment enough.

He revved up the engines while Des took Larry below for a scrub, a rubdown and a change of clothes. Almost any other man would have borrowed almost any kind of long trousers, at that point. Not Larry. He chose a pair of Desperate's shorts and came up, dry and neatly dressed again, but with legs a pale lime color.

"This," he said with genuine mirth, "is something so good I didn't think it should be missed! Wait till I get hold of the manager of the store that sold me those green britches!"

Even the admiral couldn't quite resist that: he smiled. His exhibition of good humor was, however, transient.

Toward noon the *Poseidon* followed a channel that led windingly through a series of banks to the end of a small key, which they rounded. On the key, in a cleared area, was a new bungalow.

"That," Crunch called down, "is the house Hughie built. The veteran with one leg. Only he's out."

"How can you tell?" Virginia asked.

"Because he flies a flag when he's in, daytimes. And it has lights when he's there, nights."

"What flag?" the admiral inquired.

"The American flag, naturally."

The seadog snorted. "Which should go up and come down with the sun, not with the owner's errands! That means, I presume, we've still got our cargo?"

Virginia, at that point, was tired of her father's criticism. "Oh, for heaven's sake!" she said. "What of it! Good night, dad! I remember, once, you said you were on an ammunition ship in an air raid!"

"Matter of regulations, that's all," the admiral replied crisply. "Not a question of peril."

"But Crunch and Des didn't know what it was!"

"Business to know. Their ship. Their cargo."

The girl shrugged unhappily and gave up the argument.

After lunch, inland fishing was abandoned because it was slow and because another project had developed: exploration.

The *Poseidon* moved slowly into the salt "rivers" and "lakes" which make that part of South Florida more a seascape than a landscape. Some of the lakes were mere ponds; some were two or three miles in length and half as wide. The waterways between were narrow. In one, the mangrove became a high tunnel and the captain and mate had to take down the outriggers and lash them to the deck before they could proceed. Orchids were blooming, and air plants, on the overhanging limbs along the narrow waterways. Great, slaty herons flew along these covered passageways ahead of the boat. A 'gator or croc splashed into the water in the distance.

"This," the admiral said, "is interesting." So far as Crunch could recall, it was his first word of approval.

Toward midafternoon the enthralled explorers came out on the fifth lake, and Crunch decided to head back, because he was uncertain of the way beyond. Des and the passengers were examining an egret which was watching them from the shore a few yards away, as calmly as a barnyard duck.

So it was Crunch, alone, who saw the boat. A fishing cruiser, like their own, with outriggers down. A battered-looking boat, unfamiliar to Crunch. He hoped that the people on board weren't novices; it was easy to get lost in these waters. And then the cruiser, which had been skirting the far shore, disappeared.

Crunch thought she had gone behind a mangrove island. But she did not reappear. He thumped on the canopy for Des to take over, and went below. He came back with a special chart and binoculars. All he could see through the glasses was unbroken shore line. And that chart showed no creek or waterway in the vicinity. The course out of that particular "lake" lay a mile and a half to the northeast. The only other known communicating passage was the one from which the *Poseidon* had just emerged.

But there was, obviously, another waterway of some sort, and the people on the sun-bleached fishing boat knew about it. Crunch was not particularly surprised. From time to time new "creeks" and "rivers" were found in this region—waterways concealed from the air by a mangrove roof and from the lakes by the fact that they entered them at an angle in the irregular wall of mangrove.

It would be interesting, the skipper felt, to explore something new even to him. Besides, the admiral enjoyed it, and this whole trip had been designed with the admiral's psychology in mind. Without any further thought, Crunch headed at the point where he had seen the cruiser vanish.

It was only when he had crossed most of the lake that he remembered Mr. Cutter. He frowned. Would poking into an unknown creek constitute "suspicious" behavior? He thought not. Anyway, wouldn't the people on the other boat have seen the *Poseidon*? Probably—for a minute, anyway. In which case, they would hardly have turned into the unknown creek if it had anything to do with lawlessness.

Crunch admitted to himself that there was a chance the *Poseidon* had not been observed. He weighed sending out radiophone news in the code he had been given, that he'd encountered a "suspicious event" in the waters of what was called, by the few who ever saw it, East Coot Lake. He thought he would be foolish to do anything of the sort. What was suspicious about a fishing boat poking into an uncharted channel in the broad light of afternoon?

Of the two mistakes in judgment Crunch made on that trip, the one

he made now was the worse: he drew near shore, cut the engines, and
began to search the green wall for an opening.

Behind a mangrove slightly taller than any others nearby, Crunch
noticed an indentation. He slowed the *Poseidon* almost to a stop, and
the wind, nonexistent in the creeks, but palpable on the lake, edged
her away from the shore. The water was still deep enough and a current appeared to flow from behind the big tree.

He notched up the gas and swung in. Des came farther out in the
stern cockpit and looked up inquiringly.

"Another boat, our size, went in here a while back."

"Another boat!" The mate was instantly anxious.

Crunch grinned. "Couldn't be anybody but anglers. Tourists. After all,
they must have seen us. Let's look."

Des said, "Shouldn't we—maybe—"

"Not yet, anyway." His mate also had thought of Mr. Cutter's request and warning.

Des shrugged and said no more.

On the deck, forward, the three passengers watched as what appeared to be solid mangrove suddenly showed a covered passage that
ran almost parallel with the lake shore for about a hundred feet and
then turned. It was narrow; branches on both sides scraped the
Poseidon as she went in and the trees closed overhead. The first turn
was made with difficulty.

Larry, who had gone up to the bows with a boat hook to shove in
the event shoving was needed, now called, "Somebody cleared out this
bend a while back."

Crunch looked with interest and faint misgiving at the ax marks on
certain branches and at snags obviously manhandled out of the waterway and onto the shore. He also began to think of the possibility of
meeting the other boat coming out. It would be a nice trick to back the
Poseidon down the riverlike tunnel. And "river," he presently noticed,
was a suitable name for this one; it had current, and the current flowed
against a tide coming in elsewhere.

The admiral joined Larry, and Virginia came up on top beside Crunch.
"At least," she said in a low voice, "Dad enjoys this. And you've saved
the eeriest one for the last."

"I've never been in it," Crunch answered. "Saw another boat disappear and went over to see where."

"Look at that 'gator!" The admiral pointed.

It was a big 'gator and it lay turgidly in the weeds and shade, on the
muddy edge of the clear water, the very clear, deepening water.
Crunch believed it was fresh water. He glanced down at the segment

of a map of the region. No glades-draining streams came in here. All that showed was two spots of water, like sink holes, but bigger, further ahead; ponds observed and photographed from the air, he imagined. But this waterway apparently linked them.

The next turn showed more ax work and after that the first pond came. It was only a couple of hundred yards in diameter, and an opening beyond invited. So Crunch pushed ahead on a second, tunnellike creek, which opened out into a second, larger pond. The *Poseidon* moved into it and slowed as Crunch cut the engines.

"Holy cow!"

Larry had said that. Crunch had expected, more or less, to meet up with the fishing boat in the second pond. But he had not had time to examine the whole shore, part of which had been masked by a slanting clump of very thick, old mangrove trees at the end of the outlet. He whirled now and saw what had caused Larry to make that exclamation with that particular sound—and he knew how enormous his blunder had been.

Astern and to port, behind the tall trees, inshore, hidden from above by an enormous overhang of the mangrove, was not only the boat but a helicopter. Trees and brush had been cut back to augment a natural cavity in the verdure. Boat and airship were moored by ropes to ths shore. And there were men, men standing in frozen stupefaction, on board both.

Crunch remembered now, with the utmost vividness, Cutter's earnest orders that no one be "tagged" or "investigated," and Cutter's grim words about losing other agents in other ports. He hadn't any doubt that these were the men Cutter sought.

Without very much confidence, Crunch waved casually toward the aircraft and the weatherbeaten boat; he engaged his engines and began to back. It was his obvious intention to leave the pond. He had decided, in a split second, that parley was worse than useless: a boat entering an unknown creek might be interesting, only; but a hidden helicopter was not merely suspicious, it was all but damning. The one chance was to act as if they didn't know how damning it was.

The men who had seen the invasion of their pond and reacted with such amazement now began to move quickly, as muffled orders were given them.

"What is it?" the admiral yelled at Crunch. "Who are they?"

It was an opportunity. Crunch pantomimed exaggeratedly, shrugging his shoulders, spreading his hands. "Probably hunters!" he yelled back, loudly enough to carry. "We've got to start home, now."

"They don't look like hunters," Virginia said quietly. "And you don't act as if they were, Crunch. You act scared."

His blue eyes met hers for an instant. "I'm plenty scared! If they let us back in the creek, I'll say thankful prayers daily for the next year."

"Do you know who they are?"

He watched the men. They were getting out of sight. The *Poseidon* hadn't far to go, but he didn't dare enter the creek at any speed. It was too winding for that and speed, in any case, would have indicated fear, hence suspicion.

He said to Virginia, "What could it be, with a boat and a 'copter hidden in this backwash? Smugglers. Nothing else."

"Will they—do anything to us?"

"Search me. They won't like their spot known by anybody, that's a cinch!"

He was watching the inlet now, and the approaching trees which guarded it. Once the trees were between the two parties, he could breathe again. He had about a hundred and fifty yards to go.

It wasn't a tommy gun that fired. It was heavier. It was carried by the smugglers to discourage pursuit—or to destroy it. It stood under the nameless boat's canopy and they had been waiting for the *Poseidon* to get where they could use their machine gun. Bullets threw white water ahead and moved in and tore holes in the planks above water, but below the men on the bows. Splinters flew high and Larry and the admiral fell flat. Virginia cried out and Crunch shoved her to the decking as he cut the engines. There was no use running at that range with that weapon. And he thought of the dynamite. *A bullet in there!*

The burst, actually, was a short one.

The admiral got up. "Well, I'll be a so-and-so!" he said. His expression was calm, thoughtful.

Larry got up. He pulled a sliver of wood from one of his husky, pale green legs. His face was tense.

A voice came from shore through a small megaphone, remarkably clear and loud in the sudden quiet. "Just pull back to the middle of the lake and anchor."

"You better," the admiral called from the bow.

Crunch backed and Des, shaking a little, let go an anchor. Crunch cut his engines.

The men were very busy now. They moved the tripod that supported the machine gun farther out into their cockpit and brought round a dinghy.

The megaphone spoke again. "All you—get up on the forward deck! Stay in sight! And keep your hands up!"

There was nothing else to do.

The dinghy was small, but four men crowded into it. The heavy machine gun was trained on the *Poseidon* before they took off; they came heavily armed. A thin, brown-skinned one who rowed; two black-haired men who might have been brothers, biggish and loutish, with revolvers; and a rather fat man of about fifty, in gray slacks and a loud shirt, who sat in the stern. As he came near he looked with keen attention at the five people on the *Poseidon's* bow.

He said a mocking, "Good afternoon. Very unfortunate you should have found the way here." There was an accent; Crunch couldn't decide what kind. He was thinking that if the next step would be simply to start shooting, everyone could go overboard.

He said that much. "One shot, and we all dive. For them."

The admiral looked unbelievingly from the dinghy to Crunch. "You mean to say you think they might simply—"

"I don't know what they might do. I merely said if they start shooting, dive and try to upset them."

The boat rowed around the *Poseidon*. The fat man kept his lips pursed. He seemed to be amused, but not pleasantly amused. His crew merely stared at the people on the cruiser, stared with cold rage, and held their guns.

"See what's aboard," the fat man presently said. He looked up. "Any others? Lurking below?"

Crunch shook his head.

Virginia's father stepped forward. "Look here. We're perfectly innocent anglers. Came in here because we saw you come in—"

The fat man looked toward his boat and then at the man who rowed. "Fool," he said.

It seemed to shrink the rower. He glanced at the fat man with fear and replied, "I was watching the entrance. You can run aground easy."

The fat man kicked him in the shins. And the dark-skinned oarsman said nothing. He did not even rub the shin.

"I am an admiral in the United States Navy," Virginia's father then said. He made it sound as only an admiral can. "You have fired on us and damaged us, held us up, and now you're going to board us. I hope you realize what you're doing?"

"It's you who don't realize," the fat man answered.

"I demand safe passage out of here."

The dinghy was close now. The fat man was staring at the girl. "Very attractive," he observed clearly.

Larry said, "Listen here, camembert—"

The fat man's eyes hardened. "It may be," he said, "we shoot you four. But not the girl."

Crunch spoke—quickly, quietly and with force. "Look. You wouldn't be smart to shoot anybody. We're expected back. It's known where we went, in general. It's known that your gang is here—"

"Ah?"

"—and if we do not return this evening—"

The man smiled. "It will also be known that a charterboatman like you is capable of caring for himself and party, over a night. You found good fishing. Or you had a little difficulty with the motors. You came up here, so, perhaps you even were lost. You made yourselves comfortable. You will be out in the morning."

"Then why didn't we radio?"

The fat man said, "Paul, Guvard, go on board. Take all guns. All ammunition. Destroy the radio."

The pair climbed aboard and went cautiously below. In the dinghy, the fat man relaxed and waited until the havoc was finished. Paul and Guvard handed out the *Poseidon's* arms—a forty-five, a heavy rifle for sharks, and a light rifle. Three boxes of ammunition followed.

The fat man piled them at his feet. He nodded and had the dinghy rowed forward alongside the *Poseidon*. For another minute, he contemplated the five people.

"I am, naturally, very angry," he said. "When I am angry, there is a payment. In anger, I am still a man of business. I shall not kill you; the captain is correct. It would embarrass me, much as I should enjoy the novelty of killing an admiral. Our airplane cannot leave until late in the night, however, and only two can fly in her. The lake is about fifteen feet in depth. For my anger and to give my companions time to go elsewhere, I shall sink your boat before we depart. That will a little repay me for not being able again to use this excellent place, which was difficult to find and which I spent time and money to make useful. I shall leave the dinghy, and you have one of your own. In the two, you should be able, tomorrow, before it is again dark, either to reach the coast or to locate another fishing party. It will be unpleasant—the insects—but not dangerous. If you did not have on board so pretty a young woman I think I would make the price higher for being found here by you. You are, meantime, quite harmless where you are. A chance plane would merely see a cruiser in an odd spot and"—he looked toward the sun—"the chance of such planes will be small, very soon."

He nodded again and the dinghy rowed toward shore.

It was about what Crunch had expected, and about, he thought, what he deserved. He looked first at Des. Des, with a sad expression, was gazing at the *Poseidon*, eyes moving from one detail to another. They were going to sink the boat that had been the livelihood of the mate and his skipper for a long, long time. It was a good boat. They hadn't been able to keep insurance enough to replace her at the present market. Crunch knew what Des was feeling, but as their eyes met there was no reproach in the mate's.

Crunch next looked at Virginia, who was watching her father and Larry. He expected wrath and bluster from the admiral. There wasn't any sign of it; he watched the departure of the dinghy with calm narrowed eyes. There was even a peaceful look about him. He pivoted slowly after a long stare at the machine gun which was trained on the *Poseidon*.

The admiral looked at Larry. Larry was obviously angry, obviously alarmed. He met the stare of the girl's father, measured it, seemed a little surprised, and smiled.

"A very bright, fat, nasty piece of cheese," he said.

The admiral didn't reply. He turned further, gazed at Crunch and seemed satisfied, looked at Des and understood what Des was thinking, and didn't bother to weigh his daughter's state of mind. He apparently knew what it would be.

"Well!" he said.

Crunch almost grinned. "You think they may have made a mistake?"

"What mistake?" Virginia asked.

"Not shooting us," her father replied.

"They made another," Des said slowly, "I think."

The admiral glanced at the mate with some surprise. "Yes?"

"They didn't search very well."

"It occurred to me," Crunch nodded.

"And to me," said the admiral. He walked toward the top controls as if they were on a bridge, the bridge of a fighting ship.

Larry eyed the aircraft and the boat. "What would you say? About three hundred yards?"

Des said, "About."

"And no moon?"

"None," the mate replied.

"And a case of dynamite. And caps. And the ship has plenty of wire. And there's fire fuse."

Virginia said, "And an old man who organized the Navy's first underwater demolition school." She looked toward shore. "Mistake, all right."

The admiral was now standing with an arm around Virginia. "You swim, Larry, of course?"

Larry nodded.

"There are probably 'gators aplenty in here."

Crunch said there probably were. He added that they usually didn't bite a swimming man.

"I wouldn't like to hurt anybody," the admiral went on. "But I'd risk getting hurt to even things. It's peculiar how civilians trust a few guns. In the Pacific, we've swum in under all calibers and unlimited numbers of guns, and left a wad of trouble, and swum out. I thought—two steps. A big charge under those leaning mangroves should block the creek. And a light one under that helicopter will spoil it for flying."

"And then what?" Crunch asked.

"We can talk just as well," the admiral said softly, "if we start busying ourselves getting some supper. This looks too much like a parley. Virginia, you and Des start a galley fire. Crunch, I can't answer that 'And then what?' When that fat oaf talked about killing, he was a man who was used to killing. He might decide to do it, anyhow. If we block them in here, it's going to be very mean for everybody. We'll have to figure a little. There ought to be tactics."

They brought folding chairs into the stern cockpit and arranged a bridge table there, under the eyes of the man behind the machine gun. They switched on a portable radio, loud, in the manner of whistling to keep up courage. The admiral made out of paper, and donned, a chef's hat. Wearing it, he went below, but not to cook. He opened the dynamite. He started to work, whistling with the radio.

Crunch and Des kept watch on the men in the boat and the aircraft. There were, they thought, seven or eight men. And they were making preparations for dinner, also. But not with any such seeming of nervous gaiety as the *Poseidon* showed. They were glum. Undoubtedly they were the men who had cleared the way for the cruiser, in weeks of sweating labor amongst the insect-swarming maze of mangrove.

The *Poseidon's* company ate in plain view.

Once, the admiral stared at the other boat. "It's entirely possible they might change their minds and start firing," he said. "If they do—dive, on the far side. Keep the boat between you and the guns. Swim on across the lake and hide in the mangroves, if you make it."

"People," said Des, "who do that, die anyhow, sometimes. Mosquitoes bleed 'em to death. Poison 'em. Our repellent wouldn't last the night, for all of us."

"Better," the admiral said placidly, "than being shot like a fish in a rain barrel." He ate, and admired the sunset. "There probably," he said, "isn't another spot like this in the world! Ordinarily, the beauty of it would be overwhelming."

His daughter gazed at him with a certain awe.

Crunch said, "There may be several such spots around here. They find 'em from time to time. Years back, in the days of the plume hunters, a guy found a creek that led to a lake with a bird rookery in it. Nobody else could find it. And he took about twenty thousand dollars' worth of scalps from that rookery every year."

"Scalps?" Virginia repeated.

"That's what they called bird skins with the feathers attached. They shot the birds, left the carcasses for the 'gators or ants; and, of course, since it was nesting that brought the birds to the rookeries, the young ones starved. That's how the egrets and the ibises were nearly wiped out."

"Interesting," said the admiral.

He stared again at Crunch. He grunted to himself. He eyed Larry again, and Des. His lips turned upward slightly, as if he was pleased.

Darkness came swiftly, and with darkness a call floated from the megaphone. "Turn on your lights!"

Crunch yelled back. "You broke the connections!" It wasn't true.

There was a curse and some audible but not understandable talk, then a long silence. A searchlight hit the water, lifted, and fanned over the *Poseidon*. They had foreseen that and they were on deck. The light snapped off, which, also, they had anticipated. After half an hour, it came on again, suddenly; still prepared, they were all in view. It came again in fifteen minutes, and Des had gone below.

"Where's the fifth man?"

Des showed. Darkness ensued. Obviously, they were reluctant to use their searchlight. Not often, but once in a while a commercial plane came that way by night. Sometimes such planes flew high. They might pass unobserved, but not unobserving.

Time passed and the light flickered on again after perhaps an hour. Crunch was absent now, and Larry. The shore inquired.

"Trying to sleep," the admiral bawled back.

"Show them up."

The two men appeared after a while, looking tousled. The light died again.

"So," the admiral said calmly. "Now, hunh?"

Des and Larry swam toward the creek. On two life preservers, lashed together, they pushed their load. In an emergency, if the light was swept over the pond, they could plunge the contraption under and swim down and keep it there for a while.

Ahead, against the stars, loomed the treetops where leaning mangroves hung over the opening. It didn't take them long to push their raft from the *Poseidon* to the trees; it merely seemed eternity. And when Des kicked an underwater root, he nearly cried out. But he reached with his foot again, and made sure it was a root, and went on.

Larry touched. "Sand," he whispered. "We'll go ashore here."

Slowly, painstakingly, they crept through the tangle. They had selected before dark the hurricane-tilted root mass of a clump of large trees. And they had half a case of dynamite on the raft.

Everything on shore was dank and slippery. They passed a bottle of mosquito repellent in the darkness. It kept the insects at humming distance. They found the root mass and investigated its base.

"Ought to topple," Larry said. "This is the spot."

They reconnoitered to make sure that the lights on the inshore boat could not be seen from any near point. They could not be. That meant a fire fuse wouldn't be seen from the boat.

Crunch was more afraid of the aftermath than the swim. And he, like the others—perhaps with the admiral excepted—was very much afraid of swimming in the dark in that water. He tasted, and it was sweet.

"Like old times," the admiral whispered, as they swam away from the stern. They headed toward the shore well above the helicopter. As they went, they payed out insulated wire.

When they came near the aircraft, they could see plainly what was going on. It was not much. The thin, dark-skinned man who had been kicked in the shins was now at the machine gun on the boat. Light from below revealed him clearly. The rest of the men sat about or lay below. Away from the bugs. There was nobody on the helicopter. It was no trick, except for the audacity of being there, to lash a glass jar containing dynamite and a cap to a pontoon.

Then, their feet swinging in the warm current, their hands clinging to the pontoon, they edged around for a further look. The light on the boat was dim but pervasive. It fell upon the shore-side walls of leaves and spread faintly on the water opposite. Nobody would be able to swim up close to the boat.

They had half hoped against that, but half expected it. They exchanged a signal by hand grips—and swam back toward the *Poseidon*. Crunch went the whole way with a cold belly and icy legs, expecting to hear a tail thresh, to feel teeth. Nothing happened. Virginia was at the ladder. She helped them aboard and they dried themselves. Then they put on their clothes. And then they waited.

They began to expect the light. They began to pray silently for the return of Larry and Des. It was a long wait.

But the next probing of the beam found everyone on board. Larry and Des had to struggle to keep from panting. But the light went off fairly soon.

"We couldn't do anything about the boat," the admiral said. "Couldn't swim in. Too much light."

"Then," Larry said, "I'll go."

Crunch spoke too. "And I."

"I think I'd better," the admiral said. "I may be a shade old, but—"

"I'm skipper." Crunch said the words shortly. There was no argument after that.

To swim ashore again was almost more than he could endure. Warm water, a pleasant night, but not a place to swim. Following the admiral's instructions, he and Larry, armed with nothing more than marlin billies, crept onto the land at the opposite end of the boat from the one where the helicopter was moored. They pushed into the tumult of darkness, leaves, roots, branches and bugs. They moved painfully toward the nearest thick cover behind the gunner. Then they went up the slanting trunk of a tree. The boat could not be directly approached by water; but the very thing that made it safe in daytime, the overhang of foliage, gave it a special vulnerability at night from the shore side, as the admiral had pointed out. Crunch crouched tensely on his part of the huge tree, hidden by branches ten feet above the topside deck of the boat, not slapping the incessant, pricking misery of mosquitoes, hardly breathing; and he reflected that everything, from now on, was the admiral's idea: there would be a time to act presently—a signal of the time which Des and Larry had set, a job to do then, and a method to get away, with luck. Crunch grinned tautly and got set.

The blast was stupendous. It lit up the green shore with stark clarity; the concussion would have knocked the two men out of their trees save for the fact that they were already in the air, dropping to the decks below.

Larry had chosen his target: the gunner. He had no trouble at all, as the admiral had predicted. The blast sent the man sprawling. The football coach landed on him and he had a marlin club in his hand. The billy came down while the night was still loud with a continuous cracking and splashing as the dynamited trees went over.

Larry stepped to the machine gun, worked at it rapidly, and threw overboard, as far away as he could, part of its mechanism. The gun itself followed, with its tripod.

In the meantime Crunch dealt with the searchlight on the canopy. He, too, swung a marlin billy, and the light was soon unfit for use again ever.

Men were moving, below. Yelling. Crunch peered down. Larry had stepped to the companionway and was standing there in the murk, panting a little. He glanced up, saw Crunch's head, and gestured. Crunch nodded and straightened. He looked toward the bow and a hatch was lifting. Since he was barefoot, he didn't make any noise. He approached from the hinge side of the hatch cover, which went on up, after the man beneath it had tried to look around. The hatch dropped open and Crunch struck. As he struck he grabbed and got the man's collar. That held long enough for him to reach under the chin and one arm. He pulled the man up and out. He'd dropped the gun in his hand, but there was another in his hip pocket.

Crunch took it. He slammed the hatch cover, hooked it and raced to the forward edge of the canopy.

Larry had already slugged the first man up and disarmed him. Crunch could see, in the light from below decks, the coach's naked back as he bent over the man, taking two guns, straightening, turning.

A third man appeared at the top of the short ladder and aimed at the coach. Providentially—or possibly because of the attentive admiral's sense of timing—the electrically detonated charge went off in that instant. It ruined the aim of the third man. It lifted the helicopter a few feet, dropped it heavily, and the aircraft began to settle; but no one saw that. Crunch dived on the third man, from the air above, like a giant bat. The billy fell and the man's gun dropped. Crunch scooped it up and yelled, "Okay!"

He and Larry dived over. A minute's work, maybe.

They swam under water as far as they could, knowing the half dozen more men, raging and stupefied, would soon dare to come out on deck and would fill the night with bullets.

The blast could have been arranged to set fire to the helicopter and Crunch had suggested that.

The admiral had shaken his head. "Some of us, right at that point," he said, "will be swimming. Don't want to light the water."

Swimming, Crunch was glad of that foresight.

He porpoised, caught a breath, was briefly aware of the sting of a bullet in the nearby water, swam under the surface for some yards, broke again for air and saw Larry's fishlike emergence nearby, and ducked again.

They covered about half the distance that way and then joined up, gasping. Bullets were still buzzing in the air, stinging into the water, ricocheting. Once in a while a shot whacked into the *Poseidon*. They swam not toward her, but ahead of her dim silhouette. There, in the *Poseidon*'s dinghy, out of likely range, they located the admiral and his daughter and the mate. They were hauled aboard and the little boat settled down low in the water. But it still had freeboard.

The shooting suddenly stopped.

Both Crunch and Larry panted for a long while before they told how they'd wrecked the light and jettisoned the machine gun. Virginia was crying. Des was stiff and silent as he listened. But the admiral kept busy with a handkerchief, drying out the loaded guns they had taken.

"If they have another machine gun," he said, "they'll rake the *Poseidon* where she is. Right now, they'll talk things over. Find out what's what. If we could get a line to a tree on the far shore we might be able, without starting the engines, to haul your boat to a new position. It's dark as Bligh's brig now."

There wasn't line enough to reach shore. But, working in the dark, with furious anxiety, they rowed the anchor forward, dropped it, hauled up the *Poseidon*, and repeated. Gradually, the lights on the inshore boat retreated and the sound of voices grew faint.

For quite a long time, nothing happened. Nothing more than an intermittent fusillade from the inshore boat that was aimed at the spot where the *Poseidon* had been.

On the *Poseidon*, Crunch panted for a while and got on some clothes. The admiral finished oiling the guns they had taken. There were only two. Two had been lost from their belts, in the hard underwater swim. Virginia, her breath uneven, tried to help Larry dry himself in the darkness and Crunch could hear her murmurs.

"Oh, darling! I was horribly afraid! It was so dangerous!"

Crunch could also hear Larry's bland, slightly winded responses. "The way your old man figured it, it wasn't so risky. After all, the blasts shocked the devil out of them. And us dropping like monkeys from the trees."

The number of lights increased on the opposite shore. One of them presently began to move along the water.

"Going over to look at the helicopter," the admiral said.

The lights moved at the speed of a rowed dinghy and remained awhile in the vicinity of the aircraft. Then they came back and passed the boat. Des remarked with understandable pride, "They're going to check our other blast."

The men spent perhaps fifteen minutes at the creek mouth. Then the dinghy went back to the larger boat. More time passed and it returned to the creek. It was far out of practical range for the revolvers and the admiral had no intention, in any case, of using his small store of ammunition for such shooting.

A second trip was made to the creek. Soon thereafter the sound of axes came clearly to their ears.

"That fat man," the admiral said, "is no fool. He's hardly wasted a minute. Probably the men he has with him now are the men who cleared out the channel in the first place. If they can get past our block and leave one of their own, they still have a chance to get away."

"With the stuff, too," Crunch said. He had told earlier that night and very apologetically of Cutter's visit and his own asinine failure to make use of what he knew. "The T-man said it wasn't bulky."

"Just the same," Des muttered, "they're mad enough to do something to us."

The admiral's voice was laconic, "Naturally. Not in the dark, because they know we have guns now, and they don't know our position. At dawn. Which reminds me that I'd better start work again."

He was gone a long time. When the admiral reappeared, he carried more glass jars and more insulated wire. Crunch could barely make out the man and his burden against the starlight, but he saw that the admiral was in shorts.

"One more swim tonight, and this one's on me."

Larry, Des and Crunch said in unison, "I'll go."

The admiral's laughter was brief. "Nope. Tricky set, and no likelihood of being jumped. An old guy can pull this one, and I've got the experience."

They handed him down into the warm, night-gurgling water, passed one of the jars to him and payed out wire. He was gone a long time and they could not see him or tell by sounds whether what they heard was his swimming or fish or other creatures. He reappeared at the ship's side unexpectedly. "Second load," he murmured, and was gone again.

Des said what everybody felt. "It takes something to keep on swimming around this pond."

"Dad," said Virginia softly, "has something."

Finally the admiral came back aboard. He dropped, as all had; panted as all had. "Didn't even get bitten by a little croc!" he said. There was a smile in his voice. "That's that!"

Then they waited. The hours passed. Crunch handed out chocolate and potato chips. And, later, fruit juice in cans, from the refrigerator.

The wind dropped. The trees ceased groaning and shushing. The sound of splashes was clearer. Once, Crunch said, "Tarpon."

And once again, at a plopping smack, Des murmured, "Snook."

There was a false grayness and a genuine gray. The axes at the creek mouth were still biting into the dynamited timber. They could see, finally, the faint blur of the weatherbeaten side of the distant boat. Then, unsurely at first, a moving object.

"That'll be a visit," the admiral said. "They'd like to fix the *Poseidon* if they can."

The dinghy came through the dusky morning. Crunch got the glasses and peered. "Damn!" he exclaimed.

"What?" asked Larry.

"Far as I can make out, they've got armor. Galvanized-iron sheets, or something. They must figure to row up and start shooting from behind it."

The dinghy, deep in the water, came on. In front of the iron sheeting were branches, so it was impossible to spot the watching men. The *Poseidon's* company waited breathlessly. There was a sudden shot. Everyone noticed, though no one mentioned it, that the shot caused Larry to step in front of Virginia automatically, unthinkingly.

"Waking us up," the admiral said. "Meaning a parley."

The dinghy came closer. When it was about a hundred yards off, the fat man's accented voice came through the megaphone.

"We're coming aboard again. We've got rifles here and they'll tear through the sides. If you want to fight we'll oblige. If you don't want any more trouble just open your seacocks. I would like to shoot. I will settle for settling your boat! I am primarily a business man."

The last phrase winged through the morning. There was a flurry of shooting. Things on the *Poseidon* split, splintered, crashed and danced. The ship's company ducked. A hole came through the side near Crunch's head.

"Fire one," the admiral ordered.

Des, who had hurried below, touched a wire to one of the batteries.

The charge was some distance from the dinghy—perhaps a hundred feet. Nevertheless, as it sent up a fountain of water and smoke and a racing wave, it all but upset the small boat, threw a small sea aboard, and its shock wave shook down some of the sheet-iron armor.

It was not necessary to fire two. The second mine was in close, but the dinghy did not come closer. The dawn was filled with cursing. The fat man screamed. And soon he had his boat about. It withdrew. With its going, the battle for the nameless pond was over.

A quarter of an hour later, the engines of the smuggler's cruiser started. The *Poseidon's* company watched while moorings were cast off and the boat was backed from under the trees. It moved slowly around the point to the outlet and turned and disappeared. For a time, they could hear its engine grinding fitfully as it negotiated the reopened barricade. Immediately after that there was another kind of sound, the ringing of axes again. And they could see perturbations amongst the treetops as trees already cut for felling, slowly dropped across the creek, astern of the fugitive craft.

"They're gone," Virginia said at last, in a low, unbelieving voice.

Her father hugged her. "Yeah. Gone."

"We beat them!"

His smile was barren. "Call it a draw. We drove 'em out. We stopped them from flying their stuff inland in that 'copter." He eyes roved to the canted aircraft. One motor was under water. "But we didn't capture even one, let alone the gang. Not a very effective action all told."

The mate's eyes bugged. "Golly!" Des said.

Larry took his girl up forward and the canopy hid them. After a while, the admiral stepped up on the gunwale to peer. He came back to the stern, his eyes—for an admiral's eyes—sentimental.

"Necking," he said. "Imagine."

Crunch, who was working on some assorted gear, asked, not without irony, "That's not against regulations?"

The tall gray-eyed man chuckled. Then he laughed. "Oh, Lord," he said. "What a superfluous gesture!"

Crunch didn't get it, and his expression showed the fact.

"I loved Virginia's mother," the admiral began, "as much as any man can love a woman. But marriage, Crunch, lasts a long time, even," he added in a sad parenthesis, "if she dies fairly young. And marriage, skipper, is life's greatest blessing. It is also, sometimes, life's most irritating ordeal. I liked that Wood boy on sight. But Virginia's a handful, and I had to know whether or not he could take it."

Crunch said, "Oh."

"Flying over from Manila, I decided the best way to see what made the guy tick was to take the view that I thought he was a twirp and the romance was an infatuation. You know—heckle. In marriage, you need to be able to bear heckling."

Crunch thought of his beloved Sari and grinned faintly. "There are times—"

"So I went to work on him, and including you and your excellent mate, unfortunately, but necessarily. Figured you both had fished sticky customers before and could bear up. Larry did all right, don't you think?"

Crunch nodded.

The admiral chortled again. "Especially, putting on shorts after those damned pants dyed him green! Only a man with spirit could do that!" Now his eyes looked toward the place where the smugglers had been moored. "It sure was needless planning! Our Larry ticks good, Crunch."

"Yeah." Crunch's blowtorch blue eyes held on the admiral's. "Yeah," he repeated. "Your Virginia picked a real, ticking guy."

For an instant the admiral's gaze was averted. He coughed. "Father of an only daughter wants to be sure. I'm an old fool!" He reverted to his ordinary tone. "What the deuce are you doing?"

"Getting hand lines ready. I'm a fool, too, admiral. First I carried an uninspected case as cargo. Though without it—"

"Without it," the admiral answered, "we'd have had to fire the aircraft and the boat. Did it once. Drilled into the gas tanks of a Jap torpedo boat. Got away all right."

Crunch sighed softly. "Maybe," he said, "you'll give Des and me a few lessons. We've been in a couple of spots before, where they'd have come in handy. But anyhow, I ignored what Cutter said. Followed the boat. All my fault. And now we gotta fish because I depended on Ed's Yacht Motel for grub and there isn't even lunch on board, and we could be stuck here for several days."

The admiral chuckled again. "Right! Bait me one of those rigs and I'll start."

He presently threw over a line and jigged it slowly. "Do you think I should go forward and tell Larry I'm one of the most hysterical football fans Annapolis ever graduated? Or just let 'em neck?"

"Fish," Crunch answered.

The admiral nodded. "Good advice. I'm hungry." He gave his wrist a jerk and began hauling in line, hand over hand. "Snapper," he said. "Two pounds, anyhow. I seem to like fishing, Crunch, nearly as much as football. Sure hated to make out that sail bored me! First sailfish I ever caught!"

Crunch cut bait.

They were not marooned for days. Hughie had seen them turn from his island. He had forgotten to raise his flag, that day. And when, in the evening, he heard on the radio that the *Poseidon* was missing, he hurried to the main keys in his launch, where he reported seeing the boat turn into a certain river mouth.

A plane found her at noon and men had hacked through the block in the creek before dark. It was Cutter, himself, who skidded onto the pond in a fast outboard to report that the fat man and his associates, along with something like a half million dollars' worth of narcotics, had been taken in East Coot Lake, Cutter listened with fascination to their story, and ate a second plate of fried snapper before it was all told.

"The fat man," he said at last, "has been operating a long while and we've lost several agents, trying for him. One was my brother." He ate pensively. "A smart, ruthless operator. Only he shouldn't have taken on a United States admiral, a football coach, and a couple of Florida boat-men. Particularly"—he glanced at Crunch's bare arms—"one who used to be a pugilist." Cutter surveyed the ship's company with a certain amount of amazement, and suddenly pointed at Larry. "Man! Your legs! Infected! Looks like gangrene!"

"It'll wear off in time, I hope," Larry answered.

And Virginia said, "What you think is swelling, Mr. Cutter, is just muscle." She explained about the Kelly-green pants.

"The place where you people have the most muscle," Cutter said as he dumped fish bones overboard, "is where it counts most; upstairs."

"I made some sour mistakes," Crunch demurred. He winked at the admiral. "For instance, I'll never admire myself as a judge of character, again!" The admiral chuckled.

There was a faint hail from far away.

"Got the channel open," the T-man said. "Hoist your anchor; you can get through now." As he went over the side he paused and stared. "Shot your boat up pretty bad. But the reward'll take care of repairs and then some."

"Reward?" Des gaped.

"Five G's—for capture or information leading to capture. You people gave us the information. Plus."

It was Virginia who reacted first to the stunning effect of that news. "Crunch," she said, "I'm so happy I could kiss you! And you, too, Des!"

"Why not?" said her father. "You've practiced all day."

S A I L F I S H ,   H O !

THE LIGHT went red. The car stalled. "Oh . . . no!" The driver's words tolled like bells. They spoke anguish greater than the event and a resignation that seemed out of character. He was too rugged a man, too bold, too clearly accustomed to command for such emotion at such ordinary provocation. A big man, with an indelible tan and fire-blue eyes corner-hatched in the way of every sailor. His yachting cap wasn't necessary to identify him as a true man of the sea.

"No gas?" the driver's companion asked. He, too, was strong, seafaring and—overanxious. Anxiety, however—moderate anxiety—was one of his two usual conditions. The other was an apparent blankness. He had been christened Desmond. Few knew that. Kids—when he'd been a kid—inevitably called him Desperate. Everybody did now. And perhaps the nickname had influenced his demeanor.

"Plenty of gas," Crunch Adams had grunted. Crunch was skipper of the fishing yacht, *Poseidon*. He whacked the steering wheel with a hand hard enough to break it, a hand that had once been a fighter's.

The light slipped green to yellow to red. Cars on the Palmetto Expressway exploded past them, drag-racing, in effect. A third lane, trapped by Crunch and Des, played coded profanity on their horns. No southern courtesy on Florida highways—or any highways. Crunch wrenched the ignition key. The starter ground feebly. The engine caught. And gave up halfway across the intersection. Crunch threw it in neutral and used momentum to steer it toward the shoulder. It halted, short, and the skipper leaped out. Raising the engine hood, he stared angrily.

"Generator," he muttered. "Been running on the battery. Need new brushes. New *car*, you want to know the truth. Great chance!"

Des scrutinized the region, a fringe area of Miami. Unfamiliar.

Crunch came up, kicked the car moodily and said, "Okay. Maybe they got a tow car. Won't have the parts, though. Not for our damned antique. Mean a wait."

Three hours and three buses later, they entered a pretty street and marched morosely toward the Adams cottage.

Sari appeared on the porch. She had therefore been waiting and watching. Sari was in a checked gingham dress which would have fitted her on the honeymoon she and Crunch had postponed at first and long ago canceled. A red band stacked her dark curls charmingly and she was smiling. The smile, Crunch recognized, was her arranged one. And now it faltered.

"Where's the car?" she asked.

They told her. And told her about their failed mission. She led them to the living room and tried to brighten her face as she watched Crunch light a cigarette. But her face refused to co-operate. She spoke slowly, striving to change sounds of misery and anger to a tone of encouragement. "So Mr. Sellers wouldn't wait *two days* for the *Poseidon*?"

"'Not one hour.' A quote," Crunch said.

"But when you get the *Poseidon* back in the water, he'll—"

Crunch looked at Des. Des shook his head slowly.

Sari was incredulous. "You've had him this same month for years and years! What sort of person would—would drop you when you merely hauled in the *Poseidon* for two of his days to replace a split plank? That you *could* have patched except you're too reliable for half measures!"

Crunch was more bitter, more sarcastic than he'd ever been. "Nice drive up the Sunshine Parkway. Cool, but bright. Nice house in Palm Beach, Mr. Sellers has. On the water. Knock out a few walls and you could play football. But Mr. Sellers was not so nice. The *Poseidon* had been 'stove-in,' as he called it. A brand-new boat *could* get a smashed plank, Mr. Sellers agreed. But he noted the *Poseidon* is *not* brand-new. Very old, he said. Des and I pointed out she had all the newest gear—the radio phone, electronic gadgets, extensible outriggers, diesels—of new boats. No go. She would not be ready when promised. Breach of contract, in effect, Mr. Sellers said. He dislikes changes of plan. And detests begging. Not mature, he told us. No skipper should crawl around begging," he said.

"About then"—Des filled a silence—"Crunch walked out. Luckily for Mr. Sellers. Those rich people can't stand frustration. And Crunch can't stand being called a beggar."

Sari had listened with sorrow. But she had found, in that time, the strength for which she'd struggled, and she now wore an expression of confidence. "Oh, well!" she said casually. "You'll get some Bimini or Keys charter soon. Business is certain to be good. The season is very big."

Crunch shook his head, met her eyes, started to ask what new thing was worrying her—and didn't need to.

A young man appeared. Two inches taller than his over-six-feet father, broad of shoulder, dark-haired like his mother, but with his old man's blow-torch-blue eyes. A cast of face entirely his own: sensitive in some third way. Mildly humorous. Intellectual. A face of great quietude, of inner resource and individuality. Bill was the Adams's only heir. He was not spoiled by that, however. Charter boatmen haven't the means or, generally, the nature that spoils kids.

Bill carried a thick book, finger in his place, and he sensed the heavy air of depression. But he was too young, still, to postpone his own concerns.

"Having a wake?" He grinned. "Mother, did you tell Dad about the tuition hike?"

He was too late to catch her flickered warning.

Crunch spoke, with new anguish. "Tuition? Up? How much?" His gaze ricocheted, Bill to Sari. "So *that* was what was worrying you! . . . How much?"

Bill answered steadily, but his color had changed. "Five hundred bucks more next semester. I couldn't add it to my loans, Dad, or my scholarship. I tried. The Medical School isn't endowed like some. And Miami U. is poor." His father was sweating now, and panting a little. Bill—a second-year medical student—thought, *heart attack*. "You better sit down, Dad," he murmured.

Crunch stared at him hotly, realized what Bill imagined, snorted a rude word, went to the phone and dialed violently.

"Hello. Johnson's Shipyard? Crunch Adams. Mr. Johnson around? Yeah, I'll wait." Time. "Hello, Abel? Yeah. You still need a superintendent? Two hundred a week for me, right? And a job for Des? Yeah, I know she'll be ready Thursday. So put her up for sale. . . . No, I'm not kidding. You're also a yacht broker, aren't you? Then sell the *Poseidon*. Bear in mind she's mortgaged up to her outriggers."

Bill threw the book on the floor to turn Crunch from the phone. "Before you quit guiding," he yelled, "I take a year off school and work!"

Sari murmured, "No, Bill. No good!"

Crunch glared at his big son, said a few more words to Abel Johnson and hung up. He rose and stalked out of the front door. Oranges on six trees were showing yellow; in a live oak, certain cattleyas, Christmas orchids, had hatched a dozen blooms. He saw no fruit or flower.

Indoors, Des found a way to speak. "You gotta stop him, Sari!"

Bill was nearly as frantic. "He *can't* sell the *Poseidon*! Why, it's like selling *me*!" He faced his mother. "We were even born on the same day, you always said. Me. And the boat."

"For Crunch"—Desperate's tone was weird—"a shore job would be like—like—like working in a graveyard. Digging your own hole. Sari, no kidding—"

She shook her head, which set her tears running zigzag down her cheeks. "Bill, go back and study. The one thing that could kill Crunch is for you *not* to become a doctor." Her tall son considered a refusal. Scrubbed it. Knew his mother. So he left and she went on. "Des, you sweet dope, *I* can't try to change Crunch's mind! Look at it his way. The house is mortgaged, too. Then, Mr. Sellers' month cancelled. And now, the car!"

"I could maybe scrounge up a loan."

"And pay it—how?"

He evaded that. "Fishing, for Crunch, is *living*, not just making *a* living. Sari, you know that, so you—"

She put a hand on the mate's rigid arm. "I'm his wife. Whatever Crunch does, I have to be on his side. *For* him. So he can never hear me say, or even realize I could say, 'I told you so.' "

Des backed up like a hit boxer. "All the old years? You'd let *them* go down the drain? The reputation Crunch built up as a deep-sea guide? Sari! We've had other rough spots. You gotta change his mind!"

"No, Des. Whatever Crunch does, which is *this* important, I'm for. Even if it sets me against you. You were never married, after all. So you don't know—"

"You never had a twin sister," Des responded instantly, unaware that those words only added to Sari's sense of failure, for she'd tried hard to find a girl suitable for Des.

She gave up, ran into the big bedroom and locked its door.

Des was still there when the phone rang. A standing zombie. He noticed the noise at about the fifth ring and managed a sort of hello.

The response was merry. "Hi! Des? Though you all must be out." Mr. Williams, the seventy-eight-year-old dockmaster, and still working.

"Family's busy," Des said. "Me. I'm here." A call from the dockmaster would be a business call. "Maybe you forget, the *Poseidon* won't be ready till Thursday."

"Didn't. Why this call? Tough for you an' Crunch. Anyhow, just got a letter from some guy lives in East Aurora. Near Buffalo. He wants two weeks, starting Friday. Best of everything, and sounds like he can afford it. Fresh-water fisherman, never tried salt. I thought you and Crunch—"

Des started to speak, started to grin, "Hold on a while."

"Call me back. Busy here."

"Right."

Des found Crunch lying in the grass beside the back fence, trying to outstare the sky. He told him and waited.

"Okay," the captain finally said. "We'll take the two weeks. About earn that tuition rise. *Then* we'll sell the boat."

The mate's blazing hope was sniffed out. Crunch meant it.

"Tell Mr. Williams, also, on charters after this one. Tell him to keep an eye out for somebody who might want a first-class, sports-fishing cruiser at a bargain price."

"But, after two weeks *solid*, maybe we could get with it."

"Do me a favor, Des. Get your big mouth closed, for once."

The man came down the dock that warm and gusty Friday meeting, followed by a boy carrying a hamper of lunch. A taxi waited to take the boy back to the fancy restaurant named on the hamper.

Not a distinguished-looking man, this Oliver Wilson. In his early forties, he was bald where his mousey hair had given up. He was neither tall nor short; he had no paunch, but no visible brawn, either. His nose, mouth, chin and eyebrows were of such ordinariness as to be assumed, not observed. He walked timidly, as if he didn't want to be noticed. Given a gray suit and a gray felt hat, Mr. Wilson would be that famous "bystander"—forever around, but never remembered as present.

In a way, Crunch thought, only his clothes and other accoutrements changed the picture. Slacks, sports shirt, neckerchief, straw hat with strap, rope-soled canvas shoes, big binoculars in a de luxe case and an array of camera gear—all were brand-new and all very expensive. Even so, the old proverb fell down. Oliver Wilson was a man clothes did not and could not make.

Mr. Wilson followed the mate into the cockpit of the *Poseidon*.

The ever-changing yet changeless rites of embarkation began. Mr. Wilson watched with emotions Des judged to be intense, mixed, yet pretty nearly concealed. Lines were cast off and the *Poseidon* made her transit of Government Cut and followed the channel markers out toward the big, red, barnacled buoy at the place where ships should turn.

Des commenced putting out the baits. He began to explain and his customer responded with bright-eyed, near-breathless attention:

"We'll put a balao on one outrigger. Outriggers, by the way, are to troll baits out beyond the wake and to allow slack line to fall from the clothespin it's pinched into—on a halyard—so a billfish will have time to hit and turn and pick it up. We'll put some mullet on the other outrigger—left one, to you. Starboard, really. Crunch and I always call it 'left' and 'right' because anglers face the stern and some people don't know the proper names. If a billfish starts following—or hits—you gotta get on that rod, fast. A sail can take a mullet, but being bigger than a balao, it could be attractive to a marlin. We have a cut bait on the center line, fishing straight back. Covers all possibilities. You hold that center rod and sit in the middle fighting chair. If we get a hit—or a follow—on an outrigger line, I'll grab your rod and you can go for the one then in business. There's a difference about hooking billfish, and others—"

Mr. Wilson seemed to be accumulating excitement. "I've *read* about it! The sailfish, and so on, don't grab and swallow. They bat to kill and come back?"

"Right. Since you've never fished in salt water, I'll help you if there's need."

"I'd appreciate that," Mr. Wilson said.

Mr. Wilson was actually trembling as he took the comfortable center chair and reached to grasp the light rod. Des first thought to set it in the gimbal at the front edge of the chair—and didn't when the customer settled it correctly, touching nothing and in no likelihood of doing so, even with a hit, since he held the tip away from any object in bending range. There was a silence. The outrigger baits made two small individual wakes and the center strip flickered closer in and dead astern.

"What," Mr. Wilson asked deferentially, "keeps this strip bait from twirling? And winding up my line?"

"The way it's cut, the beveled edges."

Des took another strip from the ice and showed Wilson its trim and how the hook was imbedded and how it was affixed to the long, stainless-steel leader. The leader, in turn, could be clipped to a swivel on a length of doubled line—a double line that became the conventional single strand on Wilson's reel.

"Even the best guides," Des went on, "sometimes can't pare a strip so it won't spin. In that case, you have to try reshaping till it swims flat, or chuck it away."

"Naturally. Very skillful thing, that—sculpturing!" Mr. Wilson was beginning to relax a little, though his curiosity increased. "Incredible—to think you need a hook as big as these are. And a whole fish or a strip eight inches long, say. With a *wire* trace and as much line, doubled—just for *fishing*! Gives a person like me a scare. These heavy rods and all. If you've only wet a line in brooks, rivers, lakes—I mean." He smiled at the sky and the sea. "This *is* the Gulf Stream, I suppose?"

Des glanced over the side. "Stream's a little farther out than usual. Crunch is heading for it."

"It can't be true—what I've read—that you can actually see the *edge* of it?"

Des asked his man to stand, and pointed. "See the green water in toward shore—that becomes pale blue as the reef slopes down toward us? Okay. Now, look north, astern, but a little to your right."

Mr. Wilson looked. What he saw was a meandering line of indigo, distinct from the azure water fitted against it. A border definite as a shore, almost. When he slowly gazed eastward, he found no opposite edge. Only the same purple-blue, unchanged to the horizon. "I didn't believe it!" he finally said, almost in a whisper. "How wide—"

"Here? Fifty-five miles, about." Des saw the next questions being born. "Across to the Bahamas. Bimini, this latitude. Goes down to maybe three thousand feet. Runs at an average of two-three knots or sea miles an hour."

"Yes. I understand about knots. Golly! All *that* channeled through *this* narrow spot! And through the space between Key West and Cuba, right? Then—moving north. Spreading. Fogging the Grand Banks. Making the British Isles habitable, though they're as far north as Labrador. France, too. Warming all Europe. And the whole business boiling by—*right here*! But why the rim? Why doesn't it mix?"

"The Gulf Stream does mix with inshore water, but its northing current creates a visible border because it heaves forward against the relatively stagnant, inshore water. Which is at least somewhat murky, while the Stream is crystal-clear. That contrast, plus the Stream's motion, makes the visible edge. And," he added, "weeds usually collect along that edge."

Mr. Wilson looked and beheld his first patch of golden sargasso weed— just before Crunch, on the canopy at the top controls, swung the *Poseidon* a little to troll her three baits as near the hundred-yard "island" as possible, without bringing them into the weeds.

Suddenly Des said sharply, "Get set!"

"What's that?" Mr. Wilson's words overlapped.

"Dolphin," Des said. "Nice one."

It came from under the gilded weeds in long leaps, like a skipped stone. But it was too big to be thrown—a yard long or more. It hit the center bait and closed its jaws and felt the hook and lost its mind.

A short run bent Mr. Wilson's rod double, or nearly. Then came an explosion on the mauve surface; into the sunlit air, twisting, somersaulting, a vivid being was flung. Flung repeatedly, its motions too fast to be seen completely, its colors incandescent, the sight, magic. One jump. Two. Three, four, five—and it vanished, leaving a marred place amidst the waves. Mr. Wilson's reel began a wail, a warning that was incessant though it changed pitch with the acceleration of the fish.

"It's getting all my line!" the angler gasped. "I'm going to lose it!"

"Plenty left," Des reassured.

There was, Mr. Wilson then realized. And when the dolphin came about, leaping again, but far from the boat, he stood up and used the flex of the rod with only an occasional, swift spin of the reel handle to keep taut contact with his prize.

For a while, the angler failed to exert all the pressure his tackle would allow. But gradually, testing it and himself, Mr. Wilson discovered that point at which Des had set the drag originally—the point at which added effort merely caused the spool to slip and so gained him nothing. The watching guides understood perfectly their customer's succession of surprises—his realization that what had seemed to him a very heavy rod was light for the fish he'd hung, his tentative addition of pressure till the drag finally slipped and his astonishment at the pull necessary to cause that. But, for an inland angler, he was showing his evident expertise in that— while, at the same time, taking to this new sport like, Des jubilantly thought, a duck to water or—he revised—a pelican to *salt* water.

"It's so big!" the angler murmured repeatedly. "And so fast! And it gets so far out! Even now. And—"

It did something else. It suddenly swam toward the boat, faster than this angler, or any, could reel. And it swam on *past* the boat—a living rocket of green-blue-gold—which, as if by conscious plan rather than from instinct, gave it enough slack line to continue around the bow of the *Poseidon*. Which it did.

"What in the name of—"

No time for talk; Des merely gestured and gave a hand.

Mr. Wilson was assisted to the gunwale and onto it. Rod in one hand, the other jumping along the monkey rail, he was conducted to the deck forward, where he stood on a hatch cover, incredulous, yet, when told, raising his rod high to clear the harpoon pulpit. And he battled the next set of leaps from that place, only to find he had to make a return trip on the other side of the cruiser as the fish, still seventy or eighty yards away, completed the full circuit.

In the stern cockpit again, with his fish obviously tiring, Mr. Wilson panted and tried to recover. "I thought it was *something* to follow a trout, pool-to-pool, down a brook. Big deal! But this! Ropes and rigging to pass around! Boat rocking! Fall in—and what? Get wet? Waders full? *Sharks* eat you!" He ran out of nervous steam and steadied to the war in progress. He finally frowned. "Maybe I've snagged a log—lost him?"

"Dolphins are flattish. Turn sidewise when you pull on 'em, sometimes. Adds a lot of resistance." Des was amused.

Ultimately, he gaffed the fish. As expected. A female of thirty-one pounds.

A king mackerel came next. And in another hour, a barracuda. With that one, Mr. Wilson conjured up what he'd read about its awful teeth and its terrible menace, listening appreciatively when Des set him right:

"'Cudas will occasionally hit something that plops into the water, suddenly. Before they can see what it is. A man's hand. An oar blade. But as long as they do know what's in the water, making a fuss—swimming, say, and human—they let it be. So Crunch and I think, like most men who know 'cudas, the people who claim they were bitten by them were either foolish or were hit by sharks."

Mr. Wilson then went to fetch his brand-new expensive camera from a day bed. After considerable fussing and much reference to printed directions, he took some shots of Des and the fish. "Promised myself I'd bring proof back. Proof I'd actually done all this."

"If you want," Des suggested, "I can, when we get chances, snap a few of you and maybe, in the background, something you've hooked that's in the air."

Time came for lunch and the food was everything promised by the name of the restaurant stencilled on the hamper. Crunch didn't come down to eat with them, though. He took handed-up dishes where he steered on the canopy. And, lunch finished, he didn't offer to switch places with Des. Didn't want to, Des knew.

With the sky clearing and the sun high, fishing fell off. To zero, for the *Poseidon*. By and by, with the baits still triple-tracking and no takers, Des thought Mr. Wilson should take a turn at talking about himself, his life, whatever.

Des struck a reticence there. Oliver's business was "finance." With no elaboration. East Aurora was a "nice, interesting" town. People living there played polo, raised polo ponies. Money there. Great golfing, though Oliver didn't play. Wonderful place in the spring and fall, but cold in winter. Family? Only a sister, in Buffalo. No, not married. Very pretty girl, he supposed. Smart. Twenty-seven years old. Unusual name of Aria.

Des wondered why, with his money, he hadn't tried ocean angling long ago or, at least, made farther journeys in search of other kinds of trout, salmon, char and so on. But he didn't ask. A loner, it seemed to Des. And shy, for sure. A thoroughly nice guy, Des was certain, who merely happened to be reticent, like some New Englanders they'd fished with.

Wilson said suddenly, "Haven't they hooked something, Mister Mate, on that boat?" He pointed.

Des turned, peered and grinned. "Sure have. It's the *Sea Sweeper*. Ted Collins, skipper. Looks like it might be a sail, too. Incidentally, how about giving up this Mister business? People we like to fish with call us Des and Crunch. Okay?"

"Why, of course! And I'm—Oliver."

"Nothing else? Not Ollie, even?"

"I wasn't the kind of kid," the man answered, eyes on the distant cruiser, "that other kids bothered to find a special name for. And later, well—I guess I *look* so much like an 'Oliver,' nothing else would seem to fit as well."

Des stood up and hailed Crunch. "How about barging over toward the *Sea Sweeper*. Hung a sail, looks like. Oliver, here, hasn't ever seen one."

Crunch nodded and changed course.

Des suggested, "Chance to try out those glasses you brought aboard."

Oliver Wilson was slightly startled, then he understood. Des brought the pigskin case and Oliver took out, polished and adjusted the binoculars. Presently, he gave a hushed exclamation and added, "I think it *is* a sail! Have a look."

Des examined the glasses before lifting them to his eyes and screwing them to his different focus. They were, he realized, the finest binoculars he'd ever held. And with them, he soon could say, "A sail, perhaps. Billfish. Not very big. Here. Crunch'll bring you near enough to see the show, without getting in their way."

For fifteen minutes, Oliver watched wordlessly. Motionless, too, save that he hit the plastic-covered upholstery of his chair arm, now and then, when the fish leaped. Only—and that fact became evident early in his breathless watch—it wasn't a sail, at all.

Marlin. White marlin, Des told him.

When the marlin had been defeated and, at last, boated, Oliver handed back the glasses with a smile so radiant he might have been the lucky winner himself.

"Imagine! A *marlin*! Actually caught—and me seeing it!"

Other boats engaged other fish and Oliver watched those battles, too—without ever drawing attention to the fact, disappointing to Crunch and Des, that the *Poseidon* was not among the fortunate craft.

Des changed baits, tried trolling them at various distances, used all his wiles—without result. It was, in fact, a slow afternoon.

The sun began a trial gilding of a few clouds and Crunch turned in toward the channel, marked at its mouth by the faintly flashing, hoarsely hooting buoy. Des gave up, then, his sustained hope. Oliver would have to wait another day for another fish. And that, of course, was when a sail rose behind the "left" outrigger.

"It's *one*, isn't it?" Oliver's eyes were wide, frenzied even, but fixed steadily on the area behind and slightly below the dancing balao. There—blurred shape, brownish, at first, but now turning deep navy blue—it rose and extended for a distance that was fantastic to Oliver. From it, next, a cutwater emerged, a fin, the slightly unfolded sail, aimed at the bait. And soon, at the monster's near end, a black, rod-like object bobbed out and seemed to be stabbing and slashing at the bait, but not connecting.

The line to the halyard finally straightened a trifle, as the bill did bat the balao.

"Knock it out!" Des shouted.

To his amazement, Oliver did so, reeling in line till it ran tautly from the rod's tip to the clothespin in which it had been pinched and was held, high on its halyard, by the long, slanting outrigger. Line taut, Oliver whipped the rod in an arc, dislodging it from the clothespin and so sending a drift of slack down to and upon the sun-sharp sea.

Oliver then waited, counting a slow ten to himself. And struck like a veteran. But with no answering pull of a hooked sailfish. So he reeled, as hard as he could, sending the untouched bait racing up from the depths to which it had settled and causing it to begin overtaking the steadily moving *Poseidon*. But the sail failed to give chase—in spite of this tempting simulation of a meal, stunned by its bill. The fish never did return, though Oliver dropped back and reeled in, repeatedly.

"What'd I do wrong, Des?" Oliver asked.

For once, the mate had no criticism. "Nothing," he answered pensively. "Nothing at all. You acted like a veteran." He held up a palm. "The fish did wrong."

Just having a sailfish follow and hit was fabulous for Oliver. "I saw it!" he kept saying. "Plainly! After *my* bait. A sailfish! *Me!* Imagine!"

"You'll soon do more—" Des grinned—"than *see* a sail. Catch one. In the next thirteen days, catch several. I hope."

"One," Oliver smiled, "would do. To see what that kind of fight is like. Be the high point of my life!" And he added, "this day is, so far."

The chartered time began to pass: hot, sunny weather and cool clear periods, with the northwest wind coming fast from the continent and piling up the Gulf Stream in massive shapes of blue; gray mornings and afternoons with chilly rain, too. The *Poseidon* went out in every temper of sea, but sailfish eluded her skipper, mate and their angler, though the catch of lesser species was good.

To Des, the passing days were separate griefs, numbered and diminishing toward the final, tragic end. He continued to talk with Oliver, while Crunch remained taciturn. He seldom traded posts with Des, spending his entire day up topside, even eating his frugal lunch there.

Des understood what Crunch was trying to do. He was drilling into his brain, all day and every day, the false idea that he was weary of the sea, ready to retire from it and take a secure land job. What shocked Des was the skipper's steady loss of assurance, of command, and his frequent and unprecedented uncertainty about little things, like where to fish today or how much bait to buy. Trifles, devastating to Des because they revealed how Crunch would be as an employed man, no longer a master. He'd age in no time.

Life at the Adams home was quiet now. Meals were up to Sari's high level, and maybe a bit above, for morale. Bill was on hand for dinner, usually, but otherwise in his room studying or at classes.

Sometimes at dinner, or later in the evening, they'd talk about Oliver and his fishing. But Des gave up trying to make even such talks into what they once had been, the happy, excited, often shrewd, sometimes regretful reliving of the day.

Des had a surprise in the making, one he'd planned to spring after Oliver had finished his two weeks and gone north. But, on the evening of the eleventh day, Des decided his hopeful attempt shouldn't be delayed that long. Crunch was so gloomy that Des feared he might reach a state in which nothing could change his mind. So, after a nearly wordless meal, Des got everybody's attention by saying, more loudly than he'd meant, "Maybe we aren't quite so bad off as we thought, back when Crunch phoned about selling the boat." With that, he produced his wallet and withdrew a sheaf of bills, which he handed to Sari.

She fanned them out. Twenties. Eleven of them. "Two hundred and twenty dollars!" she said, startled.

"Tips," Des murmured—casually, almost.

Crunch was angry. "For the Lord's sake, Des! You didn't hit Oliver for *tips*? He's already paid the top rate, in advance."

Des flushed and felt anger, too. "I never 'hit' anybody for a tip, Crunch! And you know it! The first day, coming through Government Cut, the guy sort of shyly slipped me a twenty. I told him to keep it. He told me he knew it was customary. I saw the numbers on the bill, then, and said it wasn't any custom at all. He pushed it. That first twenty, I said, would ride for the week ahead. He laughed. Next afternoon, same deal. I *really* tried to make him keep the dough, that time. No dice. Every trip in, twenty bucks."

Crunch was partially satisfied. "Rolling in it, that guy, you can see. Still, if he adds twenty a day to the charter, he'll fork out two hundred and forty extra."

"And," Des said earnestly, "when he says good-bye to you, Crunch, *you'll* get a nice thing, I know. He asked me if it was okay to give the skipper a parting present."

For a minute, Des believed it might work. Crunch's face had relaxed. His fingers drummed steadily on the polished wood of the dining table. He added and subtracted figures, almost in a fashion that could be followed, as if he were jotting them down on paper, not reviewing them in his head.

Sari held her breath, her eyes intent on her husband. Bill watched his father, too.

"I never did like this tipping business," Crunch began. "Maybe, for a mate, it's okay. For me, it could be an insult. I accept it, when not accepting would hurt feelings. Or when a guy is so damned pleased with life, on account of some big catch, and so rich that tipping me is an added kind of fun for him. And me. Then, okay. You have two hundred and twenty here. Will get two-eighty. Suppose Oliver hands me another hundred? Even two? Where are we? We can take out of the two-week charter money the five hundred Bill has to have. Four-eighty more would pay the bill we owe Johnson for recent and past hauling and repairs. Pay for putting the car back in shape. And leave us—*where*? Without a single charter on the books, since we quit being open for work and got mortgaged to the eyeballs. Ten years ago, I'd say, *gamble*. If we were signed up for a couple of long-term jobs, I'd say, hang on for a while, yet. But the way it is now, I want to *know* we'll be able to run a car, live under a roof, eat and put a man through med school."

No one said anything for a while. Bill tried then. "I said, Dad, I could take a term off. Get a job. Other guys do that."

"And I, son, said no to that. Right?"

Bill nodded.

"I should have retired from the sea-captain business before we got in this deep." Crunch shoved back his chair and went outdoors to not see the ripening oranges and to not observe the orchids blooming on the oak.

The fish that, to Crunch's anger, had eluded them—the major trophy of most Gulf Stream anglers—showed up on the twelfth day of Oliver's charter. It was a big sail and it materialized behind the center bait on a cloudy, breezy afternoon, coming up from deep water, fast, and hitting the cut strip hard.

Oliver, who'd seen a puzzling chocolate blur become, in a second, a deep-blue enormity that slammed his bait with its pointed club, hadn't time enough to throw off the drag. Even to shout out what he'd seen— and not understood. He did throw the reel on a free spool, as he'd been instructed. But this fish had different rules.

Crunch yelled, "Leave it on!" too late.

The reel spool accelerated, unaffected by drag. Oliver tried with his thumb to keep it from overrunning and burned himself, though he put pressure on the metal side of the reel, not the whizzing line. He threw on the drag at Crunch's shout. The reel backlashed. The sail leaped.

Des, in the cockpit, and Crunch, topside, shut their eyes—at least, figuratively. A snarled reel freezes. Against line without play, a sail need merely move to break free. Oliver, however, wasn't giving up. Seizing line above the reel in his right hand while also using that hand to hold the rod, pressing the butt into his belly for stability, he combined the bowing of the rod with swift, back-and-forth lunges to give and to take what line he could while the sail leaped. With his free hand, he tried to pick out the snarl—and managed that feat, barely in time.

As the final loop came free, the sail ran. Now, however, the drag was set and Oliver watched the diminishing diameter of his spool, glancing now and then out to sea where an occasional flash of ripped-up spray showed the line was nearly horizontal and racing toward an indeterminate distance. No fish could be seen. Just that wet-bowstring effect as line snapped clear of paired waves.

"Terrific!" Crunch shouted.

Oliver turned his head. "Done it before. Casting for bass. Backlashed. Hooked one. Got the tangle out in time."

Crunch shook his head, wonderingly. With a bass and a casting rod, maybe. With a sailfish eight feet long, you did not set the hook, whether by design or by the present accident, and *then* pick out a backlash. Your fish continued a foot or two farther than you could walk in your boat and your bent rod could yield and then your line parted.

Des came out of a stupor as running line continued to pierce and slit the sea. "Your thumb's bleeding."

"Nothing. Shouldn't we chase it?"

Des eyed the melting reel and looked up at the skipper, gestured a full turn. Crunch nodded and went swiftly to the controls.

Before the engines could explode to speed, the reel quit its diminuendo-crescendo.

"Never mind!" Des shouted. "It's stopping!"

And it was. The sounds that reels alone can make were less loud and soon sporadic. Telltale, dramatic sounds that carry the bone-tingling message of how fast, how evenly or with what sweeps of power a hooked fish is rushing away from hands that try to hold it by a thin and lengthening tether. The message ended. The sail leaped—so far away that Oliver forgot his job and for an instant merely gaped. Then he recalled himself, used the tackle as if it were a baton and controlled the faraway, flinging, twisting, head-shaking fish that looked small from this distance.

"How much line, for pity's sake, Des? That fish must be a quarter-mile off."

"Not quite." The mate grinned. "But near it. Six hundred and fifty yards on the reel. A good two hundred left. About a quarter-mile at that. *Watch* it!"

The far-off, almost dreamlike leaps had given a clue to what now occurred. The fish remained on the surface or near it, flashing through waves and emerging over troughs, coming head-on toward the boat.

Des yelled, "Reel!" with no need; Oliver was winding like a madman. Nevertheless, his best speed and the multiplying factor built into the reel did not add up to a quarter of the speed of the charge.

Nearer and nearer and dead on course, the sail came, till the skipper could imagine the expression in the glaring, egg-like eyes.

"Going to ram!" Des yelled.

A sail? Crunch thought. Ram? Never. A marlin, possibly.

There was no time for reflection. The fish was close in, still on course, coming very fast. Its big bill seemed centered on the *Poseidon's* stern. Just before the expected crash, it dipped down into the sea to gain more speed and came leaping up and out, inches short of the propellers. It came straight at Oliver Wilson.

He ducked. The mass of blue and silver violence shot up over the stern, rammed through empty air where Oliver had been an instant before and plunged toward the sea beyond the gunwale. Its tail struck mahogany as it crashed overboard, lay in violent convulsions for a moment, and then sounded.

"It tried to *kill* me!" Oliver said with a shaky voice. But he resumed the battle, somehow. His reel gave line in surges, not horizontally as before, but in vertical drives, straight down, with brief pauses.

Crunch called, "Drag too tight?" He was nervous.

Des said, "Raise the rod a bit so you lose a few inches."

Oliver lifted hard, quickly. The reel yielded. Des eyed the rod tip. Then turned and looked up.

"Okay. Ever see a sail try to commit *murder*, Crunch?"

The captain shook his head. "Saw a marlin ram. But this fish. I don't think it was after Oliver. Just charging blind—and totally nuts."

"A good thing he ducked!"

Sweating, Oliver said, "What else was there to do? When it dove down and turned my way, under water—" He stopped. "Coming up, I think!" He reeled.

It came up. It leaped. And it sounded again. But it began to do those things less violently and with less speed.

Des became fairly confident then. "You'll have the Tournament record

for this year," he said. "For sure." Then he observed, "You'll want that
baby in your office. Mounted, I mean. Or your den at home."

The question about mounting this enormous sailfish went unanswered.
Oliver began to gain line steadily. In time, Des donned gloves and prepared to take the leader, now partly above water, with caution, and then,
with violence, the bill. But the huge sail, now close, every movement
visible, made one final effort and sounded. In the violet depths, it escaped.

The line snicked and that slightly jogged the tip of the rod. Then the
rod went dead. Oliver drew a breath, reeled furiously and discovered the
truth. So he quit his hard effort and wound slowly until he lifted above
the water the broken end of his line. Des glanced up to see Crunch,
white, shaken, as he turned slowly back to the controls.

Only their customer seemed unaffected. Rather, affected in a different
fashion. He sat down in the center fighting chair and spoke in a hoarse
whisper that had an exultant, not a shattered, tone. "So that's what it's
like! Now, I know!"

Des couldn't imagine a response.

"I suppose," Oliver went on, presently, "I put too much pressure on
for too long. Line gave out from strain. An old hand would have eased
up as time passed?"

It was Crunch who explained to Oliver why the great sailfish had been
lost. Not owing to failure of the line, but to sheer accident. Fifty yards
down, as the fish bored into deeper water on its final dive, the line had
encountered another object.

"Maybe a cruising shark. Some other fish. Most likely a plank, log,
snag, sinking slowly. Taut line—sharp fin, or whatever, broke it. Not
your fault."

Oliver was relieved and returned to exulting over the fight, without
regretting the loss.

Maybe, Crunch thought, he didn't really understand the magnitude of
his tough luck. For the sailfish would surely have taken the prize for the
biggest that year and might, Crunch believed, have set a new world record for the Atlantic species.

Crunch ground out the burn of his own disappointment. Doing that
helped, too. "Anyhow, tomorrow's another day," he said. "You'll maybe
get one, not that big, but something to mount for your office."

Oliver looked at the captain oddly. Embarrassedly, Crunch thought.
Tried to say something and couldn't. Thrust out his unimpressive chin
and frowned.

"Not fishing tomorrow," Oliver finally made himself say. "Or the day
after."

Crunch couldn't blame the guy. Losing the great sail had, after all, hit him hard. The skipper nodded with understanding.

Oliver stared at him then and said, almost sharply, "I'm not quitting because of what happened. You see"—he considered a moment, then laughed ruefully—"it'll come out, anyhow, and it doesn't matter. Had a wire from my sister Aria this morning. She's flying down to get me. May meet the *Poseidon* when we come in."

To *get* him? Was he some sort of nut? Did his sister manage the family fortune? Crunch revealed his bafflement. And had it resolved.

"I'm a fake, Crunch, a fake millionaire. I'm actually a bank clerk—and out of work. Oh, not using up embezzled funds or anything. It was my money, my savings, but I ran out of funds last night. All I have is a few bucks and a plane ticket to Buffalo. Reservation for tonight, too.

"Let me explain. To begin with, I've been a fishing bug since I was a kid. All my vacation time has gone into the fishing I could afford around my area. Nights, to tying flies and such. And to reading. I've been reading about Gulf Stream fishing almost since I *could* read. And dreaming of doing it, too. I mean, of being a millionaire who could put up in the best spots, own the finest equipment, hire the best boat and guides—"

"—and even tip the mate twenty bucks a day," Crunch cut in. "That, you get back—eventually." He felt his flush of humiliation. "We've spent it, but we'll return it. You've already *paid* for two more days fishing. We, my wife and I, can put you up. So—"

But Oliver's mouth was set and his head shaking. "No. Let it ride. Spoil the whole thing, to renege on any part. It was making a dream come true and it's been all I imagined. Times fifty! You see, I'm in 'finance,' all right. Teller in a branch of a big Buffalo bank. And I wasn't so much fired as I quit." Oliver's eyes looked back at the situation and the look made him smile. "For the last five years, my boss, the cashier, has had me boning up on a specialty. One that, he let me believe, would get me out of the cage and behind a desk. I'm a graduate accountant, no CPA, though. *Yet* I studied small business management and financing. See?"

Crunch nodded, though he wasn't very clear on the matter. Oliver amplified. "Take your business. Small one. Cinchy, no doubt. Probably darn few charter boatmen are very good with money." The skipper's snort halted him, but only briefly. "Okay. Suppose you get tangled up, doughwise. In hock. Up to your chin. How many federal agencies are there that *you* know you could turn to? I can think of, offhand, at least twenty. Then there are state agencies. And also banks themselves. Most small businessmen don't realize that banks, nowadays, are set up to assist small business, as well as big. You probably know that, though! Bankers no doubt, fish—"

Crunch started. Bankers fish. Some top South Florida bankers fished on the *Poseidon* regularly. But it hadn't occurred to Crunch that they and their banks would be interested in helping, in his circumstances. It was a new thought.

Oliver left the topic behind. "Dad taught me fishing. He was a fireman. Died trying to get some horses out of a burning barn. Mother went soon after. I was fifteen. My sister was sent to live with an aunt. She's a trained nurse. What I'm getting at is that another guy in the bank was jumped over me for that small-business advisory job. So I got mad. Told the boss a few things. Walked out. Then, in my boarding-house room, it hit me. I mean—the dream. To fish the sea. To be rich enough. And I'd saved a fair sum. It would give me the whole works for at least two weeks, I figured." He grinned. "Miscalculated by a couple of days. That Gemini-Plaza sure is expensive! And that's all. You wouldn't understand. I guess—"

"I think I do," Crunch replied very slowly and very quietly. "Understand a lot of things." His gaze traveled by habit over the sea stern and his eyes contracted. "Dolphin after the center bait," he said.

And while Oliver scrapped with a living jewel that is crystalized from the sea, Crunch ran over some of his reflections.

The information about the ways of financing a small business was new and interesting. Crunch had never even applied the term "small business" to his trade, but it fitted. All that, however, was secondary. What principally ran through his head like flame was the result of a humiliation. The little guy standing there, keeping a tight and fast-worked rein on a dolphin, had the plain guts to take a dream and make it happen—without caring for the cost, the loss of his savings or his job. Whereas, he, Crunch, was so gutless that he'd been ready to give up, not a dream, but his way of life, just because things were tough.

After he gaffed Oliver's dolphin and rebaited, he went up to the side of his mate.

His face produced a double take, followed by a hollow question. "What happened?" That seemed wrong. "I mean—what's the matter?" Des asked.

"Nothing." Crunch answered. "Absolutely nothing. You go down and mate a while. Soon be time to quit, though."

Des descended, shaking. Either the old skipper had come back home or else Crunch had cracked up.

Des wasn't entirely sure which.

The usual crowd was on the Gulf Stream dock when Crunch backed the *Poseidon* into her berth and Des threw the mooring lines. In the mob,

Crunch saw Sari, which slightly surprised him because she rarely met them nowadays. She realized he had spotted her and waved something. Paper or an envelope, he thought. And before he cut the engines, he also noticed a girl beside Sari. A tall blond.

Just then, Oliver came up from the cabin where he'd changed into his expensive new clothes. And as the engines died, he called up, "That's my sister, Aria. The one with pale hair standing by that elegant-looking brunette. Come to take her nutsy brother back home." He laughed.

Moments later, Crunch was embracing the "elegant-looking brunette" and she was trying to tell him something. She managed to, finally.

"It's a letter from Mr. and Mrs. Edgar Macey. That nice Detroit couple. They want you for a month, starting next week. Keys cruise, then Bimini, Berry Islands. Asked for a collect phone call. I didn't phone, because I thought, maybe, with this new business coming in, you might at least consider—well—"

Crunch shook his head. "It was all settled before we came in, Sari. I almost turned yellow—right?" He watched her eyes light up and then caught at a bit of paper slipping from Sari's hand.

"A binder," she whispered. "In case you possibly could take them, when it's so late for asking such a thing."

Crunch missed the "binder," but rescued it from the planking. A check for a thousand dollars.

He hugged Sari again. And fragments of talk reached their ears. The girl with long, palely gold hair was saying. ". . . no, Oliver. Not to take you *back*. Though the bank would. They think you showed what they'd thought you lacked—terrific initiative. But when I realized what you'd done, I took out *my* savings. A trained nurse can get a job anywhere. I like it here. And if you wanted to be here that much, why *you* could find a job, too."

"She's charming," Sari said. "Your Oliver's sister. We've been chatting for the last half hour."

Crunch nodded. His eyes held, then, as they rose above his wife's dark curls. Mr. Williams had finally carried out the repeated orders. A large, metal sign on a stanchion gave the name of the *Poseidon* and her skipper, with relevant information. It now also bore an added sign that said: FOR SALE.

Crunch left Sari, pushed through the crowd and took down that notice. Underneath, other words were now disclosed: FOR CHARTER.

He started back when he noticed Des, straddling the gap between the dock and the boat, a large king mackerel in his hands, set for tossing ashore with the rest of the fish Oliver had caught that day.

But Des wasn't moving. And he didn't know any more that he was holding a twenty-pound fish. Or was straddling open water and might fall into it. Or know even where he was, to judge by his stare.

Crunch followed it and found its target. Aria Wilson.

Unusual name, Crunch reflected. As was Sari's. Unusual girl, too, from what he'd gathered.

Crunch grinned broadly and called, "Des! Snap out of it before you get wet! She's real. Single. Oliver'll give you her phone number—soon as they get a phone!"

Slowly. Des budged his eyes. Gradually, the sense of what had been said filtered into his mind. With which he became a little limp and almost fell overboard. To regain his balance, he dropped the fish.

But Crunch, who had expected some such fumble, caught it.

THE PUBLISHED
CRUNCH AND DES
STORIES

Collections

I. *The Big Ones Get Away* (1940) Farrer and Rinehart, Inc., New York.

II. *Salt Water Daffy* (1941) Farrer and Rinehart, Inc., New York.

III. *Fish and Tin Fish* (1944) Farrer and Rinehart, Inc., New York.

IV. *Selected Short Stories of Philip Wylie* (1945) Editions for the Armed Services, Inc., New York.

V. *Crunch and Des: Stories of Florida Fishing* (1948) Rinehart and Company, New York.

VI. *The Best of Crunch and Des* (1954) Rinehart and Company, New York.

VII. *Treasure Cruise and other Stories* (1956) Rinehart and Company, New York.

VIII. *Crunch and Des: Classic Stories about Saltwater Fishing* (1990) Lyons & Burford, New York.

The Stories

TITLE	FIRST PUBLISHED	COLLEC-TIONS	DATE
"Widow Voyage"*	*Saturday Evening Post*	I, V	June 10, 1939
"Hooky Line & Sinker"*	*Saturday Evening Post*	I, VI	June 24, 1939
"The Old Crawdad"*	*Saturday Evening Post*	I, VI	Aug. 19, 1939
"The Big Ones Get Away"	*Saturday Evening Post*	I	Sept. 23, 1939
"Blowing East"*	*Saturday Evening Post*	I	Oct. 14, 1939
"There He Blows!"	*Saturday Evening Post*	I	Nov. 11, 1939
"The Visiting Fire-Eater"	*Saturday Evening Post*	I, VI	Dec. 23, 1939
"Fresh-Water Mermaid"	*Saturday Evening Post*	I	Mar. 23, 1940
"The Reelistic Viewpoint"*	*The Big Ones Get Away*	I	1940
"Salt Water Daffy"	*Saturday Evening Post*	II	April 6, 27, 1940
"Crunch Goes Haywire" ("Crunch Catches One")	*Saturday Evening Post*	I, VI	Feb. 17, 1940
"The Missing Mariners"	*Saturday Evening Post*	II	Aug. 4, 1940
"Light Tackle"*	*Saturday Evening Post*	II, VI	June 1, 1940
"The Hex on Mr. Hicks"	*Saturday Evening Post*	II	July 20, 1940
"Spare the Rod"*	*Saturday Evening Post*	II	Sept. 28, 1940
"Fifty-Four, Forty and Fight"*	*Saturday Evening Post*	II	Nov. 23, 1940
"Hull Down"	*Saturday Evening Post*	II, VI	Feb. 1, 1941
"Fire on the Beach"	*Saturday Evening Post*	IV, V	May 10, 1941
"The Expert"*	*Saturday Evening Post*	III, VI	June 7, 1941
"Fish Bites Man"*	*Saturday Evening Post*	III, VI	July 19, 1941
"The Way of All Fish"*	*Saturday Evening Post*	III, VI	Sept. 6, 1941
"Bimini Hall, or Mr. Gale Reaps the Whirlwind"	*Saturday Evening Post*	III	Oct. 11, 1941
"A Day Off for Desperate" ("Des Takes a Holiday")	*Saturday Evening Post*	III, VI	Nov. 22, 1941

"Crunch and the Golden Lure"	*Saturday Evening Post*	IV	Jan. 3, 1942
"Shake up Cruise"	*Saturday Evening Post*	III	Mar. 21, 1942
"Three-Time Winner"	*Saturday Evening Post*	IV, V	May 2, 1942
"A Sales Talk from Sari"*	*Saturday Evening Post*	III	Oct. 17, 1942
"She Wanted a Hero"	*Saturday Evening Post*	III, VI	July 15, 1942
"One-Legged Gull"	*Saturday Evening Post*	IV	Jan. 16, 1943
"The Man Who Had Been Around"*	*Saturday Evening Post*	III, VI	Mar. 13, 1943
"Crunch Catches a Megrim"	*Saturday Evening Post*	IV	May 29, 1943
"Trophy"	*Saturday Evening Post*	IV	Aug. 14, 1943
"The Snarling Santa Claus"	*Saturday Evening Post*	IV, V, VI	Oct. 2, 1943
"Once on a Sunday"*	*Saturday Evening Post*	III, VI	Nov. 13, 1943
"Nothing to Report"	*Fish and Tin Fish*	V	1944
"Shoals"	*Fish and Tin Fish*	V	1944
"Crazy Over Horse Mackerel"	*Fish and Tin Fish*	V	1944
"The Annapolis Landlubber"	*Fish and Tin Fish*	V	1944
"War Paint for the Poseidon" ("A Matter of Paint Scraping")	*Saturday Evening Post*	V	Feb. 19. 1944
"The Shipwreck of Crunch and Des"*	*Saturday Evening Post*	IV, V, VI	June 3, 1944
"A Diet of Fish"	*Argosy*	V	June, 1944
"Beauty and the Poor Fish"	*Argosy*		July, 1944
"Strike Three"	*Saturday Evening Post*		Sept. 9, 1944
"Mr. Pike and the Tin Fish"	*Argosy*		Nov. 1944
"Bait for McGillicudy"	*Argosy*	V, VI	Mar. 1945
"Off Tackle"	*Argosy*		Jan. 1945
"Fresh Water Nightmare"	*Argosy*		May, 1945
"Too Much Fish for Rugmund"	*Argosy*		July, 1945

"Winter Vacation"	*Saturday Evening Post*		Jan. 19, 26, Feb. 1, 8, 15, 1946
"Eve and the Sea Serpent"	*Saturday Evening Post*	V, VI	Dec. 7, 1946
"Doc. Cutney's Bonefish Marathon"	*Argosy*		Jan. 1947
"By Hook — or Crook"	*Argosy*		Mar. 1947
"Fair-Caught"*	*Saturday Evening Post*	V	Mar. 8, 1947
"Sharks Make Good Models"	*Argosy*		Feb. 1948
"Key Jinx"	*Saturday Evening Post*	V	Feb. 28, Mar. 6, 13, 20, 27, 1948
"Sporting Blood"	*Saturday Evening Post*		Dec. 4, 11, 18, 1948
"The Sixth Sense"	*Saturday Evening Post*		Aug. 27, 1949
"Smugglers' Cove"*	*Saturday Evening Post*	VII	Sept. 9, 1950
"Company for Christmas Dinner"*	*Saturday Evening Post*		Dec. 23, 1950
"The Man Who Loved to Joke"	*Saturday Evening Post*	VII	Mar. 10, 1951
"Dead Man in the Water"	*Saturday Evening Post*		Feb. 23, 1952
"The Bad Luck Kid"	*Saturday Evening Post*		Apr. 26, 1952
"Plane Down — Hurricane Area"	*Saturday Evening Post*	VII	Aug. 16, 1952
"Danger at Coral Key"*	*Saturday Evening Post*	VII	Apr. 25, May 2, 9, 1953
"The Affair of the Ardent Amazon"*	*Saturday Evening Post*	VII	Jan. 30, 1954
"Treasure at Tandem Key" ("Treasure Cruise")	*Saturday Evening Post*	VII	Mar. 10, 17, 24, 31, Apr. 7, 1956
"Sailfish, Ho!"*	*Argosy*		July, 1966

* In this volume.

SC